lonely pla

P9-EMH-959

Daly City Public Library

Jamaica

DISCARDED

Negril &
West Coast
p135

Montego Bay &
Northwest Coast
p107

Ocho Rios, Port Antonio &
North Coast
p73

South Coast &
Central Highlands
p156

Kingston, Blue Mountains &
Southeast Coast
p36

THIS EDITION WRITTEN AND RESEARCHED BY
Paul Clammer, Brendan Sainsbury

917.292
LON
2014

HOLGER LEUE/GETTY IMAGES ©

**PORT ANTONIO
PAGE 93**

DOUGLAS PEARSON/GETTY IMAGES ©

**NEGRIL
PAGE 138**

ON THE ROAD

Contents

Welcome to Jamaica

Jamaica has long been a jewel in the Caribbean tourism industry crown, but there's far more to discover than just beaches and all-inclusive resorts.

Jah's Garden

Ask any expat Jamaican what they miss about their island, and the answer is inevitably the landscape itself, that great green garden that constitutes one of the most beautiful islands of the Caribbean. Jamaica begins with crystalline waters flowing over gardens of coral, lapping onto soft sandy beaches, then rising past red soil and lush banana groves into sheer mountains. This is a powerfully beautiful country, captivating to the eyes and soul. Jamaican culture can be a daunting subject for foreigners to understand, but ultimately it's a matter of appreciating this land and how its cyclical rhythms set the pace of so much island life.

Adventure Playground

Jamaica cries out to be explored – underwater, on hikes, river-bound with a raft, underground with a lamp strapped to your head, or on the road by car or bicycle. Getting away from the (admittedly beautiful) beaches allows you to see sides of the island that many tourists miss. We want to stress: outdoor activities in Jamaica hardly require you to be as fit as Usain Bolt. There's no physical effort involved when you raft (someone else poles), and even folks in moderate health can accomplish the country's most famous hike through the lush mountains to the top of Blue Mountain Peak.

Island Riddims

With Bob Marley, Jamaica gifted us the first global superstar from the developing world. But he didn't spring from nowhere – this tiny island has musical roots that reach back to the folk songs of West Africa and forward to the electronic beats of contemporary dancehall. Simply put, Jamaica is a musical powerhouse, a fact reflected not just in the bass of the omnipresent sound systems, but in the lyricism of the patois language and the gospel sounds from the island's many churches. Music is life in Jamaica, and you'll soon find yourself swaying along with it.

Caribbean Flavors

Like many aspects of Jamaica culture, the food is a creole, born somewhere between the Old and New Worlds. African spice rubs have evolved into delicious jerk, while yam, rice and plantain form the basis of rich stews and the fish that abound in local waters. Throw in the astounding array of tropical fruits that seem to drip from the trees, washed down with a shot of rum, and you can see (and taste) how the Jamaican cultural story retains its original voice while adapting to the setting – and of course rhythms – of the Caribbean.

Why I Love Jamaica

By Paul Clammer, Author

Before visiting Jamaica, I hadn't realized my preconceptions of the country were firmly out of date – somewhere between the troubles of the 1970s and Bob Marley's last LP. Touching down for the first time, the scales fell from my eyes. I've rarely been to a country so viscerally alive (Kingston dancehall street parties have to be experienced to be believed) and so achingly beautiful: just how many waterfalls hidden in rainforests can one country have? Smooth like rum and hot like a spicy plate of jerk, Jamaica ensnared me instantly. The media might call it dangerous, but the worst crime you're likely to encounter is having your heart stolen.

For more about our authors, see page 224

Above: Rastafarian reggae artist

Jamaica

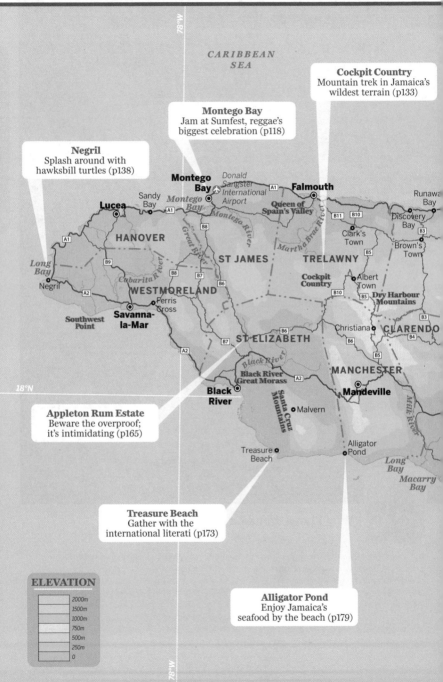

Cockpit Country
Mountain trek in Jamaica's
wildest terrain (p133)

Montego Bay
Jam at Sumfest, reggae's
biggest celebration (p118)

Negril
Splash around with
hawksbill turtles (p138)

Appleton Rum Estate
Beware the overproof;
it's intimidating (p165)

Treasure Beach
Gather with the
international literati (p173)

Alligator Pond
Enjoy Jamaica's
seafood by the beach (p179)

ELEVATION
2000m
1500m
1000m
750m
500m
250m
0

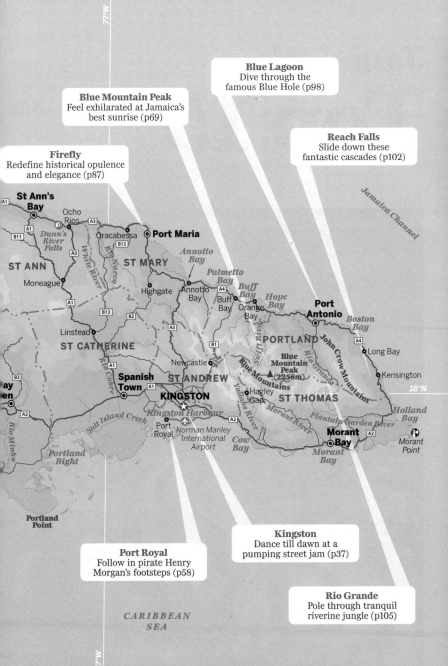

Blue Lagoon
Dive through the
famous Blue Hole (p98)

Blue Mountain Peak
Feel exhilarated at Jamaica's
best sunrise (p69)

Reach Falls
Slide down these
fantastic cascades (p102)

Firefly
Redefine historical opulence
and elegance (p87)

77°W

**St Ann's
Bay**

A1

Ocho
Rios   A3

*Dunn's
River
Falls*   Oracabessa   B13   ● **Port Maria**

A1   *Jamaica Channel*

B11

ST ANN   *White River*   *Rio Nuevo*   **ST MARY**

A3   *Annotto
Bay*

Moneague ●   A1   Highgate   Annotto   *Palmetto
                                                    Bay   Bay*

                   B13   B2   A3   Buff   *Buff   *Hope
                                                    Bay   Bay*   Bay*

Linstead ●   Orange   **Port
                                                    Bay   Antonio**   *Boston
                                                                          Bay*

ST CATHERINE   B1   **PORTLAND**   *Rio Grande*   *John Crow Mountains*   A4   Long Bay

                   Rio Cobre   Newcastle ●   Kensington ●

ay ●   **Spanish
                Town**   A1   **ST ANDREW**   ▲ **Blue   18°N
                                              Mountain
B3   ●   **KINGSTON** ★   Peak
en ●   *Kingston Harbour*   (2256m)   Hagley   *Morant River*
        A2   Gap   **ST THOMAS**
                          Port   *Norman Manley* *Yallahs River*   *Plantain Garden River*   *Holland
Rio Minho   Royal   International   Bay*
                                  Airport*   *Cow   **Morant**   A2
        Portland   *Bay*   **Bay**   ◉
        Bight   *Swift River*   ●   *Morant
                                                            Morant   Point
                                                            Bay*

*Portland
Point*

*CARIBBEAN
SEA*

Kingston
Dance till dawn at a
pumping street jam (p37)

Port Royal
Follow in pirate Henry
Morgan's footsteps (p58)

Rio Grande
Pole through tranquil
riverine jungle (p105)

77°W

Jamaica's
Top 15

Reggae Grooves

1 If there's any cultural trend that defines Jamaica to the rest of the world, it's reggae music – quite literally the soundtrack of the island. The reggae calendar is dominated by two huge events that celebrate the country's love of 'riddims,' both worth planning your trip around – Rebel Salute (p89) held every January in St Ann, and then Reggae Sumfest (p118), held in Montego Bay in the middle of the broiling Jamaican summer. Break out a sweat amid the throbbing mass of bodies and the nonstop dancing. Reggae Sumfest

Best Beaches

2 Jamaica's beach experiences are as varied as the island's topography. The tiny, delicate Lime Cay (p60), only reachable by boat from Port Royal, is perfect for snorkeling and picnics. Hellshire Beach (p60) heaves with Kingstonians and reverberates with loud music, its wooden shacks doing a roaring trade in fried fish. The north coast's Winnifred Beach (p98) draws the locals with its azure waters and weekend parties, while Negril's Seven Mile Beach (p138) is criss-crossed by jet-ski riders, and its long crescent of white sand lined with the bodies of sun worshippers. Seven Mile Beach, Negril

SHELBY SOBLICK/GETTY IMAGES ©

MARK BASSETT/ALAMY ©

RICK ELKINS/GETTY IMAGES ©

Reach Falls

3 On Jamaica's east coast, past stretches of jungle and beach that are completely off the radar of most tourists, you'll find, up in the hills, one of Jamaica's most beautiful waterfalls (p102) – and this is an island with a lot of beautiful waterfalls. Hire a guide (you'll need one, trust us) and clamber up slippery rocks, over neon-green moss and into cool mountain pools of the freshest spring water. In some areas you can dive under watery tunnels and through blizzards of snowy-white cascading foam.

Climbing Blue Mountain Peak

4 A night hike to reach Jamaica's highest point (p69) by sunrise, your path lit by the sparks of myriad fireflies, is an experience unlike any other. As you climb, the vegetation becomes less and less tropical, until you're hiking amid stunted trees draped with old man's beard (lichen) and giant ferns. In the pre-dawn cold at the summit, you wait in rapt silence as the first rays of the sun wash over the densely forested mountain peaks all around you, illuminating the distant coffee plantations and Cuba beyond.

Kingston Nightlife

5 Whether you're attending a nightclub or a street dance (p53), expect a sweaty, lively, no-holds-barred event. Dress up to the nines and follow the locals' lead. At a street dance, two giant speakers are placed facing each other, the street pounding with the bass, while nightclubs provide a similar indoor experience. Expect to be pulled into the melee as the locals will want to see how well you can dance, and bump and grind the best you can; the dancing will be some of the most explicit you'll ever see.

Negril

6 So you've walked on the snowy sands of Seven Mile Beach, wandered past the nude sunbathers, seen the sun sink behind the cliffs, plunged into the ocean to scrub your soul and fended off all the hustlers in Negril (p138). How about topping off all of these experiences by donning some scuba gear, getting PADI-certified and watching sea turtles dance their slow ballet in the cerulean waters of Jamaica's westernmost resort? If a full aqualung isn't your thing, just get your snorkel on amid the darting rainbow-colored fish.

MICHAEL LAWRENCE/GETTY IMAGES ©

Bob Marley Museum, Kingston

7 Marley's creaky home (p46) is crammed with memorabilia, but the visitor is drawn to his untouched bedroom, adorned with objects of spiritual significance to the artist, the small kitchen where he cooked I-tal food, the hammock in which he lay to seek inspiration from the distant mountains, and the room riddled with bullet holes, where he and his wife almost died in an assassination attempt. The intimate surrounds and modest personal effects speak eloquently of Marley's turbulent life.

Perfect Hotels in Treasure Beach

8 The greatest, most interesting variation of accommodations in Jamaica can be found in Treasure Beach (p173), on Jamaica's south coast. Here, instead of huge all-inclusive resorts, you'll find quiet, friendly guest houses, artsy enclaves dreamed up by theater set designers, Rasta retreats favored by budget backpackers and private villas that are some of the classiest, most elegant luxury residences in the country. Aside from beds and bathrooms, some places offer interesting extras such as cooking classes, rooftop yoga, farm-to-table banquets and movie nights.

DOUG PEARSON/GETTY IMAGES ©

Rafting the Rio Grande

9 No less a celebrity than Errol Flynn started the habit of sending discerning tourists on romantic, moonlit rafting trips through the Rio Grande Valley (p103), from Berridale to Rafter's Rest at St Margaret's Bay. These days the experience isn't quite as exclusive as it was when Mr Flynn was running the show – the Rio Grande rafting trips are actually quite affordable as Jamaican tourism activities go – but if the moon is full, you can still pole onto the waters, which turn silver and unspeakably romantic.

Appleton Rum Estate

10 Red Stripe is the alcohol everyone associates with Jamaica, but you may find that rum, the local spirit, provides a more diverse boozing experience. We're not saying Appleton produces the best rum on the island, but it is by far the most commonly available, bottled as several different varieties, and you can sample all these examples of the firewater at the Appleton Rum Estate (p165) in the Central Highlands. A lot of rum is served, so don't expect to accomplish much else on one of these day trips!

Sipping Coffee in Mandeville

11 Mandeville (p169) is the fifth-largest city on the island and the unofficial capital of the cool Central Highlands. This is an area that has been settled by many retired Jamaicans who have made their fortunes overseas, as well as many Western volunteers and aid-agency workers. As such, Mandeville has a cosmopolitan feel for a town of its size. Rub shoulders with the local intelligentsia at the Bloomfield Great House, which serves excellent pub fare, and sip some locally grown coffee as the mountain mists are dispelled by the golden sunlight. Picking coffee

Maroon Culture

12 The mysticism of Jamaican culture springs vividly to life in the Maroon settlements where escaped African slaves doggedly resisted the British colonizers in the 17th and 18th centuries and ultimately won their autonomy. Still protected by a 1739 treaty, the Maroons of Accompong (p166), Moore Town (p103) and Charles Town (p105) proudly preserve their old way of life and locals will happily show you around where land is community owned, bush medicine is still practiced and old Maroon trails in the hills can be still be hiked. Moore Town

CHRISTOPHER P BAKER/GETTY IMAGES ©

STUART DEE/GETTY IMAGES ©

Playing Pirates at Port Royal

13 The sleepy fishing village of Port Royal (p58) only hints at past glories that made it pirate capital of the Caribbean and 'the wickedest city on Earth.' Stroll in the footsteps of pirate Sir Henry Morgan along the battlements of Fort Charles, still lined with cannons to repel the invaders; become disorientated inside the Giddy House artillery store, tipped at a jaunty angle; or admire the treasures in the Maritime Museum, rescued from the deep after two thirds of the town sank beneath the waves in the monstrous 1692 earthquake. Fort Charles

Cockpit Country

14 The Cockpit Country of the island's interior is some of the most rugged terrain in the Caribbean, a series of jungle-clad round hills intersected by powerfully deep and sheer valleys. The rains gather in these mountains and the water percolates through the rocks, creating a Swiss cheese of sinkholes and caves. You can hike around the edges of Cockpit Country on old roads or forest paths, but to get the full wilderness experience hire a guide and tackle the hot, tough, perennially overgrown Troy–Windsor trail (p132). Good Hope Estate

Crocodile-spotting in Black River Great Morass

15 This is one of our favorite ways of exploring wild Jamaica: setting off by boat in the Black River Great Morass (p162), gliding past spidery mangroves and trees bearded with Spanish moss, while white egrets flap overhead. Your tour guide may tell you about the local women who sell bags of spicy 'swimp' (shrimp) on the riverside, and point to a beautiful, grinning American crocodile, cruising by.

Need to Know

For more information, see Survival Guide (p205)

Currency
Jamaican dollar (J$) and US dollar (US$)

Language
English and patois (pah-*twa*)

Visas
Not required for American, Canadian, UK, EU, Australian and Japanese citizens for stays of up to 90 days.

Money
ATMs, banks and moneychangers widely available in large cities, rarer in rural areas. US dollars (US$) preferred currency at larger hotels, resorts and restaurants.

Cell Phones
US phones must be set to roaming. Local SIM cards work in unlocked phones for most other countries.

Time
Eastern Standard Time (GMT/UTC minus five hours)

When to Go

Montego Bay
GO Dec–Mar

Ocho Rios
GO Jan–Apr

Negril
GO Feb–Apr

Port Antonio
GO Feb–May

Kingston
GO Mar–May

Tropical climate, wet & dry seasons
Tropical climate, rain year-round

High Season
(Dec–Mar)

➡ Expect sunny, warm days, especially on the coast. Little rainfall, except in Port Antonio and the northeast.

➡ At night it can become chilly, particularly in the mountains.

Shoulder Season
(Apr & May)

➡ Good time to visit; weather is still pretty dry (again, except in Port Antonio).

➡ Rates drop for accommodations.

➡ Far fewer tourists, especially in the big resorts/cruise ports.

Low Season
(Jun–Nov)

➡ Sporadic heavy rainfall across the island, except the south coast.

➡ Heavy storms, including hurricanes, gear up August to October.

➡ Many of Jamaica's best festivals happen in midsummer.

Useful Websites

Lonely Planet (www.lonely planet.com/jamaica) Succinct summaries on travel in Jamaica, plus the popular Thorn Tree bulletin board.

Jamaica National Heritage Trust (www.jnht.com) Excellent guide to Jamaica's history and heritage buildings.

Jamaica Gleaner (www.jamaica-gleaner.com) The island's most reliable newspaper.

Visit Jamaica (www.visit jamaica.com) The tourist board's version of Jamaica. Listing information may be outdated.

Important Numbers

Jamaica's country code is ⏀876, which is dropped if dialing in the country.

Ambulance	⏀110
Directory assistance	⏀114
International operator	⏀113
Police	⏀119
Tourism board	⏀929-9200

Exchange Rates

Australia	A$1	J$89
Canada	C$1	J$86
Euro zone	€1	J$121
Japan	¥100	J$105
New Zealand	NZ$1	J$68
UK	UK£1	J$136
US	US$1	J$85

For current exchange rates see www.xe.com.

➡

Daily Costs

Budget: less than US$100

➡ Everything is cheaper outside Kingston, Montego Bay, Negril and Ocho Rios

➡ Plate of jerk: US$3.50

➡ Route taxi fare: US$1 to US$2

➡ Double rooms: US$50

Midrange: US$100–200

➡ Admission to major attractions: US$20

➡ Short taxi ride: US$20

➡ Meal at mid-range restaurant: $20

➡ Share villas to score luxury rooms for midrange rates

Top end: more than US$300

➡ Private taxis for transport

➡ Fine dining: from US$30

➡ Luxury accommodations: from US$200

Opening Hours

Opening hours vary throughout the year. We've provided high-season opening hours; hours will generally decrease in the shoulder and low seasons, with the hours of restaurants, bars and clubs being particularly variable.

Banks 8.30am–1.30pm and 3.30pm–4.30pm Monday to Friday

Restaurants midday–2.30pm and 7.30pm–midnight

Cafes 7.30am–8pm

Bars and Clubs 10pm–4am

Shops 9am–1pm and 4pm–8pm Monday to Saturday

Arriving in Jamaica

Donald Sangster International Airport, Montego Bay (MBJ; ⏀952-3124; www.mbjairport. com) Taxis are US$10 to US$20 to downtown Montego Bay, US$80 to US$100 to Negril, US$100 to US$120 to Treasure Beach. Route taxis run from near the gas station at the airport entrance to the Hip Strip (J$100).

Norman Manley International Airport, Kingston (KIN; ⏀924-8452; www.nmia.aero) Taxis are US$30 to US$35 to New Kingston. Bus 98, opposite the arrivals hall, runs to Kingston Pde (J$100).

Getting Around

Public transportation in Jamaica consists of buses, minibuses and route taxis; they run between Kingston and every point on the island.

Bus Cheap travel between towns, but often overcrowded and dangerously driven. More expensive and reliable scheduled coaches also available.

Car Useful for traveling at your own pace, or for visiting regions with minimal public transportation. Cars can be hired in every town or city. Drive on the left.

Route taxi Run set routes within and between nearby towns and cities. Cheap and convenient.

For much more on **getting around**, see p213

If You Like...

Diving & Snorkeling

Major dive centers are concentrated on the northwest coast; snorkeling opportunities can be found almost anywhere. Dive or snorkel and you'll soon discover a plethora of vibrant small fish and good visibility.

Montego Bay It gets green points due to protected waters at Montego Bay Marine Park & Bogue Lagoon. (p109)

Ironshore Shares operators with Montego Bay. Sights such as The Point and the underwater tunnel at Widowmakers Cave are highlights. (p116)

Negril The calm waters that characterize Negril make it a good place for newbies seeking scuba certification. (p140)

Ocho Rios A reef stretches from Ocho Rios to Galina Point and makes for fine diving and snorkeling expeditions. (p76)

Music

Jamaica is per capita one of the most musically influential nations in the world. From local sound-system parties to international festivals, beats and bass are always in the background here.

Kingston parties Downtown Kingston's sound-system parties are the stuff of legend, with the brashest dancehall on the streets. (p37)

Reggae Sumfest The world's definitive reggae experience features both the best of old sweet sounds and dancehall's raucous 'riddims.' (p118)

Rebel Salute Held on the north coast in January, this is the biggest roots reggae festival in Jamaica. (p89)

Alpha Live! Spot upcoming Kingston talent at weekly open bands sessions at the most musically-influential boys' school on the island. (p46)

Historic Sites

Jamaica's complex story can be explored in a variety of ways, from its beautiful colonial architecture to community tourism projects recounting history from the bottom up.

Falmouth This friendly little town on the north coast boasts the greatest concentration of historic buildings in all Jamaica. (p126)

Port Royal Just a skip away from Kingston is this old haven of pirates and streets of Georgian architecture. (p58)

Outameni A fantastically comprehensive museum and multimedia and dramatic production that examines the wide sweep of Jamaican history and ethnicities. (p129)

Accompong The isolated outpost of the living Maroons, descendants of escaped slaves who have retained deep African cultural roots. (p166)

Wildlife

Jamaica is unexpectedly rich in wildlife, from American crocodiles and a diverse, multihued bird population, to the marine fauna, including dolphins and sea turtles, that inhabits the surrounding waters.

Black River Great Morass Nothing makes a boat trip into a Jurassic-looking swamp cooler than dozens of prehistoric-looking crocodiles. (p174)

Windsor birding Head into the daunting jungles of craggy Cockpit Country with trained ornithologists in search of birdlife. (p133)

Rocklands Bird Feeding Station In Anchovy, this quirky grassroots tourism project is for birders who want to catch sight of Jamaica's hummingbirds. (p132)

Canoe Valley Wetland A series of isolated, lonely roads lead to this lovely window onto Eden, where jungle vines frame a pool sometimes frequented by manatees. (p62)

ANTHONY PIDGEON/GETTY IMAGES ©

SHANE LUITJENS/ALAMY ©

Food & Drink

When home is a garden island populated by a cultural mélange of Africans, Chinese, Indians, Spanish and English, you should probably expect food to evolve in some interesting ways.

Boston Bay The supposed birthplace of jerk, Jamaica's most famous spice rub, is the best place to sample it. (p101)

Appleton Rum Estate Sip the strong stuff in the Central Highlands and realize how much flavor rocket fuel can have. (p165)

Fine Kingston dining The nation's capital is the place to sample haute Caribbean cuisine. (p50)

Blue Mountain coffee Take a 'bean to cup' tour of the plantations above Kingston that grow some of the world's most exclusive coffee. (p66)

Waterfalls & Rivers

Jamaica's rivers have historically been the country's most important arterials. Today, they're also a playground for tourists, visiting the Caribbean's most dramatic waterfalls.

YS Falls Deeply secluded in St Elizabeth parish, you'd be forgiven for thinking YS Falls emerged out of Eden. (p166)

Martha Brae River Be gently poled down this emerald-green tunnel, a silent riverine paradise close to MoBay. (p128)

Reach Falls These tall falls, which cascade through pools into lush jungle, may be the most beautiful in Jamaica. (p102)

Dunn's River Falls They may be slightly overcrowded, but it's still tons of fun to clamber up these slippery falls. (p76)

PLAN YOUR TRIP IF YOU LIKE...

Top: YS Falls (p166)
Bottom: Jerk chicken

Month by Month

January

January is prime tourist season, when the rains are few and the weather is pleasantly sunny and warm.

☆ Rebel Salute

The biggest Roots Reggae concert in Jamaica goes down on the second Saturday in January at Richmond Estate in St Ann on the north coast. Details at www.rebelsaluteja.com.

☆ Air Jamaica Jazz & Blues Festival

Locally and internationally acclaimed artists perform a variety of musical genres in a splendid outdoor setting near Rose Hall, Montego Bay. Held in the last week of January. Details at www.jamaicajazzandblues.com.

February

The weather continues to be dry and the sun continues to shine as some of the important cultural festivals on the island occur in the east.

★ Fi Wi Sinting

This festival (the name means 'It is ours') has grown into the largest celebration of Jamaica's African heritage, with music, crafts and food, Jonkanoo dancing, mentos music and storytelling. Held in Hope Bay, Portland parish. Details at www.fiwisinting.com.

★ Jamaica Carnival

This carnival draws thousands of costumed revelers to the streets of Kingston, MoBay and Ochi. Sometimes spills over into March. Details at www.bacchanaljamaica.com.

March

You may find Jamaica less crowded, yet still blessed with good weather, as the high tourism season comes to an end. In the capital, thoughts turn to getting fit.

🏃 Boys & Girls Championships

Held during the last week before Easter, this century-old four-day event is a crown jewel of Jamaican athletics. Around 30,000 spectators (and talent scouts), crowd the national stadium to try to spot the next Usain Bolt. Details at www.issasports.com.

🏃 Kingston City Run

In the first weekend of March, Kingston straps on its running shoes and takes part in the popular charity-fundraising Kingston City Run. Details at www.kingstoncityrun.com.

April

While this is the beginning of the Jamaican shoulder season, the weather stays largely dry even as the crowds, and accommodations rates, start to plummet.

🍴 Trelawny Yam Festival

In ruggedly beautiful Albert Town: yam-balancing races, best-dressed goat and donkey, the crowning of the Yam King and Queen – how can you resist? Perhaps the most idiosyncratic, unique festival on an island full of 'em. Details at www.stea.net.

May

The rainy season really

gears up in May, although things stay dry in the south for the nation's top literary festival.

Calabash International Literary Festival

This innovative literary festival draws some of the best creative voices from Jamaica, plus highly touted international intelligentsia, to Treasure Beach. Details at www.calabashfestival.org.

Jamaica Observer Food Awards

The venerable *Observer*'s affair is the Caribbean's most prestigious culinary event. International talent and attention turn towards Kingston, where local restaurateurs bring their top game to the kitchen. Details at www.jamaicaobserver.com/foodawards.

June

A soupy combination of heat and humidity from the rains begins to take hold, but sea breezes on the coast and mountain chill in the interior keep things fresh.

Caribbean Fashion Week

You may not be able to access some of the most exclusive tents here, but the vibe of Caribbean Fashion Week can be felt all across Uptown and the posher suburbs of Kingston. Details at www.caribbeanfashionweek.com.

July

Phew. It's hot. And not just the weather: one of the island's best music festivals heats up the events

calendar. The rainy season continues.

☆ Reggae Sumfest

The big mama of all reggae festivals, held in late July in Montego Bay, this event brings top acts together for an unforgettable party. Even if you're not attending, you're attending – the festivities tend to take over MoBay. Details at www.reggaesumfeset.com.

August

It's as hot as Jamaica gets, and about as humid too. In fact, the rains may be coalescing into ominous storm clouds. Yet the celebrations on the island aren't slowing down.

Independence Day

August 6 marks Jamaica's independence from the British Empire, and occurs with no small fanfare and delivery of dramatic speeches, especially in the Kingston area. Celebrations mark the event island-wide.

October

Now the rains are coming in hard, and there may be hurricanes gathering off the coast. On the plus side, accommodations run dirt cheap.

Jamaica Coffee Festival

Thousands of coffee lovers converge on the spacious lawns of Devon House in Kingston during the first week of October to slurp up Jamaica's world-famous coffee in an orgy of beverages, liqueurs, ice cream, cigars and classic Jamaican chow.

November

The rains are beginning to slacken off, although the northeast is still getting drenched. This is the end of low-season rates.

Restaurant Week

Jamaican restaurant week has been building over the years, and organizers clearly hope it will grow in international cachet. It shows off the dishes of participating restaurants from Kingston, Ocho Rios and Montego Bay. Details at http://go-jamaica.com/rw.

December

The weather becomes refreshingly dry again, and resorts start raising their prices accordingly. During Christmas, thousands of Jamaicans fly in from the US, Canada and the UK to spend time with family.

☆ LTM National Pantomime

The Jamaican take on social satire is raw, irreverent and amusing, and presented at this annual song-and-dance revue in Kingston from December through January. This is some of the best theater in the Caribbean. Details at www.ltmpantomine.com.

National Exhibition

Kingston's National Gallery shows works by Jamaica's newcomers and old hands at this biennial display; one of the most anticipated cultural events in the Caribbean. The current cycle hits on even-numbered years. Details at www.natgalja.org.jm.

Itineraries

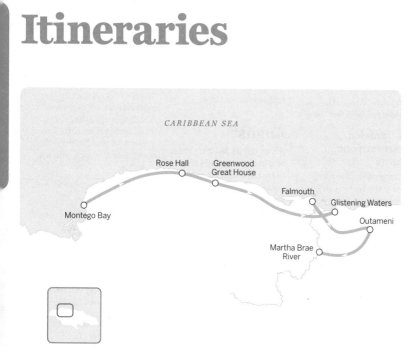

CARIBBEAN SEA

Rose Hall

Greenwood
Great House

Falmouth

Glistening Waters

Montego Bay

Outameni

Martha Brae
River

Montego Bay & Around

Start in **Montego Bay**, the gateway to Jamaica for about 80% of international travelers. Hit Doctor's Cave Beach for water sports and head downtown to Sam Sharpe Sq, taking in the historic architecture and the hustle of a real Jamaican city. Are you exhausted by all that energy, or did it invigorate you? Either way, finish up with a fine meal on the Hip Strip.

Spend the next morning relaxing on Montego Bay's beaches and maybe enjoy a cold Red Stripe and plate of jerk for lunch, but don't linger too long. Heading east from MoBay you'll find two great houses: the more (in)famous **Rose Hall** and the more authentic **Greenwood Great House**; we recommend the latter. Grab lunch on the north coast and relax on the beach before taking a nighttime boating expedition at **Glistening Waters**.

The next day give yourself a crash course in Jamaican history with a walking tour of **Falmouth** and its faded Georgian buildings. Then catch the incredible cultural show at **Outameni**. Finish this itinerary with a rafting trip down the **Martha Brae River**.

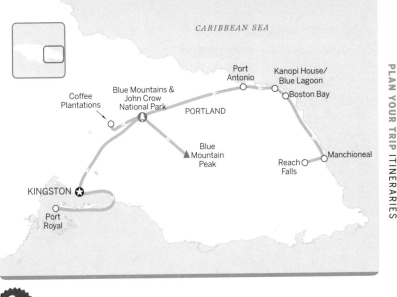

Kingston, Blue Mountains & Portland

3 WEEKS

Touch down in **Kingston** for three days of sightseeing, excellent food and rip-roaring nightlife. Don't miss the National Gallery. Take in historic Devon House, enjoying Jamaica's best patties and ice-cream while you're there. Afterwards head up to Bob Marley Museum. After hours, enjoy dinner and live music at Red Bones Blues Cafe, segueing elsewhere into a dancehall party and some of the liveliest nightlife in the Caribbean. For a captivating day trip, visit **Port Royal**, the earthquake-shattered former haunt of pirates and privateers.

Those hills looming over the city are calling, so slip into the Blue Mountains. Enjoy the breathtaking scenery and crisp mountain air from hiking trails in **Blue Mountains & John Crow National Park**. The main event here is making an early-morning ascent of **Blue Mountain Peak**, Jamaica's highest mountain. If you are truly adventurous, whiz down from the highlands on a bicycle tour; if such a trip seems like a bit too much, enjoy a pleasant day seeing how the Caribbean's most prized coffee rises from bean to brewery at the one of several **coffee plantations**.

Descend from the Blue Mountains to Portland parish, on the prettiest stretch of the north coast. Walk the atmospheric streets of **Port Antonio**, taking lodging in one of the many intimate spots to the east of town or within the port's atmospheric historic district. East of Port Antonio, you'll find appealing communities with stellar beaches and attractive places to stay.

You can explore this terrific stretch of coast quickly or slowly, but it lends itself to some lingering. In the course of, say, five days you could go diving in the **Blue Lagoon** and stay at gorgeous **Kanopi House**, take a visit to **Boston Bay**, the home of jerk cooking, stop in **Manchioneal**, a terrific base for visiting the sublime **Reach Falls**, one of the best waterfalls on the island.

The Sunny South

Start your trip in **Bluefields**, where you'll find some exceptional stretches of beach and the mausoleum of reggae star Peter Tosh. We recommend shacking up in one of the local Rasta-run homestays, where you can begin to slip into the laid-back rhythms of the south coast.

Linger at this quiet fishing beach for a day or three, then continue on to **Black River**, a sleepy port town with lovely historic buildings and vintage hotels. This is the gateway for boats into the mangrove swamps of the **Black River Great Morass**, a gorgeous wetlands where crocodile sightings are common. A trip up the river will take up a day of your time; afterwards visit the Ashton Great House.

In the morning head north to **Middle Quarters** for an unforgettable lunch of pepper shrimp at a crossroads eatery and an afternoon at the lovely **YS Falls**. Wet your whistle at the **Appleton Rum Estate**, then head south to **Treasure Beach**. Stay awhile in the welcoming embrace of this tight-knit community (folks seem to easily lose a month here). Be sure to take a boat trip to one of the planet's coolest watering holes, the Pelican Bar, perched on stilts on a sandbar 1km out to sea.

From Treasure Beach, visit **Lover's Leap** for an astonishing view of the coastlands. You could spend a day here walking around the sweet pastureland of **Back Seaside**. Continue along the coast to the fishing village of **Alligator Pond**. Far from packaged tourism, here you can enjoy traditional village life and unspoiled scenery at its best. You'll also enjoy a seafood feast at a truly extraordinary beachside restaurant, Little Ochie.

If you have your own car, preferably a 4WD, and are a confident driver, head east from Alligator Pond on the 'lonely road.' This really is an isolated stretch of road, but you'll find wild, empty beaches here and, after many potholes, **Alligator Hole**, a small preserve where manatees can be spotted.

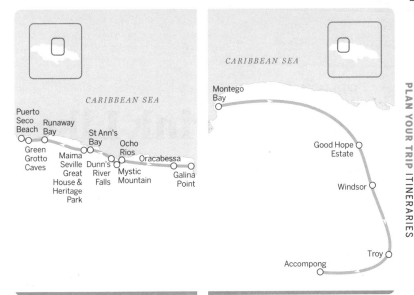

Ocho Rios & the Central Coast

1 WEEK

Start this trip in the tourist town of **Ocho Rios**. Give yourself two days to chill out around Ocho Rios, taking full advantage of the tourist menu of activities, especially **Mystic Mountain** and the amazing **Dunn's River Falls**.

Drive along the coast towards **Oracabessa** to see sights associated with James Bond author Ian Fleming, such as the lovely hotel of Goldeneye; and **Galina Point** for Noël Coward, whose former estate Firefly is now an excellent museum.

Turning back, head past Ocho Rios before stopping in at St Ann's Bay to see the Columbus and Marcus Garvey monuments, then on to the **Maima Seville Great House & Heritage Park**, which can be explored on horseback.

Now head to **Runaway Bay**, where you can eat well, sleep well and base yourself for an exploration of the awesome **Green Grotto Caves** before continuing on to Discovery Bay and the simple charms of **Puerto Seco Beach**.

A Taste of Cockpit Country

1 WEEK

From Montego Bay, head out to the **Good Hope Estate**, a beautiful house and working plantation. Enjoy horseback riding, lunch on the terrace and tremendous views.

On narrow roads, travel through cane fields to **Windsor**. Check into a lodge and wake to the sound of birds, then head off to explore Windsor Caves with a Rastafarian guide, or pay a visit to the Windsor Great House to learn about its environmental protection and bird-banding efforts.

Get ready for some challenging but rewarding hiking. From Windsor you can hire a guide and walk the old military trail connecting Windsor (in the north) with Troy (in the south)...but be ready for some gnarly trails. Exhausted and exhilarated, head east to Clark's Town, then **Troy**. This part of the journey is made for soaking up the scenery. Continue south and make sure to stop at **Accompong**, where you can meet Jamaica's remaining Maroons (descendants of escaped slaves).

It's possible to get around on this tour via route taxi, but you'll get the most out of it by renting a 4WD.

Eat & Drink Like a Local

One of the best ways to learn about Jamaica is through its food, so why not eat your way around the island? Ackee and saltfish for breakfast, curried goat for lunch and an I-tal vegetarian dinner will teach you more about Jamaica than a month at any all-inclusive resort. Jamaica's tropical climate means good, fresh food abounds throughout the year, but keep an eye out for foodie festivals.

The Year in Food

Portland Jerk Festival (July)

A celebration of everything smoked and spicy held across Portland parish, the spiritual home of Jamaican jerk.

Jamaica Coffee Festival (October)

Farmers, roasters and baristas alike gather together in Kingston to celebrate everything coffee, from Blue Mountain bean to cup.

Port Royal Seafood Festival (October)

A fisherman's haul of splendid seafood (and music) in Jamaica's old pirate capital, a stone's throw from Kingston.

Jamaica Restaurant Week (November)

Held across Kingston, Montego Bay and Ocho Rios, this is Jamaica's biggest festival of the island's culinary arts.

Eating in Jamaica

Jamaican Favorites

Ackee & saltfish The Jamaican breakfast of champions. Ackee fruit bears an uncanny resemblance to scrambled eggs when cooked, while the salty, flaky fish adds a savory depth to the pleasing blandness of the ackee. Usually served with johnny cakes and *callaloo* (a spinach-like vegetable).

Breadkind A sort of catch-all term for starch accompaniments, which can include yams, breadfruit, *bammy* (cassava flatbread), *festival* (sweet fried cornbread), johnny cakes (dumplings) and steamed bananas, among others. While not technically breadkinds, rice and peas (rice and beans) is also a major addition.

Brown stew Often more of a sauce than a stew, brown stew dishes are a nice combination of savory and sweet (and slightly tangy); it's a good choice for those who don't like hot food.

Curry All kinds of curry are popular in Jamaica, but goat curry is king, chopped into small bits with meat on the bone. While the curry has Indian roots, it's not as hot as its motherland cuisine.

Escoveitch Imported from Spain by Spanish Jews, escoveitch is a marinade – most commonly used on fish – made of vinegar, onions, carrots and Scotch bonnet peppers.

Jerk The island's signature dish, jerk is the name for a tongue-searing marinade and spice rub for meats and fish, and for the method of smoking them slowly in an outdoor pit over a fire of pimento wood for its unique flavor. Every chef has a secret ingredient, but allspice, a dark berry which tastes like a mixture of cinnamon, clove and nutmeg, is essential.

Oxtail Simmered with butter beans and served with rice, stewed oxtail is a national obsession.

Patties Delicious meat pies; fillings can include spicy beef, vegetables, fish and shrimp. A Jamaican favorite is a patty sandwich – a patty squeezed between two thick slices of coco bread (a sweet bread baked with coconut milk). Juici Patties and Tastee Patty are reliable national fast food chains selling patties and other Jamaican takeaway dishes.

Rundown chicken Cooked in spicy coconut milk, and usually enjoyed for breakfast with johnny cakes. Some say the dish is named for the method by which the chicken is caught.

Fish tea 'Warm up yuh belly' with this favorite local cure-all. Essentially, fish broth.

Fruits & Vegetables

'All fruits ripe' A Jamaican expression meaning 'all is well,' which is also the state of Jamaican fruit. This island is a tropical-fruit heaven. Sampling them all and finding your favorites is a noble, healthy and rewarding task. Don't just taste the obvious, like coconut, banana, papaya and mango. Savor your first star apple, soursop, *ortanique*, naseberry or tinkin' toe.

I-tal Thanks to the Rastafarians, Jamaica is vegie-friendly. The I-tal diet (derived from 'vital') has evolved an endless index of no-nos. For instance: no salt, no chemicals, no meat or dairy (the latter is 'white blood'), no alcohol, cigarettes or drugs (ganja doesn't count). Fruits, vegetables, soy, wheat gluten and herbs prevail. Because of the popularity of the I-tal diet many restaurants offer I-tal options on their menus. Popular dishes include eggplant curry, whipped sweet potatoes and steamed vegetables.

Drinks

Nonalcoholic Drinks

Coffee Jamaican Blue Mountain coffee is considered one of the most exotic and expensive coffees in the world. It's relatively mild and light-bodied with a musty, almost woody flavor and its own unmistakable aroma. Most upscale hotels and restaurants serve it as a matter of course. The majority of lesser hotels serve lesser coffees from other parts of the country or – sacrilege! – powdered instant coffee. Be careful if you ask for white coffee (with milk), which Jamaicans interpret to mean 50% hot milk and 50% coffee.

Tea 'Tea' is a generic Jamaican term for any (usually) hot, nonalcoholic drink, and Jamaicans will make teas of anything. Irish moss is often mixed with rum, milk and spices. Ginger, mint, ganja and even fish are brewed into teas.

Cold drinks A Jamaican favorite for cooling off is 'skyjuice,' a shaved-ice cone flavored with sugary fruit syrup and lime juice, sold at streetside stalls. You may also notice 'bellywash,' the local name for limeade.

Ting A bottled grapefruit soda, Ting is Jamaica's own soft drink, although Pepsi is pretty popular too (Coca Cola is surprisingly difficult to find).

Coconut water Sold straight from the nut from streetside vendors, along with its white 'jelly.'

Roots tonics Made from the roots of plants such as raw moon bush, cola bark, sarsaparilla and dandelion, roots tonics are widely available in small shops, or sold roadside in handmade batches. They taste like dirt...but in a good way.

Alcoholic Drinks

Rum Jamaica is proud of its rum – the smooth and dark Appleton rum is the most celebrated brand and is great sipped or mixed. You can even visit the estate (p165) where it's made. Wray & Nephew's white overproof rum carries a knockout blow – it may come in a shot glass, but if you down it in one go you're heading home early. Mix it with ginger beer, or even milk ('cow and cane').

PRICE RANGES

The following price structure is based on the cost of an average meal at a Jamaican restaurant. Be aware of restaurants adding 16.5% government tax and a further 10% service charge to the bill.

⇒ **Budget**
$ less than US$15 (J$1600)

⇒ **Midrange**
$$ US$15 to US$25 (J$1600 to J$2600)

⇒ **Top end**
$$$ more than US$25 (J$2600)

JAMAICAN FRUIT PRIMER

ackee	Its yellow flesh is a tasty and popular breakfast food, invariably served with saltfish.
cho cho	Also known as christophine or chayote; a pulpy squashlike gourd served in soups and as an accompaniment to meats. Also used for making hot pickles.
guava	A small ovoid or rounded fruit with a musky sweet aroma. It has a pinkish granular flesh studded with regular rows of tiny seeds. It is most commonly used in nectars and punches, syrups, jams, chutney and even ice cream.
guinep	A small green fruit (pronounced gi-nep) that grows in clusters, like grapes, and can be bought from July through November. Each 'grape' bears pink flesh that you plop into your mouth whole. It's kind of rubbery and juicy, and tastes like a cross between a fig and a strawberry. Watch for the big pip in the middle.
jackfruit	A yellow fruit from the large pods of the jackfruit tree. Jackfruit seeds can be roasted or boiled.
mango	A lush fruit that comes in an assortment of sizes and colors, from yellow to black. Massage the glove-leather skin to soften the pulp, which can be sucked or spooned like custard. Select your mango by its perfume.
naseberry	A sweet, yellow and brown fruit that tastes a bit like peach and comes from an evergreen tree. Also known as sapodilla.
papaya	Cloaks of many colors (from yellow to rose) hide a melon-smooth flesh that likewise runs from citron to vermilion. The central cavity is a trove of edible black seeds. Tenderness and sweet scent are key to buying papayas.
Scotch bonnet pepper	Celebrated for its delicious citrus sparkle just before your entire mouth and head go up in flames, Scotch bonnets are small hot peppers that come in yellow, orange and red.
soursop	An ungainly, irregularly shaped fruit with cottony pulp that is invitingly fragrant yet acidic. Its taste hints at guava and pineapple.
star apple	A leathery, dark-purple, tennis-ball-sized gelatinous fruit of banded colors (white, pink, lavender, purple). Its glistening seeds form a star in the center. The fruit is mildly sweet and understated.
sweetsop	A heart-shaped, lumpy fruit packed with pits and a sweet, custardlike flesh.
ugli	A fruit that is well named. It is ugly on the vine – like a deformed grapefruit with warty, mottled green or orange skin. But the golden pulp is delicious: acid-sweet and gushingly juicy.

Beer Red Stripe is Jamaica's famous beer, a crisp and sweet antidote to spicy jerk creations. Real Rock is a slightly heavier, local lager, while Dragon Stout is also popular. Heineken and Guinness are brewed locally under license.

Self-Catering

Food at grocery stores is usually expensive, as many canned and packaged goods are imported. Dirt-cheap fresh fruits, vegetables and spices sell at markets and roadside stalls island-wide. Wash all produce thoroughly! You can always buy fish (and lobster, in season) from local fisher folk.

Cooking Courses & Tours

Liven up your kitchen by learning how to cook Jamaican-style. Good places include Treasure Beach Cooking (p179; in Treasure Beach) and Hotel Mocking Bird Hill (p100; near Port Antonio).

To travel and taste at the same time, join a specialist culinary tour. Those offered by Jamaica Cultural Enterprises (p47) in Kingston and Falmouth Heritage Walks (p127) in Falmouth are particularly recommended. Don't forget coffee tasting in the Blue Mountains (p66), and the tours offered by the Appleton Sugar Estate and Rum Factory (p165).

Plan Your Trip

Outdoor Activities

Jamaica might be in the Caribbean, but it offers a lot more than just sunbathing on a beach, from mountain biking and rafting to horse riding and bird-watching. Get a natural high hiking in the mountains or dive below the waves to explore shipwrecks and coral.

Bird-Watching

All you need in the field are a good pair of binoculars and a guide to the birds of the island. Expect to pay anywhere from US$25 for an hour's jaunt to US$75 for a good half-day of bird-watching in the bush.

Where to Go

Good spots include:

➡ **Black River Great Morass** (p162)
➡ **Blue Mountains** (p66)
➡ **Cockpit Country** (p133)
➡ **Negril Great Morass** (p150)
➡ **Rio Grande Valley** (p103)

When to Go

The best time for bird-watching in Jamaica runs from December to June; at this time of year birds can be expected to show off their best plumage. This is also the dry season, so you're less likely to be drenched in your binoculars. A good online resourse is the Caribbean Birding Trail (www.caribbeanbirdingtrail. org), a conservation and eco-tourism organization that covers the Caribbean Basin.

Operators

Suggested operators include the following:

➡ **Ann Sutton** (☎904-5454; asutton@ cwjamaica.com) Based in Marshall's Pen in

Best of the Best

Best Wall Dive
The Point (p116) Swimming amid sharks and shoals along this coral-clad sea-wall

Best Wreck Dive
The *Kathryn* (p77) Diving alongside the wreck of a minesweeper on a reef near Ocho Rios

Best Long Hike
Blue Mountain Peak (p69) Getting to the top just in time for the best sunrise in Jamaica

Best Short Jaunt
Back Seaside (p161) Having a stroll amid the low hills and soft breezes near Treasure Beach

Best River-Rafting
Rio Grande (p105) Heading up into the jungle-clad, rain-soaked green tunnels of the eastern parishes

Best Wildlife-Viewing
Black River Great Morass (p162) A boat trek from Treasure Beach, past jumping dolphins, up the river by sunning, grinning crocodiles

Mandeville, has been leading major bird tours in Jamaica for more than 30 years.

➡ **Arrowhead Birding Tours** (www.arrow headbirding.com) Tours of one to eight days from Kingston.

➡ **Hope Gardens** (p47) Bird-watching tours on the first Saturday of every month.

➡ **Hotel Mocking Bird Hill** (p100) Hotel outside Port Antonio, known for its highly regarded custom birding tours.

➡ **Rocklands Bird Sanctuary** (☑952-2009) Near Montego Bay.

Caving

Jamaica is honeycombed with limestone caves and caverns, most of which boast fine stalagmites and stalactites, underground streams and even waterfalls. The Jamaican Caves Organisation (p204) provides resources for the exploration of caves, sinkholes and underground rivers. The group regularly sends out expeditions to survey the island's caves. Expect to pay a guide at least US$50 per person for a short, half-day exploration of a cave; if you want to go deeper and longer into spelunking territory, rates for guides start at US$70 to US$85 for full-day treks.

Where to Go

You can find guided tours at these caves:

➡ **Fox Caves** (p104), Rio Grande Valley

➡ **Green Grotto** (p92), Discovery Bay

➡ **Roaring River** (p154), Savanna-la-Mar

➡ **Windsor Caves** (p134), Cockpit Country

The following are for advanced cavers:

➡ **Coffee River Caves** (p168), Troy

➡ **Gourie Caves** (p168), Christiana

➡ **Peterkin-Rota Caves** (p133), St James

Cycling

You can hire bicycles at most major resorts and many smaller guest houses. For anything more serious, you should consider bringing your own mountain or multipurpose bike. You will need sturdy wheels to handle the potholed roads. Check requirements with the airline well in advance. Remember to always have, at a minimum, a flashlight for the front of your bike and reflectors for the rear. If you're in the fixed-gear bicycle camp, note that Jamaica's many hills and unpredictable traffic make riding a 'fixie' extremely difficult.

Good online resources include the **Jamaican Cycling Federation** (www.jamaica cycling.com; 14C Benson Ave, Kingston) and **St Mary's Off-Road Bike Association** (SMORBA; ☑470-8139; www.smorba.com).

Operators

The downhill tour from Hardwar Gap (1700m) in the Blue Mountains is very popular (but not for the fainthearted).

Blue Mountain Bicycle Tours (☑974-7075; www.bmtoursja.com; 121 Main St, Ocho Rios) offers pickup from Kingston or Ocho Rios and transfer to Hardwar Gap. Other tours available around Ocho Rios. Also try **Mount Edge B&B** (p64).

Diving & Snorkeling

Diving has been a part of the Jamaican tourist landscape since the late 1960s, when the first facilities opened in Montego Bay, even then the tourism capital of the island. Thanks to nearby reefs and the MoBay marine park, the northwest coast from Negril to Ocho Rios remains the epicenter of Jamaican diving culture. By law, all dives in Jamaican waters must be guided, and dives are restricted to a depth of 30m.

Where to Go

Dive Sites:

➡ **Airport Reef** (p116)

➡ **Rose Hall Reef** (p116)

➡ **The Throne** (p140)

Snorkeling Sites:

➡ **Belmont Beach** (p157)

➡ **Seven Mile Beach (Long Beach)** (p138)

When to Go

It's best to go from January to April, when the weather is driest and least prone to storms.

Operators

Montego Bay

➡ **Dressel Divers** (p117)

➡ **Jamaica Scuba Divers** (☑Falmouth 342-617-2500, Negril 957-3039) Based out of

APPROXIMATE DIVING COSTS

1-tank dive US$50

2-tank dive US$95

Snorkeling excursion around US$30

PADI or NAUI certification course around US$420

Rental of masks, fins, snorkels, buoyancy control devices and regulators usually an extra $15.

Falmouth, Negril and Runaway Bay, but does excursions to MoBay.

➡ **Resort Divers** (p117)

Negril

➡ **Marine Life Divers** (p140)

➡ **Sundivers Negril** (☑957-4503; www.sundiversnegril.com; Point Village Resort, Long Bay)

Ocho Rios

➡ **Garfield Diving Station** (p77)

➡ **Resort Divers** (p77)

Fishing

Deepwater game fish run year-round through the Cayman Trench, which begins just over 3km from shore on the western side of the island. The waters off Jamaica's north coast are also particularly good for game fishing; an abyss known as 'Marlin Alley' teems with game fish. Charters can be arranged for US$500 to US$550 per half-day or US$900 to US$1200 for a full day through hotels or directly through operators in Montego Bay, Negril, Ocho Rios and Port Antonio. A charter includes captain, tackle, bait and crew. Most charter boats require a 50% deposit.

When to Go

Summer (June to August) is good for game fishing, but major tournaments go off in Montego Bay in late September and October.

Operators

Port Antonio

➡ **Errol Flynn Marina** (p213)

Montego Bay

➡ **Montego Bay Yacht Club** (p213)

Hiking

Hiking is a great way of seeing the Jamaican interior, but keep in mind it's always best to head into the jungles and the mountains with a guide. It's easy to get lost out here, and it's good to have a contact who can vouch for you with locals. Expect to pay at least US$45 a day for local expertise, and possibly a good deal more to head into particularly difficult terrain.

Where to Go

The most developed area for hiking is in Blue Mountains & John Crow National Park, followed by the Rio Grande Valley in Portland parish, where some of the hikes venture into the Blue and John Crow Mountains. The remote Cockpit Country, with its jungle-clad limestone hills, is perhaps the most dramatic landscape on the island; small community-tourism outfits are growing in that region.

➡ **Best Short Trek** The one to the summit of Blue Mountain Peak (p69). Reaching it at sunrise is one of the Caribbean's most exhilarating experiences. The view out over the entire island (and as far as Cuba if the day's clear) more than compensates for having to get up at an inhuman hour.

➡ **Best Long Trek** A trek from Troy, in South Cockpit Country, to the Windsor Caves in North Cockpit Country (p132). This hike traverses some of the most beautiful yet simultaneously difficult terrain in the country. Attempting it without a guide is genuinely risky.

➡ **Best Bird-Walking** Head out in the area around Windsor, in North Cockpit Country, with the biologists of the Windsor Research Centre (p134). It's a fun walk (although you need to be fit) and the accompanying scientific expertise is priceless.

When to Go

It's best to go from January to April, when the weather is driest and least prone to storms.

Operators

➡ **Grand Valley Tours** (Map p94;☑993-4116, in the USA 401-647-4730; www.portantoniojamaica.com/gvt.html; 12 West St) Treks to Scatter and Fox Caves as well as hikes to Moore Town, Nanny Falls, Nanny Town and along the White River Trail.

DON'T WANDER OFF THE TRACK

Wherever your walk carries you, be sure to stay on the established trails: the mountainous terrain in Jamaica is too treacherous to go wandering off the track as thick vegetation hides sinkholes and crevasses. You should seek local advice about trail conditions before setting out, and take a good guide even if you know the route.

If you're heading into the back-country, don't forget the following:

⇒ hiking boots
⇒ mosquito netting
⇒ bug spray
⇒ drinking water
⇒ sunblock

⇒ **Jamaica Conservation & Development Trust** (☎960-2848; www.jcdt.org.jm; 29 Dumbarton Ave, Kingston 10) Responsible for the management and supervision of the Blue Mountains & John Crow National Park. Can advise on guides and routes.

⇒ **Original Trails of the Maroons** (☎475-3046; www.jamaicanmaroons.com) This is an excellent ecotourism collaboration between an expat and the local Accompong community. It offers cultural tours of Accompong, and arranges tours with local guides into the rugged interior of the Cockpit Country.

Horse Riding

Horse riding is a popular attraction, particularly along the coast where you can ride your horses into the sea, or to explore some of the larger plantations. Expect to pay US$60 to US$70 for a two-hour excursion. Reliable operators include:

⇒ **Braco Stables** (p130), near Falmouth
⇒ **Chukka Caribbean Adventure Tours** (p78), Ocho Rios
⇒ **Hooves** (p78), St Ann's Bay
⇒ **Rhodes Hall Plantation** (p140), Negril

Rafting

Errol Flynn first saw the fun of coasting down the river on a raft of bamboo poles lashed together. Today, you sit on a raised seat with padded cushions, while a 'captain' poles you through the washboard shallows and small cataracts.

Where to Go

The best river-rafting in Jamaica is in the mountainous interior of the northwest, near the Great River and Martha Brae River (p128). Both of these are within easy day-tripping distance of Montego Bay and Ironshore. On the other side of Jamaica, head to the Rio Grande Valley (p105), which sits within day-trip distance between Kingston and Port Antonio in the east.

When to Go

The best time to go rafting is in the dry season (December to April), when the waters aren't too swollen. If you want a white-water experience, head here in summer.

Operators

⇒ **Mountain Valley Rafting** (☎956-4920; Lethe Estate; 1-/2-person US$50/80) For trips along the Great River, in the interior, within easy day-trip distance of Montego Bay and Ironshore.

⇒ **Rafters Village** (☎940-6398, 952-0889; www.jamaicarafting.com; 66 Claude Clarke Ave, Montego Bay; per raft 1-2 people US$60) For trips along the Martha Brae, near Falmouth on the northwest coast, within easy day-tripping distance of Montego Bay and Ironshore.

⇒ **Rio Grande Experience** (☎993-5778; Berridale; per raft US$65) For trips along the Rio Grande, in the eastern interior, within day-tripping distance of Port Antonio and, to a lesser extent, Kingston.

Surfing & Kiteboarding

The easterly trade winds bless Jamaica with good summer surfing. The sport's home on the island is undoubtedly the **Jamnesia Surf Club** (☎750-0103; http://jamnesiasurf.com), which operates a surf camp at Bull Bay, 13km east of Kingston.

Boston Bay (p101), 14km east of Port Antonio, has consistent good waves and a small beachside shack from which you can rent boards cheaply.

Kiteboarding Jamaica (p129) at Glistening Waters near Falmouth is home to Jamaica's nascent kiteboarding scene.

Regions at a Glance

Ocho Rios, Port Antonio & North Coast

Activities
Landscape
History

Adrenaline Heaven

The Ocho Rios area arguably has the most activities packed into a relatively small space in Jamaica. Besides Dunn's River Falls, the country's most popular waterfall, the north coast boasts a mountaintop adventure park, good diving spots, horse-riding adventures, ATV safaris and zipline tours that attract active travelers.

Scenic Waters

Reach Falls is surely one of the most beautiful cascades in the Caribbean. Afterwards, raft up the Rio Grande or relax on lovely, lonely Long Bay. Compared to the crowded northwest coast, fewer tourists explore the outdoors in Portland parish.

Colonial Jamaica

Explore early colonial settlements at Maima Seville Great House in St Ann's Bay, the Windward Maroon stronghold of Moore Town, and the Fi Wi Sinting festival which explores Jamaica's deepest African roots

p73

Kingston, Blue Mountains & Southeast Coast

Nightlife
History
Hiking

Dance Downtown

Kingston never sleeps and you can join a party any night of the week, from formal nightclubs to sound system parties consisting of giant speakers set up at either end of a street to stage shows featuring the biggest names in dancehall and reggae. Make sure you come to Downtown parties with a friendly local.

Pirates & Ruins

Visit Port Royal in search of past pirate glory, stroll amid the ruined buildings of Spanish Town, the island's former capital, or take a walking tour through the streets of Downtown Kingston; understanding the history of this city is reading the history of the nation writ small across the streets of its capital.

Blue Mountains

As well as the island's most popular hike – the night-time climb up to the island's highest point at Blue Mountain Peak – the Blue Mountains offer numerous trails to suit all abilities. Mornings afford some of the best wildlife-spotting in Jamaica.

p36

Montego Bay & Northwest Coast

Activities
History
Hiking

MoBay Water Sports

The beaches in Montego Bay are OK, but there's better sand elsewhere; we really recommend swimming in the Glistening Waters and rafting up the Martha Brae. The infrastructure for guided activities is more developed here than elsewhere on the island.

Old Falmouth

Cheerfully chaotic Falmouth is the most historically preserved town in Jamaica, while near Ironshore there are protected great houses and the excellent history/culture show put on at Outameni.

Spelunking & Birding

Head deep into Cockpit Country, south of Montego Bay, to find fascinating caves and some of the best birding in Jamaica near Windsor and Albert Town. For an easier challenge, you can go on light hill walks in the area near Lethe.

p107

Negril & West Coast

Activities
Eating
Nightlife

Dawn to Dusk

Sure, you can go water-skiing and parasailing and cliff-diving and all that, but a lot of the joy of Negril is at the end of an active day, watching that perfect sunset every evening, and doing nothing at all.

Sunset Dinners

Negril has a plethora of good eating options, from simple, beach-satisfying fare on Long Bay to the classier confines of the fusion and high-end restaurants of the West End. Sunsets off the island's west coast make for some of the most romantic dining experiences in Jamaica.

Party Negril

If you're looking for a beach party in Jamaica, you can't really do much better than Negril. From folks getting 'sedate' on the beach to riproaring, rum-fueled parties, there's a lot to keep you entertained.

p135

South Coast & Central Highlands

Landscape
Culture
Relaxing

Great Outdoors

From the extensive cave networks of the Central Highlands to the glorious cascades of YS Falls, and even gentler options like the rolling pastureland near Lover's Leap, there's a lot to keep you outdoors.

Maroon Culture

Accompong, in dramatic South Cockpit Country, is the best place in Jamaica to interact with the Maroons. For intellectual pursuits, hit Treasure Beach during the Calabash International Literary Festival. Many members of the island intelligentsia are attracted to the laid-back resorts in and around Treasure Beach.

Chillin' Time

You know what? Crocodiles are relaxing. Look how laid-back they are, chilling on Black River. Even more relaxing? Picking the perfect Treasure Beach accommodations and losing yourself for days, weeks, months...

p156

On the Road

Kingston, Blue Mountains & Southeast Coast

Best Places to Eat

➡ Andy's (p51)
➡ Sonya's Homestyle Cooking (p51)
➡ Kushites (p51)
➡ Moby Dick (p50)
➡ Gloria's (p59)
➡ Terra Nova Hotel (p52)

Best Places to Stay

➡ Reggae Hostel (p48)
➡ Neita's Nest (p49)
➡ Jamnesia Surf Camp (p57)
➡ Strawberry Hill (p71)
➡ Lime Tree Farm (p68)
➡ Mount Edge B&B (p64)

Why Go?

Kingston is Jamaica undiluted and unadulterated, its raw energy contrasting sharply with the languor of resorts and villages elsewhere on the island. The launching pad for some of the world's most electrifying music, spirited clubs and riotous street-system parties attest that the beat is still alive and bumping. Kingston's cosmopolitan makeup has given rise to fine international dining but its dynamic galleries and museums remain unapologetically Jamaican.

Kingston is the ideal base for exploring Jamaica's southeast corner. The region offers the breadth of the Jamaican experience – while there are beaches in easy striking distance of the capital, the island's history is thrown into relief by the faded pirate glory of Port Royal and the grit of Spanish Town, and the majestic, forest-covered Blue Mountains allow you to escape into nature and hike old Maroon trails or taste a gourmet cup at a working coffee plantation.

When to Go

Kingston

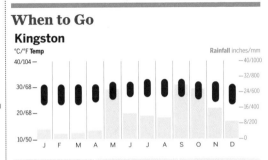

Feb Carnival and Reggae month offer plenty of chances for music and partying.	**Nov–Apr** Best time for sightseeing; in December the island's choice lineup of stars appears at Sting.

Dec–Mar & Jul–Sep Best time for surfing (there are few waves outside these seasons).

KINGSTON

POP 662,400

Squeezed between the Blue Mountains and the world's seventh-largest natural harbor, Kingston simultaneously impresses you with its setting and overwhelms you with its size, noise and traffic. This is the island's cultural and economic heart, a lively crucible of music and politics. Like a plate of spicy jerk washed down with a cold Red Stripe beer, a visit to Kingston is essential to taste the rich excitement of modern Jamaica.

Kingston is a city of two halves. Downtown is home to historic buildings, the courts, banks, street markets and one of the Caribbean's greatest art museums. Centered around Parade, it has a shabby charm and runs down to a bayside park. To the west lie the ghettoes of Trench Town and Tivoli Gardens, where many houses don't have running water and the rule of law can sometimes be thin at best.

By contrast, Uptown holds the city's best hotels and restaurants, largely confined to New Kingston, with its cluster of tall buildings around Emancipation Park. In addition to two of the city's most essential sights, the Bob Marley Museum and Devon House, its diplomatic and commercial status assures Uptown a definite cosmopolitan suaveness. Further out, in the foothills, are Kingston's most exclusive neighborhoods, with expansive views over the capital.

Uptown and Downtown seldom mix, but taken together they form a compelling and sometimes chaotic whole. Kingston is certainly never boring – we encourage you to jump right in.

History

When the English captured Jamaica in 1655, Kingston was known as Hog Crawle, little more than a site for raising pigs. It took an earthquake that leveled nearby Port Royal in 1692 to spur the town planners into action and turn Kingston into a going concern.

In the 18th century, Kingston became one of the busiest ports in the western hemisphere, and a key trans-shipment point for the slave trade. By 1872, it became the colony's official capital.

In 1907 an earthquake leveled much of the city, sending Kingston's wealthier elements uptown. Downtown became a breeding ground both for the new Rastafarian movement, and labor unions and political parties alike.

In the 1960s the port was expanded and attempts were made to spruce up the waterfront. But as cruise ships docked in Kingston Harbour, the boom also drew in the rural poor, swelling the shantytowns.

Unemployment soared, and with it came crime. The fractious 1970s spawned politically sponsored criminal enterprises whose trigger-happy networks still trouble the city. Commerce began to leave Downtown for New Kingston, and the middle class edged away as well.

KINGSTON, BLUE MOUNTAINS & SOUTHEAST COAST KINGSTON

KINGSTON IN...

Two Days
Visit the Bob Marley Museum to see where Jamaica's favorite son rested his natty dreads, and the National Gallery of Jamaica for a crash course in Jamaican art; tour beautiful colonial manse Devon House; eat a meal to remember at the Red Bones Blues Café or try Andy's for the best jerk in town. At night, hit the town for some sweaty after-hours excitement at the Famous or Quad.

Four Days
Go to Port Royal for a peek into Jamaica's pirate past, and catch a boat to the tiny island of Lime Cay for sun worship. Soak in some history by taking a stroll around Downtown Kingston and see what influenced the young Bob Marley at the Trench Town Culture Yard & Village, or see what his son Ziggy's up to at Tuff Gong Recording Studios. Attend a sound-system party at Weddy Weddy Wednesdays or Rae Town's Oldies Night (Sunday).

One Week
Head to Hellshire Beach Recreation Area for a Kingstonian beach experience; or head up into the Blue Mountains to commune with nature and maybe trek the tallest peak in Jamaica.

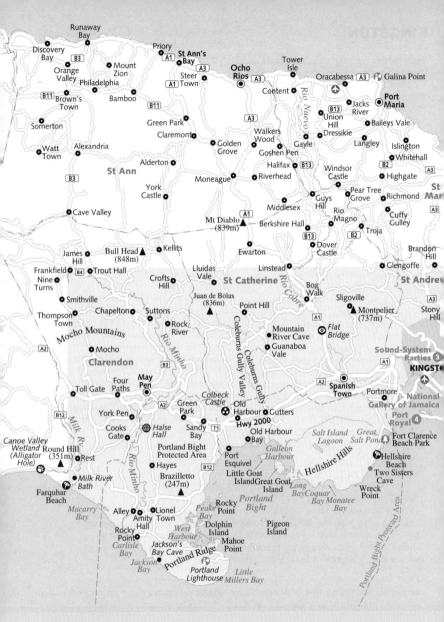

Kingston, Blue Mountains & Southeast Coast Highlights

❶ Delving into the life of Jamaica's most revered contemporary hero at his former home and studio, the **Bob Marley Museum** (p46)

❷ Appreciating the vision of Jamaican artists at the internationally acclaimed **National Gallery of Jamaica** (p40)

❸ Getting into the groove at the **sound-system parties** (p53) of Weddy Weddy Wednesdays, or Rae Town's Oldies Night

❹ Retracing the steps of Blackbeard and Henry Morgan at the former pirate capital of the world, **Port Royal** (p58)

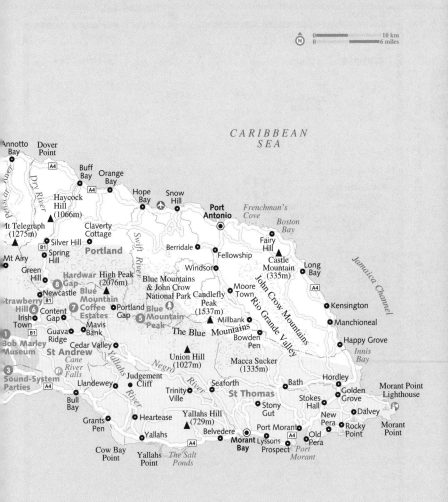

CARIBBEAN
SEA

Annotto
Bay

Dover
Point

A4

Buff
Bay

Orange
Bay

Haycock
Hill
(1066m)

Hope
Bay

Snow
Hill

Port
Antonio

Frenchman's
Cove

Boston
Bay

Mt Telegraph
(1275m)

Claverty
Cottage

Silver Hill

B1

Portland

Berridale

Fellowship

Fairy
Hill

Castle
Mountain
(335m)

Long
Bay

Jamaica Channel

Mt Airy

Spring
Hill

Windsor

Green
Hill

8 Hardwar
Gap

High Peak
(2076m)

Blue Mountains
& John Crow
National Park

Moore
Town

John Crow Mountains

A4

Kensington

Newcastle

B1

Blue
Mountain
Coffee
Estates

Candlefly
Peak
(1537m)

Rio Grande Valley

Strawberry
Hill **6**

Content
Gap

7

Portland
Gap

Blue **5**
Mountain
Peak

Manchioneal

Irish
Town

Millbank

Happy Grove

1

Mavis
Bank

Guava
Ridge

Bob Marley
Museum

The Blue Mountains

Bowden
Pen

Innis
Bay

St Andrew

Cedar Valley

Cane
River
Falls

3

Sound-System
Parties

A4

Llandewey

Union Hill
(1027m)

Macca Sucker
(1335m)

Hordley

Morant Point
Lighthouse

Yallahs River

Negro River

Judgement
Cliff

Seaforth

Bath

Golden
Grove

Bull
Bay

Trinity
Ville

St Thomas

Stony
Gut

Stokes
Hall

Dalvey

Morant
Point

Grants
Pen

Heartease

Yallahs Hill
(729m)

New
Pera

Rocky
Point

Cow Bay
Point

Yallahs

Belvedere

Morant
Bay

A4

Lyssons

Old
Pera

A4

Port
Morant

Prospect

Yallahs
Point

The Salt
Ponds

CARIBBEAN
SEA

N

0 ━━━━━━ 10 km
0 ━━━━━━ 6 miles

5 Setting out before dawn to experience the greatest high in Jamaica, **Blue Mountain Peak** (p69)

6 Rewarding yourself with a meal, spa treatment or night of romance at one of Jamaica's

best hotels, **Strawberry Hill** (p71) near Irish Town

7 Seeing a red berry transformed into the world's best coffee bean at one of the **Blue Mountain coffee estates** (p66)

8 Cycling from **Hardwar Gap** (p70), quickening your pulse with a rip-roaring descent from the high mountains, through coffee plantations and villages

Kingston

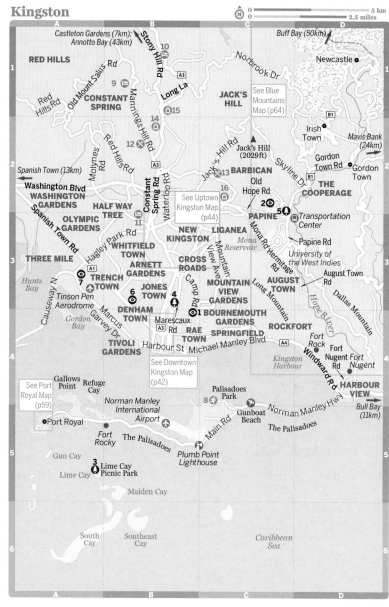

Kingston's troubled image has deterred tourists ever since, but modernization in the 1990s, and the ongoing expansion of the port and other signs of rejuvenation, suggest that the capital's prospects are finally on the up again.

Sights

Downtown

★ **National Gallery of Jamaica**   ART GALLERY
(Map p42; ☑ guided tours 922-1561; www.natgalja.

Kingston

art, including during the superb National Biennial temporary exhibition that takes place on alternate, even-numbered years between mid-December and March.

★ **Liberty Hall**   MUSEUM
(Map p42; ☎948-8639; http://libertyhall-ioj.org.jm; 76 King St; adult/child J$400/200; ⊙9:30am-4:30pm Mon-Thu, to 3:30pm Fri) At the end of a tree-lined courtyard, decorated with cheerful mosaics and a mural depicting Marcus Garvey, stands Liberty Hall, the headquarters of Garvey's UNIA (United Negro Improvement Association) in the 1930s. The building now contains a quite excellent multimedia museum about the man and his work, which allows the visitor to appreciate Garvey's impact as a founder of pan-Africanism.

As in Garvey's day, Liberty Hall has a community outreach program, holding after-school programs for neighborhood children and computer literacy classes. There's also a superb reference library with a focus on Garvey, African history and its diaspora.

Institute of Jamaica   MUSEUM
(JCDT; Map p42; ☎922-0620; www.instituteofjamaica.org.jm; 10-16 East St; adult/child J$400/200) The Institute of Jamaica is the nation's small-scale equivalent of the British Museum or Smithsonian, housed in three separate buildings. The institute hosts permanent and visiting exhibitions. Buy your ticket at the Natural History Museum, accessed by a separate entrance around the corner on Tower St.

Downstairs there is a small exhibition on natural history and agriculture, while upstairs holds a temporary exhibition space. The small but informative Museum of Music on the top floor displays traditional musical instruments and traces the history and development of Jamaica's music, from Kumina, mento and ska to reggae and dancehall. Next door, the Africa Collection features weapons, carvings and some exquisite craftwork from various African countries.

The temporary exhibitions are often the best, so check online for details. Recent highlights have included 'Jamaica 50', about independence, 'Historic Rastafari' and 'Reggae and Social Change.'

The central building also holds the **National Library** (Map p42; www.nlj.org.jm), which incorporates the Caribbean's largest repository of books, maps, charts and documents on West Indian history.

org.jm; 12 Ocean Blvd; admission J$400, 45min guided tour J$2000; ⊙10am-4:30pm Tue-Thu, to 4pm Fri, to 3pm Sat) The superlative collection of Jamaican art housed by the National Gallery is the finest on the island and should on no account be missed. As well as offering a distinctly Jamaican take on international artistic trends, the collection attests to the vitality of the country's artistic heritage as well as its present.

The collection is organized chronologically, introduced by Taíno carvings and traditional 18th-century British landscapes, whose initial beauty belies the fact that their subjects include many slave plantations. Ten galleries represent the Jamaican school, from 1922 to the present. Highlights include the boldly modernist sculptures of Edna Manley, the vibrant 'intuitive' paintings of artists like John Dunkley, David Pottinger and revivalist bishop Mallica 'Kapo' Reynolds. Later galleries chart the course of 'Jamaican art for Jamaicans' up to the recent past, including abstract religious works by Carl Abrahams, Colin Garland's surrealist exercises, ethereal assemblages by David Boxer, and the work of realist Barrington Watson.

Temporary exhibition spaces frequently offer up the best of contemporary Jamaican

Downtown Kingston

N 0 ————— 200 m
0 ————— 0.1 miles

TRENCH TOWN

National Heroes Park (500m);
New Kingston (4km);

Dumfries St

Blount St
Oxford St
Upper Rose La
Slipe Pen Rd

Bond St
Pink La
Rose La
West St
Charles St

Orange St
Chancery La
Upper King St
North St
Church St
Upper Mark La
Duke St
Upper Johns La
East St

6

Spanish Town
(23.5km)

Beeston St

Spanish Town Rd

Liberty Hall

Love La

1

Salt La
Young St
Heywood St
N Parade

14

W Parade
13

Downtown
Bus Terminal (200m)

W Queen St

Parade
(William
Grant Park)

E Parade

3

10

Statue of
Queen
Victoria

12

Beckford St
S Parade

7

Marcus
Garvey Ave

Pechon St
West St
Matthews La
Princess St
Luke La
Orange St
Peters La
Temple La

Johns La
Georges La
Hanover St

Darling St

Church St

Tinson Pen
Aerodrome
(3.2km);
Portmore
(10.2km)

11

Tower St

Tower La

5 **8**

Water La

Long-Distance
Bus Terminal

Water St

18

19

16

15

Harbour St

Port Royal St

Rae Town (2km);
Norman Manley
International Airport
(20.5km);
Port Royal
(25.5km)

**National Gallery
of Jamaica** **2**

King St
Church St
Ocean Blvd

Little Port
Royal St

Nethersole Pl

Ocean Blvd

Derelict Wharves **9**

17

20

21

Downtown Kingston

Parade　　　　　　　　　　　　　SQUARE
(William Grant Park; Map p42) William Grant Park, more commonly known as 'Parade,' is the bustling heart of Downtown, and originally hosted a fortress erected in 1694 with guns pointing toward the harbor. The fort was replaced in 1870 by Victoria Park, renamed a century later to honor Black Nationalist and labor leader Sir William Grant. The north and south entrances are watched over by cousins and political rivals **Norman Manley** (Map p42) and **Alexander Bustamante** (Map p42), respectively. A large fountain stands at its center.

At North Parade, the distinguished **Ward Theatre** (Map p42; www.wardtheatrefoundation.com; North Parade), built in 1911, once hosted the annual Boxing Day pantomime – a riotous, irreverent social satire. Sadly, the building has fallen into disrepair over the years, although there are plans to restore it to its former glory. For now, you can admire the cracked sky-blue facade with white trim.

The gleaming white edifice facing the park's southeast corner is **Kingston Parish Church** (Map p42), which replaced an older church destroyed in the 1907 earthquake. Note the tomb dating to 1699, the year the original was built. The tomb of Admiral Benbow, commander of the Royal Navy in the West Indies at the turn of the 18th century, is near the high altar, while plaques commemorate soldiers of the colonial West Indian regiments.

The crenelated redbrick building facing East Parade is the 1840 **Coke Memorial Hall** (Map p42), named after the founder of the Methodist churches in the Caribbean, Thomas Coke.

South Parade, packed with street vendor stalls and the blast of reggae, is known as 'Ben Dung Plaza' because passersby have to bend down to buy from hawkers whose goods are displayed on the ground. King St leads from here to the waterfront, and to Edna Manley's *Negro Aroused* statue (Map p42; King St), depicting a crouched black man breaking free from bondage (a replica; the original is in the National Gallery of Jamaica).

Coronation Market　　　　　　　MARKET
(Map p42) This huge cast-iron-framed hall hosts the biggest market in the English-speaking Caribbean. It holds a special place in Jamaican culture as both 'stomach' of the country, and the old heart of Kingston's commerce; indeed half the country appears to be shopping here (except on Sunday). It's a brilliant and lively show of noise, produce and commerce, but leave your valuables at home and watch out for pickpockets.

Tuff Gong
Recording Studios　　　　RECORDING STUDIO
(Map p40; ☏ 923-9380; www.tuffgong.com; 220 Marcus Garvey Dr; tour J$700) Tuff Gong is one of the Caribbean's largest and most influential studios. Bob Marley's favorite place to record, it's run by his son Ziggy. Visitors are welcome to take a 45-minute tour with the entire music production process explained, provided you call in advance, but if someone's recording, you may not be allowed to see all sections of the studio.

Trench Town Culture Yard COMMUNITY PROJECT
(Map p40) Trench Town, which began life as a much-prized housing project erected by the British in the 1930s, is widely credited as the birthplace of ska, rocksteady and reggae music. It has been immortalized in numerous reggae songs, not least Bob Marley's 'No Woman No Cry,' the poignant anthem penned by Marley's mentor, Vincent 'Tata' Ford, in a tiny bedroom at what is now the

Uptown Kingston

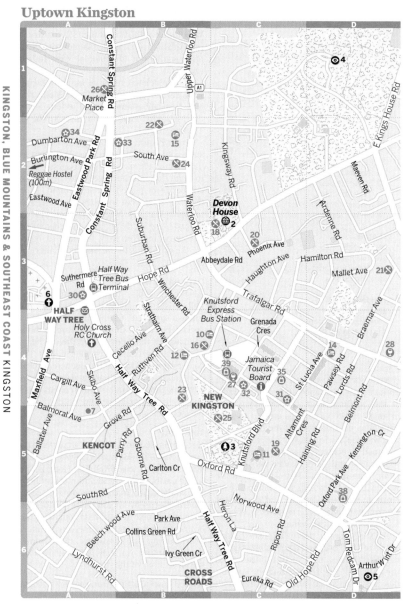

Trench Town Museum (Map p40; ☎ 859-6741; www.trenchtowncultureyard.com; 6-10 Lower First St; yard & museum J$1000, with guided neighborhood tour J$1500; ☺ 8am-6pm).

The museum is stocked with Wailers memorabilia, along with the rusted-out car-cass of a VW bus that belonged to the Wailers in the 1960s and the small bedroom that was Bob and Rita Marley's home before superstardom. Tours can be rather brisk, with visitors steered towards the gift shop.

Uptown Kingston

Also on site is the Trench Town Development Association, responsible for transforming the home into a community-based heritage site, and dedicated to promoting social justice and self-reliance. It is allied with the nearby **Trench Town Reading Centre** (www.trenchtownreadingcentre.com; First St), established to arm the neighborhood youth with knowledge rather than guns.

Visits are best arranged in advance – it's safe to visit, but we don't advise wandering elsewhere around Trench Town on your own.

National Heroes Park
PARK

(Map p40) The 30-hectare, oval-shaped National Heroes Park hosts National Heroes Circle, dedicated to Jamaica's seven national heroes. Sir Alexander Bustamante, Norman Manley and Marcus Garvey are all buried here, along with symbolic memorials to Nanny, Sam Sharpe, and Paul Bogle and George William Gordon of the 1865 Morant Bay Rebellion.

Other celebrated Jamaicans buried here include Michael Manley, 'Crown Prince of Reggae,' Dennis Brown, and 'Miss Lou,' the revered Patois poet Louise Bennett.

Alpha Boys School
MUSIC SCHOOL

(Map p40; ☑ 928-1345, 930-2200; www.alphaboys school.org; 26 South Camp Rd; donation requested; ☺ Fri 4-5pm) Few have had the impact on modern Jamaican music like Alpha Boys School and their students. A nonprofit residential school for at-risk boys, Alpha is where many of Jamaica's musical pioneers in jazz, ska and reggae (from the Skatalites to Yellowman) got their start. The band is still a primary source of local talent, with weekly public performances at their welcome center forming part of the school's 'Alpha Live!' program. The band also play regularly at Devon House.

Roktowa
ART GALLERY

(Map p42; ☑ 922-9229; www.roktowa.org; 8 Pechon St; ☺ 9am-5pm Mon-Fri) This innovative gallery-cum-art-workshop in an old Red Stripe factory is a sprawling warehouse project aimed at rejuvenating the surrounding area and channeling local creativity. Roktowa (aka 'Rock Tower') artists include potters, sculptors and painters, with residencies available for visiting artists. Outreach projects work with local communities, and there are yoga classes and a café.

Jewish Synagogue
SYNAGOGUE

(Map p42; ☑ 922-5931; www.ucija.org; cnr Duke & Charles Sts; ☺ service 10am Sat) Jamaica's only synagogue is an attractive white building dating from 1912. It's usually locked, though on weekdays there is often someone in the little office around the back who will open it up for a small donation. The hall adjacent to the synagogue houses a well-presented exhibition on the history of Jamaica's Jewish community.

◉ Uptown

★ Bob Marley Museum
MUSEUM

(Map p44; ☑ 876-927-9152; www.bobmarley museum.com; 56 Hope Rd; adult/child J$2000/1000; ☺ 9:30am-4pm Mon-Sat) The

---

MARLEY'S GHOST

Although Bob Marley (1945–81) was born and buried in Nine Mile in St Ann parish, it was from Kingston that Jamaica's most famous son made his mark on the global music scene.

Bob and his mother moved to Trench Town in 1955, at the time a desirable neighborhood and fertile spot for the emerging music scene, where he met Bunny Livingston and Peter Tosh. In 1963 they formed the Wailin' Wailers, scoring a number-one hit with their first single, *Simmer Down*. On signing to Island Records in the early '70s (and becoming Bob Marley and the Wailers) they began to receive international acclaim with albums *Burnin'* and *Catch a Fire*, though Peter Tosh and Bunny Wailer quit soon after. In 1975 Marley moved into the house at 56 Hope Rd, now a museum.

During the 1970s, Bob, his wife Rita and his manager were shot at in Hope Rd by a gang, just before a major concert. Remarkably, everyone survived (and Marley even played at the concert), but afterwards Bob and Rita went into exile in Britain for two years. In 1978 Marley made his legendary homecoming when messages of peace and unity were being all but drowned out by open street warfare. On April 22 he played the 'One Love' peace concert, attended by 100,000 people.

During his world tour in 1980 Marley was diagnosed with cancer and died in a Miami hospital eight months later. While some argue that Marley was not the greatest-ever reggae musician, he was the developing world's first global superstar, and there's no denying that his music has touched more people worldwide than many other artists.

large, creaky, colonial-era wooden house on Hope Rd, where Bob Marley lived and recorded from 1975 until his death in 1981, is the city's most-visited site. Today the house functions as a tourist attraction, museum and shrine, and much remains as it was in Marley's day.

The hour-long tour provides fascinating insights into the reggae superstar's life after moving uptown. His gold and platinum records are there on the walls, alongside Rastafarian religious cloaks, Marley's favorite denim stage shirt, and the Order of Merit presented by the Jamaican government. One room is entirely wallpapered with media clippings from Marley's final tour; another contains a replica of Marley's original record shop, Wail'n Soul'm. Marley's simple bedroom has been left as it was, with his favorite star-shaped guitar by the bed.

The former recording studio out back is now an exhibition hall with some wonderful photos of Bob, and a theater, where the tour closes with a 20-minute film. There's another recording studio inside the house, which his sons occasionally use for solo projects.

★ **Devon House** MUSEUM
(Map p44; ☑ 929-6602; www.devonhousejamaica.com; 26 Hope Rd; admission J$700; ☺ 9am-4:30pm Tue-Sat) This beautiful colonial house was built in 1881 by George Stiebel, the first black millionaire in Jamaica. Antique lovers will enjoy the visit, whose highlights include some very ornate porcelain chandeliers. Note the trompe l'œil of palms in the entrance foyer and the roundabout chairs, designed to accommodate a man wearing a sword. Amid the grand surroundings, Stiebel even managed to discreetly tuck a gambling room away in the attic. Admission includes a mandatory guided tour.

The tree-shaded lawns of Devon House attract Kingstonians who come here to canoodle and read. The popular former carriage house and courtyard are home to the famous Grog Shoppe restaurant, the island's best ice cream and a few quality shops.

For Emancipation Day (August 1), Devon House puts on a rousing celebration complete with roots plays, a maypole ritual and a booming sound system.

Emancipation Park PARK
(Map p44; Knutsford Blvd) This grand open space, opened in 2002, is a fine place for a stroll or a spot of people-watching over a takeaway pattie. Check out the controversial statue *Redemption Song,* by Laura Facey Cooper. It depicts a couple of nude, 3m-tall slaves gazing to the heavens – play art critic and pass approving or prurient comments as you see fit.

Hope Gardens GARDEN
(Map p40; Old Hope Rd; ☺ 5:30am-6:30pm) These 18-hectare gardens, replete with manicured grounds, exotic plants and beautiful flowers, date back to 1881 when the government established an experimental garden on the site of the former Hope Estate. The spacious lawns, towering palms and flower-scented walkways provide a lovely respite from the urban jungle. Other attractions include an orchid house, greenhouses, ornamental ponds and a privet-hedge maze.

King's House NOTABLE BUILDING
(Map p44; ☑ 927-6424; W Kings House Rd; ☺ by appointment 9am-5pm Mon-Fri) FREE The official residence of the governor-general, the representative of the Queen of England, King's House was initially the home of the Lord Bishop of Jamaica. It was heavily restored after the 1907 earthquake. The dining room contains two particularly impressive full-length portraits of King George III and Queen Charlotte by Sir Joshua Reynolds.

Sculpture Park PARK
(Map p40; 237 Old Hope Rd) FREE This sculpture garden, on the grounds of the University of Technology, features nine sculptures by acclaimed Caribbean artists. These include Laura Facey's sculpture of a woman's torso stretched in a yoga position, and Basil Watson's *The Compass,* depicting humanity shaping the environment with the use of technology.

St Andrew Parish Church CHURCH
(Map p44; Half Way Tree Church, cnr Hagley Park & Eastwood Park Rds) This brick church is more popularly known as the 'Half Way Tree Church.' The foundations of the existing church were laid in 1692. The exterior is austere and unremarkable, but the stained-glass windows and organ are definitely worth a peek. Outside, there's a very atmospheric graveyard.

☞ **Tours**

Jamaica Cultural Enterprises CULTURAL TOURS
(☑ 540-8570; www.jaculture.com) Very well-respected cultural tours in and around Kingston, including the Blue Mountains.

Excellent themed tours include history, food, music and art, either as a group (from US$65 per person) or tailor-made.

Sun Venture Tours CITY TOURS
(Map p44; ☑ 960-6685, 408-6973; www.sunventure tours.com; 30 Balmoral Ave, Kingston) Offers a city tour of Kingston, starting either at the Bob Marley Museum or Tuff Gong Studios, and incorporating a walking tour of Port Royal and a visit to Devon House (US$65 per person for four people or more). Sun Venture also offers hiking tours of the Blue Mountains and Maroon country, excursions to coffee plantations and more.

★☆ Festivals & Events

Befitting a Caribbean capital city, Kingston is the site of engaging festivals and events all year round.

**Jamaica School of Dance
Concert Season** DANCE
(☉ Jan) Creative, Caribbean-themed dancing at the Little Theatre.

Carnival CARNIVAL
(www.bacchanaljamaica.com; ☉ Feb) A week of costumed revellers taking to the streets, two carnival camps – Jamaica Carnival and Bacchanal Jamaica – paint- and rum-throwing, parades, all-night parties and live reggae, calypso, and particularly soca. Highlights include J'Ouvert, an epic night-long party, and the Road March, when the two camps parade through the streets of New Kingston in carnival costume.

Boys & Girls Championships SPORTS
(www.issasports.com; National Stadium; ☉ Week prior to Easter) A highly charged youth athletics contest as scouts from around the world arrive to get a glimpse of future champions. A great atmosphere, as locals fill the stands to overflowing.

Kingston on the Edge ART
(www.kingstonontheedge.com; ☉ Jun) Week-long urban art festival featuring the best of new painting, photography and sculpture, as well as gallery shows, concerts and readings.

**World Reggae Dance
Championships** DANCE
(www.jcdc.gov.jm; ☉ Aug) The finals of the reggae, dancehall and reggaeton dance competition, with troupes of young dancers battling it out among themselves at the Ranny Williams Entertainment Centre.

Caribbean Heritagefest CULTURE
(www.jcdc.gov.jm; ☉ mid-Oct) A two-day event at the Jamworld Entertainment Complex at Portmore, southwest of Kingston. It features food and crafts fairs, folk theater, traditional dance and drumming, and musical performances.

Devon House Christmas Fair FAIR
(☉ Dec) Devon House promotes a colorful display of arts, crafts and culinary delights in the week before Christmas.

Biennial Art Exhibition ART
(www.natgalja.org.jm; ☉ Dec-Mar) Exhibition featuring the very best of contemporary Jamaican art, held in even-numbered years.

LMT National Pantomime THEATER
(☉ Dec) Annual event at the Little Theatre, with traditional Jamaican song and dance, saucy humor and fabulous costumes.

🛏 Sleeping

Many lodging options cater more to business travelers than tourists, and rates don't vary much year round. Most hotels are in Uptown, with some of the more luxurious retreats further up in the hills.

★**Reggae Hostel** HOSTEL $
(Map p40; ☑ 920-1596; www.reggaehostel.com; 8 Burlington Ave; dm US$15-30, d US$70; ⓟ ❄ @ ⓢ) Close to Halfway Tree, this excellent hostel has a relaxed, friendly vibe. Dorms are simple with fans, while private rooms (one with its own bathroom) are spacious and have air-con. There's a communal kitchen, patio bar (with Sunday barbecue) and helpful staff. Highly sociable if you're looking for people to hook up with to go to a dancehall street party or weekend beach trip.

Mikuzi Guest House GUESTHOUSE $
(Map p44; ☑ 978-4859, 813-0098; www.mikuzi jamaica.com; 5 Upper Montrose Rd; r US$50-80, ste US$90; ⓟ ❄ ⓢ) Friendly yellow colonial-era guest house with comfortable rooms – all bright colors and funky furnishings, most with kitchenettes. All but the 'backpacker rooms' have air-con. There's a cushion-strewn gazebo in the lush garden for relaxing in. It's just off Hope Rd, a stone's throw from the Bob Marley Museum, and has a sister outfit near Port Antonio.

City View Hotel BOUTIQUE HOTEL $
(Map p40; ☑ 969-4009; www.cityviewjamaica.com; Mannings Hill Rd, St Andrew; r incl breakfast US$90;

THE YARDS

Much of Kingston's growth in recent decades has been in the 'yards' – acres of cheap and substandard housing west of Parade, originally conceived as 'model communities' when built in the 1960s. Most famous among them are Trench Town and Tivoli Gardens.

During the 1970s the middle classes debunked to the suburbs, and the JLP (Jamaica Labour Party) and PNP (People's National Party) curried favor among the ghetto constituencies by patronizing area leaders who in turn encouraged their gangs to recruit voters and intimidate political opponents at election time. Today, a large percentage of the gangs' incomes come from drug- and gun-running. The most famous leaders of recent years was Christopher 'Dudus' Coke, who ran Tivoli Gardens and brought a perverse sense of security to the area until the government stormed the ghetto in 2010, with great loss of life.

It's easy to tell which party rules behind the stockades: no-nonsense wall murals act as territorial markers. While people from neighboring areas can freely enter the turf of the 'opposition' most of the time, tempers easily flare and it's best to visit with a trusted local (ironically, local security for street parties is usually excellent).

The **People's Action for Community Transformation** (PACT; ☑ 920-0334; www.jamaica-kidz.com/pact; 2-6 Grenada Cres) is a coalition of 26 community-based nongovernmental organizations working to improve life and community relationships in Kingston's inner city.

P ❊ 🛜) This family-run pocket of splendor in upper St Andrew offers an intimate experience combined with a panoramic view of Kingston. The five rooms, named after Jamaica's different parishes, feature delightful antique furnishings. The genial hosts treat guests like family. There's a typical Jamaican breakfast (ackee and saltfish, callaloo, dumplings, and fresh fruit).

Indies Hotel
HOTEL **$**

(Map p44; ☑ 926-2952; www.indieshotel.com; 5 Holborn Rd; s/d US80/90; P ❊ @) This family-friendly 'home away from home' is highly rated for its cheerful ambience and accommodating atmosphere. Rooms cluster around a green courtyard, but try to take an upstairs room for brighter sunlight. A small restaurant serves economical pizzas and great fish and chips and the attractive patio is a good spot for alfresco dining.

Hotel Prestige
HOTEL **$**

(Map p44; ☑ 927-8244; 70 Sandhurst Cres, Liguanea; s US$55, d US$55-70; P ❊ 🛌) In a quiet residential neighborhood in Liguanea, this renovated hotel is a decent option. The spotlessly kept rooms with their black-and-white tile floors, utility furniture and plastic flowers conjure images of Miami in the 1960s. Some have a private veranda. A large dining terrace shaded by mango trees affords views toward the Blue Mountains.

★ Neita's Nest
GUESTHOUSE **$$**

(Map p40; ☑ 469-3005; www.neitasnest.com; Stony Hill, Bridgemount; s/d US$80/120; 🛜) A delightful art-filled bed-and-breakfast tucked up high in Stony Hill and with great views from the terrace of Kingston and the mountains. Cosy rooms and a gracious host who welcomes you into the family make this feel like a perfect retreat away from the city. Dinner is available on request (and is recommended).

Moon Hill
BOUTIQUE HOTEL **$$**

(☑ 620-8259; www.moonhilljamaica.com; 5 Roedeen Cl, Jack's Hill; s US$75-90, d US$150-180; P 🛜 🛌) A great combination of seclusion and close proximity to the capital's attractions, this luxurious four-bedroom villa located in the Blue Mountain foothills is ideal for romantic or small-group getaways. The airy bedrooms feature firm queen- and king-size beds, all freshened by a cool breeze from the mountains. The Jamaican and international menu uses fresh produce from the on-site organic garden.

Eden Gardens
HOTEL **$$**

(Map p44; ☑ 946-9981; www.edengardensjamaica.com; 39 Lady Musgrave Rd; r US$140; P ❊ 🛜 🛌) Set amid lush vegetation – a nod to its name – this condo and wellness center complex attracts those who like to mix business with pleasure. Each of the spacious, light rooms comes with fully equipped kitchenette and large desk, while the Therapeutic Spa has a full range of massages and other treatments. Long-stay discounts available.

Knutsford Court Hotel HOTEL $$
(Map p44; ☑929-1000; www.knutsfordcourt. com; 16 Chelsea Ave; s US$114-186, d US$148-196, ste US$205; P ⊛ ✳ @ 🛜 🌊) Agreeable hotel with a garden setting, popular with Jamaican families and businesspeople. The rooms – some with private balconies and work desks – are clean and well appointed. Rates include continental breakfast, served in the Melting Pot Restaurant, which offers exemplary Jamaican fare and room service at other times.

★**Spanish Court Hotel** BOUTIQUE HOTEL $$$
(Map p44; ☑926-0000; www.spanishcourthotel. com; 1 St Lucia Ave; r US$239-245, ste US$282-1212; P ✳ @ 🛜 🌊) A favorite with the discerning business elite. Thoroughly modern rooms have Jamaican-designed furtniture and come with iPod docks. Relaxation options include the rooftop pool, gym and a spa with a full range of treatments. The Gallery Café serves a selection of gourmet coffees and snacks, while the restaurant has beautifully presented international and Jamaican dishes.

Jamaica Pegasus HOTEL $$$
(Map p44; ☑926-3690; www.jamaicapegasus. com; 81 Knutsford Blvd; s/d US$180/204, ste US$276-492; P ⊛ ✳ 🛜 🌊) This glitzy 17-story property overlooking Emancipation Park is a long-established feature of the business travel scene. On Wednesday there's poolside happy hour (6pm to 7pm) featuring a complimentary buffet of Jamaican finger foods and rum punch. Rooms were undergoing a refit when we visited – preliminary results looked good. For an unparalleled view, ask for a room facing the mountains.

Terra Nova All-Suite Hotel HOTEL $$$
(Map p44; ☑926-2211; www.terranovajamaica. com; 17 Waterloo Rd; ste incl breakfast US$265-505; P ✳ @ 🌊) Although this colonial mansion dates from 1924, the spacious junior suites here have a great contemporary feel. The suites vary from regular to ultra-luxe, but king-size beds are standard – and thumbs up for the marble bathrooms, some of which have Jacuzzis. The restaurant is the venue for one of the city's top Sunday brunches.

✖️ Eating

As in other matters, Kingston is Jamaica's capital of food; it is here that the national cuisine was born and it is here that it continues to thrive and evolve. Let your taste buds run free!

Most of the notable eateries, which include international and fusion cuisine, are found in Uptown Kingston, where the culinary adventurer is spoiled for choice.

✖️ Downtown

Swiss Stores CAFE $
(Map p42; cnr Church & Harbour Sts; meals J$700; ⏱lunch) Pasta, pepperpot soup, Black Forest ham sandwiches and wine inside a welcome bubble of air-con – what more could you ask of a jewelry store! The stools aren't conducive for lazy lingering, but all the items on the small menu are fresh and tasty and the Blue Mountain coffee comes in a cup the size of a soup tureen.

Chung's JAMAICAN $
(Map p42; cnr Mark Lane & Harbour St; meals J$700; ⏱lunch Mon-Fri) In spite of the name, this simple canteen-style place – a favorite of Downtown office workers – serves only Jamaican specialties. Choose your mains, such as stew peas, fried chicken or curry goat, and then either take your overflowing container to the bustling dining area next door or go picnic on the waterfront.

★**Moby Dick** JAMAICAN $$
(Map p42; 3 Orange St; meals J$1100-2000; ⏱9am-7pm Mon-Sat) Don't let the plastic tablecloths fool you, this Muslim-run former sailors' hangout has been popular with besuited lawyers and judges for nearly a century. The curried goat (J$1100) is outstanding, as is the conch version (J$1700) when available, served with roti, rice and salad and washed down with one of the excellent fresh fruit juices.

✖️ Uptown

★**Hot Pot** JAMAICAN $
(Map p44; 2 Altamont Tce; meals J$500-1000; ⏱7am-4pm) A thoroughly unpretentious restaurant offering unfussy but indisputably delicious Jamaican home-style cooking, with dishes such as ackee and saltfish, escoveitch fish and garlic chicken. Wash it down

with a fresh tamarind juice, coconut water or a Red Stripe. Highly recommended.

★Andy's
JERK **$**

(Map p40; 49 Mannings Hill Rd; meals J$700; ⊙lunch & dinner) If you're after the best, authentically prepared jerk chicken and pork in Kingston, then Andy's is well worth the travel. This nondescript corner stop gets particularly busy in the evenings, when locals line up for their meats accompanied by fried breadfruit, festival, sweet potato or plantain.

★Kushites
I-TAL **$**

(Map p44; ☑375-0642; www.facebook.com/KushitesVegetableCuisine; 11 Phoenix Ave; meals from J$700; hmidday-10pm; ☑) Vegan and I-tal food in pleasant leafy surroundings, with thick wooden tables and bright fabrics, coupled with an inside 'riad' dining room serving Moroccan-style cuisine. The menu is inventive – try the delicious raw, gluten-free 'pizzas,' washed down with freshly squeezed juice.

Sweetwood Jerk
JERK **$**

(Map p44; Knutsford Blvd; jerk from J$400; ⊙lunch & dinner) This lively jerk center, opposite Pegasus Hotel, is popular with Uptown office staff and gets particularly busy after work. Spicy, flavorful meaty offerings can be enjoyed in the outdoor sitting area facing Emancipation Park. Accompaniments include festival, sweet potato and particularly

---

PATTY, GLORIOUS PATTY

Patties – pastries with spicy beef, chicken, lobster, shrimp, cheese or vegetable filling, often consumed as part of a coco-bread 'sandwich' – are a Jamaican institution. They're cheap (around J$120), filling and delicious, and sold by the Juici Patties, Tastee Patties and Mother's franchises. Juici has an edge over its rivals by not limiting itself to patties; the larger branches serve ultra-filling hominy and peanut porridge for breakfast, and lunch mains such as salt fish with callaloo or cabbage. Try its **downtown branch** (Map p42; cnr Harbour & King Sts) or the more-upscale **Devon House Bakery** (p52) in Uptown Kingston.

---

good fried breadfruit. This is one of the few jerk joints in Jamaica to feature jerk lamb.

★Sonya's Homestyle Cooking
JAMAICAN **$$**

(Map p44; ☑968-6267; 17 Central Ave; mains around J$1200; ⊙6:30am-6pm Mon-Fri, 7:30am-6pm Sat, 8:30am-7pm Sun) A place that's famous for big traditional Jamaican breakfasts, washed down with fresh juices; the Sunday buffet (8:30am to midday) is particularly popular. For lunches and early dinner, there's good pepper pot soup, curry goat, oxtail and beans, stew pork and fry chicken.

Guilt Trip
FUSION **$$**

(Map p40; ☑977-5130; 20 Barbican Rd; meals J$1600-2500; ⊙dinner) The name alludes to the imaginative, decadent desserts, the unrestrained consumption of which will leave you feeling very indulgent. That's not all: the chef constantly experiments with Caribbean-French fusion cuisine, so you'll be constantly surprised by concoctions like coconut curry sea bass with mango and chestnut salsa, and roast chicken with whiskey sauce. The experience is worth dressing up for.

Chez Maria
LEBANESE **$$**

(Map p44; 7 Hillcrest Ave; meals J$750-1800; ⊙lunch & dinner; ☑) Whether you sit in the garden beneath the mango tree or grab a table on the front terrace, you'll be treated to fine Lebanese and Italian cuisine. The mezes, notably the hummus, are excellent and are complemented by homemade pita bread. A host of shawarmas and kebabs awaits if you still have an appetite. Alternatively, go for some of the best pizza in town or the outstanding penne a la vodka.

So-So Seafood Bar & Grill
SEAFOOD **$$**

(Map p44; 4 Chelsea Ave; meals J$1200-2000; ⊙lunch & dinner) A casual place, known for its mellow after-work scene (the bar is good for chilling before your meal), its modest menu belies the quality of the menu. The garlic shrimp and stew fish are particularly good, as is the weekly conch soup (Thursday and Friday), and delicious mannish water (miscellaneous goat-part soup) on Sunday.

Grog Shoppe
JAMAICAN **$$**

(Map p44; Devon House; meals J$1500-2500; ⊙11am-10pm Mon-Sat) Lodged in an expansive brick building that used to be the servants' quarters for Devon House, this atmospheric choice has the look and feel of a

UPTOWN QUICK EATS

Devon House Bakery (Map p44; Devon House; patties from J$200-450; ⊙10am-10pm; ✍) Those in the know swear by patties served up in this small bakery located next to Devon House I-Scream (p52). We're inclined to agree that they're some of the best in Jamaica. Lobster patty, anyone? An array of tempting cakes and juices is also available at this excellent option for a picnic on the grounds.

Café Blue/Deli Works (Map p40; Sovereign Centre, Hope Rd; meals J$700-900; ⊙8am-8pm Mon-Sat, 9am-3pm Sun) Always full of Uptowners with laptops, this bright, air-conditioned cafe serves an array of delicious though not cheap Blue Mountain coffees, as well as cakes, filled bagels and sandwiches. The smoked marlin baguette (J$500) is consistently superb. Next door, you can choose from a number of Jamaican specials (J$500 to J$650), consumed in a lively canteen setting.

Cannonball Café (Map p40; www.facebook.com/CannonballCafe; Loshusan Shopping Centre, Barbican Rd; meals J$500-700; ⊙7am-7pm Mon-Fri, 9am-5pm Sat & Sun; ☎) Popular and busy cafe with wireless internet, serving excellent Blue Mountain coffee and cakes. Light dishes – quiches, sandwiches and salads – are also on offer here. Also branches at 134 Constant Spring Rd and 20 Barbados Ave.

Devon House I-Scream (Map p44; Devon House, 26 Hope Rd; scoops J$250; ⊙10am-10pm) Some of the island's best ice cream in over 20 flavours – check out their signature Devon Stout.

colonial pub. A separate dining room serves good Jamaican specialties, while the pub menu features burgers, crab cakes and other finger food.

South Avenue Grill   INTERNATIONAL **$$**
(Map p44; 20A South Ave; meals J$1100-2900; ⊙lunch & dinner) Meat-heavy menu of Jamaican and Italian dishes in an attractive open-air setting. The steaks are good but pricey. Formerly known as Gaucho's Grill.

★**Terra Nova**
All-Suite Hotel   INTERNATIONAL **$$$**
(Map p44; ☎926-2211; 17 Waterloo Rd; Sun brunch J$2500; ⊙lunch & dinner; ✍) The European menu has hints of the Caribbean as well as Jamaican favorites such as pepperpot soup and grilled snapper. However, the bigger draw for well-heeled Kingstonians is its famous Sunday brunch, comprising an all-you-can-eat buffet. Gorge yourself on curry goat, jerk chicken, pasta salads, ribs and more. The only downside is that there's only so much you can eat!

Red Bones Blues Café   FUSION **$$$**
(Map p44; ☎978-8262; 1 Argyle Rd; mains US$20-40; ⊙midday-1am Mon-Fri, from 6pm Sat) This restaurant, bar and live-music venue has long been a behive of cultural and culinary activity. Inside, the walls are beguilingly bedecked with photographs of jazz and blues legends. The menu offers Jamaican twists on European tastes (callaloo strudel, anyone?) with good fish, pasta and salads. Leave room for the sweet potato pudding!

Taka's East
Japanese Restaurant   JAPANESE **$$$**
(Map p44; ☎960-3962; Market Pl, 67 Constant Spring Rd; meals J$2500-4500; ⊙lunch & dinner Wed-Sun, dinner Tue) Part of the upmarket cluster of restaurants known as the Market Place, this Japanese restaurant serves an exquisite selection of authentic, imaginative sushi. Though the menu is fish-heavy, noodle dishes abound and the vegetable tempura hits the spot. The heavily air-conditioned interior will make you glad there's a dress code: no sleeveless shirts or shorts.

Akbar   INDIAN **$$$**
(Map p44; ☎926-3480; 11 Holborn Rd; mains J$900-2500; ⊙lunch & dinner; ✍) Kingston's best Indian restaurant draws crowds for its gracious service, garden graced by a fountain, and pricey but well-executed menu that includes tandoori and vegetarian dishes, complemented by excellent Indian breads. Be sure to insist on extra spiciness, if fire's what you crave. Offers a buffet lunch special (J$1500).

🍷 Drinking & Nightlife

Kingston is the best town in Jamaica for bar-hopping and clubbing, and you'll never want for after-hours action.

Many bars, nightclubs and sound systems feature regularly scheduled events and theme nights, making it possible to get a groove going every night of the week. For listings, check out the Friday Observer and keep an eye out for flyers advertising one-off events. Drinking and music invariably go hand-in-hand in Kingston, though at sound-system parties your choices will be limited to rum, Red Stripe and Guinness.

Without question, the high point of Kingston's nightlife is its free outdoor sound system parties. A raucous combination of block party, dance-offs between neighborhood groups, fashion show and all-out stereo war, sound-system parties can be heard blocks away and go well into the night. They kick off around 11pm, but plan to arrive for 1am when they really get going; things usually shut down at 4am. Sound-system dances are unforgettable cultural experiences.

It's perfectly safe to attend street parties, as the neighborhoods are responsible for security and people don't take kindly to violence spoiling the event, but it's best to come with a local and to leave obvious valuables behind.

Bars

⭐ Red Bones Blues Café   BAR

(Map p44; www.facebook.com/RedbonesBlues Cafe; 1 Argyle St; ⊙11am-1am Mon-Fri, 7pm-1am Sat) This could easily become your favorite Kingston spot – it's a hip open-air bar with cool ambience and great music. There are quality live bands throughout the week, including blues, jazz and reggae, showcasing well-chosen local and international talent, as well as regular poetry slams. Oh, and the food is great too.

Tracks & Records   BAR

(Map p44; ✆906-3903; www.facebook.com/UB Tracks; Market Pl, 67 Constant Spring Rd; ⊙11.30am-11.30pm) Music meets athletics at this doubly-punning sports bar owned by Usain Bolt. The atmosphere is lively, with plenty of drinks and bar food, plus some surprisingly good karaoke, and live music on 'Behind the Screens' Tuesday.

Deck   BAR

(Map p44; 14 Trafalgar Rd; ⊙from 4:30pm) This cavernous open-air bar, festooned with fishing nets, is a long-standing favorite with the older crowd for its easygoing atmosphere and good bar food. On Fridays things get particularly lively during the ever-popular oldies After-Work Jam.

KINGSTON, BLUE MOUNTAINS & SOUTHEAST COAST KINGSTON

KINGSTON'S WEEKLY PARTY PLANNER

Monday	**Hot Mondays** At Limelight (Map p44; ✆908-0841; Half Way Tree Entertainment Complex, 5-7 Hagley Park Rd; ⊙midnight-5am)
	Uptown Mondays At Savannah Plaza (Map p44; Half Way Tree); dancehall sound system.
Tuesday	**Behind the Screen** At Tracks & Records
Wednesday	**Weddy Weddy Wednesdays** At Stone Love HQ (Map p44; Half Way Tree); one of the best Uptown sound systems.
	Retro Night At Quad (p54).
	Inclusive Wednesdays At Medusa (p54).
Thursday	**I Love v.O.D.k.a.** At Privilege (Map p44; ✆622-6532; www.clubprivilegejm.com; 14-16 Trinidad Tce; admission J$1000; ⊙10pm-4am Thu-Sat).
Friday	**After Work Jam** At Deck.
	Friday Night Party At Privilege (Map p44; ✆622-6532; www.clubprivilegejm.com; 14-16 Trinidad Tce; admission J$1000; ⊙10pm-4am Thu-Sat).
	Club Night At Fiction (p54).
Saturday	**Privilege Saturday** At Privilege (Map p44; ✆622-6532; www.clubprivilegejm.com; 14-16 Trinidad Tce; admission J$1000; ⊙10pm-4am Thu-Sat).
	Club Night At Fiction (p54).
Sunday	**Oldies Night** Sound system playing the best of reggae outside the Capricorn bar in Rae Town.

Cuddy'z
SPORTS BAR

(Map p44; www.facebook.com/cuddyzsportsbar; 25 Dominica Dr; ⊙ 11:30am-1am Mon-Thu, 11:30am-2am Fri & Sat, 1pm-11pm Sun) This hip establishment is the creation of the 'Big Man Inna Cricket,' Courtney Walsh. TVs in each booth and a lively bleachers section with an oversized screen make this a great place to catch the latest football, cricket and baseball games.

Medusa
BAR

(Map p44; 96 Hope Rd) The airy upstairs deck makes for relaxing evening drinking and Inclusive Wednesdays (all-you-can-drink for J$1000) are particularly popular with local students. It's behind Treasure Hut Shopping Plaza.

Nightclubs

Famous
NIGHTCLUB

(☑ 988-8801; www.facebook.com/FamousNightclubJa; Gerbera Ave, Portmore; J$1000; ⊙ 10pm-4am) Reputedly the largest nightclub in the Caribbean, this superclub and self-styled mecca of dancehall in Portmore has a Coliseum-style dancefloor, huge soundstage and lightshow. Ladies night (free entry) is on Thursday, but on no night consider turning up before midnight.

Quad
NIGHTCLUB

(Map p44; ☑ 754-7823; www.facebook.com/QuadNightClub; 20-22 Trinidad Tce; admission J$1000; ⊙ 4-10pm Tue & Thu; 4pm-5am Wed, Fri & Sat) A superclub with four different levels. On the main floor is the more tasteful Spirits Lounge (food available). Every Wednesday, Friday and Saturday, two clubs open up: the top-floor Deja Vu Lounge, which draws crowds for an oldies mix; and Club Vision Z, which plays rocking dance beats until 5am. In the basement is Taboo, with 'exotic' dancers.

Fiction
NIGHTCLUB

(Map p44; ☑ 631-8038; Unit 6, Market Pl, 67 Constant Spring Rd; admission J$100; ⊙ 6pm-4am Mon-Sat) Pretty young things rub shoulders (and not just shoulders) with each other at one of Kingston's most popular elegant new clubs, which wouldn't look out of place in Miami.

☆ Entertainment

Streetside billboards advertise upcoming live concerts and sound system parties. Sports lovers should make their way to Sabina Park or the National Stadium for big events.

Sabina Park
SPORTS

(☑ 967-0322; South Camp Rd) *The* place for cricket in Jamaica. The 30,000-seat arena hosted its first Test match in 1929. The atmosphere during international Tests makes it a must – whether or not you're a fan.

National Stadium
SPORTS

(☑ 929-4970; Arthur Wint Dr) Big-name concerts, track-and-field events and matches featuring the Reggae Boyz, Jamaica's national football – soccer – team.

Little Theatre
THEATER

(Map p44; ☑ 926-6129; www.ltpantomime.com; 4 Tom Redcam Dr) Puts on plays, folk concerts and modern dance throughout the year. The National Dance Theatre Company performs July to August. Pantomime from late December through April.

Caymanas Park
SPORTS

(☑ 988-2523; www.caymanaspark.com; Caymanas Dr, Portmore; admission J$150-350; ⊙ Wed & Sat) The horse races at Caymanas Park in Portmore, one of the best race tracks in the Caribbean (and immortalized in several classic ska songs), make for a lively outing and a real slice of traditional Jamaican life; get a local to explain the complicated betting system. Take bus 17A, 18A or 20A from Half Way Tree.

🔒 Shopping

Kingston has it all, from modern shopping malls to street craft stalls. Good crafts are found Downtown, whereas Devon House is your port of call for specialty shops. Art galleries and souvenir shops are scattered around Uptown, though many are to be found in shopping malls off and along Hope Rd.

Two of the largest shopping centers are Sovereign Centre (Map p40; 106 Hope Rd) and New Kingston Shopping Centre (Map p44; Dominica Dr).

Patoo
SOUVENIRS

(Map p40; Manor Hill Plaza, 184 Constant Spring Rd) Local treasures – Tortuga puddings laced with rum, Busha Brown sauces, ceramic tableware, decorative ornaments and batik sarongs.

Bookland
BOOKSTORE

(Map p44; 53 Knutsford Blvd) Stock includes a strong selection of titles on Jamaica and the Caribbean, including guidebooks. Good black literature section.

Bookophilia   BOOKSTORE
(Map p44; 92 Hope Rd) Very good selection of books and magazines. The Blue Mountain coffee and muffin counter makes you want to linger longer.

Crafts Market   SOUVENIRS
(Map p42; cnr Pechon & Port Royal Sts; ⊘ Mon-Sat) Stall upon stall of wood carvings, bead jewelry, wickerworks, batiks, handbags and Jamaican clothing.

Rockers International   MUSIC STORE
(Map p42; ☑ 922-8015; 135 Orange St) The best pick of reggae music in town, both CDs and LPs. Find your Burning Spear, Horace Andy and John Holt here.

Mutual Gallery   ART GALLERY
(Map p44; ☑ 929-4302; 2 Oxford Rd) Excellent little gallery at the base of North Tower, with constantly changing exhibits of Jamaica's most exciting modern art.

Techniques Records   MUSIC STORE
(Map p42; ☑ 967-4367; 99 Orange St) Oldies, dancehall and traditional Jamaican music.

Grosvenor Galleries   ART GALLERY
(Map p40; ☑ 924-6684; 1 Grosvenor Tce) Excellent contemporary art by exciting new artists.

Contemporary Art Centre   ART GALLERY
(Map p44; ☑ 927-9958; 1 Liguanea Ave) Good selection of contemporary art.

ⓘ Information

DANGERS & ANNOYANCES
Kingston carries a fearful reputation before it, but in practice visitors can safely enjoy the city as long as a few common-sense guidelines are followed.

New Kingston and upscale residential areas such as Liguanea and Mona are generally safe for walking, as are most main roads and Downtown. Avoid wandering at night, and stick to main roads where possible. Watch out for pickpockets in market areas.

Trench Town, Jones Town, Denham Town and Tivoli Gardens and west of Parade, Downtown, are areas best explored with a local guide.

EMERGENCY
Ambucare (☑ 978-2327) Private ambulance service.
Emergency (☑ 119)
Police Headquarters (☑ 922-9321; 11 East Queen St); Half Way Tree (142 Maxfield Ave, Half Way Tree); Cross Roads (Brentford Rd, Cross Roads)

St John Ambulance (☑ 926-7656) Free ambulance services in Kingston.

INTERNET ACCESS
Most hotels and plenty of coffeeshops provide free wi-fi access. Digicel and LIME shops offer island-wide USB modems for laptops (from J$3600).

MEDICAL SERVICES
Andrews Memorial Hospital (☑ 926-7401; 27 Hope Rd) Well-equipped private hospital with well-stocked pharmacy.
Liganea Drugs & Garden (134 Old Hope Rd) Uptown pharmacy.
Monarch Pharmacy (Sovereign Centre; ⊘ 9am-10pm Mon-Sat, 9am-8pm Sun)
University Hospital (☑ 927-1620; University of the West Indies campus, Mona) The best, most up-to-date public hospital with 24-hour emergency department.

MONEY
Uptown, there are half a dozen banks along Knutsford Blvd and around Halfway Tree. Most banks have foreign-exchange counters as well as 24-hour ATMs. There are also ATMs along Hope Rd, particularly by the shopping malls.

POST
Post Office (⊘ 8am-5pm Mon-Thu, 9am-4pm Fri, 8am-1pm Sat); Main post office (Map p42; ☑ 876-922-2120; 13 King St); Half Way Tree (Map p44; 18 Hagley Park Rd)

TOURIST INFORMATION
Jamaica Conservation & Development Trust (☑ 960-2848; www.jcdt.org.jm; 29 Dumbarton Ave, Kingston 10) Responsible for the management and supervision of the Blue Mountains & John Crow National Park. Can advise on guides and routes.
Jamaica Tourist Board (www.visitjamaica.com) Offices offering maps, brochures and limited travel advice in Uptown (p209) and Norman Manley International Airport (Arrivals hall).

ⓘ Getting There & Away

AIR
Norman Manley International Airport (p212), 27km southeast of Downtown, handles international flights. Domestic flights depart and land at Tinson Pen Aerodrome (p213) in west Kingston.

CAR
From the North Coast
The A3 leads to Kingston via the Stony Hill and Constant Springs. The more scenic but difficult B3 takes you to Papine from Buff Bay via the Blue Mountains but is sometimes closed due to landslides.

POPULAR BUS ROUTES IN KINGSTON

All bus fares within Kingston are J$100.

BUS	DESTINATION	FREQUENCY	DEPARTURE POINT
1/1A	Hellshire Beach	hourly	Parade/Half Way Tree
21B/22, 22A	Spanish Town	hourly	Half Way Tree/Parade
42/42A	Constant Spring	hourly	Parade/Half Way Tree
60, 68	Papine	hourly	Parade/Halfway Tree
61	Gordon Town	several daily	Parade
74/76	Barbican	hourly	Parade/Half Way Tree
97	Bull Bay	hourly	Parade
98	Airport, Port Royal	every 30min	Parade
99	Harbour View	hourly	Parade
500/600/700	Parade	every 30min	Half Way Tree

From the West

Spanish Town Rd enters Kingston at the Six Miles junction. For Uptown Kingston, veer left on Washington Blvd, which later changes its name to Dunrobin Ave and joins Constant Springs Rd.

From the East

Windward Rd passes the turnoff for Port Royal and the airport. For New Kingston turn right on Mountain View Ave or South Camp Rd (the latter has helpful 'follow the hummingbird' signs directing the way).

PUBLIC TRANSPORTATION

Buses, minibuses and route taxis run between Kingston and every point on the island. They arrive and depart primarily from Downtown **long-distance bus terminal** (Map p42; cnr Port Royal St & Water Lane). Buses (fewer departures on Sunday) depart when full and are often packed beyond capacity.

Comfortable Knutsford Express (p214) buses run from their own terminal in New Kingston, with several departures per day to Ocho Rios (J$1600, two hours), Falmouth (J$2200, three hours), Montego Bay (J$2450, four hours), Savannah-la-Mar (J$1500, two hours), Mandeville (J$2000, two hours) and Negril (J$2700, five hours). Buying tickets more than 24 hours in advance gets a J$200 discount. Be at the bus station 30 minutes before departure to register your ticket.

Minibuses to Port Antonio (J$450, two hours) arrive and depart from outside **Half Way Tree Bus Terminal** (Map p44).

If you're traveling to Kingston, find out where you will be dropped before boarding a bus.

Getting Around

TO/FROM THE AIRPORT

Bus

Bus 98 operates between the international airport (arrivals hall) and Parade, Downtown (J$100, 35 minutes, every 30 minutes). For Tinson Pen Aerodrome, take bus 22 or 22A from Parade (J$100, 20 minutes, hourly).

Taxi

Between the international airport/Tinson Pen Aerodrome and New Kingston costs about US$35/15 (J$3850/1650).

Car

Driving in Kingston isn't for the faint-hearted. Be prepared for erratic and aggressive driving. Don't drive Downtown after dark. All hotels and shopping centers offer parking, but secure car parking is nonexistent Downtown.

Most car-rental companies offer free airport shuttles. Some reputable companies with offices at Norman Manley International Airport:

Avis (924-8293; www.avis.com)

Budget (759-1793; www.budget.com)

Island Car Rentals (924-8075; www.island carrentals.com)

PUBLIC TRANSPORTATION

Buses, minibuses and route taxis arrive and depart from **North** (Map p42) and **South Parade** (Map p42) in Downtown, Half Way Tree bus station in Uptown, Cross Roads (between Uptown and Downtown) and Papine, at the eastern edge of town off Old Hope Rd.

Jamaica Urban Transport Co Ltd (JUTC; www.jutc.com; fares J$80-170) operates a fleet of white and yellow Mercedes-Benz and Volvo buses.

MINIBUSES FROM KINGSTON

DESTINATION	COST (J$)	DURATION (HR)	FREQUENCY
Mandeville	300	1½	5-6 daily
May Pen	200	1	6-8 daily
Montego Bay	650	4½-5	6-8 daily
Ocho Rios	400	2	8-10 daily
Port Antonio	450	2	6-8 daily
Santa Cruz	400	2	6-8 daily

Most are air-conditioned. JUTC buses stop only at official stops.

Minibuses and route taxis ply all the popular routes (J$50 to J$80), stopping on request. It's easy to confuse white route taxis with red license plates with identical chartered taxis.

TAXI

Taxis are numerous in Kingston except when it rains, when demand skyrockets. Use licensed cabs only, which have red PP or PPV license plates. Taxis have no meters, so confirm the fare in advance (New Kingston to Downtown is about J$500).

Reputable 24-hour radio taxi firms:
Apollo Taxis (☑ 969-9993)
El Shaddai (☑ 925-1363)
On Time (☑ 926-3866) Biggest radio taxi company in Jamaica.

AROUND KINGSTON

Whether it's Downtown's perpetual slope toward the harbor or the Blue Mountains beckoning from high above Uptown, there's something about Kingston's topography that tempts the visitor to take a break from the intensity of city life.

Most popular among day trips is a visit to Port Royal, a former pirate's den of iniquity, easily combined with a visit to Lime Cay, the best (and closest) swimming spot in the area. Other good seaside options include Hellshire Beach – a quintessential Kingstonian seaside experience – and Bull Bay, a rapidly growing surfing community. If it's greenery you crave, Castleton Gardens, a half-hour drive north of Kingston, are the finest botanic gardens in Jamaica. Finally, Jamaica's second city and former capital, Spanish Town, is noted for its Georgian architecture as well as the red brick splendour of St Jago de la Vega, the oldest Anglican cathedral outside of England.

Castleton Gardens

These fine gardens (☉ 9am-5pm) FREE, 27km north of Half Way Tree, are spread over 12 hectares on the banks of the Wag Water River. They date back to 1862, when 400 specimens from Kew Gardens in London were transplanted on the former sugar plantation owned by Lord Castleton. More than 1000 species of natives and exotics are displayed.

Bull Bay

Bull Bay is 14km east of Downtown Kingston (bus 97 from Parade, J$100, 30 minutes). It's a nondescript place, but nearby is Jamaica's most notable surf camp and an interesting Rastafarian community.

Jamnesia Surf Camp   SURFING
(☑ 750-0103; http://jamnesiasurf.com; Cable Hut Beach; camping per person US$15, s/d from US$35/45) This surf club with accommodation and a chilled vibe is a great place to catch the swell. There are plenty of boards to rent, decent basic rooms with shared kitchen facilities and a rustic outdoor bar that has live music on alternate Saturdays. Multinight lodging packages are also offered, including meals and surf shuttle.

Bobo Hill   RASTAFARIAN COMMUNITY
(Ethiopia Africa Black International Congress; ☑ 578-6798) Bobo Hill, or the Ethiopia Africa Black International Congress, is the home of the Bobo Ashanti and sits on Queensbury Ridge above Bull Bay. About 100 fundamentalist Rastafarians live here, making a living from farming or selling natural-fiber brooms in Kingston. Other than that, they disassociate themselves from 'Babylon' and don't venture outside their commune.

Guests with a sincere interest in the Bobo's beliefs are welcome as long as they respect 'manners and principles.' Guests are greeted by the head priest or female elder and given a spiel rich in clever metaphor that offers a fascinating insight into Rastafarian philosophy. Menstruating women aren't allowed inside the commune.

Overnight guests must contribute 'something' and 'come to salvation' through performing duties on 'campus.'

It's little more than 1km uphill from the bridge on the A4. You'll need a 4WD and to call ahead as the Bobo prefer advance notice.

Port Royal

POP 3000

Once the wealthiest, and 'wickedest', city in the New World, the pirate capital of the Caribbean – and for more than 200 years the hub of British naval power in the West Indies – Port Royal today is a sleepy fishing village, yet one replete with historic buildings.

There are few hints of the town's former glory, though landmarks such as Fort Charles have been given a new lease on life by the Jamaica Heritage Trust. Restaurants serving the freshest fish in Kingston, and doubling as party spots after hours, along with the white-sand beach of Lime Cay, make this one of the best-loved spots near Kingston.

History

The English settled the cay in 1655 and built five forts here to defend Kingston Harbour. Buccaneers – organized as the Confederacy of the Brethren of the Coast – established their base at Port Royal, using it for government-sponsored raids against the Spanish.

The lawless buccaneers were big spenders. The wealth flowing into Port Royal attracted merchants, rum traders, prostitutes and others seeking a share of the profits. Townsfolk invested in the expeditions in exchange for a share of the booty and by 1682 Port Royal was a prosperous town of 8000 people.

At midday on June 7 1692, a great earthquake shook the island, followed by a huge tsunami, and two-thirds of the town disappeared underwater. Around 2000 people died instantly, and numerous survivors were claimed by the pestilence that followed. Many claimed the destruction was God's vengeance for the town's lax morals.

Port Royal never truly recovered. Piracy was outlawed, and the town was overshadowed by the growing city of Kingston. In the 18th century, Port Royal instead began a 250-year tenure as headquarters of the Royal Navy in the West Indies; Admiral Lord Nelson was quartered here for a spell. In 1838 Jamaica ceased to be a separate naval command and, with the development of steam warships in the early 20th century, Port Royal's demise was sealed.

◎ Sights & Activities

★ Fort Charles   FORT

(☑967-8438; adult/child J$200/100; ⊙9am-4:45pm) Jamaica's latitude and longitude are measured from the flagstaff of Fort Charles, a weathered redoubt originally laid in 1655, and the only one of the town's forts to survive the 1692 earthquake. Originally washed by the sea on three sides, the fort is now firmly landlocked due to the gradual silt build-up.

At its peak, 104 guns protected the fort. Many cannons still point out from their embrasures along the restored battlements. In the center of the courtyard stands the small, well-presented **Maritime Museum**, containing a miscellany of objects – from glassware and pottery to weaponry – retrieved from the sunken city. Horatio Nelson, who later became Britain's greatest naval hero, lived in the small 'cockpit' while stationed here for 30 months.

Behind the museum is the raised platform known as **Nelson's Quarterdeck**, where the young Nelson was kept on watch for enemy ships amid fears of a French invasion. A plaque on the wall of the King's Battery commemorates his time here.

A small red-brick artillery store, the 1888 **Giddy House**, sits alone just behind the fort. The 1907 earthquake briefly turned the spit to quicksand and one end of the building sank, leaving the store at a lopsided angle. Next to the Giddy House is a gun emplacement with a massive cannon – which also keeled over in 1907.

St Peter's Church   CHURCH

(Main Rd) Built in 1725 of red brick, this church is handsome within, despite its cement faux-brick facade. Note the floor paved with original black-and-white tiles, and the beautifully decorated wooden organ loft built in 1743. The place is replete with memorial plaques. Come dressed up for a Sunday service.

Old Naval Hospital   NOTABLE BUILDING

Behind the old garrison wall off New St stands the dilapidated two-story Old

Naval Hospital, built by Bowling Ironworks in Bradford, UK, shipped to Port Royal and reconstructed at this site in 1819. Though it suffered considerable damage from Hurricane Gilbert, the Jamaica National Heritage Trust has plans to renovate it.

Old Gaol House   HISTORICAL SITE
(Gaol Alley) The only fully restored historical structure in town is the sturdy Old Gaol House, made of cut stone on Gaol Alley. It predates the 1692 earthquake, when it served as a women's jail, and has since survived a host of disasters, including 14 hurricanes and two major fires.

✦ Festivals & Events

Port Royal Seafood Festival   FOOD
(☉ Oct) The Port Royal Seafood Festival, held each year on National Heroes Day, the third Monday in October, is a rollicking good time with plenty of food and live music.

🛏 Sleeping

Admiral's Inn   GUESTHOUSE $
(☎ 353-4202; Henry Morgan Blvd; d J$5000; ❄)
Rooms inside this cheerful yellow family-run guest house have fridges and microwaves, and you can chill in the garden while the owners cook your fish supper. Trips to Lime Cay can be organized. Follow the road round past Gloria's Top Spot and past the park on your right-hand side. The guest house is on the left.

**Grand Port Royal Hotel
Marina & Spa**   HOTEL $$$
(☎ 480-5226; www.grandportroyalhotel.com; 1 Port Royal; r US$180-350; P ❄ 🛜 ☒) Formerly Morgan's Harbour, this hotel in the grounds of the old naval dockyard (which featured in the Bond film *Dr No*) was undergoing a complete refit when we visited. Expect high-end rooms with balconies, top restaurant and waterside bar overlooking Kingston's largest marina, as well as spa facilities. Day rates are also available.

✗ Eating & Entertainment

On the main square are several food stalls serving good fried fish.

★ Gloria's   SEAFOOD $
(5 Queen St; stew fish J$1000; ☉ lunch & dinner)
This informal restaurant fills daily with locals who drive here from miles around. Get here early, particularly on Friday night and Sunday lunchtime. Gloria's fish is nothing

Port Royal

short of glorious – a large plate of melt-in-your-mouth perfection, accompanied by *bammy*, festival or rice. The brown stew fish is particularly good.

Y-Knot   SEAFOOD $
(meals J$1000-1500; ☉ lunch & dinner) On a large deck over the water, this spot serves particularly good conch soup, as well as sumptuous grilled chicken, fish, shrimp and lobster. The bar draws a younger crowd on weekends for drinking and dancing.

Gloria's Top Spot   SEAFOOD $$
(Foreshore Rd; meals J$1100-1400; ☉ lunch & dinner) Run by the children of the dearly departed Gloria, this restaurant perches by the water, with a large, attractive upstairs dining area that's particularly popular with tourists

DON'T MISS

LIME CAY

The idyllic **Lime Cay** (Map p40) is one of half a dozen or so uninhabited, white-sand-rimmed coral cays about 3km offshore from Port Royal. Immortalized in the final showdown of the movie *The Harder They Come*, it's ideal for sunbathing and snorkeling. Shacks sell food and drinks.

Arrange a trip from **Morgan's Harbour Yacht Marina** (Wednesday to Sunday only, J$1000, minimum four people). You might talk the local fishers into taking you for a reduced rate on their motorized boats ('canoes'); agree a round-trip rate first and only pay half until they come to pick you up, or risk getting stranded.

and large groups. Things get lively on Friday and Saturday nights when gussied-up locals pile in to flirt and dance to the latest sounds.

❶ Getting There & Away

From Kingston's Parade take bus 98 (J$100, every 30 minutes, less frequently on Sunday).

Hellshire Beach Recreation Area

White-sand beaches fringe the Hellshire Hills southwest of Kingston. **Fort Clarence Beach Park** (adult/child J$250/150; ⊙10am-5pm Mon-Fri, 8am-7pm Sat & Sun) is popular with Kingstonians on weekends. It has clean sand, showers, toilets and secure parking. A restaurant and bar are open weekends only, but there are regular dancehall events.

Further on is Fisherman's Beach, a funky fishing and Rasta 'village' with dozens of brightly painted huts and stalls selling beer, jerk and fish. It's a lively place on weekends, with sound systems on Sunday nights. In the morning, fishing pirogues come in with their catch. On any day of the week, though, it's a fascinating visit, a slice of the 'real' Jamaica up close.

Bus 1 (J$100, 30 minutes), minibuses and route taxis (J$200) run from Kingston's Parade; bus 1A (J$00, 35 minutes) from Half Way Tree.

Portland Bight Protected Area

Created in 1999, this 1876-sq-km **protected area** (PBPA; www.portlandbight.com.jm) comprises Jamaica's largest natural reserve with 210 sq km of dry limestone forest and 83 sq km of wetlands, as well as precious coral reefs (two-thirds of the protected area lies offshore). This vital habitat is managed by the **Caribbean Coastal Area Management Foundation** (CCAM; ☑ 986-3344; www.ccam.org.jm).

Although CCAM has planned to move forward with 'community tourism' programs, employing local fishermen to lead guided boat tours and hikes, the area is currently under threat from a government-led plan to develop the area into a huge trans-shipment port with a Chinese consortium – a plan being resisted by local environmental groups.

Spanish Town

POP 160,000

Spanish Town was Jamaica's capital for more than 300 years. Now circled by ghettoes, it's very much Kingston's poor neighbor, although its historic center contains the Caribbean's most extensive assortment of Georgian architecture, albeit in a sad state of repair, its greatest cathedral and Jamaica's national archives. Parts of Spanish Town are regularly affected by gang violence. Take local advice, but consider this a day trip only.

History

Founded in 1534, Villa de la Vega was Spain's second permanent settlement in Jamaica. Although it grew modestly, its population was never large, and it was ransacked several times by English pirates. Eventually, in 1655, an English invasion fleet landed and captured the city. The English destroyed much of the town, then they renamed it 'Spanish Town' and made it their capital. For the next two centuries, the town prospered as Jamaica's administrative capital but it was eventually outpaced by Kingston, which took over as the island's capital in 1872.

❍ Sights

Emancipation Square   SQUARE

Spanish Town's finest old buildings enfold this square, also known as Parade Sq. Dominating the north side is the elaborate Rodney Memorial, built for Admiral George Rodney, the commander-in-chief of the West Indian Naval Station who saved Jamaica from a combined French and Spanish invasion fleet in 1782. He stands within a cupola temple, with sculpted panel reliefs showing the battle scenes.

The building behind the memorial is the **National Archives** (☑984-2581; ☺9am-4:30pm Mon-Thu) FREE, with national documents dating back centuries, including the proclamation of the abolition of slavery.

On the eastern side of the plaza is the 1762 redbrick House of Assembly. It has a beautiful wooden upper story with a pillar-lined balcony. The Assembly and Supreme Court sat here in colonial days, when it was the setting for violent squabbles among feuding parliamentarians.

On the square's south side are the fenced-off Courthouse Ruins, dating from 1819 but destroyed by fire in 1986.

On the west side of the plaza is the porticoed Georgian red-brick facade of the ruins of the Old King's House, a once-grandiose building erected in 1762 as the official residence of Jamaica's governors.

Today the stables, to the rear, house the **People's Museum of Crafts & Technology** (☑922-0620; adult/child J$300/100; ☺9:30am-4:30pm Mon-Thu, to 3pm Fri). A reconstructed smith's shop and eclectic array of artifacts – from Indian corn grinders to early sugar-processing and coffee-making machinery – provide an entry point to early Jamaican culture. A model shows how Old King's House once looked and the outdoor section features carriages used in colonial times.

St Jago de la Vega Cathedral   CHURCH
Built in 1714, this is the oldest Anglican cathedral in the Caribbean, boasting an impressive beamed ceiling, and a magnificent stained-glass window behind the altar. The church stands on the site of one of the first Spanish cathedrals in the New World, built in 1525. Note the gargoyles with African features, considered unique in the world, above the south window.

Iron Bridge   LANDMARK
At the bottom of Barrett St, turn left onto Bourkes Rd and follow it east to the narrow Iron Bridge spanning the Rio Cobre. The span was made of cast iron prefabricated at Colebrookdale, England, and was erected in 1801 on a cut-stone foundation that dates to 1675. The only surviving bridge of its kind in the Americas, it is still used by pedestrians, if barely.

✗ Eating

Cecil's   JAMAICAN $
(☑984-1927; 35 Martin St; meals J$450-650; ☺breakfast, lunch & dinner Mon-Sat) Curry goat, oxtail and beans, brown stew chicken and a host of chow mein dishes served on plastic tableclothes under dim lighting.

La Cocina for Mom's Cooking   JAMAICAN $
(Shop 31, St Jago Shopping Centre, Bourkes Rd; meals J$300-450; ☺lunch) Popular lunch spot cooking up a slightly Spanish take on Jamaican favorites such as stew pork, red pea soup and curry mutton.

ⓘ Information

Parts of Spanish Town are heavily affected by gang violence. Beware pickpocketing, especially at the market, and avoid driving near the market and exploring away from main downtown streets.
Police (☑984-2775; cnr Oxford Rd & Wellington St)
Post Office (☑info 984 2409; cnr King & Adelaide Sts)
Scotiabank (☑984-3024; 27 Adelaide St)
Spanish Town Hospital (☑984-3031; Bourkes Rd) Has a 24-hour emergency department.

ⓘ Getting There & Away

From Half Way Tree take bus 21B; from Parade, 22, 22A (J$100). In Spanish Town, buses, minibuses and route taxis leave from the **municipal bus terminal** (Bourkes Rd). Taxis depart from the taxi stand to the east of the bus terminal on Bourkes Rd.

May Pen & Around

May Pen
POP 48,500
The capital of Clarendon parish, 58km west of Kingston, is a teeming market and agricultural town. Expect pandemonium on Friday and Saturday when the market is held south of the main square, with terrible congestion adding to the general mayhem.

⊙ Sights

Halse Hall   NOTABLE BUILDING
(☑986-2215; ☺tours by arrangement) Halse Hall is a handsome great house 5km south of May Pen. The house was once occupied by Sir Hans Sloane, the doctor and botanist whose

WORTH A TRIP

CANOE VALLEY WETLAND

This is a lovely government-owned **wildlife reserve** (☑377-8264; ⊙Mon-Sat) FREE also known as Alligator Hole. It's notable for its family of manatees that inhabit the clear water, and its crocodiles. They live amid dense reeds in jade-blue pools fed by waters that emerge at the base of limestone cliffs, and are not always easy to see. Waterfowl are abundant.

There's a small visitor center with displays on local wildlife. You can take an hour-long trip by canoe with a guide for J$1000 (tip expected).

The turnoff is signed 1.5km north of Milk River Bath on the B12. Otherwise take the beautiful 17km-long coastal road from **Alligator Pond**, which is often deserted. The road conditions can be poor after autumn rains.

collection of Jamaican flora and fauna formed the nucleus of what later became the Natural History Museum in London. Today, it is owned by the bauxite concern Alcoa Minerals, but tours can be arranged in advance.

★ Festivals & Events

Denbigh Agricultural Show AGRICULTURE
The annual Denbigh Agricultural Show is held on the Denbigh Showground, 3km west of town, on Independence weekend in early August. It's a muddy, smelly, noisy and enjoyable affair, with farmers from each parish showcasing the fruits of their labor, from yams to livestock. Live entertainment and food vendors round out the bill.

⊨ Sleeping

Hotel Versalles HOTEL $$
(☑986-2709; hotelversalles@cwjamaica.com; 42 Longbridge Ave; r J$8000, ste J$10000; P❄@☎) This modern hotel, 1km southwest of town, has modestly furnished rooms, suites and studios. Take the second left at the Mineral Lights Roundabout.

❶ Getting There & Around

The **transportation center** (Map p40; Main St), 200m southeast of the main square, has frequent buses, minibuses and route taxis to and from Kingston (J$150, one hour), Ocho Rios, Mandeville, Negril and Milk River.

Milk River Bath

This well-known **spa** (☑449-6502; adult/ child per bath J$400/200, hotel guests free, massages J$1000-4500; ⊙7am-10pm), operating since 1794, is fed from a saline mineral hot spring that bubbles up at the foot of Round Hill, 3km from the sea. The waters are a near-constant 33°C (92°F).

The spa, which is attached to the Milk River Hotel, is owned by the government. Public and private baths are available. Many recommend drinking the waters as a tonic, but they're the most radioactive spa waters in the world; bathers are limited to only 15 minutes, though you are allowed three baths a day. About 200m north of the spa is the open-air Milk River Mineral Spa Swimming Pool.

Beyond Milk River Bath, a dirt road leads 2.5km to the black-sand Farquhars Beach, where you can watch fishermen tending their nets and pirogues.

Milk River Hotel (☑449-6502; hotelmilk river@yahoo.com; Clarendon; d without/with bathroom J$6000/8000) is a rambling white-porched hotel with shady verandas and 20 modestly furnished, pleasant rooms. Jamaican favorites are served in a cozy dining room; full board is available.

Farquhars Beach has two good eateries: Dian's Three Star Seafood Restaurant, a sky-blue shack serving steamed fish and basic Jamaican fare; and Jaddy's Rasta shack at the end of the beach, great for fried fish, fish tea and dumplings.

A bus operates from May Pen (J$150, 45 minutes) twice daily.

BLUE MOUNTAINS

Deriving its name from the azure haze that settles lazily around its peaks, this 45km-long mountain range looms high above the eastern parishes of St Andrew, St Thomas, Portland and St Mary. The Blue Mountains were formed during the Cretaceous Period (somewhere between 144 and 65 million years ago) and are the island's oldest feature. Highest of the highlights, Blue Mountain Peak (p69) reaches 2256m above sea level, and no visit to the area should neglect a predawn hike to its summit for a sunrise view.

Unsurprisingly, the Blue Mountains' largely unspoiled character owes much to the difficulty in navigating around the area. Roads are narrow and winding, and some are dirt tracks that are utterly impossible to pass without 4WD, especially after heavy rains. If you are spending time in the area, it is highly advisable to rent a hardy vehicle, contact a tour guide or make arrangements with your hotel.

History

With dense primary forests and forbidding topography, the prospect of life in the Blue Mountains has discouraged all but the most determined settlers. During the 17th and 18th centuries, these same formidable qualities made the territory the perfect hideout for the Windward Maroons, who from their remote stronghold at Nanny Town resisted enslavement and British colonialism for more than 100 years. But this region's primary claim to fame has always been coffee cultivation; it has been a mainstay since the very first coffee factories were erected around Clydesdale in the mid-18th century. Meanwhile, back down at sea level, the southeast coast of St Thomas parish is notable for its long history of protest and rebellion, and the independent spirit of the region has kept it at odds with the government even to this day. The Blue Mountains & John Crow National Park was gazetted in 1993 in recognition of the region's ecological and cultural importance.

ⓘ Information

The Blue Mountains & John Crow National Park protects 782 sq km and is managed by the **Jamaica Conservation & Development Trust** (JCDT; ☑ 960-2848; www.blueandjohncrow mountains.org; 29 Dumbarton Ave, Kingston). The park includes the forest reserves of the Blue and John Crow Mountain Ranges and spans the parishes of St Andrew, St Thomas, Portland and St Mary. Ecotourism is being promoted and locals are being trained as guides. Camping is only permitted at designated sites. Camping 'wild' is not advised.

There is a national park entrance fee of US$5, payable at the **ranger stations** (☺ 9am-5pm) at Holywell Recreation Area and Portland Gap (for Blue Mountain Peak), and at the Kingston office of the JCDT. Although it's quite possible to enter without a ticket, we do urge you to pay as funds go directly to supporting trail maintenance, ranger salaries and conservation work. The JCDT can

also advise on guides and hiking routes, and sell copies of the excellent *Guide to the Blue and John Crow Mountains.*

Irish Town

Mammee River Rd climbs to Irish Town, a small village where the coopers lived during the 19th century. Potatoes are still an important crop, reflecting the Irish influence. Largely famous for one of the Caribbean's most luxurious resorts, it also contains St Mark's Chapel (Map p64), an attractive white clapboard church restored after damage from Hurricane Gilbert. The pleasant Observation Deck Gallery (Map p64; ☑ 944-8592; ☺ Thu-Sun) features sculpture and painting by local artist Tiffany Recas; it can be found just below the town. A little further up the road, the excellent Cafe Blue (meals J$700; ☺ lunch), the offshoot of the popular Kingston institution, serves sumptuous gourmet sandwiches and Blue Mountain coffee, while the adjoining Crystal Edge (meals J$1000; ☺ lunch) specializes in Jamaican favorites, such as curry goat, and is popular for Sunday brunch.

From Irish Town, a dirt road runs up to the fundamentalist Rastafarian commune called Mount Zion Hill, consisting of just over 50 adults and children who rely on subsistence farming for a living. Though fierce in their rejection of Babylon, the residents can be seen on Papine Sq every Saturday when they come down to hold a Nyabinghi Sabbath Service consisting of drumming and dancing.

Newcastle

The road climbs to 1220m where you suddenly emerge on a wide parade ground guarded by a small cannon. The military encampment clambers up the slope above the square. Newcastle was founded in 1841 as a training site and convalescent center for British soldiers. Since 1962 the camp has been used by the Jamaica Defense Force.

Note the insignia (which dates back to 1884) on the whitewashed stone wall, commemorating those regiments stationed at Newcastle. Visitors are allowed only around the canteen, shop, roadways and parade ground.

A steep dirt road runs from the parade ground up to St Catherine's Peak (one hour). You need to get permission first from the military encampment.

Blue Mountains

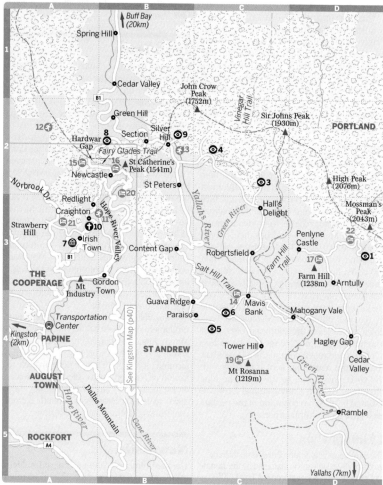

Three kilometers above Newcastle you reach Hardwar Gap (1700m), at the crest of the Grand Ridge – the start on an exhilarating cycle track.

◎ Sights & Activities

Craighton Coffee Estate   COFFEE ESTATE
(www.craightonestate.com; 1hr tour per person J$2000; ⊙9am-4pm) Just north of Newcastle, you can take a one-hour tour of the attractive 200-year-old Craighton Estate Great House and coffee plantation. During the tour, your knowledgeable guide explains to you the basics of coffee cultivation and a mildly steep walk leads you up to a gazebo surrounded by coffee bushes, with wonderful views of the mountains and the villages below. Tasting is included.

🛏 Sleeping & Eating

★ **Mount Edge B&B**   GUESTHOUSE $
(☎351-5083, 944-8151; www.17milepost.com; r J$4000-6000, with shared bathroom J$3000-4000; ℗@⊚) ✿ This quirky mountainside maze of brightly painted rooms and rustic bathrooms is a great budget option. Some rooms (as well as the chill-out lounge) have great views over the valley

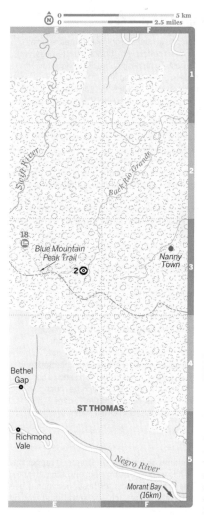

Blue Mountains

in a hammock or in the terrace tiki bar that hangs over a burbling river.

Gap Café Bed & Breakfast　　B&B **$**
(☑ 319-2406; r J$6000) Just below the entrance to Holywell Recreation Area, here's a cosy Hansel and Gretel–style, one-bedroom, self-catering cottage with a veranda. The **cafe** (open for breakfast and lunch Thursday to Sunday; dinner by reservation only) is a fabulous place to take in the vistas. Dine alfresco on a wooden terrace, sampling the succulent curry goat and smoked pork chops, as well as lighter fare in the form of fancy sandwiches.

Heritage Gardens　　GUESTHOUSE **$$**
(☑ 960-8627/0794; www.heritagegardens jamaica.com; cottage J$15000) Set 400m east of Newcastle parade ground, this is a simple yet exquisite three/four-bedroom, fully equipped wooden cottage (with kitchen, lounge and live-in caretakers), set in a circa-1750 coffee estate　with wonderful views towards Kingston. The old coffee-drying barbecues are now laid out as gardens.

below and the gardens that produce organic veggies for the EITS Café. Birding and cycling tours are on offer. Meal packages can be arranged and weekly and monthly rates are negotiable.

★ **Rafjam Bed & Breakfast**　　GUESTHOUSE **$**
(☑ 944.8094; www.rafjam.net; Red Light; r US$35-40, 2-bedroom cottage US$140) This popular budget guest house sits next to the hamlet of Red Light, surrounded by nature and with lovely views. Rooms are charming if simple, but the welcome is a warm one. Bird-watching and guides for hiking can be arranged, or chill out

A SEED-TO-CUP TASTE OF BLUE MOUNTAIN COFFEE

Coffee grows best on well-watered, well-drained slopes in cooler, tropical climates, such as Jamaica's Blue Mountains region. Its distinctly flavored coffee, with its lack of bitterness, is acclaimed by connoisseurs as among the world's best. To be designated 'Blue Mountain,' it must be grown – and roasted – at a certain altitude in a prescribed area.

In 1728, at Temple Hall Estate north of Kingston, governor Sir Nicholas Lawes introduced Arabica coffee to Jamaica from neighboring St Domingue (modern Haiti), and other planters followed suit, prompted by the growing demand in Europe. After the Haitian Revolution, many French planters settled in Jamaica, bringing their expertise with them, expanding and refining the industry. During the peak years of 1800–1840, production rose to 17,000 tons a year and Jamaica became the world's largest exporter.

Emancipation in 1838 brought an end to many of the plantations. Many ex-slaves left the estates and planted their own coffee. As steeper slopes were planted, coffee quality began to decline. The end of Britain's preferential tariffs for Jamaican coffee further damaged the industry at a time when high-quality coffee from Brazil was beginning to sap Jamaica's market share. By the close of WWII, Jamaica's coffee industry was on its last legs, prompting the Jamaican government to establish quality guidelines for coffee cultivation, thus saving the plantations.

There has been a resurgence in the popularity of Blue Mountain coffee in the last decade, largely thanks to interest from Japan, where it is a treasured commodity and sells for US$140 or more per kilogram. More than 80% of Blue Mountain coffee is sold to Japan at a preferential rate.

Sadly, this profitability only encouraged deforestation at home. Tearing down trees brought coffee farmers more valuable land, but also chased away migratory bird populations and has made Blue Mountain coffee especially vulnerable to hurricane damage. Over the past few years the industry's small farmers have been particularly hard hit by natural disasters, highlighting the need both for greater regulations and greater investment.

Currently 26 large and small estates are certified to produce Blue Mountain coffee, with quality guaranteed by the Jamaica Coffee Industry Board. Several estates offer plantation and factory tours, allowing you to learn about this most treasured drink from seed to cup, and come away with your own beans to enjoy at home – food miles don't come much shorter than this. Estates worth checking out are the **Mavis Bank Coffee Factory** (p68, in Mavis Bank), **Craighton Coffee Estate** (p64, Newcastle) and **Old Tavern Coffee Estate** (p67, Section).

EITS Café ORGANIC **$$**
(☎ 944-8151; breakfasts J$800, salads J$500, mains from J$1400) The acronym in the name of the restaurant at the Mount Edge B&B stands for Europe In The Summer – a reasonable summation of what the menu is attempting, with fresh organic vegetables and a 'farm to table' attitude.

Holywell Recreation Area

Spanning Hardwar Gap, this **area** (Map p64; ☎ 960-2848; www.greenjamaica.org.jm; admission US$5; ☉ 9am-5pm) protects 120 hectares of remnant woodland, lush with dozens of fern species, epiphytes, impatiens, violets, nasturtiums, wild strawberries and raspberries. The mist-shrouded uppermost slopes are densely forested with rare primary montane forest, dominated by pine trees. The bird-watching is fabulous. The manned ranger station is a short distance beyond the entrance. The orientation center hosts occasional live entertainment such as traditional music and dance, plus outdoor games, storytelling and a treasure hunt for the kids (contact the Jamaica Conservation & Development Trust (p55) for information). On the last Sunday in February, the Misty Bliss mountain festival is held here, involving Maroon drumming, food and storytelling.

Well-maintained, easy hiking trails lead off in all directions through the ferny dells, cloud forest and elfin woodland. The 2.4km Oatley Mountain Trail, best seen with a guide (US$20) who can point out the different flora, leads to a river good for bathing. The 2km Waterfall Trail leads down along a stream to the Cascade Waterfalls – more trickle than cascade, due to recent landslides.

Camping (per person J$423) is allowed. You can also rent rustic **cabins** (1-/2-bedroom cabins J$4233/5926) with basic kitchens. Bring your own bedding and food (there's a gas ring and fridge) and reserve cabins in advance, particularly on weekends and holidays.

Section & Clydesdale

Heading northeast from Holywell, the road drops steeply toward the hamlet of Section and then curls its way down to Buff Bay, 29km north (impassible at the time of writing due to landslides). A turnoff to the right at Section leads 1.5km to the ridge crest, where the main road loops south and drops to Content Gap, eventually linking up with the road from Gordon Town to Mavis Bank. A steep and muddy dirt road to the left drops to the simple **Silver Hill Coffee Factory** (Map p64).

Clydesdale (Map p64) is a derelict old coffee plantation and a good spot for camping. The much-battered waterwheel and coffee-mill machinery are partially intact. There is a small waterfall where you can skinny-dip and a natural pool in the Clydesdale River below, rumored to have healing properties.

From Section take the horrendously potholed road south towards Guava Ridge; the turnoff for Clydesdale is about 1km above the hamlet of St Peters. Then you will cross over the Chestervale Bridge above the Brook's River and take the left, steeply uphill road at the Y-fork. It's a terribly rocky drive, suitable for a 4WD only.

⊙ Sights

Old Tavern Coffee Estate   COFFEE ESTATE
(Map p64; ☎924-2785) Old Tavern Coffee Estate lies about 1.5km southwest of Section. Dorothy Twyman and her son David produce the superb Blue Mountain coffee. The Twymans welcome visitors by prior arrangement. You're treated to a lesson on coffee growing and production as well as a tasting session of two of the three arabica bean roasts: dark, medium-dark and medium. Additionally, they produce the rare peaberry variety with a mild, subtle flavor.

The late Alex Twyman emigrated to Jamaica from England in 1958 and started growing coffee a decade later, his son now keeping up the tradition. Dorothy oversees the roasting, meticulously performing quality control by taste. The environmentally con-

scious Twymans keep their use of chemical pesticides and fertilizers to a minimum and compost all by-products before returning them to the soil

Cinchona Gardens   GARDEN
(Map p64; tip to caretaker expected) A dilapidated old house sits atop these 2.5-hectare gardens, fronted by lawns and exquisite floral beds. It's a little run-down, but the views are fabulous: to the north stand the peaks, but you can also peer down into the valleys of the Clyde, Green and Yallahs Rivers. The Panorama Walk begins to the east of the gardens, leading through a glade of towering bamboo and taking in the juniper cedar, camphor and eucalyptus trees, as well as a striking display of orchids.

It was the cultivation of Assam tea and cinchona (whose quinine – extracted from the bark – was used to fight malaria) that led to the founding of Cinchona Gardens in 1868. The grounds were later turned into a garden to supply Kingston with flowers. In 1903 the Jamaican government leased Cinchona to the New York Botanical Gardens and, later, to the Smithsonian Institute.

Finding Cinchona can be difficult without a guide. From Clydesdale you can either hike (1½ hours) or drive uphill along the muddy dirt track for about 3km. There are several unmarked junctions; ask for directions at every opportunity. Don't underestimate the awful road conditions; a 4WD with low-gear option is absolutely essential. Alternatively, you can drive up the more populated route via Mavis Bank, though the road conditions can be as atrocious.

🛏 Sleeping

Starlight Chalet & Health Spa   HOTEL
(Map p64; ☎969-3070; www.starlightchalet.com; s/d US$80/90, ste US$95-285) This plantation-style retreat is set amid a flower-filled hillside garden with dramatic alpine vistas, at the turnoff for the Silver Hill Coffee Factory. A great base for birding and hiking, it also offers massages at the no-frills spa, nature walks and yoga; book ahead of arrival. Off-season, you'll have the place to yourself. Pickups are available – the road is atrocious.

Gordon Town & Guava Ridge

Gordon Town, at 370m, is a hamlet centered on a wide square with a police station and tiny courthouse. It began life as a staging post for Newcastle in the days before the Mammee River Rd was cut from the Cooperage. Turn right at the square and cross the narrow bridge to reach Guava Ridge, a ridge-crest junction for Content Gap and sights to the north, while Mavis Bank and Blue Mountain Peak are straight ahead.

Part dirt road, part footpath, the Bermuda Mt Trail begins in Gordon Town and follows the Hope River Valley for part of the way before leading northwest to Redlight via Craighton.

A road signed for 'Bellevue House', 50m east of Guava Ridge, leads through pine and eucalyptus forests to the coffee plantation of Flamstead (Map p64; ☑960-0204) – visits by prior appointment. This former great house of Governor Edward Eyre was a lookout from which Horatio Nelson and other British naval officers surveyed the Port Royal base. You can admire the awe-inspiring views over the Palisadoes and Kingston Harbour.

Mavis Bank

Mavis Bank, around a one-hour drive from Kingston, is a tidy little village in the midst of coffee country.

◉ Sights & Activities

Mavis Bank Coffee Factory COFFEE ESTATE
(Map p64; ☑977-8015; tour J$1000; ⊙10am-2pm Mon-Fri) Established in 1923 and located 1km southwest of Mavis Bank is the largest coffee factory in Jamaica, producing Blue Mountain coffee sold under the 'Jablum' label. Ask the chief 'cupper' to demonstrate 'cupping' (tasting), the technique to identify quality coffee. You can tour the factory to see the coffee beans drying (in season) and being processed; call in advance. At the end of the 'from the berry to the cup' tour you can purchase roasted beans at bargain prices.

Farm Hill Trail HIKING
This trail begins beside the Anglican church, crossing Yallahs River and Green River and leading uphill for 8km (1½ to two hours) to Penlyne Castle and on to Blue Mountain Peak.

🛏 Sleeping

Forres Park
Guest House & Farm GUESTHOUSE $$
(Map p64; ☑927-8275; www.forrespark.com; cabin US$75, r US$90-220; ℗) This guest house is a

top choice for bird-watchers. All rooms have balconies and the plushest sports a whirlpool tub. Excellent meals are cooked on request and available to nonguests. You can rent mountain bikes and enjoy the on-site spa treatments after tackling the steep, rewarding hiking trail. Tours and guided hikes offered by appointment.

★ **Lime Tree Farm** BOUTIQUE HOTEL $$$
(Map p64; ☑881-8788; www.limetreefarm.com; d cottage with full board US$326; ℗) This combination of a small working coffee farm with exclusive all-inclusive lodging is hugely appealing. It offers three large, luxurious cottages with jaw-dropping mountain views as well as fine meals consumed in the attractive open-air lounge. All-inclusive packages comprise wine with dinner, transportation to and from Kingston and a variety of bird-watching and hiking tours.

Hagley Gap & Penlyne Castle

The ramshackle village of Hagley Gap sits abreast a hill east of Mavis Bank and is the gateway to Blue Mountain Peak (p69). The road forks in the village, where a horrendously denuded dirt road to Penlyne Castle begins a precipitous ascent.

Penlyne Castle is the base for the 12km hikes to and from Blue Mountain Peak. Most hikers stay overnight at one of several simple lodges near Penlyne Castle before tackling the hike in the wee hours.

Bring warm, waterproof clothing. One minute you're in sun-kissed mountains; the next, clouds swirl in and the temperature plunges.

Penlyne Castle is reached via a 5km dirt road that ascends precipitously from Hagley Gap. Only 4WD vehicles with low-gear option can handle the dauntingly narrow and rugged road.

🛏 Sleeping

Jah B's Guest House GUESTHOUSE $
(Map p64; ☑377-5206; bobotamo@yahoo.com; dm/r J$20/30; ℗) This friendly place, run by a family of Bobo Rastas and particularly popular with shoestring travelers, has a basic but cozy guest house with bunks and simple rooms. Jah B's son Alex himself cooks I-tal meals amid a cloud of ganja smoke and a nonstop volley of friendly banter; he can help arrange transfers from Kingston.

HIKING IN THE BLUE MOUNTAINS

The Blue Mountains are a hiker's dream, and 30 recognized trails lace the hills. Many are overgrown due to lack of funding and ecological protection programs, but others remain the mainstay of communication for locals.

The most popular route is the steep, well-maintained trail to 'The Peak,' which in Jamaica always means Blue Mountain Peak.

These trails (called 'tracks' locally) are rarely marked. Get up-to-date information on trail conditions from the main ranger station at Holywell. If a trail is difficult to follow, turn back. Mountain rescue is slow and you could be lost for days. When asking for directions from locals, remember that 'jus a likkle way' may in fact be a few hours of hiking.

If you're hiking alone, normal precautions apply:

➡ Wear sturdy hiking shoes

➡ Bring snacks, plenty of water and a flashlight (torch)

➡ Let people know where you're headed

➡ Buy the 1:50,000 or 1:12,500 Ordnance Survey topographic map series, available from the **Survey Department** (☎ 750-5263; www.nla.gov.jm; 23 1/2 Charles St, Kingston)

Guides can be hired at the guesthouses in Hagley Gap, Penlyne Castle or through most local accommodations for J$5000/7000 per half/full day, while guided hikes in the Blue Mountains are also offered by the following:

➡ **Forres Park Guest House & Farm** (Map p64; ☎ 927-8275; www.forrespark.com)

➡ **Jamaica Conservation & Development Trust** (p63) – manages trails in the national park and can recommend hiking guides

➡ **Mount Edge B&B** (p30)

Whitfield Hall   GUESTHOUSE **$**
(Map p64; ☎ 878-0514; www.whitfieldhall.com; camping per tent US$103, dm US$20, s/d US$30/55; ℗) Nestled amid pine trees, this former plantation dating from 1776 is an atmospheric but basic option (it's electricity-free), with shared bathrooms and kitchen. The dark, cavernous lounge has a huge fireplace and smoke-stained ceiling. Camping is allowed on the lawn beneath the trees. Order a large breakfast (US$8) or lunch/dinner (US$9) in advance.

Blue Mountain Peak

From Penlyne Castle to the summit of Blue Mountain Peak at 2256m is a 950m ascent and a three- or four-hour hike one way. It's not a serious challenge, but you need to be reasonably fit.

Most hikers set off from Penlyne Castle around 2am to reach the peak for sunrise. Fortified with breakfast of coffee and cereal, you set out single file in the pitch black along the 12km round-trip trail (you'll need a flashlight and a spare set of batteries, just in case). The first part of the trail – a series of steep scree-covered switchbacks named Jacob's Ladder – is the toughest. Midway, at Portland Gap, there's a ranger station and cabin, where you pay the US$5 park fee.

As you hike, reggae music can be heard far, far below, competing with the chirps of crickets and katydids. Myriad peeny-wallies flit before you, signaling with their phosphorescent semaphore.

You should arrive at the peak around 5:30am, while it is still dark. Your stage is gradually revealed: a flat-topped hump, marked by a scaffolding pyramid and trig point (in the cloud it is easy to mistake a smaller hump to the left of the hut near the summit – Lazy Man's Peak – for the real thing). If the weather's clear, Cuba, 144km away, can be seen from the peak, which casts a distinct shadow over the land below. After a brief celebratory drink and snacks, you'll set off back down the mountain, passing through several distinct ecosystems – stunted dwarf or elfin forest, with trees like hirsute soapwood and rodwood no more than 2.5m high, an adaptation to the cold, followed by cloud forest, dripping with filaments of hanging lichens and festooned with epiphytes and moss and dotted with wild strawberries, while further down you encounter bamboo and primordial

ℹ️ GETTING AROUND IN THE BLUE MOUNTAINS

Traveling by your own vehicle is the best way to enjoy the Blue Mountains, as public transportation between villages is infrequent and it's difficult to reach many points of interest. Many mountain guest houses will arrange transfers.

By Car

The roads in the Blue Mountains consist of endless switchbacks; they are narrow, sometimes overgrown with foliage, and can be badly rutted. Many corners are blind. Honk your horn frequently and watch out for reckless local drivers.

The main routes are usually fine for most vehicles, but the further you get from the beaten track, piste quality can deteriorate quickly (especially after heavy rains), making a sturdy 4WD with a low gear option a better option. Where relevant, road conditions are noted in the text.

From Kingston, Hope Rd leads to Papine, from where Gordon Town Rd (B1) leads into the mountains. Papine is your last opportunity to fill up with gas, so make sure you have a full tank. At the Cooperage, the road splits in two. Mammee River Rd forks left steeply uphill for Strawberry Hill resort (near Irish Town) and Newcastle. Alternatively Gordon Town Rd continues straight from the Cooperage and winds east up the Hope River Valley to Gordon Town, then steeply to Mavis Bank and Hagley Gap (for Blue Mountain Peak). The B1 continues across the mountains all the way to Buff Bay. A 4WD is recommended; this road is sometimes closed by landslides, so check before setting out.

By Public Transportation

Buses run hourly from Halfway Tree in Kingston up Hope Rd to Papine (J$100, 20 minutes), from where you connect to the Blue Mountains. Minibuses and route taxis depart from near the Park View Supermarket on the main square in Papine. There are two main routes: to Mavis Bank and Hagley Gap via Gordon Town (for Blue Mountain Peak), and to Newcastle and Section via Irish Town. Frequency of service depends on demand, but there's at least one morning run and one in the afternoon for the two main routes.

Sample fares include Mavis Bank (J$250, 1½ hours), Irish Town (J$150, 45 minutes) and Newcastle (J$250, 1¼ hours). Be prepared to haggle if you want to charter a route taxi. There is no regular bus service up the B1 to Buff Bay.

By Mountain Bike

An exhilarating way to see the Blue Mountains is by mountain bike – the sturdier the better as the going can be steep and arduous. Blue Mountain Bicycle Tours (p78) in Ocho Rios offers pickup from Kingston or Ocho Rios, transfer to the Hardwar Gap and an exhilarating downhill cycling tour. Potential stops include a coffee-roasting facility. Up to 43 cyclists. Mount Edge B&B (p30) offers a similar tour with smaller groups, also from Hardwar Gap. Always check the bike's condition before setting out.

giant tree ferns. Your guide points out Blue Mountain coffee growing and you arrive at your accommodations in time for brunch.

Don't hike without a guide at night. Numerous spur trails lead off the main trails and it is easy to get lost. Although hiking boots or tough walking shoes are best, sneakers will suffice, though your feet will likely get wet. At the top, temperatures can approach freezing before sunrise, so wear plenty of layers. Rain gear is also essential, as the weather can change rapidly.

The **Jamaica Conservation & Development Trust** (Map p64; ☑ 960-2848, 960-2849; www.jcdt.org.jm; 29 Dumbarton Ave, Kingston 10; tent J$170, dm J$423) maintains two basic wooden cabins halfway up the trail at Portland Gap (4km above Abbey Green, Map p64). You can camp outside, where there's a cooking area and water from a pipe. Bring your own tent, sleep on a bunk bed (BYO sleeping bag) or on the floor (foam mats available for rent; J$150). Reserve in advance.

SOUTHEAST COAST

Jamaica's southeast corner, the parish of St Thomas, is one of the least-developed parts of the island, which is part of its charm. Don't

DON'T MISS

STRAWBERRY HILL

One of the finest resorts in Jamaica and record mogul Chris Blackwell's pet, **Strawberry Hill** (Map p64; ☎ 946-1958; www.islandoutpost.com/strawberry_hill; r/ste/villa incl breakfast & transfers US$355/455/595; ⓟ❄🛜🛍) is a luxury retreat just north of Irish Town. Gaze at Kingston and the harbor 950m below from a deckchair by the infinity-edge pool, roam the bougainvillea-draped grounds or relax at the Ayurvedic spa.

The Caribbean-style cottages range from well-appointed mahogany-accented studio suites, each with canopied four-poster beds with heated mattresses, to a four-bedroom, two-story house built into the hillside. A sumptuous breakfast is included in the rates, as are transfers. Bird-watching, hiking and other tours are available, and Strawberry Hill also hosts a calendar of special events throughout the year.

Many Kingstonians make the tortuous drive to Strawberry Hill for some of the finest nouvelle Jamaican cuisine on the island (dinners US$25 to US$55, Sunday brunch J$3000). Reservations required.

be surprised if you come across obeah circles in isolated villages – this parish is strongly associated with the practice.

Yallahs & Around

Southeast of Bull Bay and the parish boundary between St Andrew and St Thomas, the A4 from Kingston makes a hairpin descent to Grants Pen, then winds through scrub-covered country until it reaches the coast at Yallahs. The excellent jerk stands of Yallahs' Main St are a cheerful pit stop. Past Yallahs, a series of long, dark-gray beaches, with colorful pirogues drawn up, extends eastward to Morant Bay, and a pitted dirt road only navigable by 4WD heads north into the mountains to Hagley Gap.

East of Yallahs, two large salt ponds are enclosed by a narrow, bow-shaped spit of sand. The ponds are exceedingly briny due to evaporation and legend has it that they were formed by the tears of an English planter whose beloved married his brother. Algae flourishes and often turns the ponds a deep pink, accompanied by a powerful smell of hydrogen sulfide ('bad egg gas').

Morant Bay

POP 9400

Morant Bay, the town that played a pivotal role in Jamaica's history, squats on a hill behind the coast road. These days, it's a nondescript place with a lively central market, its sugar-producing heyday long behind it. Most of the town's early colonial-era buildings were burned in the Morant Bay Rebellion

of 1865, led by the town's national hero, Paul Bogle, but a couple of gems remain.

October 11 is Paul Bogle Day, when a party is held in the town square and a 10km road race sets out from Stony Gut.

☉ Sights

Just east of Morant Bay lies the attractive, palm-fringed Lyssons Beach – one of the few public beaches in Jamaica with free access for locals (though paid parking).

Courthouse & Around   HISTORICAL BUILDING
Port Morant's courthouse was rebuilt in limestone and red brick after being destroyed in the 1865 rebellion and burned down again in early 2007, its ruins standing defiant behind an empty plinth that once bore an Edna Manley statue of Paul Bogle, his hands clasped over the hilt of a machete. Bogle is buried beside the courthouse alongside a mass grave holding the remains of many slaves who lost their lives in the rebellion.

Diagonally across from the courthouse is a handsome, ochre-colored Anglican church dating to 1881.

❶ Information

Police station (7 South St) Next to the old courthouse.
Scotiabank (23 Queen St) Opposite the Texaco gas station.

❶ Getting There & Away

Buses serve Kingston (J$160 to J$250, two hours, three daily) and Port Antonio (J$160 to J$300, 2½ hours, two daily). Minibuses and route taxis arrive and depart from beside the Shell gas station on the A4 at the west end of town.

Retreat

A small beachside residential community about 5km east of Morant Bay, Retreat draws Kingstonians on the weekends. It sits between two of the few pleasant beaches along Jamaica's southern coast. The aptly named Golden Shore Beach is hidden from view from the road. Watch for the hand-painted sign. Further east is Prospect Beach, a 'public bathing beach.'

Bath

This village, 10km north of Port Morant by a very attractive road, lies on the bank of the Plantain Garden River, amid sugarcane and banana plantations. The town owes its existence to the discovery of hot mineral springs in the hills behind the present town in the late 17th century, which attracted socialites for a time. Minibuses and route taxis run daily from the downtown bus terminal in Kingston (J$250, 90 minutes).

⊙ Sights & Activities

Bath Fountain   HOT SPRINGS
(Massages J$2000, Bath House 20min bath for 1/2 people J$350/550; ⊙ Bath House 8am-9:30pm) Local legend says that a runaway slave discovered hot springs here that cured the leg ulcers he'd had for years. In 1699 the government bought the spring, and formed a corporation to administer mineral baths for the sick and infirm. The water's high sulfur and lime content, and slight radioactivity, have therapeutic value for skin and rheumatic problems.

You can walk to the free hot springs 50m north of the Bath Hotel and Spa, though you'll sadly have to fend off the attentions of 'guides' offering massages. Alternatively have a peaceful soak in the spa at the Bath Fountain Hotel & Spa. The homey spa also offers a variety of massages. Arrive early on weekends. To get here, turn up the road opposite the church in Bath and follow the road 3km uphill.

Bath Botanical Garden   GARDEN
(⊙ dawn-dusk) FREE At the east end of town is an old limestone church marking the entrance to a somewhat rundown horticultural garden established in 1779. Many exotics introduced to Jamaica were first planted here, including the famous breadfruit brought from the South Pacific by Captain Bligh in 1793. Every September, Bath's Breadfruit Festival commemorates what's now a firm Jamaican staple.

Bath Fountain–Bowden Pen Trek   HIKING
This one-day trek, a former Maroon trading route – for experienced hikers only – leads from Bath Fountain up over Cuna Cuna Gap to Bowden Pen. Obtain Sheets 19 (St Thomas parish) and 14 (Portland parish) of the Ordnance Survey 1:12,500 map series from the Survey Department (p209) for more detailed information or hire a guide from the JCDT.

🛏 Sleeping & Eating

Bath Fountain Hotel & Spa   HOTEL $
(☑ 703-4154; r with shared/private bathroom J$3600/4450, deluxe r J$6000; P) Your only option is this 18th-century pink colonial hotel that contains the spa baths on the ground floor. The clinically white bedrooms are modestly furnished. There's a small restaurant serving Jamaican dishes as well as breakfast.

Ocho Rios, Port Antonio & North Coast

Includes →

Ocho Rios................. 76

East of Ocho Rios 84

South of Ocho Rios... 88

West of Ocho Rios..... 88

Dry Harbour
Mountains................. 92

Port Antonio............. 93

East of Port Antonio . 98

Rio Grande Valley.... 103

West of Port
Antonio 105

Best Places to Eat

➡ Toscanini (p82)

➡ Whalers (p81)

➡ Boston Bay jerk stands (p101)

➡ Dickie's Best Kept Secret (p97)

➡ Mille Fleurs (p100)

Best Places to Stay

➡ Reggae Hostel (p80)

➡ Gee Jam (p100)

➡ Ambassabeth Cabins (p103)

➡ Great Huts (p101)

➡ Cottage at Te Moana (p80)

Why Go?

Ocho Rios, Jamaica's third-largest town, dominates the north coast's tourist scene. Cruise ships land passengers in huge numbers here, and if the town can sometimes feel a little like a theme park, visitors are at least drawn for good reason – the surrounding area features some of the most beautiful (and popular) natural attractions on the island. From working plantations to sights unveiling the breadth of Jamaican history, there's plenty to keep you occupied.

By comparison, sleepy Portland is by far the least developed resort area in Jamaica, yet also the most rugged and scenic. Forested mountains with deep gorges and rushing rivers spread their fingers towards fringes of white sand and cool-blue surf that rolls into beach-lined coves. The folks are friendly and the hustle small. From Port Antonio, you can explore gorgeous but untouristed beaches, or head into the mountains and rainforest for hiking and birding.

When to Go
Ocho Rios

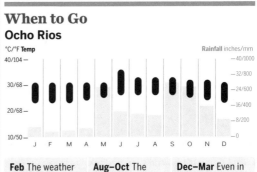

Feb The weather is (relatively) dry and you'll have a chance to see the Fi Wi Sinting festival.

Aug–Oct The rains are vicious, but you'll get good wind for serious adventure surfing.

Dec–Mar Even in the high season this region doesn't see as many crowds as the rest of Jamaica.

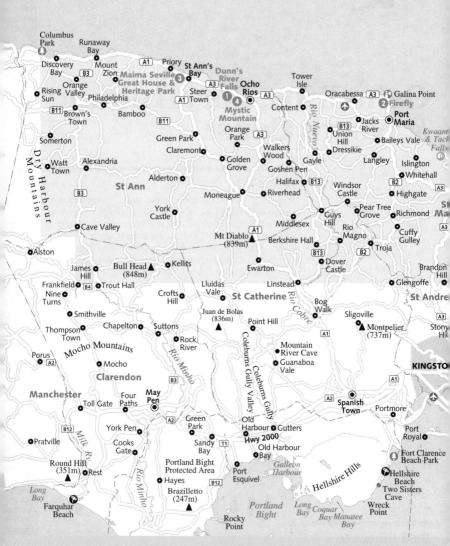

Ocho Rios, Port Antonio & North Coast Highlights

1 Climbing one of the world's most famous waterfalls, **Dunn's River Falls** (p76)

2 Savoring the jaw-dropping view from author Noël Coward's well-preserved former home, **Firefly** (p87)

3 Exploring Jamaica's first Spanish settlement, **Maima Seville Great House & Heritage Park** (p89), on horseback

4 Admiring panoramic views of the coast from the chairlift and zipping down Jamaica's longest

canopy line at **Mystic Mountain** (p76)

5 Wandering the streets of picturesque **Port Antonio** (p93)

6 Listening to the stories of the elders of the Windward

CARIBBEAN
SEA

N

0 — 10 km
0 — 6 miles

nnotto Bay
Dover Point
Buff Bay
Orange Bay
A4
A4
Hope Bay
Snow Hill
Port Antonio
5
Frenchman's Cove
Winnifred Beach
10
Boston Bay
9
Rio Grande Valley
7
Berridale
Fairy Hill
Long Bay
A4
Dry River
River
Haycock Hill (1066m)
Claverty Cottage
Silver Hill
B1
Telegraph (1275m)
Spring Hill
Portland
Windsor
Fellowship
Castle Mountain (335m)
Mt Airy
Green Hill
High Peak (2076m)
Swift River
Blue Mountains & John Crow National Park
Moore Town
6
Rio Grande Valley
John Crow Mountains
Jamaica Channel
Reach Waterfall
8
Kensington
Manchioneal
Newcastle
Content Gap
Portland Gap
Candlefly Peak (1537m)
Irish Town
B1
Guava Ridge
Mavis Bank
Millbank
The Blue Mountains
Happy Grove
Innis Bay
Cedar Valley
Blue Mountain Peak (2256m)
Bowden Pen
St Andrew
B1
Yallahs River
Negro River
Union Hill (1027m)
Macca Sucker (1335m)
Llandewey
Judgement Cliff
Seaforth
Hordley
Morant Point Lighthouse
A4
Bull Bay
Trinity Ville
St Thomas
Bath
Stokes Hall
Golden Grove
Grants Pen
Heartease
Stony Gut
New Pera
Dalvey
Yallahs Hill (729m)
Port Morant
Rocky Point
Morant Point
Yallahs
Belvedere
A4
Morant Bay
Lyssons
Old Pera
CARIBBEAN SEA
Cow Bay Point
Yallahs Point
The Salt Ponds
A4
Prospect
Port Morant

Maroons at **Moore Town** (p103)

7 Rafting merrily down the Rio Grande past former banana plantations in verdant **Rio Grande Valley** (p103)

8 Contemplating the wonderful primordial **Reach Waterfall** (p102) from the pools below

9 Stuffing your face with fine Jamaican jerk and shredding

some waves with local surfers at **Boston Bay** (p101)

10 Enjoying **Winnifred Beach** (p98), the white-sand beach hugging a pretty cove

OCHO RIOS

POP 17,000

Wrapped around a small bay with post-card-worthy snugness, Ocho Rios is a former fishing village that the Jamaica Tourist Board developed for tourism in the mid-1980s. The frequent docking of cruise ships at the central pier that commands the town's focus gives 'Ochi' a decidedly 'packaged' feel, spiced up by the regular entreaties of 'guides' and souvenir sellers. However, it's also endowed the town with an international eating scene and two distinct kinds of nightlife: rough-and-ready dancehall clubs and beach sound systems versus karaoke nights and all-you-can-drink swimwear parties. The choice is yours. The town makes an excellent base for active, solvent travelers who wish to explore the north coasts and partake in slick, well-managed 'adventures' such as zip-line tours, horseback riding and waterfall climbing.

History

The name Ocho Rios is a corruption of the Spanish term *chorreros* ('swift water'). Not only was the area west of Ocho Rios the site of Columbus' first landing in Jamaica and the first Spanish settlement, it also saw Spain's last stand in Jamaica at nearby Rio Nuevo. It was here that the British instituted huge slave-run sugar and pimento (allspice) plantations, crops that defined the region until the mid-20th century, when bauxite mining and tourism took over.

◉ Sights

★ **Dunn's River Falls** WATERFALL
(☑ 876 974-2857; www.dunnsriverfallsja.com; adult/child US$20/12; ⊙ 8:30am-4pm Sat-Tue, 7am-4pm Wed-Fri) These famous falls, 3km west of town, are Jamaica's top-grossing tourist attraction. Great throngs of people can sometimes make it can seem more like a theme park than a natural wonder, but this doesn't make the climb up the falls any less exhilarating. You clamber up great tiers of limestone that step down 180m in a series of beautiful cascades and pools. The water is refreshingly cool, with everything shaded by tall rainforest.

Guides can help with the climb (tip expected), but aren't strictly necessary. The current is strong in places but the ascent is easily achieved by most able-bodied people. Swimwear is essential. There are changing rooms, and you can rent lockers (J$500) and jelly shoes (J$500). The park also includes food stalls, restaurant, kid's playground, and a hard-selling craft market.

Try to visit when the cruise ships aren't in dock, and ideally when the gates open in the morning. Route taxis (J$100) from Ocho Rios to St Ann's Bay can drop you at the entrance.

★ **Mystic Mountain** AMUSEMENT PARK
(www.rainforestbobsledjamaica.com; adult/child US$47/23; ⊙ 9am-4pm) Mystic Mountain is one of Ochi's biggest attractions, featuring a series of zip-lines crisscrossing the forest in a superb canopy tour, as well as the signature 'bobsled' ride through the dense foliage.

The park begins with the Sky Explorer chairlift through the forest, with views of the coastline along the way. As well as the adrenaline rushes of the bobsled and zip-line, there's also an excellent exhibition on Jamaican sport, a contemporary Caribbean restaurant and an infinity pool with water slide.

Prices add up quickly: a Sky Explorer and Bobsled combo is US$69; a Sky Explorer and Zip-line combo is US$115, whereas a combination of all three is US$137. Avoid the park on cruise ship days.

Mystic Mountain is 3km west of Ocho Rios; to get here, catch a route taxi heading towards St Ann's Bay (J$100).

Dolphin Cove DOLPHIN ENCOUNTER
(☑ 974-5335; www.dolphincovejamaica.com; admission US$45, dolphin packages US$69-195; ⊙ 8:30am-5:30pm) This cove, popular with cruise passengers and adjacent to Dunn's River Falls, allows you to swim with dolphins. Basic admission includes an aquarium, mini-zoo, snorkeling with stingrays, and paddling in glass-bottomed kayaks.

There are several dolphin 'packages,' including stroking the animals to free-swimming. Note that the Jamaica Environmental Trust and cetacean conservation organizations oppose the display of these highly intelligent animals, which in the wild travel hundreds of kilometers a day in complex social groups. Most dolphins on display in Jamaica were wild-captured.

Coyaba River Garden & Mahoe Falls GARDEN
(www.coyabagardens.com; Shaw Park Rd; admission adult/child J$1000/500; ⊙ 8am-6pm) *Coyaba* being the Arawak word for 'paradise,' this garden seems aptly named, its walkways and trails leading past pools and streams through the best-kept gardens in Ocho Rios. The thoughtful Coyaba Museum traces Jamaica's

history, and there are splendid panoramic views from Ysassi's Lookout Point, adjoining the Mahoe Falls, an attractive waterfall suitable for swimming. Coyaba is nearly 2km west of St John's Church (on the A3); follow the signs.

Shaw Park Gardens
GARDEN
(www.shawparkgardens.com; admission J$1000; ⊙8am-5pm) This is a tropical fantasia of ferns and bromeliads, palms and exotic shrubs, spread out over 11 hectares centered on an 18th-century great house. Trails and wooden steps lead past waterfalls that tumble in terraces down the hillside. A viewing platform offers a bird's-eye vantage over Ocho Rios. The gardens are signed from opposite the public library on the A3.

Island Village
ENTERTAINMENT CENTER
(☑974-8353; village/beach free/J$200; ⊙9am-midnight) Since its 2002 opening, this self-contained entertainment park, has changed the face of Ocho Rios. The 2-hectare development claims to resemble a 'Jamaican coastal village.' It doesn't remotely, but you'll still find a peaceful beach, upscale craft shops, a cinema, Jimmy Buffett's Margaritaville bar (p82) and **Blue Mont** (Island Village; meals J$700; ⊙breakfast, lunch & dinner) cafe, and an amphitheater for live performances.

🏊 Beaches

Ocho Rios Bay
BEACH
(admission J$200; ⊙8am-5pm; 🧒) The main beach of Ocho Rios, popular with tourists, is the long fenced-off crescent known variously as Turtle Beach and Ocho Rios Bay, stretching east from the Turtle Towers condominiums to the Renaissance Jamaica Grande Resort. There are changing rooms and palms for shade.

Island Village Beach
BEACH
(admission J$250; ⊙6am-6pm) Island Village Beach, located at the west end of Main St, is a peaceful, smaller beach with lockers, towels, beach chairs and umbrellas for hire. Also on offer is a complete range of water sports.

Fishermen's Beach
BEACH
FREE Immediately west of Island Village Beach is the tiny public Fishermen's Beach, with colorful fishing boats and several eateries serving fresh fish and more.

Mahogany Beach
BEACH
FREE The small and charming Mahogany Beach, 1km east of the town center, is par-

ticularly popular with locals; it comes to life on weekends with loud music, smells of jerk cooking and impromptu football matches.

🏃 Activities

Virtually the entire shoreline east of Ocho Rios to Galina Point is fringed by a reef, and it's great for snorkeling and scuba diving. One of the best sections is Devil's Reef, a pinnacle that drops more than 60m. Nurse sharks are abundant at Caverns, a shallow reef about 1km east of the White River estuary; it has many tunnels plus an ex-minesweeper, the *Kathryn*. Most resorts have their own scuba facilities. As well as operators listed here, upscale hotels also offer water sports.

Garfield Diving Station
DIVING
(☑395-7023; www.garfielddiving.com; Turtle Beach) Ocho Rios' longest-running water sports operator with 29 years' experience. Dive packages include one-tank dives (US$50), PADI certification courses (US$420) and wreck dives. Other activities offered include snorkeling excursions, glass-bottom boat rides, and jet-ski rental. Boat charter is available for deep-sea fishing (half day for up to four people US$500).

Cool Runnings
WATER SPORTS
(☑376-4310; www.coolrunningscatamarans.com; 1 Marvins Park, Ocho Rios) Specializes in catamaran cruises, including the **Dunn's River Falls Cruise** (US$80; ⊙12:30-4pm Mon-Wed, Fri & Sat), which includes an hour's snorkeling and entry to the falls, and **Catamaran Sunset Sail** (US$65), with drinks and buffet dinner.

Resort Divers
DIVING
(☑881-5760; www.resortdivers.com; Royal DeCameron Club Caribbean, Runaway Bay; 1-/2-tank dive US$50/95, snorkeling US$30) Dive packages available with pickup from your accommodation for an additional US$10 to US$15.

Island Village Beach
WATER SPORTS
(Island Village; ⊙8am-4pm) Rents snorkeling gear (J$1500 per day), kayaks (single/double J$1000/1500 per hour), windsurfing gear (J$5000 for 30 minutes) and Hobie Cats (J$3500 for 30 minutes).

👉 Tours

The Ocho Rios area offers more organized outdoor adventure tours than any other Jamaican resort area. All operators offer transportation from hotels.

Ocho Rios

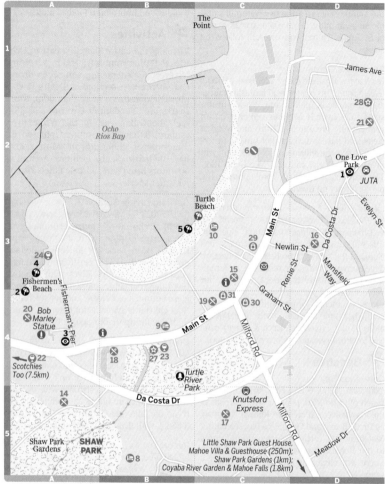

Chukka Caribbean

Adventure Tours ADVENTURE TOURS
(☑ 972-2506; www.chukkacaribbean.com/jamaica; tour incl lunch/high tea US$29/39) Established adventure specialist offering horseback-riding tours, river tubing, zip-line canopy tours, ATV safaris, trips to Bob Marley's birthplace at Nine Mile and even dog-sleigh tours.

Hooves HORSE RIDING
(☑ 972-0905; www.hooves-jamaica.com; half-day horseback tour incl refreshments J$6000) Offers guided horseback tours from the Maima Seville Great House to the beach, with a bare-back ride into the sea (beginners welcome) and the 'honeymoon ride,' which includes a beach meal with fizz. Reservations required.

Blue Mountain Bicycle Tours CYCLING
(☑ 974-7075; www.bmtoursja.com; 121 Main St; Blue Mountain downhill tour adult/child US$108/75) Exhilarating downhill cycling tour of the Blue Mountains, week-long eco-adventures in Portland and tours of Kingston.

✸ Festivals & Events

Fat Tyre Festival SPORTS
(www.smorba.com; ☉ Feb) This rip-roaring mountain-bike race and festival is the

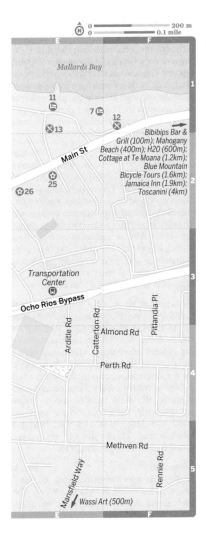

Ocho Rios

nation's premier mountain-biking festival, and is definitely not for the weak of heart (or calves).

Follow Di Arrow   MUSIC
(☺ Feb) Annual dancehall music event featuring big local artists, held at James Bond Beach on the last weekend in February.

Bacchanal Jamaica   CARNIVAL
(www.bacchanaljamaica.com; ☺ Easter) Part of the nationwide carnival season. Celebrated in a big way in Ocho Rios, this riotous all-night party featuring soca music is held at Chukka Cove.

Beach J'ouvert   MUSIC
(☺ Apr) Popular soca music night held at James Bond Beach during the carnival season, with all-night revelry and paint throwing.

Ocho Rios Jazz Festival   MUSIC
(www.ochoriosjazz.com; ☺ Jun) This eight-day event every June (which actually tries to cover the whole island, with events in Kingston, Port Antonio, Montego Bay, Negril and the south coast) draws some of the biggest names in jazz and stages concerts under the stars.

🛏 Sleeping

Villas of varying ranges of opulence are represented by Sun Villas (☏ 888-625-6007, 544-9497, in the USA 941-922-9191; www.sunvillas.com; 1410 South Lake Shore Dr, Sarasota, FL), Jamaican Association of Villas & Apartments (JAVA; ☏ in the US 800-845-5276; www.villasinjamaica.com) and Royal Plantation (☏ in the UK 800-022-3773, in the USA 877-845-5275; www.uniquevillasofjamaica.com).

★Reggae Hostel   GUEST HOUSE $
(☏ 974-2607; www.reggaehostel.com; 19 Main St; r US$60, dm US$20; P❄🛜) A new offshoot of the popular Kingston hostel, this relaxed guest house is perfectly located in the centre of Ocho Rios. There's a good mix of simple private rooms (air-con) and dorms (fan only), and a rooftop bar and lounge area that's ideal for socializing. The manager is a font of local knowledge for backpacker-friendly excursions.

Little Shaw Park Guest House GUEST HOUSE $
(☏ 974-2177; www.littleshawparkguest house.com; 21 Shaw Park Rd; r US$45-55, apt US$65, ste US$75; P❄🛜) This retreat, set among beautifully tended lawns and a garden overflowing with bougainvillea, remains a popular option. The furniture is somewhat worn, and the cheaper rooms (fan only) are spacious but rather dark, but the studio apartments with kitchens are great value for money. While away the day in the gazebo or one of the hammocks. Meals available on request.

Mahoe Villa & Guest house   GUEST HOUSE $
(☏ 974-6613; 11 Shaw Park Rd; r without/with bathroom US$30/40; P🛜) This large guest house on the hill up to Cinchona, run by the effusive Michael and replete with original works of art, is decent value for money. The spic-and-span, fan-cooled rooms share a communal kitchen, and a chilled vibe prevails.

Rooms   RESORT $
(☏ 974-2008; www.roomsresorts.com; Main St; r incl breakfast US$88-112; P❄@🏊) In the center of Turtle Beach, this family-friendly resort has all the trappings of an all-inclusive without being one. Everything (apart from breakfast) – from meals to internet access and water sports – costs extra, but the location is superb, the beachfront pool and gym are bonuses and the spacious rooms boast sea or pool views.

★Cottage at Te Moana   COTTAGE $$
(☏ 974-2870; www.harmonyhall.com; cottages US$150-170; P❄) With its small cliff-top garden overhanging a reef, this exquisite reclusive property with two delightful cottages offers a wonderful alternative to Ochi's resorts. Think wicker furniture and artistic aesthetics. Both cottages have fully equipped kitchens, separate living areas, plus verandas with hammocks. Steps lead down to a coral cove good for snorkeling, and kayaks are available. Three-night stay minimum.

Mystic Ridge   RESORT $$
(☏ 974-8050; www.mysticridgejamaica.com; 17 DaCosta Dr; r US$125, ste US$145, apt US$260; P❄🛜🏊) This modern hilltop resort (formerly Crane Ridge) features spacious and cheery suites and two-bedroom apartments. The airy June Plum restaurant serves Jamaican dishes with an emphasis on fresh fruit. There's a pool-side bar and the very relaxing Samambaia spa, plus a shuttle service to the beach. Special entry packages to Mystic Mountain are also available to guests.

Hibiscus Lodge   HOTEL $$
(☏ 974-2676; www.hibiscusjamaica.com; 83 Main St; r US$150-192; P⊖❄@🏊) A stairway descends alongside a cliff overhang, past flowering gardens overflowing with bougainvillea, and down to a private sunning deck, perfect for a spontaneous jump in the sea. A small gallery of contemporary Jamaican art complements the main building nicely. Rooms are modestly furnished; deluxe ones are worth the extra expense for their large private balconies. There's also a breezy bar and the Almond Tree (p82) restaurant.

Silver Seas   HOTEL $$
(☏ 974-2755; www.silverseashotel.com; 66 James Ave; r US$135; P❄🏊) Ocho Rios' first-ever luxury resort is somewhat worn and creaky, but wonderfully atmospheric and welcoming to families. Inside the colonial-style building with a cavernous hall with creaky wooden floors, each well-kept room has a large, private patio with a stellar ocean view. Dining takes place on the waterfront patio and there's good snorkeling to be had off the jetty.

★Jamaica Inn   GUEST HOUSE $$$
(☏ 974-2514; www.jamaicainn.com; ste US$523-823, cottages US$1112-1586; P⊖❄🛜🏊) Winston Churchill's favorite hotel (echoed in the colonial-era prints and furnishings) this exquisite family-run 'inn,' tucked in a private cove, exudes patrician refinement. There's a library and a bar with a warm clubby feel, and on-site spa. Dining requires a jacket

and tie for men. Water sports include scuba diving, snorkeling and fishing. Breakfast, half- and full-board available on request.

Blue House
GUEST HOUSE $$$

(☑ 994-1367; www.thebluehousejamaica.com; White River Bay; r US$180-260; P ❋ @ ☎ ☎) This gem offers luxurious bedrooms in cool blue hues. The separate two-bedroom Cozy Cottage provides even greater seclusion, with its private patio and hammock hidden behind a curtain of flowers. Darryl the Barefoot Chef cooks up superb fusion cuisine, drawing on Chinese and Indian influences, and the lavish three-course dinners are worth every penny.

Couples Sans Souci Resort & Spa
RESORT $$$

(☑ 994-1206; www.couples.com; A3; d US$735-745, ste US$756-1341, cottages US$1391; P ☻ ❋ @ ☎) On the A3, east of town, this resort has a sublime setting in a secluded cove. The top-end suites have spa baths and one of the two beaches is for nude bathing. Rates include gourmet dining, trips to Ochi's attractions, and all the golf you can play. Charlie's Spa is set on mineral springs rumored to have rejuvenating powers. The huge range of water sports on offer includes scuba lessons.

✖ Eating

Ocho Rios has a good range of international cuisine and several economical Jamaican restaurants; many places are open late. After dark, you'll find many smoking oil-drum barbecues along the roadside, particularly in the area surrounding the clock tower.

★ Whalers
SEAFOOD $

(Fishermen's Beach; meals J$800-1000; ☺ breakfast, lunch & dinner) Rising up above the wooden shacks on tiny Fishermen's Beach, adjacent to Island Village and awaft with ganja smoke, this cheerful eatery with an upstairs terrace is the best place in town for fresh fish dishes. Besides the fish that comes in steamed, brown stew or escoveitch form, there is delicious conch soup (lunchtimes only) and breakfast specials such as ackee and saltfish. Great, if occasionally grungy.

Ocho Rios Jerk Centre
JERK $

(☑ 974-2549; 16 DaCosta Dr; meals J$550-1000; ☺ lunch & dinner) Its deserved popularity further boosted by it being the official Knutsford Express stop, the liveliest jerk joint in town serves excellent jerk pork (J$390), chicken (J$390) and conch (J$850), as well

as BBQ ribs. There are daily specials, the best being curry goat (J$450) and goat head soup (J$100). Grab a Red Stripe and watch sports on the big-screen TV while you're waiting for your jerk. 'Spicy Fridays' feature weekly DJ sets (free entry) and the last Friday of the month is Retro/Soca Nite.

Lion's Den
JAMAICAN $

(☑ 848-4413; A3; meals J$650-1000; ☺ breakfast, lunch & dinner) West of town between Dolphin Cove and Dunn's River Falls, this place looks like a tourist trap but is worth a stop for the excellent, well-priced Jamaican fare and unique, artistic decor. The dining room resembles a Rastafarian chapel with hand-carved columns and wicker 'tree limbs' reaching to the ceiling. The menu boasts local specialties such as curry goat, stew pork and dumplings, and fried chicken.

Scotchies Too
JERK $

(☑ 794-9457; Jack's Hall Fair Ground; meals J$500-700; ☺ lunch & dinner) This roadside offshoot of the famous jerk center in Montego Bay lies adjacent to an Epping Gas station just west of Dunn's River Falls. Its pork and chicken, smoked over pimento wood, water the mouths of locals and visitors alike; the jerk sausage is also worth investigating. Accompaniments include roast breadfruit, festival (sweet fried cornbread) and yam.

Centre Spot
JAMAICAN $

(☑ 876 323-0042; 75E Main St; meals J$400-500; ☺ breakfast & lunch) This unassuming hole-in-the-wall place whips up local favorites such as curried goat; specials include the ever-popular cow head, tripe and beans and cow foot. For breakfast, if you're hungry consider the porridge – a cup of the cornmeal or peanut variety really sticks to your ribs – or the ackee and saltfish.

World of Fish
SEAFOOD $

(☑ 876 974-1863; 3 James Ave; meals J$850; ☺ lunch & dinner Mon-Sat) Popular with locals, this casual and economical eatery has been serving fried fish, stew fish and steamed fish for years. Get it with bammy (cassava flatbread), rice and peas or festival.

Healthy Way
VEGETARIAN $

(☑ 876 974-9229; Ocean Village Plaza; meals J$650; ☺ breakfast & lunch Mon-Sat; ✍) A vegetarian kitchen and health-food store selling herbs, teas, I-tal juices and supplements, plus hearty chow such as a delicious tofu cheeseburger, stew peas and large fruit plates to go.

Tropical Kitchen
BAKERY $

(Main St; ⊘ breakfast, lunch & dinner; 🍴) Cakes, pastries and the best potato pudding on the north coast.

Juici Patties
JAMAICAN $

(1 Newlin St; patties J$80-120; ⊘ breakfast, lunch & dinner) The local branch of the best patty chain on the island, serving coco bread as well as cheese, beef, chicken, shrimp and lobster patties.

Almond Tree Restaurant
INTERNATIONAL $$

(📞 974-2813; Hibiscus Lodge, 83 Main St; meals J$1200-3000; ⊘ breakfast, lunch & dinner) Providing a splendid perch for a sunset dinner, this cliff-top spot features a dining pavilion that steps down the cliffside. Candlelit dinners are served alfresco. The menu ranges from seafood and continental fare, such as steaks and cheeseburgers, to steadfast Jamaican dishes.

Evita's
ITALIAN $$

(📞 974-2333; Eden Bower Rd; meals J$1400-2500; ⊘ lunch & dinner; 🍴) This slightly overpriced charmer sits high above Ochi in a romantically decorated 1860s house – an airy setting with exquisite views. The Italian-Jamaican menu includes jerk spaghetti, the ackee and callaloo 'Lasagna Rastafari' and the delectable, fish- and seafood-filled 'Lasagna Capitano.' Lighter dishes include a selection of salads; half-portions of the pasta dishes are also available.

Bibibips Bar & Grill
INTERNATIONAL $$

(93 Main St; meals J$1000-3000; ⊘ lunch & dinner) This popular, touristy oceanfront bar and restaurant with a porch overlooking Mahogany Beach serves up a range of tasty seafood, burgers, jerk and barbecue dishes that don't quite live up to their pricing. Wash it down with a cocktail from the extensive list.

★ Toscanini
ITALIAN $$$

(📞 975-4785; Harmony Hall; meals J$3300-4600; ⊘ lunch & dinner Tue-Sun; 🍴) One of the finest restaurants on the island, this roadside spot is run by two gracious Italians who use the freshest local ingredients in recipes from the motherland. The proprietress greets all the guests and explains the use of local herbs in the cooking. The daily menu ranges widely, encompassing such appetizers as prosciutto with papaya or marinated marlin and mains such as garlic lobster pasta, or shrimp sautéed with garlic and Appleton rum. Leave room for sumptuous desserts such as strawberry tart or profiteroles. Treat yourself!

Passage to India
INDIAN $$$

(📞 795-3182; Soni's Plaza, 50 Main St; meals J$1800-3200; ⊘ lunch & dinner Tue-Sun, lunch Mon; 🍴) On the rooftop of a duty-free shopping center, Passage to India offers respite from the crowds below in addition to very good northern Indian fare. The naan is crisp, the lassis flavorful, the curries sharp, and the menu divided into extensive chicken, mutton, seafood and vegetarian sections. Tandoori options are also on offer.

🍷 Drinking & Nightlife

There's a healthy bar scene and a decent choice of nightspots, but in general Ochi lacks the after-hours verve of Negril or the authenticity of Kingston. Nonetheless, it's not hard to find a good party atmosphere somewhere on any night of the week.

Many all-inclusive resorts sell night passes permitting full access to meals, drinks and entertainment.

Jimmy Buffett's Margaritaville
BAR

(📞 876-675-8800; Island Village; ⊘ 11am-4am) This corporate franchise has turned getting drunk into big business. The music is loud and the signature margaritas don't come cheap, but many tourists find the orchestrated good-time vibe to be irresistible. Admission is charged for special events, such as Wednesday's Wet'n'Wild Pool Party (J$2000, half-price entry for guests in swimwear). Although Margaritaville 'goes until you say when,' things wind up earlier when there's no ship in town.

Ocean's 11 Watering Hole
BAR

(Fisherman's Point) With its prime spot on the pier, it's little surprise that Ocean's 11 is popular with cruise-ship passengers, who knock back the potent cocktails and cheer each other on during Tuesday night karaoke. The upstairs space doubles as a small art gallery and coffee shop, and serves excellent Blue Mountain coffee, which you can also purchase by the pound.

H2O
BAR

(Shop 22, Coconut Grove Shopping Centre; ⊘ midday-4am) Run by reggae singer Tanya Stephens, this inviting resto-bar specializes in vegetarian and seafood dishes during the day, and fills up by night when locals and visitors alike stream in for the music events. Live band karaoke takes place on Friday nights, the H2O Flow event on Saturdays features appearances from local and international artists, while Sunday is the night to live out the glory days of reggae, ska and mento.

John Crow's Tavern   SPORTS BAR
(10 Main St) The big TV above the bar screens the latest football games and the outdoor terrace is perfect for a beer, burger and a spot of people-watching.

Nexus   NIGHTCLUB
(8 Main St; ☺9pm-4am Tue & Fri, 7-11pm Sun) Rooftop lounge that comes to life on cruiseship days. Tuesday is Ladies' Night, Friday features local DJs and the street reverberates with the pounding beats. Live bands on Sunday play a mix.

☆ Entertainment

On the A3 east of town, the **White River Reggae Park** infrequently hosts sound systems. **Priory Beach** has a regular Sunday sound system on the beach (7pm onwards). Also look for posters around town advertising live music or sound systems at **Reggae Beach**.

Amnesia   DANCEHALL
(☑876 974-2633; 70 Main St; admission J$350-550; ☺Wed-Sun) A classic Jamaican dancehall, this remains the happening scene. Theme nights include an oldies jam on Sunday, ladies' night on Thursday and an after-work party on Friday. This is all leading up to Saturday's dress-to-impress all-night dance marathon. Expect lots of sweat, a tightly packed dance floor and some of the raunchiest dancing you've ever seen.

Blitz   DANCEHALL
(60 Main St; admission J$500; ☺10pm-6am Tue & Fri) Though this is essentially an after-party for the Ocean 11's karaoke crowd on Tuesday, on Friday be prepared to wind and grind your way through the batty-rider and puss-boot–clad local crowd at the weekly 'Thank God It's Friday' (admission free for women) dancehall event. Big names perform occasionally.

Roof Club   DANCEHALL
(7 James Ave; admission J$300) The gritty Roof sends earth-shattering music across the roofs of town; it's the place to get down and dirty with the latest dancehall moves. It can get rough.

🔒 Shopping

Sellers hawk mix CDs of the latest sounds on Turtle Beach and along Main St, where crafts

vendors also sell their goods, though for the more exceptional souvenirs you'll have to travel further out.

Olde Craft Market   CRAFTS
(Main St) A better (and less expensive) choice than the rows and rows of identical crafts at other craft parks, this market features quality ceramics and art, as well as the usual T-shirts with chirpy Jamaican slogans and Rasta tams with fake dreadlocks attached.

Harmony Hall   ART
(☑975-4222; www.harmonyhall.com; ☺10am-5:30pm Tue-Sun) Art gallery featuring the best of local art, located 7km east of Ocho Rios. Renowned for its Christmas, Easter and mid-November craft fairs, and regular exhibitions.

Ocho Rios Craft Park   SOUVENIRS
(Main St) For all your tacky T-shirt, batik, wooden sculpture and crafts-made-of-coconut-shells needs. Some of the sellers also sell quality music-mix CDs.

Wassi Art   CRAFTS
(☑546-3197; Bonham Spring) Excellent pottery and ceramics. Free tours are offered, detailing the entire process including clay processing, painting and firing.

Reggae Yard   SOUVENIRS
(Island Village) Reggae wear in Rasta colors, Usain Bolt T-shirts, and a good selection of reggae music.

Vibes Music Shack   MUSIC STORE
(Map p78; Ocean Village Plaza) Reggae and dancehall CDs, as well as some mento and calypso.

ℹ Information

DANGERS & ANNOYANCES
Good humor and a firm 'no' should be enough to deal with the persistent taxi drivers, hustlers and would-be tour guides. Avoid the area immediately behind the produce market, south of the clock tower and the seedy, poorly lit James Ave, a hang-out strip of ill repute. Use caution at night anywhere.

EMERGENCY
Police Station (☑974-2533) Off DaCosta Dr, just east of the clock tower.

INTERNET ACCESS
Computer Whizz (Shop 11, Island Plaza; per 30min/1hr J$150/250; ☺8:30am-7:30pm Mon-Sat) Has 10 computers as well as wi-fi access for those with own laptops.

MEDICAL SERVICES

Kulkarni Medical Clinic (☑ 974-3357; 16 Rennie Rd) Private practice, between RBTT and Jamaica National Bank, used by upmarket hotels in the area.

Pinegrove Pharmacy (☑ 974-5586; Shop 5, Pinegrove Plaza; ☺ 9am-8pm Mon-Sat, 10am-3pm Sun)

St Ann's Bay Hospital (☑ 972-2272; Seville Rd) The nearest hospital.

MONEY

There are numerous banks along Main St, including Scotiabank. All have foreign-exchange facilities and ATMs.

POST

Post Office (Main St; ☺ 8am-5pm Mon-Sat) Opposite the Ocho Rios Craft Park.

TOURIST OFFICE

Tourist Information (☑ 974-7705; Shop 3, Ocean Village, Main St; ☺ 9am-5pm Mon-Thu, to 4pm Fri) Represents the Jamaica Tourist Board. Staff can help you suss out Ochi's transportation, lodging and attractions options. Also operates an information booth on Main St, but it's open only when cruise ships are in port.

ⓘ Getting There & Away

AIR

At the time of writing, the former Boscobel Airport, about 16km east of town, had just reopened as the Ian Fleming International Airport (p213), expanded primarily to accommodate private jets, as well as chartered flights. **Jamaica Air Shuttle** (☑ 906-9026, 906-9030; www.jamaicaairshuttle. com) offers several weekly flights to Kingston.

PUBLIC TRANSPORTATION

Buses, minibuses and route taxis arrive at and depart Ocho Rios at the **transportation center** (Evelyn Rd). During daylight hours there are frequent departures (fewer on Sundays) for Kingston and destinations along the north coast. There is no set schedule: they depart when full. If heading to Port Antonio by bus, you will have to change buses at Port Maria (J$140) and possibly Annotto Bay. Sample destinations:

Discovery Bay J$150, 35 minutes.

Kingston J$320, two hours.

Montego Bay J$500, 90 minutes.

Port Maria J$140, 50 minutes.

Runaway Bay J$140, 30 minutes.

St Ann's Bay J$100, 10 minutes.

Knutsford Express (www.knutsfordexpress. com) has scheduled departures to Kingston and Montego Bay from its office in the car park of the Ocho Rios Jerk Centre. Arrive half an hour prior to departure to register your ticket.

Departures:

Kingston (J$1200, two hours) 6:20am, 10:25am, 2:30pm and 6:30pm Monday to Friday; 7:20am and 5:55pm Saturday; 9:45am and 6pm Sunday.

Montego Bay (J$1200, two hours) 7:45am, 11:20am, 3:45pm and 6:40pm Monday to Friday; 7:45am, 11:20am and 6pm Saturday; 10am and 6pm Sunday.

TAXI

JUTA (☑ 974-2292) is the main taxi agency catering to tourists. A licensed taxi will cost about US$110 for Montego Bay, and about US$100 for Kingston (US$110 to the international airport at Kingston).

ⓘ Getting Around

TO/FROM THE AIRPORT

There is no shuttle service from the airport to downtown. Local buses (J$100), and minibuses and route taxis (J$150) pass by. A tourist taxi will cost about J$2116.

CAR & MOTORCYCLE

Shopping malls along Main St have car parks, though not secure ones. Most hotels offer parking; all upmarket hotels offer secure parking. Main St during rush hour is one long traffic jam.

Outlets include:

Bargain Rent-a-Car (☑ 974-8047; Shop 1A Pineapple Place Shopping Centre, Main St)

Budget (☑ 974-1288; www.budgetjamaica.com; 15 Milford Rd)

PUBLIC TRANSPORTATION

Minibuses and route taxis ply Main St and the coast road (J$80 for short hauls; J$150 to Boscobel or Mammee Bay).

TAXI

Chartered taxis are in great abundance along Main St. Negotiate the fare before setting off, as the drivers will quote any figure that comes to mind. If you want the driver to wait for you, do not hand over the full fare in advance.

EAST OF OCHO RIOS

The seaside resorts of Ocho Rios quickly give way to isolated villas and fishing villages such as Port Maria as the coastal road winds its way east along cliffs and bluffs. The sense of leaving tourist Jamaica behind is enhanced by the drop in road quality.

Drawn by its coastal beauty and unspoiled character, two of Jamaica's most famous visitors, author Noël Coward and James Bond creator Ian Fleming, made their homes in the area. While Coward settled in Firefly (p87), with its spectacular view down on the coastline, Fleming found refuge at Goldeneye (p86), now one of the island's most elegant hotels.

Reggae Beach to Boscobel Beach

East of Ocho Rios, habitations begin thinning out along the A3. Several beaches lie hidden below the cliffs; notable among them is Tower Isle, 9km east of Ocho Rios, with its cluster of resorts. The Rio Nuevo meets the ocean about 1km west of Tower Isle.

Sights & Activities

Prospect Plantation PLANTATION
(994-1058; www.prospectplantationtours.com; tours J$2963; Mon-Sat) If you've been wondering why St Ann is called 'the garden parish,' you'll find your answer at this beautiful old hilltop great house and 405-hectare property, less working plantation and more tourist attraction, 5km east of town. On a pleasant, educational tour you'll travel by tractor-powered jitney through scenic grounds among banana, cassava, cocoa, coconut, coffee, pineapple and pimento. **Dolphin Cove** (974-5335; www.dolphincovejamaica.com) offers Prospect Plantation tours that include either a horseback (J$5418) or camelback ride (J$5418), an ostrich feeding session and a visit to Dunn's River Falls.

Harmony Hall ART GALLERY
(974-2870; www.harmonyhall.com; 10am-5:30pm Tue-Sun) A lovely pink gingerbread house on the A3 6km east of town, Harmony Hall dates to 1886 when it was a Methodist manse that adjoined a pimento estate. The restored structure is made of cut stone, with a wooden upper story trimmed with fretwork and a shingled roof with a spire. Reborn as an arts-and-crafts showcase, it holds shows in the Front Gallery throughout the year; an exhibition season runs mid-November to Easter. The Back Gallery features fine arts and crafts by local artists such as Albert Artwell and Cebert Christie. The acclaimed Toscanini (p82) Mediterranean restaurant is on the ground floor.

Reggae Beach BEACH
(admission J$100; 9am-5pm) Located east of Harmony Hall on the A3, this clean yellow-sand beach is hustler-free and popular with tourists only, due to the high admission rate. Kayaks are available for rent, and jerk chicken and fish are readily available. Raucous sound-system parties are held here now and then.

Rio Nuevo Battle Site HISTORIC SITE
(admission J$424; 10am-5pm Mon-Fri, 10am-2pm Sat & Sun) On the bluff west of the Rio Nuevo river mouth is this little-visited site where, in 1658, the English forces fought their decisive battle against the Spanish, sending them fleeing to Cuba. A plaque here records the events and there's a small exhibition on the area's historical heritage.

Boscobel Beach BEACH
This beach, 6km east of Rio Nuevo, is a hamlet dominated by Boscobel Beach Spa Resort & Golf Club, a resort especially geared towards families with young children. The Ian Fleming International Airport is located nearby.

Jamaica Beach BEACH
Between Tower Isle and Rio Nuevo, it is renowned for its dive sites offshore. The offshore reef, known as the Rio Nuevo Wall, supports turtles, barracudas and other marine life.

Getting There & Away

Minibuses and route taxis traveling between Ocho Rios and Oracabessa serve Rio Nuevo and Tower Isle (J$100).

Oracabessa

POP 10,000
Taking its name from the Spanish *oro cabeza* (golden head), Oracabessa, 21km east of Ocho Rios, is a small, one-street, one-story village with a vague aura of a Wild West town. The street itself is lined with Caribbean vernacular architecture, with wooden houses trimmed with fretwork. This was a major port for shipping bananas in the 19th century. While the boom era has passed, the town itself is far from derelict.

Below Oracabessa is the marina (formerly a banana-loading port), in the lee of a tombolo on whose western flank pirogues and fishing boats bob at anchor.

Sights

James Bond Beach BEACH
(adult/child J$500/250; 9am-6pm Tue-Sun) The attractive strip of white sand hosts large-scale annual music events, such as Follow Di Arrow, Beach J'ouvert and Fully Loaded (watch

out for event posters in Ocho Rios). During the week it's pretty quiet but on weekends, in particular, visitors flock to **Stingray City** (☑975-3354; adult/child J$4500/2500) to snorkel and swim with the resident stingrays or to take part in jet-ski safaris (J$6000) and glass-bottom boat rides (J$3000) along the coast. A small bar and restaurant provides refreshment.

Adjacent to the Bond beach is Fisherman's Beach, a rootsy alternative where one can enjoy simple I-tal and seafood fare and the occasional sound-system party.

Sun Valley Plantation PLANTATION
(☑446-2026, 995-3075; tour incl snack J$1000; ☺9am-2pm) This working plantation and botanical farm is at Crescent on the B13, some 5km south of Oracabessa. Owners Lorna and Nolly Binns offer enjoyable garden tours in a plantation setting, which teach visitors about banana and sugar-cane – two staple crops that have played an important part in the development of the area. You can opt to visit the groves of coconuts – the current main crop – and other tropical fruits and medicinal herbs.

🛏 Sleeping & Eating

Tamarind Great House GUEST HOUSE $
(☑995-3252; www.tamarind.hostel.com; Crescent Estate; d US$74-120; P☒) The hilltop setting for this 'plantation guest house' near Sun Valley Plantation is sublime, with lush valleys and mountains all around (there's a lovely walk to a local waterfall). The large bedrooms with four-poster beds open to a vast veranda. The excellent restaurant serves stick-to-your-ribs breakfasts and dinners. From Oracabessa, take Jack's River Rd; it's a rough 6km drive, but worth it.

Nix-Nax GUEST HOUSE $
(☑975-3364; dm/r US$15/30) Northeast of the town center opposite a Seventh Day Adventist church, this inimitable hostelry offers cheerful dorms, rooms, and communal kitchens. Your host, Domenica, a Harlem transplant who has run the guest house for more than 20 years, prides herself on flexible arrangements for travelers, saying that it's a 'good place for the broke and busted.'

Villa Sake GUEST HOUSE $
(☑368-1036; www.hostelsofjamaica.com; Opposite Ian Fleming Airport; r US$25-50) A small but charming hostel-style guest house opposite Ian Fleming. Villa Sake has just a handful of rooms and communal kitchen, and lounge area that virtually hangs over the waves of its own tiny private cove (there's a ladder running down the cliff to get to the sea).

★**Goldeneye** HOTEL $$$
(☑946-0958; www.goldeneye.com; ste US$850, 1-/2-/3-bedroom cottage US$1220/1520/2280, villa US$6800; P☀☎☒) Jamaica's most exclusive

---

NOËL COWARD'S PEENY-WALLY

The multitalented Sir Noël Coward first visited Jamaica in 1944 on a two-week holiday. He found peace of mind here and dubbed his dream island 'Dr Jamaica.' Four years later he rented Ian Fleming's estate, Goldeneye, at Oracabessa, while he hunted for a site to build a home.

In 1948 Coward bought a 3-hectare estate overlooking Little Bay near Galina and set to work building Coward's Folly, a three-story villa with two guest cottages, and a swimming pool at the sea's edge. He named his home Blue Harbour and invited his many notable friends, a virtual 'Who's Who' of the rich and famous. The swarm of visitors, however, eventually drove Coward to find another retreat.

While painting with his lover Graham Payn at a place called Lookout (so-named because the pirate Henry Morgan had a stone hut built atop the hill to keep an eye out for Spanish galleons), Coward was struck by the impressive solitude and incredible view. The duo lingered until nightfall, when fireflies ('peeny-wallies' in the Jamaican dialect) appeared. Within two weeks Coward had bought the land, and eight years later he had a house built. He named it Firefly.

Coward had spent 30 years in Jamaica, recording his love of the island and islanders on canvas in bright, splashy colors. When he suffered a heart attack at the age of 73, he was buried on the lawns of Firefly beneath a marble slab. Lines from his last poem, inscribed on one of Firefly's walls, are a suitable epitaph: 'When I have fears, as Keats had fears, Of the moment I'll cease to be/I console myself with vanished years, Remembered laughter, remembered tears/And the peace of the changing sea.'

property features eight villas, including Ian Fleming's abode, sprinkled across expansive grounds. Additional waterfront cottages, built of wood and stone and painted in autumnal colors, have pampering yet discreet stewards. The two restaurants serve gourmet meals and there's an entertainment room for Bond movies, but the coup de grâce is the hotel's private island with beach and water sports. Immediately east of Oracabessa.

Tropical Hut JAMAICAN **$**
(Racecourse; mains J$300-800; ☺lunch & dinner) Popular local watering hole serving delicious Jamaican dishes.

ℹ Information

Oracabessa Medical Centre (☎ 975-3304; Vermont Ave; ☺8am-2:30pm Mon & Tue, 7am-midday Wed-Sat) By the Esso gas station at the east end of town.
Scotiabank (Main St) Bank with ATM.

ℹ Getting There & Away

Minibuses and route taxis pass through, en route between Ocho Rios (J$150, 25 minutes) and Annotto Bay (for Port Antonio).

Galina Point & Little Bay

Five kilometres east of Oracabessa, the A3 winds around the promontory of Galina Point. A 12m-high concrete lighthouse marks the headland. South of Galina you'll pass Noël Coward's first house, Blue Harbour, squatting atop 'the double bend,' where the road and shoreline take a 90-degree turn and open to a view of Cabarita Island. The road drops steeply from Blue Harbour to Kokomo Beach in Little Bay.

The beach is unappealing, but the bay and around makes a more pleasant stopover than Port Maria if you wish to visit Firefly.

◎ Sights

★Firefly HISTORIC HOUSE
(☎ 997-7201, 994-0920; admission J$847; ☺9am-5pm Mon-Thu & Sat) Set amid wide lawns high atop a hill 5km east of Oracabessa and 5km west of Port Maria, Firefly was the home of Sir Noël Coward, the English playwright, songwriter, actor and wit, who was preceded at this site by the notorious pirate Sir Henry Morgan. When he died in 1973, Coward left the estate to his partner Graham Payn, who donated it to the nation.

Your guide will lead you to Coward's art studio, where he was schooled in oil painting by Winston Churchill. The studio displays Coward's original paintings and photographs of himself and a coterie of famous friends. The drawing room, with the table still laid, was used to entertain such guests as the Queen Mother, Sophia Loren and Audrey Hepburn. The upper lounge features a glassless window that offers one of the most stunning coastal vistas in all Jamaica. The view takes in Port Maria Bay and the coastline further west. Contrary to popular opinion, Coward didn't write his famous song *A Room with a View* here (it was written in Hawaii in 1928).

Coward lies buried beneath a plain white marble slab on the wide lawns where he entertained many illustrious stars of stage and screen; a pensive statue of the man graces the lawn.

🛏 Sleeping & Eating

Blue Harbour HOTEL **$**
(☎ 725-0289; www.blueharb.com; r per person US$70, full board US$120; P⛱) Once owned by Noël Coward, this is a pleasingly ramshackle retreat with a laid-back atmosphere, consisting of three villas by a tiny beach and saltwater pool. Spacious rooms feature some original furniture from Coward's day. Meals are served on a wide veranda with bay views and full board is worth it for the delicious home-cooked Jamaican specials.

Little Bay Inn HOTEL **$**
(☎ 373-5871, 994-2721; r J$2540-2963; P) On the main road, just at the turnoff for Firefly, this modest hotel offers 10 simple, fan-cooled rooms with double beds and private bathroom; the pricier rooms have TVs. There's a small restaurant and jerk center and the downstairs disco may keep you awake.

Galina Breeze HOTEL **$$**
(☎ 994-0537; www.galinabreeze.com; r US$100, ste US$120; P❄🛜) This small hotel with superb views of the coast has just 14 light, spacious rooms, all equipped with firm king-size beds and cable TV. There's a restaurant, bar, and (just outside the main gate) a decent jerk stand.

★Bolt House BOUTIQUE HOTEL **$$$**
(☎ 994-0303; www.bolthousejamaica.com; villa US$2200; P❄🛜⛱) This secluded cliffside villa is the ultimate in luxury. Offering the same spectacular views as nearby Goldeneye, it has an infinity pool, a yoga deck and

FLEMING...IAN FLEMING

Ian Fleming, inventor of James Bond, first came to Jamaica in 1942 while serving with British Naval Intelligence. In 1946 he bought a house on the shore at Oracabessa and named it 'Goldeneye,' and he wintered here every year until his death in 1964. It was here that Fleming conceived agent 007, the creation of whom the author attributes to living in Jamaica.

'Would these books have been born if I had not been living in the gorgeous vacuum of a Jamaican holiday? I doubt it,' he would write later. All 14 of Fleming's James Bond novels were written here, and five were set in Jamaica. 'I was looking for a name for my hero,' he related, 'nothing like Peregrine Carruthers or Standfast Maltravers – and I found it, on the cover of one of my Jamaican bibles, *Birds of the West Indies* by James Bond, an ornithological classic.' Without Jamaica, there would literally be no James Bond 007. The house is now part of Goldeneye hotel and can be rented.

private hiking trails on 18 hectares of land. The five rooms (four nights minimum stay) are splendidly decorated with contemporary art, and guests have access to Goldeneye's private beach. Fusion cuisine (US$60 per day) is served in the airy dining room and it's possible to dine at Goldeneye with 24 hours' notice.

ⓘ Getting There & Away

Minibuses and route taxis pass through, en route between Ocho Rios (J$150, 25 minutes) and Annotto Bay (for Port Antonio).

Brimmer Hall

This 809-hectare working plantation (☑ 994-2309; 1-hr tour J$2540; ⊘ 9am-4pm Mon-Fri), near Bailey's Vale, 10km southwest of Port Maria, grows bananas, coconuts, sugarcane, pineapple and citrus for export. It's centered on a wooden great house dating back to the 1700s, with an impressive interior furnished with oriental rugs and antique furniture, and even an original suit of armor. The one-hour plantation tours are in a canopied jitney. It is signed from the A3.

SOUTH OF OCHO RIOS

The A3 winds through sweeping pastoral country on its way south. At Moneague, the road meets up with the A1 from St Ann's Bay, continues over Mt Diablo and drops dramatically to Kingston.

Faith's Pen

From Moneague the A1 climbs steadily to Faith's Pen, 27km south of Ocho Rios. Pull into the side road parallel to the main road and choose your meal from the many shacks offering jerk pork and chicken, fried fish and fresh fruit juices. You'll be immediately surrounded by the competitive roadside cooks; insist on sampling the wares first. Shack 2 is best for soursop juice (J$250 a bottle) while shack 8 is great for jerk pork and accompaniments.

The road continues up the pine-forested slopes of Mt Diablo (839m). At 686m the A1 crests the mountain chain and begins its steep, winding descent to Ewarton and the lush Rosser Valley, beautiful when seen from these heights.

WEST OF OCHO RIOS

Mammee Bay

Formerly a favorite with Jamaican beachgoers, Mammee Bay – 5.5km west of Ocho Rios and 4km east of St Ann's Bay – has several little beaches, some hidden away, but is now firmly dominated by the monolithic Club Hotel Riu Ocho Rios. Much of the beachfront is a private residential estate, but access is offered to the public beaches.

At Laughing Waters – also called Roaring River – 1km east of Mammee Bay and 1km west of Dunn's River Falls, a river appears from rocks amid a shallow ravine about 3km from the sea and spills to a charming little beach (admission free). This is where Ursula Andress famously appeared as Honey Ryder, dripping with brine, in the James Bond movie *Dr No*. Look for the large fenced-in electrical power structure beside the A3. Follow the river to the beach. Public access to the falls is by foot, though sometimes access to the beach is blocked by guards stationed along the road.

St Ann's Bay

POP 12,400

In 1509 the Spaniards built the first Spanish settlement on the island about 700m west of St Ann's Bay, at Sevilla la Nueva. The site was abandoned within four decades and it was later developed as a sugar estate by a British planter. Other planters established sugar estates nearby, and the town grew and prospered as a bustling seaport with forts on opposite sides of the bay. Marcus Garvey, founder of the Black Nationalist movement, was born here and is honored each August 17 with a parade.

◉ Sights

Up the hill from the Columbus Monument is the exquisite Catholic church of Our Lady of Perpetual Help, built in contemporary Spanish design by an Irish priest in 1939 with stones recovered from the ruins of Sevilla la Nueva.

At the corner of Market St is the courthouse, erected in elegant cut limestone and red brick in 1866 with a pedimented porch bearing the scales of justice. Across the way is the market, which gets busy on Friday and Saturday. Further west lies quaint St Ann's Bay Baptist Church. Statues at either end of St Ann's Bay provide neat book-ends to the town's history: Columbus stands at one end, Garvey at the other.

★ Maima Seville Great
House & Heritage Park   HISTORIC SITE

(admission J$500; ⊙9am-4pm Sat & Sun) This historical park overlooking the sea, less than 1km west of present-day St Ann's, marks the site of the first Spanish capital on the island – Sevilla la Nueva – and one of the first Spanish settlements in the New World. It houses a fascinating great house, plantation remains and reconstructions of Taíno houses, African slave houses and a slave kitchen garden.

When the English captured Jamaica from the Spanish, the land on which Sevilla la Nueva had been built was granted to army officer Richard Hemming. The estate was developed for sugar, and was dominated by the Seville Great House, built in 1745 by Hemming's grandson. The family tombs are outside, and next to them a memorial to the slaves and whose remains were discovered and reburied here in 1997.

The restored house contains an engaging museum depicting the history of the site from Taíno times through the era of slavery and the colonial period.

Traces of the original Spanish buildings, including a church and the castle-house of the first Spanish governor, are visible, along with the ruins of the English sugar mills and overseer's house. This was also the site of the Taíno village of Maima; the inhabitants were forced to work as serfs under the Spanish encomienda system, and quickly died out through a combination of disease, overwork and suicide. The best way to explore the sprawling property is by joining a Hooves (p78) horseback tour that ends with a jaunt into the sea.

★ Festivals & Events

Rebel Salute   MUSIC

(www.rebelsaluteja.com) The biggest Roots Reggae concert in Jamaica goes down on the second Saturday in January at Richmond Estate.

Emancipation Jubilee   CULTURAL

(⊙Jul 31-Aug 1) Held annually on the grounds of Maima Seville Great House overnight from July 31 to August 1. Celebrations consist of dancing and traditional folk music, such as Kumina and mento.

🛏 Sleeping & Eating

There are street food stalls along Main St dishing up fish tea and jerk.

High Hope Estate   B&B $$

(☏972-2277; www.highhopeestate.com; r US$185-225; P❋@☒) This beautiful Venetian-style villa is set in large woodland grounds high in the hills above St Ann's Bay. Each of its five rooms is decorated with antiques, and three have wonderful ocean views and verandas. There's a well-stocked library for browsing and fabulous meals on request (Jamaica and Italian dishes are a speciality; cooking courses also available).

Seafood Specialist   SEAFOOD $

(cnr Jail Lane & A1; meals J$500-850; ⊙lunch & dinner) Wholesome local fare such as brown stew, plus excellent steamed or fried fish with yams and rice and peas, washed down with natural juices.

Juici Patties   JAMAICAN $

(Main St; patties J$90) Sells patties of all varieties as well as lunch mains such as saltfish and stews.

ⓘ Information

Police Station (cnr Main & Braco Sts)

Scotiabank (18 Braco St) Has a 24-hour ATM.
St Ann's Bay Public General Hospital (📞 972-2272) At the far west end of Main St, with an emergency clinic.

ⓘ Getting There & Away

Route taxis run throughout the day for Ocho Rios (J$100, 10 minutes) and Montego Bay (J$350, 90 minutes), via Falmouth.

Priory & Around

Priory, about 1.5km west of St Ann's Bay, has a small beach with water sports and several hotels. You can turn inland and head into the hills for views down the coast. Here you'll find Lilyfield Great House, about 8km east of Brown's Town.

⊙ Sights & Activities

Chukka Cove Farm   ADVENTURE CENTER
(J$7195) This former polo field west of Priory is now the home of **Chukka Caribbean Adventures** (📞 972-2506; www.chukkacaribbean.com), which offers an ever-growing list of guided excursions and adventures. The trips are sometimes a mite crowded, but the quality of service and expertise of the guides is high. Chukka works closely with a dog-rescue center, and offers 'dog-sledding' on land, the exhilarating 50km/h buggy ride pulled by a trained dog team. Other popular excursions include the three-hour Horseback Ride 'n Swim (US$79), which culminates with an exciting bareback trot into the sea; River Tubing Safari (US$65); and Zip Line Tour (US$99). Rates include transfer from Ocho Rios.

In April, Chukka Cove Farm hosts the exuberant all-night Carnival party, complete with soca music and paint throwing, though purists are grumbling about the introduction of dancehall to the event.

H'Evans Scent   ADVENTURE CENTER
(📞 564-6467; www.hevansscent.com; ⊙ 8am-5pm Mon-Fri, 9am-4pm Sat & Sun) In the tiny hill town of Free Hill, 10km south of Priory, this evolving ecotourism experiment is the brainchild of Derek Evans, better known in the UK as fitness celebrity Mr Motivator. The sprawling hilltop property is the site for four adrenalin-charged but family-friendly experiences: paintballing, ATV rides, a zip-line tour and the Screamer – a 17m giant swing that sends you hurtling across the valley. Activity package combos are available, with discounts for groups of 10 or more; if you want to sample everything on the menu, the 'Zips, ATV and

Paintball Extreme' package (J$3250) gives you access all areas. Meals are available in the bright-yellow main house.

Cranbrook Flower Forest   GARDEN
(www.cranbrookff.com; adult/child J$1000/500; ⊙ 9am-5pm) This 53-hectare botanical garden run by Chukka Cove Farm is a treat, crafted in the lush valley that carves up into the hills south of Laughlands, about 5km west of Priory. The garden is built around a colonial-era building and includes theme gardens, a hothouse orchid display, pools, and lush lawns (with croquet) fringed by banks of anthuriums and other tropical flowers.

Guided nature walks (about 90 minutes) lead to the river, reflecting giant tree ferns, spectacular torch ginger, heliconia and other exotic species, and there are perfect spots for picnicking. River tubing, horseback rides and adrenalin-packed canopy zip-line tours are available.

⏨ Sleeping

Circle B Farm Guest House   GUEST HOUSE $
(📞 913-4511; www.circlebfarm.com; dm US$22.50, r US$50) This working plantation has its own simple backpacker lodge offering several dorm-style rooms, a communal kitchen and lounge. Meals are offered on request. The farm also runs engaging tours that demonstrate its fruit production. It is reached via a turnoff after Sevilla la Nueva at Priory, 3km west of St Ann's Bay.

ⓘ Getting There & Away

Minibuses that run between St Ann's Bay and Runaway Bay can drop you off at the bus stop right in front of Chukka Cove Farm. To reach H'Evans Scent and Cranbrook Flower Forest, you'll need your own vehicle.

Runaway Bay

This bay (16km west of St Ann's) is low on cultural attractions, though sun worshippers, snorkelers and divers find much to celebrate. This one-street village, lined with all-inclusive resorts and nondescript local shops, stretches along the A1 for 3km, merging with the small community of Salem to the east.

⚐ Activities

Several small beaches are supposedly public, although most are the backyards for a few all-inclusive resorts. If you're hankering for a dip in the big blue, head to the white-sand

Cardiff Hall Public Beach, opposite the Shell gas station. There is a livelier (but littered) fisherman's beach in Salem, where the occasional sound-system party is staged on the weekend.

Runaway Bay has excellent diving. There's a wreck in shallow water in front of Club Ambiance, plus two cars and a plane offshore from Club Caribbean. A reef complex called Ricky's Reef is renowned for its sponges. More experienced divers might try the eponymous Canyon. Here, too, is the *Reggae Queen*, a 30m-long sunken tugboat. Potty Reef will have you flush with excitement; divers can't resist having their photo taken sitting on, er, King Neptune's throne.

Resort Divers   DIVING
(✐ 881-5760; www.resortdivers.com; Royal Decameron Club Caribbean, Runaway Bay; 1-/2-tank dives US$50/95) Besides standard dives, there are certification courses (from US$420), night dives (US$60), snorkeling excursions (US$30) and a plethora of other water sports on offer, such as banana-boat rides, parasailing and jet-ski rental.

🛏 Sleeping

The **Jamaica Association of Villas & Apartments** (JAVA; ✐ 974-2508, in the USA 800-845-5276; www.villasinjamaica.com) offers fully staffed beachside and hilltop villas.

Club Ambiance   RESORT $$
(✐ 973-6167; www.clubambiance.com; s/d US$156/222, 3-bedroom villa US$980; P ❋ 🛜 🏊) This lively alternative to grander all-inclusives is popular with 20- and 30-somethings and features two small private beaches, a pool with a bar and a secluded three-bedroom villa with its own swimming pool. All bright colors and kitschy art, the spacious rooms feature firm king-sized beds and tiled floors. Rooms were being refitted when we visited.

Little Savoy Guest House   GUEST HOUSE $$
(✐ 474-5889; www.jamaica-holiday.net; 150 Ricketts Dr; r incl breakfast J$8000; P ❋ @ 🏊) This grand new guest house with marble floors, faux-Grecian columns and the odd burst of color (in the shape of fresh flowers livening up the austere black-and-white exterior) is proving a hit, particularly with wedding parties. Each light, double room has its own color scheme and there's a good buffet breakfast.

Franklyn D Resort   RESORT $$$
(✐ in the USA 800-654-1337; www.fdrholidays.com; all-inclusive 1/2/3 bedrooms US$490/595/650, child

under 6/6-15/16-19 free/US$50/80; P ❋ 🛜 🏊) At this Spanish hacienda-style, all-inclusive family resort, there are kid-friendly facilities and a personal nanny assigned to each child. The resort has three restaurants and a bar, plus an oceanfront spa and waterslide. Three nights minimum stay.

🍴 Eating & Drinking

Food Fa Life   I-TAL $
(West Salem; meals J$450; ☺ closed Sun; ✐) Excellent I-tal food served from a nondescript container near Devon House I-Scream. Try the June plum juice (J$150), the ackee or the tasty vegetable stew.

Sharkie's   SEAFOOD $
(Salem Beach; meals J$1000) Locals head for this informal seafood restaurant on Fisherman's Beach for steamed and fried fish, conch (curried, soup or fritters) and nonfishy standards.

Tek It Easy   BAR $
(A1; meals J$500-700; ☺ lunch & dinner) At this economical rooftop haunt, Jamaican fare – primarily chicken and fish – competes for attention alongside the freely flowing overproof rum. There's music most nights.

★ Cardiff Hall Restaurant   INTERNATIONAL $$
(✐ 973-2671; Runaway Bay Heart Hotel; meals J$1270-2400) This cheerful restaurant serves well-made Jamaican and continental fare. The service is great and reservations highly recommended.

⭐ Entertainment

Most fun-hungry visitors make the short journey to Ocho Rios for their after-hours kicks or settle for what's on at their resort. Subsequently, most resorts offer expensive night-passes for US$50 to US$100, granting unlimited booze, food and entertainment.

Local entertainment consists of a few rum shops and insalubrious go-go clubs.

ℹ Information

Police (cnr Main St & B3)
Post office (Main St)
Scotiabank (Main St, Salem) Bank with ATM.

ℹ Getting There & Around

BUS

Minibuses and route taxis ply the A1 between Montego Bay (J$150 to J$200, one hour) and Ocho Rios (J$100 to J$150, 30 minutes). They can be flagged down anywhere in Runaway Bay.

Discovery Bay

This wide flask-shaped bay, 8km west of Runaway Bay and 8km east of Rio Bueno, is a popular resort spot for locals drawn to Puerto Seco Beach, and many of Jamaica's wealthiest families have holiday villas up in the hills here. The town itself has only marginal appeal.

A giant bauxite-loading facility dominates the town. Large freighters are fed by conveyor belts from a huge storage dome that looks like a rusty pumpkin – it was used as the villain's headquarters in the James Bond movie, *Dr No*. You can follow the road signed 'Port Rhoades' uphill 1km to a lookout point offering fantastic views over the bay.

Locals believe this to be the location where Christopher Columbus first landed on Jamaican soil in 1494, though others say it was at Rio Bueno.

◉ Sights & Activities

Green Grotto Caves CAVE
(www.greengrottocavesja.com; adult/child U$20/10; ◉9am-4pm) This impressive system of caves and tunnels, 3km east of Discovery Bay, extends for about 45km. The steps lead down into the impressive chambers, where statuesque dripstone formations are illuminated by floodlights. The Taíno people left petroglyphs carved into the walls; the caves have frequently been used as hideouts – by the Spanish during the English takeover of the island in 1655, by runaway slaves in the 18th century, and between the two world wars by smugglers running arms to Cuba.

The highlight is Green Grotto, a glistening subterranean lake 36m down. The entrance fee includes a guided one-hour tour, which is particularly family friendly. The guides conduct their tours with humor and attempt to amaze you by tapping stalactites to produce hollow drum-like sounds, as well as pointing out the different species of bat that live in the cave, and their imported predator, the Jamaican yellow boa.

Puerto Seco Beach BEACH
(admission J$500; ◉9am-5pm) The eastern side of the bay is rimmed with white-sand beaches. With its soft sand and limpid waters, Puerto Seco Beach, in the center of town, is a real charmer. Open to the public, it sports rustic eateries and bars and a fun park with a waterslide for kids not interested in sun tanning. On weekends and holidays the beach is teeming, but during the week the place is often deserted. You can rent fishing boats, sea bikes and jet skis.

Columbus Park MUSEUM
(◉9am-5pm) FREE An open-air roadside museum atop the bluff on the west side of the bay, this park features anchors, cannons, nautical bells, sugar-boiling coppers and an old waterwheel, and a diminutive locomotive once used to haul sugar at Innswood Estate. Nearby are remains of Quadrant Wharf, built in 1777 by the British, with a mural commemorating Columbus' landing. There's a branch of Scotchies here, making a popular stop for tour coaches running between Mobay and Ochi.

🛏 Sleeping & Eating

Some of the most luxurious fully staffed villas on the island are found in the hills above Discovery Bay and can be booked with the **Jamaica Association of Villas & Apartments** (✆974-2508, in the USA 800-845-5276; www.villasinjamaica.com).

Paradise Place GUEST HOUSE $
(✆862-2095; www.paradiseplace54.com; 54 Bridgewater Garden; r/apt J$5936/7819; P ❄) The pick of the Bay's budget accommodations, this attractive eight-room guest house is set back from the A1. The hot tub in the yard is a nice touch. Look for the bright murals by the white gates.

Ultimate Jerk Centre JERK $
(meals J$500-750; ◉lunch & dinner) This popular rest stop and bar opposite Green Grotto Caves caters to a captive audience. The curry goat is very good, as is the bammy and festival, but you can find far better jerk elsewhere.

❶ Getting There & Away

Minibuses and route taxis ply the A1 between Montego Bay and Ocho Rios. They depart from the Texaco gas station, opposite the entrance to Puerto Seco Beach.

DRY HARBOUR MOUNTAINS

Paved roads lead south from Discovery Bay, Runaway Bay and St Ann's Bay and ascend into the Dry Harbour Mountains. In this off-the-beaten-track area, the badly potholed roads twist and turn through scenic countryside as they rise to the island's backbone.

Only two main roads run east–west. The lower, the 'Great Interior Rd' (the B11), parallels the coast about 11km inland. It begins at Rock, 2km east of Falmouth, and weaves east to Claremont.

Brown's Town

Brown's Town is a lively market town 11km south of Runaway Bay. Many noble houses on the hillsides hint at its relative prosperity. The town is at its most bustling during market days (Wednesday, Friday and Saturday), when the cast-iron Victoria Market (cnr Main St & Brown's Town Rd) overflows with *higglers* (street vendors).

Irish estate-owner Hamilton Brown (1776–1843) financed the building of St Mark's Anglican Church (cnr Main St & Brown's Town Rd) in Victorian Gothic style. Note the fine cut-stone courthouse (Brown's Town Rd) with neoclassical-columned portico.

Minibuses and route taxis run to St Ann's Bay, Kingston and Nine Mile from the east end of Top Rd, a block off Main St.

Nine Mile

The small community where Bob Marley was born, and is now buried, is set dramatically in the midst of the Cockpits. Despite its isolated location, the village is decidedly on the beaten path for tour groups playing pilgrimages to Marley's tomb, so be prepared for hustlers. Recently started are enterprising (but illegal) coffee plantation–style tasting tours of local ganja producers.

Nine Mile Museum   MUSEUM
(☎999-7003; www.ninemilejamaica.com; admission J$1900; ☺9:30am-4:30pm) In theory, Nine Mile Museum could be such a great attraction. The plain two-room house where Marley spent his early years is touching, as is his marble mausoleum, with its candles, Bible and stained-glass windows. Unfortunately, the site's relentless plastic commercialization, and the hoary tales from guides grubbing for tips may quickly depress the casual visitor, and upset those who ever got a spiritual lift from the man's music. Adjust your expectations accordingly.

❶ Getting There & Away

Nine Mile is linked by infrequent minibuses and route taxis from Brown's Town (which is in turn served by connections to St Ann's Bay and Kingston). Chukka Caribbean Adventures (☎972-2506; www.chukkacaribbean.com; tour US$65) runs the 'Zion Bus Line' tour from Ocho Rios. By car, follow signs from Claremonet on the A1. The mountain road is beautiful but in shockingly bad condition.

PORT ANTONIO

POP 15,000

If you took an ice-cream scoop out of the rainy northeast coast and surrounded it with a mess of markets, higglers and Georgian architecture in various states of disrepair, you'd get Port Antonio. There's definitely no Margaritavilles here; just a capillary-like tangle of backstreets, browsing goats and friendly locals. Wandering past the dilapidated houses lining the Titchfield Peninsula, it's very easy to think you've roamed into some quaint colonial ghost town.

Ironic, then, that the tentacles of Jamaican tourism first found purchase in Port Antonio. The island's major banana port, its prosperity began luring visitors at the turn of the 20th

ERROL FLYNN

Hollywood idol Errol Flynn arrived in Portland parish in 1946 when his yacht *Zacca* washed ashore in bad weather. Flynn fell in love with the area and made Port Antonio his playground and home. In his autobiography *My Wicked, Wicked Ways*, he described Port Antonio as, 'more beautiful than any woman I've ever seen.'

Flynn bought the Titchfield Hotel and Navy Island, where he threw wild, extravagant parties. Port Antonio's beguiling ways inevitably attracted the attention of other stars of stage and screen, such as Clara Bow, Bette Davis and Ginger Rogers.

With his third wife, Patrice Wymore, Flynn later established a cattle ranch at Boston Estate. He also planned a lavish home at Comfort Castle and had grandiose plans to develop Port Antonio into a tourist resort. But heavy drinking and a profligate lifestyle added to his ill health, and he died in 1959 aged just 50. The wild parties are no more, but his legend lives on.

century. Celebrity visitors, led by cinematic swashbuckler Errol Flynn, descended on the town in the 1940s. When the tourist attentions moved on to the west of the island, Port Antonio reverted to bananas. As a gateway to lush Portland parish, its laid-back attitude makes it a perfect destination for travelers seeking to get away from it all.

History

Port Antonio had a slow start in life. Spanish 'Puerto Anton' never thrived, while the British town of Titchfield on the peninsula suffered throughout the 18th century from coastal fevers and raids by the local Maroons. It wasn't until 1871 that the town came into its own, when fruit shipping magnate Captain Lorenzo Dow Baker settled here. Baker established the banana trade here, turning Port Antonio into a true boomtown as the 'banana capital of the world.'

In the 1890s Baker began shipping in tourists from the US in his empty banana boats. Although Portland's banana bonanza was doomed in the 1930s by the onset of Panama disease, the arrival of movie star Errol Flynn and, later, numerous bluebloods and Hollywood stars, gave new cachet to Port Antonio as a tourist resort. The jet-set continued to visit through the 1960s, when hip new resorts were built.

Sadly, Port Antonio has been in quiet decline ever since. Tourist dollars migrated to Negril and Montego Bay, and Jamaica's banana trade has been out-competed in the world market by Latin America.

◎ Sights

Town Square & Around　　　SQUARE

Port Antonio's heart is the Town Sq, at the corner of West St and Harbour St. It's centered on a clock tower and backed by a handsome red-brick Georgian courthouse from 1895; the building is surrounded by a veranda supported by Scottish iron columns and topped by a handsome cupola, and is now a

Port Antonio

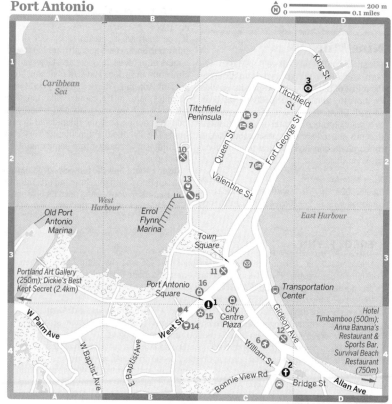

branch of National Commercial Bank. About 50m down West St is the junction of William St, where the smaller Port Antonio Sq has a cenotaph honoring Jamaicans who gave their lives in the two world wars.

On the west side is Musgrave Market (p97), decked out in yellows and blues, a quintessential chaotic developing-world market supported by thick limestone columns. Following William St south to Harbour St, you can turn left to peek inside Christ Church, a red-brick Anglican building constructed in neo-Romanesque style around 1840 (much of the structure dates from 1903). Look for the brass lectern donated by banana-magnate Captain Lorenzo Dow Baker.

On the north side of the Town Sq is the marvelously baroque facade of the Royal Mall, a three-story complex painted a striking red, now more or less a covered shopping parade decorated and designed in a plethora of styles, including Tudor and Renaissance.

Errol Flynn Marina   MARINA
(993-3209, 715-6044; www.errolflynn marina.com; Port Antonio, GPS N 18.168889°, W -76.450556°) Port Antonio has, undoubtedly, one of the finest natural harbors in Jamaica, which has been converted into a posh yacht-ing dock where sailboats moor and the well-to-do wander. At night it's a popular place for young couples to stroll along the paths that snake around a few upmarket restaurants and shopping centers – a quiet retreat from the bustle of town.

Titchfield Peninsula   NOTABLE BUILDING
Along this hilly peninsula – known locally as 'the Hill' – are several dozen Victorian-style gingerbread houses, most notably DeMontevin Lodge (p96), an ornate rust-red mansion, now a hotel. Many of the finest homes line King St, which runs down the center of the peninsula (parallel to Queen and Fort George Sts). The peninsula is a National Heritage Trust site and has been slated to receive restoration for a while now. This is a relatively well-off area, but one with a romantically sad sense of glamour gone by. Further north at the tip of the peninsula are the ruins of Fort George, dating from 1729. The parade ground and former barracks today house Titchfield School (closed to the public). Beyond the school, several George III–era cannons can still be seen mounted in their embrasures in 3m-thick walls.

Navy Island   ISLAND
This lushly vegetated 25-hectare island is popular with local day-trippers on weekends – or it was, when the ferries ran.

In colonial days the British Navy used it to careen ships for repair. In the mid-20th century Errol Flynn bought the island and built a home that became a hotel, which later fell into decay. In early 2002 the Port Authority and the Urban Development Corporation (UDC) jointly took over the island with a view to developing the jaded property as an upscale resort and ecological theme park, but nothing has come of it so far. Talk to fishermen on the docks or, more reliably, the folks at Dickie's Best Kept Secret (p97); they may be able to get you out here for a good day of stomping through the ruins.

Folly   RUIN
This rather appropriately named two-story, 60-room mansion on the peninsula east of East Harbour was built entirely of concrete in pseudo-Grecian style by North American millionaire Alfred Mitchell in 1902. Sea water was used in the concrete mix, however, causing the iron reinforcing rods to rust and the roof to collapse in 1936. What's left is a fantastically evocative ruin that deserves a place on the cover of *The Great Gatsby*. The shell of the structure remains, held aloft by limestone

columns, and makes a perfectly peculiar locale for a picnic. The orange candy-striped **Folly Point Lighthouse**, built in 1888, overlooks Woods Island.

🏃 Activities

You can charter sport-fishing boats on the docks at Errol Flynn Marina. **Reel Sensations** (☑545-2384) is a reliable operator.

Lady G'Diver   DIVING
(☑995-0246, 715-5957; www.ladygdiver.com; Errol Flynn Marina; 2-/4-dive package US$84/152) A full-service dive shop at the marina, with daily dives, retail store, PADI instruction and equipment rentals. The folks here are pioneering the largely undiscovered dive sites in the area, including Courtney's Reef and Fisherman's Reef, a series of drops, canyons and outcrops of coral.

☞ Tours

Port Antonio makes an excellent base from which to take excursions into the forests of the Rio Grande Valley and into the Maroon country towns of Moore Town and Nanny Town.

Grand Valley Tours   HIKING TOURS
(☑993-4116, in the USA 401-647-4730; www.portantoniojamaica.com/gvt.html; 12 West St) Treks to Scatter and Fox Caves as well as hikes to Moore Town, Nanny Falls, Nanny Town and along the White River Trail.

Jamaica Explorations   ADVENTURE TOURS
(☑993-7267; www.jamaicaexplorations.com) Professional outfit based at Hotel Mocking Bird Hill that aims to promote ecocultural tourism in Portland and the Blue Mountains. Tailor-made guided soft-adventure tours include walking, hiking and cultural excursions.

🎉 Festivals & Events

Portland Jamboree   CARNIVAL
(☉mid-Aug) Full on one-week carnival with jonkanoo dancing (traditional Caribbean dancing with West African roots).

**Port Antonio International
Marlin Tournament**   FISHING
(☑927-0145; www.errolflynnmarina.com; ☉early Oct) Week-long fishing extravaganza.

🛏 Sleeping

Port Antonio has relatively restricted accommodation options, but there are several exceptional choices for all budgets a short drive to the east in Fairy Hill, so it's worth keeping your search as wide as possible, see p99.

Ivanhoe's   GUEST HOUSE $
(☑993-3043; 9 Queen St; r US$50-65; ❋🛜) Fantastic views across the whole of Port Antonio from breezy verandas, spotless white rooms and bargain rates are the hallmarks of this spot, the oldest guest house on historic Titchfield Hill. Meals are cooked to order.

**Ocean Crest Guest
House B&B**   GUEST HOUSE $
(☑993-4024; 7 Queen St; r US$40-60; ❋) A favorite with the backpacker crowd, this B&B has simple rooms with tile floors and an ice-creamesque pink-and-white color scheme. We don't mind; the lounge has a large-screen TV and the balconies have a stunning view of Port Antonio and its picturesque bay.

DeMontevin Lodge   GUEST HOUSE $
(☑993-2604; 21 Fort George St; d US$50, d with shared bathroom US$40) This venerable Victorian guest house has a homey ambience that blends modern kitsch and antiques reminiscent of Granny's parlor – the place could almost be the setting of a tropical Sherlock Holmes novel. The simple bedrooms (six with private bathrooms) are timeworn, but clean as a whistle.

Hotel Timbamboo   HOTEL $$
(☑993-2049; www.hoteltimbamboo.com; 5 Everleigh Park Rd; s US$60-75; 🅿❋🛜🏊) Offering rare comfort for a Port Antonio hotel so centrally located, the Timbamboo has spacious, sunny rooms with modern furniture, carpeted floors and cable TV. Some rooms have balconies with views of the Blue Mountains. The hotel's sun deck is a great place to unwind.

🍴 Eating

Kajama's Café   JAMAICAN $
(cnr Fort George & West Sts; mains J$300-750; ☉lunch & dinner) Upstairs facing the clock tower, this restaurant has a balcony painted like an athletics track. However, after filling up with big tasty plates of Jamaican stews and rice, plus smoothies and cake for dessert, you won't feel too much like a Usain Bolt–dash to your next destination. Excellent value.

The Italian Job   ITALIAN $
(29 Harbour St; pasta J$700, pizza/slice J$900/250) The fluorescent strip lights can be a bit harsh, but this is otherwise a jolly Italian-run checked-tablecloth sort of a place, with great

pasta dishes, pizza, sandwiches and crepes for dessert. The wine isn't bad, and it's a nice change of pace from jerk and rice.

Survival Beach Restaurant   JAMAICAN $
(24 Allan Ave; mains US$5-10; ⊙breakfast, lunch & dinner; 🖉) In addition to the usual local fare, natural juices and the best jelly coconut in town, this choice shack serves a tasty dish made with coconut milk, pumpkin, Irish potato, garlic, scallion, thyme, okra, string beans and three kinds of peas, served with sides of cabbage and callaloo. Just ask for the vital I-tal stew.

★ Dickie's Best Kept Secret   FUSION $$
(🖉809-6276; dinner US$20-40; ⊙dinner) Dickie's – a tiny pointy-roofed seaside hut on western outskirts of Port Antonio – offers enormous five-course meals in rooms best described as Bob Marley meets Alice in Wonderland. They'll cook almost anything you want (provided they have the ingredients) but trust their suggestion – that anything will be delicious. Reservations essential.

Anna Banana's Restaurant
& Sports Bar   JAMAICAN $$
(🖉715-6533; Allan Ave; breakfast J$300; seafood dinners J$800-1500; ⊙breakfast, lunch & dinner) Need seafood? Jerk? An open-air bar? Head to this breezy restaurant-bar, overlooking a small beach on the southern lip of the harbor, which specializes in jerk or barbecued chicken and pork and groaning plates of conch and lobster. Hit up the pool table or toss some darts afterwards.

Ambiance Lounge   INTERNATIONAL $$
(🖉354-0800; Errol Flynn Marina; mains US $11-20; ⊙lunch & dinner) This quality restaurant on top of the marina is an airy open-sided affair. Steaks, chops and fish prepared continental style, plus a few Jamaican classics are served up, with the restaurant giving over to a lounge-bar vibe later in the evening.

🍷 Drinking & Nightlife

As well as the following, Anna Banana's beachside bar is the place to go for darts, pool and a rum punch. Friday heats up with the help of local DJs.

Roof Club   NIGHTCLUB
(11 West St; ⊙8pm-late Thu-Sun) This is Port Antonio's infamous hang-loose, rough-around-the-edges reggae bar. Young men and women move from partner to partner. You're fair game for any stranger who wants to try to

extract a drink from you. It's relatively dead midweek when entry is free, but on weekends it hops and on Thursday – 'Ladies Nite' – this place gets nuts.

Marybell's Pub on the Pier   BAR
(Errol Flynn Marina, Ken Wright Dr; ☎) Inside Errol Flynn Marina, this is a good place to while away an afternoon (or evening) away from the pace of the town, at the cabana bar or one of the tables overlooking the bay. Light meals are available.

Club La Best   NIGHTCLUB
(Map p94; 5 West St; ⊙9:30pm-late) The liveliest spot in Port Antonio, La Best assumes a different identity depending on the evening. Dance-hall throbs into the wee hours on Friday; Sunday grooves to a mellow blend of reggae and old-school R&B; ladies' night is Friday; and periodic live shows occur on Saturday.

🛍 Shopping

Musgrave Market   MARKET
(West St) There's a small craft market on the north side. Look for a stand called **Rock Bottom** selling well-made crafts and reggae-inspired duds.

Portland Art Gallery   ART
(🖉882-7732; 2 West Palm Ave) A simple gallery and studio staffed by Hopeton Cargill, a Port Antonio realist painter. He's delighted to act as an ambassador for the local art scene.

ℹ Information

EMERGENCY
Police station (🖉993-2546, 993-2527)

INTERNET ACCESS
Dekal Internet Café & Bistro (City Centre Plaza; sandwiches from JS$250, wi-fi free with an order; ⊙9am-7pm Mon-Thu, 9am-9pm Fri & Sat; ☎)

INTERNET RESOURCES
Port Antonio (www.portantoniotravel.com) The official online visitor's guide.

MEDICAL SERVICES
City Plaza Pharmacy (🖉993-2620; City Centre Plaza, Harbour St)
Port Antonio Hospital (🖉993-2646; Nuttall Rd; ⊙24hr) Above the town on Naylor's Hill, south of West Harbour.

MONEY
CIBC Jamaica Banking Centre (🖉993-2708; 3 West St)

FX Trader Cambio (☑ 993 3617; City Centre Plaza, Harbour St)

National Commercial Bank (☑ 993-9822; 5 West St)

RBTT Bank (☑ 993-9755; 28 Harbour St)

Scotiabank (☑ 993-2523; 3 Harbour St)

POST

Post office (☑ 993-2651; Harbour St) On the east side of Town Sq.

ⓘ Getting There & Around

The town center lies at the base of the Titchfield Peninsula, where the two main drags meet at a right angle in front of the main plaza and courthouse.

BOAT

Errol Flynn Marina (☑ 993-3209, 715-6044; www.errolflynnmarina.com; Errol Flynn Marina, Port Antonio; GPS N 18.168889°, W -76.450556°) Customs clearance for private vessels,

CAR

There are gas stations on West Palm Ave, Fort George St and Harbour St.

Eastern Rent-a-Car (☑ 993-4364; 16 Harbour St)

PUBLIC TRANSPORTATION

There's a **transportation center** (Gideon Ave) that extends along the waterfront, with minibuses leaving regularly for Kingston (to Halfway Tree bus station; J$450, two hours) via Buff Bay, and Port Maria (where you change for Ocho Rios). Route taxis depart constantly for Fairy Hill (J$100, 10 minutes), Boston Bay (J$150, 20 minutes), and Manchioneal (J$250, 40 minutes).

TAXI

For licensed taxis, call **JUTA/Port Antonio Cab Drivers' Co-op** (☑ 993-2684). Taxis hang out by hotels. They can also be found pretty easily in town, notably along Gideon Ave and the intersection of **Bridge St** and **Summers Town Rd**. Licensed taxis to Port Antonio cost about US$100 from Kingston and US$250 from Montego Bay.

EAST OF PORT ANTONIO

Port Antonio to Fairy Hill

The A4 meanders east of Port Antonio through thick forest, jagged-tooth bays, pocket coves and the coastal villages of Drapers, Frenchman's Cove and Fairy Hill. This is where most visitors to Port Antonio, and

indeed to Portland, will find accommodations and explore the nearby Rio Grande Valley, Nonsuch Caves and Blue Lagoon as well as the luxuriant sands of Winnifred Beach, Frenchman's Cove and San San Beach. Back in the 1950s and '60s, vacationing A-listers nicknamed this beautiful area the 'Jamaican Riviera,' and today many Jamaicans still name Portland as their favorite part of the country.

⊙ Sights

★**Blue Lagoon** LAGOON

The waters that launched Brooke Shields' movie career are by any measure one of the most beautiful spots in Jamaica. The 55m-deep 'Blue Hole' (as it is known locally) opens to the sea through a narrow funnel, but is fed by freshwater springs that come in at about a depth of 40m. As a result the water changes color through every shade of jade and emerald during the day thanks to cold freshwater that blankets the warm mass of seawater lurking below.

You may encounter boat operators eager to take you on a short boat ride (US$25) to nearby **Cocktail Beach** (where parts of the Tom Cruise vehicle *Cocktail* was filmed) and rustic Monkey Island, a short distance away.

The lagoon is accessible from the road and is technically public property, but touts in the parking area may demand an entrance 'donation' – J$200 should assuage them.

★**Winnifred Beach** BEACH

FREE Perched like a baby bird on a cliff 13km east of Port Antonio you'll find the little hamlet of Fairy Hill and a rugged dirt track. Follow that road steeply downhill and you'll reach Winnifred Beach, yet another totally gorgeous beach that puts a lot of the sand in more famous places (ahem: MoBay, Negril) to shame. It's the only truly public beach on this stretch of the coast, and has a great vibe, with food and drink stands, weekend sound systems and Jamaicans from all walks of life.

Trident Castle LANDMARK

(www.castleportantonio.com) A strange slice of Ruritania in the Caribbean, this folly on a headland 3km from Port Antonio was built in the 1970s by the (in)famously eccentric Baroness Elizabeth Siglindy Stephan von Stephanie Thyssen, also known as Zigi Fami. Resembling a rather magnificent wedding cake, it is a popular backdrop for society weddings and music video shoots. Sadly, the castle is closed to the public, but it makes one hell of a landmark from the road.

THE FIGHT FOR A FREE WINNIFRED BEACH

Since around 2007, locals have been fighting to keep this, the last public beach in the area, free. The Jamaican government has been intent on developing Winnifred into a private resort, a move which will result in the displacement of a fair few local businesses as well as putting another beach outside local access. The fight is still ongoing as of this writing; in the meantime, locals continue to keep the beach sparkling clean for visitors and some may ask you for a donation if you visit.

Frenchman's Cove   BEACH

(admission J$700; ⊙9am-5pm) This little cove just east of Drapers boasts a small but perfect white-sand beach, where the water is fed by a freshwater river that spits directly into the ocean. The area is still technically owned by the **Frenchman's Cove Resort** (www.french manscove.com). There's a snack bar serving jerk chicken and fish, bike rental (US$20 a day), alfresco showers, bathrooms, a secure parking lot and the option of taking boat tours to the Blue Lagoon (US$20). Look for the entrance opposite the San San Golf Course.

San San Beach   BEACH

(admission J$700; ⊙10am-4pm) San San is another gorgeous private beach used by residents of the villas on Alligator Head, and guests of the Goblin Hill, Fern Hill and Jamaica Palace hotels. The bay is enclosed by a reef that's wonderful for snorkeling (US$10 per day) and kayaking (US$25 per hour). Undeveloped Monkey Island (there are no monkeys – damn) is a good snorkel spot, and you can swim here from the beach if you're in decent shape.

🏃 Activities

Scuba Diving   DIVING

Good scuba diving abounds: the shoreline east of Port Antonio boasts 13km of interconnected coral reefs and walls at an average of 100m to 300m offshore. Alligator Head is known for big sponge formations and black corals. Hammerhead sharks are common at Fairy Hill Bank.

For dive tours, instruction and equipment, contact Lady G'Diver (p96) at the Errol Flynn Marina in Port Antonio.

San San Golf Course & Bird Sanctuary   GOLF

(☑ 993-7645; 9/18 holes US$50/70; ⊙8am-5pm) The 18-hole golf course is laid out along valleys surrounded by rainforest. The bird sanctuary comprises primary forest and is not developed for tourism.

🛏 Sleeping

Drapers San Guest House   GUEST HOUSE $

(☑ 993-7118; www.draperssan.com; Hwy A4, Drapers; s/d with shared bathroom US$31/62, d/tr with private bathroom US$72/90; 🛜) Run by an Italian expat, activist and font of local knowledge, this cozy little house comprises two cottages with five doubles and one single room (two share a bathroom), all with fans, louvered windows and hot water. It's all very welcoming and family-oriented; there's a comfy lounge and communal kitchen and (excellent) dinners can be served by arrangement.

Mikuzi Vacation Cottages   COTTAGE $

(☑ 480-9827, 978-4859; www.mikuzijamaica.com; Hwy A4, Fairy Hill; r US$40-60; 🛜) Mikuzi is wonderful: kind of funky, kind of romantic, set in pleasingly landscaped grounds and close to Winnifred Beach. It's a perfect hideaway, especially for couples. The property is divided between candy-bright cottages (the cheaper one lacks a kitchen), a small house and nicely kitted-out studio apartment. Meals available on request (breakfast not included).

San San Tropez   HOTEL $$

(☑ 993-7213; www.sansantropez.com; Hwy A4, San San Bay; s/d US$85/125; 🅿❄🛜🍽) This friendly Italian-run hotel has gracious, well-lit rooms and suites and a palpably European small-resort feel. The furnishings are modern and graced by bright tropical decor, there's a nice sun deck and the adjoining restaurant has splendid views and better food (meal plans are offered). Gives passes to San San Beach.

Jamaica Palace   HOTEL $$

(☑ 993-7720; www.jamaica-palacehotel.com; Hwy A4; r deluxe/superior US$170/190, ste US$230-320; 🅿❄🛜🍽) A neoclassical property overlooking Turtle Cove, Jamaica Palace almost feels more art gallery than hotel, perhaps like one of the original grande dames of the Jamaican Riviera. Cavernous rooms and suites boast crystal chandeliers, antiques and Georgian bay windows. In the landscaped grounds is a 35m-long pool shaped like the island of Jamaica.

Frenchman's Cove RESORT $$
(☑933-7270; www.frenchmanscove.com; r/ste US$110/145, 1-/2-/3-bedroom cottages US$165/260/360; P✳🛜🏊) This old great house frankly feels its age a little; back when Errol Flynn was the talk of the town we're sure this hotel was a big deal too, but today some of the stone cottages and '70s modernist condos feel a bit dated. That said, lovely staff and ready access to one of Jamaica's prettiest beaches make amends.

Moon San Villas VILLA $$
(☑993-7777; www.moonsanvilla.com; Hwy A4, Fairy Hill; r incl breakfast US$145-195; P✳🛜🏊) Sitting above Blue Lagoon, this is a tastefully decorated three-level house with a big-windowed lounge and bedrooms you could get lost in, all with wide windows, good views, fans and romantic (if frilly) decor. The bargain rates include a gourmet breakfast, access to a snorkel boat and passes for Blue Mountain Bicycle Tours (p30). French-inspired meals are offered on request.

★Kanopi House HOTEL $$$
(☑632-3213, in the USA 305-677-3525; www.kanopihouse.com; Hwy A4, Drapers; r from US$300; ✳🛜🏊) 🏄 This Blue Lagoon ecoresort deserves the accolades given in honor of its luxury and comfort. Dark-wood chalets that seemingly grow from the jungle makes it feel like you're staying in a laid-back five-star hotel carved into a banyan tree. The property makes great efforts to leave a low ecological footprint and is stuffed with elegant art. Fresh organic dinners are prepared on site.

★Gee Jam HOTEL $$$
(☑993-7000, 993-7302; www.geejamhotel.com; off Hwy A4, San San Bay; r US$495-795, ste from US$995; P✳🛜🏊) The hotel home of Gee Jam recording studios sets the standard for ultra-modern design, cuisine and exclusivity. There's a definite Manhattan penthouse vibe, with cottages connected by jungle walkways with views of the coast. Owner Jon Baker is a music-industry veteran with a taste for hip-hop and reggae – guests who've stayed here form their own Grammy Award nominees list.

★Hotel Mocking Bird Hill HOTEL $$$
(☑993-7267/134; www.hotelmockingbirdhill.com; Mocking Bird Hill Rd; r US$190-295, ste US$348-600; 🛜🏊) 🏄 The Mocking Bird is one of the most vigorous proponents of ecotourism in Portland. The property is a lovely maison at the end of a winding dirt road; all rooms are lovingly appointed with well-chosen fabrics and art, ocean views and private balconies. Meals at the Mille Fleurs restaurant are sublime. Trails through the hillside gardens are fabulous for birding.

🍴 Eating & Drinking

This stretch of road has many accommodations but few independent restaurants. Most folks eat at their hotels – which generally have restaurants open to nonguests – or are catered to by the staff of their villa.

Woody's JAMAICAN $
(Hwy A4, Drapers; mains J$300-800; ⊘lunch & dinner) This brilliant spot – with an outdoor patio and an indoor counter that doubles as a local meeting place – prepares tremendous hotdogs and burgers, grilled cheese and Jamaican dinners to order. Vegetarians are catered for by a veggie burger heaped with stewed callaloo. Charming hosts make this a winning experience.

Sir Pluggy's JERK $
(Hwy A4, Drapers; mains J$400-800; ⊘lunch & dinner) There are two things that can't be beat about Sir Pluggy's: the name and the jerk. Smell that sweet smoke, order by the pound and fill dem belly up.

San San Tropez ITALIAN $$
(☑993-7213; Hwy A4, San San Bay; mains US$12-25; ⊘breakfast, lunch & dinner) The enormous menu here has one focus: Italian food, home-cooked and cooked right. It's relatively simple stuff (if you've ever been to an Italian restaurant, you can probably recite the menu from rote memory), well-prepped and filling; the seafood and pizza are standouts. There's a large wine list as well.

★Mille Fleurs JAMAICAN $$$
(☑993-7267; Hotel Mocking Bird Hill, Mocking Bird Hill Rd; 3-course dinner US$90; ⊘7am-10pm; 🥬) This restaurant at Hotel Mocking Bird Hill offers some of the best haute Jamaican cuisine on the island, savored on a gorgeous terrace and served with a sense of elegance and intimacy. The locally sourced organic menu is influenced by what ingredients are seasonally available, includes vegetarian options and ends with a cleansing trolley of regional liqueurs. Reservations required.

Bush Bar   FUSION **$$$**
(☑ 993-7000; Gee Jam; set meal US$70; ☺ dinner)
Set in a veranda that overlooks the jungle
and the ocean and ensconced in multiple
layers of hip, the restaurant at Gee Jam offers
an immaculate Asian-Jamaican fusion expe-
rience, replete with cocktails as neon-bright
as Vegas, chilled background music and that
ineffable sense of being part of life's winning
team, the perpetual in-crowd. Call ahead.

🛍 Shopping

Gallery Carriacou   ART
(☑ 993-7267; Hotel Mocking Bird Hill; ☺ 10am-5pm
Thu-Tue) Has a fabulous array of paintings,
ceramics, sculptures and other quality works
of fine art by local artists. It also hosts work-
shops for rural children and cultural events,
so it tends to be a social anchor for this part
of the island.

R Stewart   ART
(Hwy A4, Drapers) In Drapers you'll find the
roadside gallery of renowned self-taught
artist R Stewart, who more than likely will
be working on his latest canvas at the edge
of the road. His whimsical, masterful depic-
tions of Jamaican life regularly inspire im-
pulse buys from passersby.

ℹ Information

In the little hamlet of Drapers is a small **post
office** (☺ 8am-4pm Mon-Fri, 8am-midday Sat),
and a **police station** (☑ 993-7315) just east of
Frenchman's Cove.

ℹ Getting There & Away

Route taxis run throughout the day along this
stretch of road between Port Antonio and Bos-
ton Bay – fares in either direction are unlikely
to top J$100.

Boston Bay

Boston Bay is a pocket-sized beach shelving
into turquoise waters. High surf rolls into the
bay, making it a popular place to catch some
waves. You can rent boards on the beach for
around US$15.

Boston is equally famous for its highly
spiced jerk. Today, jerk has a worldwide fan
base and is pretty much synonymous with
Jamaican cuisine, but until the 1950s it was
virtually unknown outside this area. The prac-
tice of marinating meat with jerk seasoning
was first developed centuries ago not far from
here by the Maroons, and the modest shacks

at Boston Bay were among the first to invite
attention – well worth making a detour for.

🛏 Sleeping & Eating

★ **Great Huts**   RESORT **$$**
(☑ 353-3388; www.greathuts.com; Boston Beach
Lane; African-style hut per person US$55-80, tree-
house US$163-255; 🐾) A green 'ecovillage'
meets sculpture park overlooking Boston
Bay, this is a distinctive and imaginative
collection of African-style huts and tree-
houses with open verandas, bamboo-walled
bedrooms and alfresco showers. There's a
private beach, a walking trail along the cliff,
Afro-centric library and a great restaurant/
bar with live music on Saturday. If only all
resorts in Jamaica felt this 'inclusive.'

Jerk stands   JAMAICAN **$**
(J$400-800) At the entrance to Boston Bay
you'll see a clutch of smoky jerk pits on
the roadside. Vendors vie for your custom;
they're all pretty good, though Mikey's produces a complexity of heat and sweet that has
us shuddering at the memory.

ℹ Getting There & Away

Boston Bay is 15km east of Port Antonio; buses
(J$100) leave early in the morning (8am) and
around 5pm; route taxis ($J200) are a more
convenient option.

Long Bay

Long Bay is well-named; its creamy beach
sweeps for 1.5km, with strong breezes push-
ing the waves forcefully ashore. A strong
undertow makes it bad for swimming, but
surfers love the waves.

While the strong easterlies bring good surf
it also leaves Long Bay exposed to extreme
weather. Once a big draw for backpackers,
the hamlet has a slightly forlorn hurricane-
battered air today, with many once-popular
restaurants and guest houses now closed.
Locals hope for better weather to come.

🛏 Sleeping

Blue Heaven Resort   GUEST HOUSE **$**
(☑ 892-2195; www.blueheavenjamaica.com; dm/d
J$1500/3000; ⚹🐾) A very basic Italian-run
backpackers with whitewashed rooms,
shared bathrooms and private beach access.
It's a bit unloved and run-down, but the
knock-down price makes it a fair option in a
pinch. Italian food available on request, along
with surfing gear to rent.

Hotel Jamaican Colors   HOTEL $$

(☎407-4412, 893-5185; www.hoteljamaicancolors.com; Hwy A4; s/d/q/house US$70/80/130/136, aircon supplement US$18; P ❋ ☎ ☎) This spiffy French-run hotel is located on the cliffs 2km south of Long Bay and has 12 comfortable cottages, all with plush double beds draped with mosquito netting (there's also a house for rent that can sleep five; rates based on number of guests). The open-air restaurant is great, and the owners dispense good information for surfers.

✖ Eating

Numerous rustic beachside shacks sell inexpensive Jamaican fare and double as nofrills 'rum shops' with music at night; find the one with guests, music and laughter, pop in and enjoy yourself. The following restaurants are all located on the beach. For classy French fare, head to Hotel Jamaican Colors.

Y & V Sea View Restaurant   JAMAICAN $

At the cliffside entrance to Long Bay, this shack in red, green and gold with a Bob Marley mural is a popular place for Jamaican standards – plenty of filling chicken and fish with rice and the like. Eat outside in the breeze, and then clamber down the rocks to the beach below.

Fishermans Park   JAMAICAN $

On the main road in the center of Long Bay, Fishermans Park is a lively open-sided restaurant/sports bar, with thatched seating area. Strong on fish (we also enjoyed the goat curry), with good-sized portions.

ⓘ Getting There & Away

Minibuses and route taxis run between Port Antonio and Long Bay (J$300, 25 minutes).

Reach Falls

Even in a country that abounds in waterfalls, Reach Falls stands out as one of the most beautiful places in Jamaica. The white rushing cascades are surrounded by a bowl of virgin rainforest; the water tumbles over limestone tiers from one hollowed, jade-colored pool into the next.

Once you enter the **falls** (adult/child US$10/5; ☺8:30am-4:30pm Wed-Sun) a guide will offer his services – crucial if you want to climb to the upper pools, which we highly recommend (there's a little underground, underwater tunnel a bit up the falls; plunging through is a

treat). The Mandingo Cave, the crown jewel of the falls, can be accessed at the top of the cascades, but you need to bring climbing shoes and be prepared for a long climb.

It's also possible to walk, wade and swim your way up to the edge of the falls, by an unmarked jungle path someway below the main entrance. It's an idyllic experience, with the forest and water all to yourself. Excellent local guide **Leonard Welsh** (☎849-6598) can take you, and point out plants and wildlife along the way.

The turning to Reach Falls is well-signed about 2km north of Manchioneal. Any Port Antonio–Manchioneal route taxi can drop you; it's a further 3km uphill to the falls.

Manchioneal

POP 2000

Keep heading about 2km south past Reach Falls and the road rises into a series of silly curves and waves around a vividly blue bay. Surrounding this bay is the fishing village Manchioneal (Man-kee-oh-neal), where colorful pirogues are drawn up on the wide, shallow beach. It's a center for lobster fishing and the surf is killer – July is said to be the best month.

Manchioneal is a culinary destination for roast fish or conch in foil, which you can purchase from small shacks on the beach later in the day after fishermen have come in with their catches. At the far end of the bay, Under the Rock Beach is a small cove with a bar that's a good spot to sip beer and let the day slip away. There's usually a sound system on Sunday. Another nearby private beach receives year-round visits from manatees – ask at Zion Country for details.

Three kilometers southeast of Manchioneal, Ennises Bay Beach is another great place to spend a lost afternoon. There's a refreshment stand and lovely views of the John Crow Mountains.

⌅ Sleeping & Eating

Zion Country   GUEST HOUSE $

(☎993-0435, 451-1737; www.zioncountry.com; s US$50, d without/with bathroom US$60/75) Four cute cottages built over the green cliffs overlooking Manchioneal bay and a chilled vibe lead to an excellent backpacker haven, with hammocks on the veranda and shared bathrooms. There's a small bar/restaurant with lovely views, and steep steps leading down to the beach.

Bryan's Restaurant   JAMAICAN **$**
(Main St; meals J$200-600) A rooftop eatery that offers simple but delicious Jamaican fare, served on a sunny veranda. Pay for your meal at the B&L Supermarket on the 1st floor before heading upstairs.

❶ Getting There & Away

Minibuses and route taxis run between Port Antonio and here (J$250, 40 minutes). Taxis can take you to Reach Falls for around J$1000. If you have your own vehicle, you can follow the coastal road south until it becomes the A2 heading to Kingston (beware of floods in the rainy season).

RIO GRANDE VALLEY

The Rio Grande river, fed by the frequent rains of wet Portland parish, rushes down from 900m in the Blue Mountains and has carved a huge gorge that forms a deep V-shaped wedge between the Blue Mountains to the west and the John Crow Mountains to the east. While not as remotely rugged as the Cockpit Country, the Rio Grande comes pretty close; if you need an escape from anything resembling a city, we recommend heading out here. The Maroons, descendants of escaped slaves who have retained a strong sense of their African cultural heritage, have a strong presence here; to distinguish themselves from their cousins in the Cockpit Country, they are referred to as the Windward Maroons.

Red Hassell Rd runs south from Port Antonio and enters the Rio Grande Valley at Fellowship.

Moore Town

This one-street village, 16km south of Port Antonio, stretches uphill for several hundred meters along the Wildcane River. Today it looks like any other Jamaican village, but historically it occupies a space of some importance as the former base of the Windward Maroons. The village was founded in 1739 following the signing of a peace treaty granting the Maroons their independence. Moore Town is still run semi-autonomously by a council of 24 elected members headed by a 'colonel.' The locals attempt to keep alive their lore and legends, and still bring out their *abengs* (goat horns) and talking drums on occasion, but many youth are emigrating to the cities.

Visitors expressing interest in the fascinating history of the Windward Maroons will be warmly welcomed. On arrival, it's considered polite to pay respects to the local colonel (Wallace Sterling during research; just ask around

---

OFF THE BEATEN TRACK

UPPER RIO GRANDE VALLEY
....

If you really want to get away from everything, head for **Ambassabeth Cabins** (📞395-5351; www.bowdenpenfarmers.com; cabins US$50) 🍃, a community tourism outfit in Bowden Pen that's an absolute gem. These rustic wooden cabins have running water but no electricity. You'll be treated to a true Maroon cultural experience, with indigenous folklore, Maroon cooking and local guides all on offer to take you along the **Cunha Cunha Pass Heritage Trail**. This is as educational and fun as stays in the Jamaican bush get.

The ranger station for Blue Mountains & John Crow National Park is at Millbank, 3km before Bowden Pen, near the summit ridge of the John Crow Mountains, which parallels the valley like a great castle wall. A trail leads to the **White River Falls**, a series of seven cascades, while beyond you may find the ruins of abandoned Maroon villages. Be advised that this is a tough trek through some serious rainforest, so get a Maroon guide at Ambassabeth or Millbank.

A short distance above Bowden Pen the track begins rising more precipitously and the vegetation closes in. The trail (passable on foot only) continues over the **Corn Puss Gap** and into St Thomas – a fabulous trek for the well-prepared.

To get to the Upper Rio Grande, the road to the right of the Y-junction at Seaman's Valley leads via Alligator Church to Bowden Pen, 16km or so up the river valley. The paved road ends at Alligator Church. Beyond here, the dirt road is extremely rough and narrow and you'll need a 4WD.

Valley Hikes and **Grand Valley Tours** (📞401-647-4730; www.portantoniojamaica.com/gvt.html) in Port Antonio offer tours; the latter operates a campsite just beyond Millbank.

HIKING THE RIO GRANDE

Popular hikes include those to White Valley, known for its large population of giant swallowtail butterflies; to Dry River Falls; and to Scatter Falls and Fox Caves.

Other hikes are demanding, with muddy, overgrown trails and small rivers that require fording. Don't attempt to hike off the beaten path without a guide. The Corn Puss Gap trail is particularly difficult, as is the wild path from Windsor to Nanny Town.

Various companies offer organized hikes. In Port Antonio, contact Jamaica Explorations (p96) at Hotel Mocking Bird Hill, or Grand Valley Tours (p96), which offers treks to Scatter Falls and Fox Caves as well as hikes to Moore Town, Nanny Falls and Nanny Town. **Valley Hikes** (☑993-3881; Unit 41, Royal Mall, Port Antonio) is another locally run trekking outfit. **Sun Venture Tours** (☑960-6685; www.sunventuretours.com; 30 Balmoral Ave, Kingston), based in Kingston, offers hiking and cultural tours in the area. All of these outfits can organize homestays in the Rio Grande Valley, which is preferable to rocking up on your own or camping in an area you're unfamiliar with.

Scatter Falls & Fox Caves

An excellent and easy hike takes you to Scatter Falls and Fox Caves, reached by crossing the Rio Grande on a bamboo raft at Berridale, then hiking for 30 minutes through a series of hamlets and banana groves. The falls tumble through a curtain of ferns into a pool where you can take a refreshing dip. There are changing rooms nearby as well as toilets, a campground, a bamboo-and-thatch bar, and a kitchen that serves a hot lunch – though this must be ordered in advance through Grand Valley Tours, based in Kingston.

A steep, 15-minute hike from the falls leads to the caves, which have some intriguing formations, some of which resemble Rasta dreads. The roof is pitted with hollows in which tiny bats dangle, and you can see where the falls emanate from the caves.

As the path is unsigned and you'll be passing through private property, it's imperative that you visit accompanied by a guide.

Nanny Town

This former village stronghold belonging to the Windward Maroons is perched on the brink of a precipitous spur on the northeastern flank of Blue Mountain Peak, about 16km southwest of Moore Town as the crow flies. It is named for an 18th-century Ashanti warrior priestess and Maroon leader, now a national hero. In 1734 English troops brought swivel guns into the valley and blew up most of Nanny Town, but the local Maroons remained defiant. Essentially, they proved more trouble to subdue than they were worth, and Nanny Town was granted a sort of semi-autonomy that persists to this day.

It's a tough 16km hike from Windsor, 5km north of Moore Town. There are numerous side trails, and it's easy to get lost if you attempt to hike on your own.

and someone will take you to him). If he's not about, you may be approached by one of his emissaries and asked for a small donation. Trails lead from Moore Town, including one to a series of lovely pools at Nanny Falls, about 45 minutes away.

Grand Valley Tours (p96) in Port Antonio leads trips, including a 'Moonlight at Moore Town' community tour that aims to connect visitors to the spirit of the Maroons.

Moore Town's main site of interest is Bump Grave, at the southern, uppermost end of town. Topped by a flagpole flying the Maroon and Jamaican flags, the oblong stone and plaque mark the grave of Nanny, warrior woman freedom fighter and

chieftainess of the Maroons. There's a gate protecting the grave, but it can be opened for a small donation. Also be on the lookout for the church of Mother Roberts (the building is bedecked in flowers); it's the AME Zionist Deliverance Center, and is a major destination for faith healings.

Moore Town is unsigned and lies in a hollow to the left of a Y-junction at Seaman's Valley; the road to the right continues via Alligator Church through the Upper Rio Grande Valley. In Moore Town the road dead-ends in the village. Minibuses and route taxis operate to Moore Town from Port Antonio (about J$150). A minibus from Port Antonio runs in the early morning and again in the early afternoon.

WEST OF PORT ANTONIO

Port Antonio to Buff Bay

This otherwise uninspirational stretch of coast is best noted for Somerset Falls. A loop drive, however, can be made from here up the Swift River Valley, where plantations grow cacao.

☉ Sights

Somerset Falls   WATERFALL
(☑383-6970; www.somersetfallsjamaica.com; Hwy A4; admission J$1250; ☉9am-5pm) This dark waterfall is hidden in a deep gorge about 3km east of Hope Bay. The Daniels River cascades down through a lush garden of ferns, helico-nias, lilies and crotons into glistening tear-drop black pools. Visitors have to negotiate some steep, twisty steps to get here.

The site has a touristy restaurant, bar, ice-cream shop and small menagerie, but the falls themselves are unspoiled. The entrance fee includes a guided tour through a grotto by boat to the Hidden Fall, which tumbles 10m into a jade-colored grotto. Bring a swimsuit to enjoy the large swimming area.

🛏 Sleeping & Eating

Rio Vista Resort & Villas   GUEST HOUSE $$
(☑993-5444; www.riovistajamaica.com; Rafter's Rest; r US$90-125, villa US$195-270; P❋☎☒)
This guest house sits atop a ridge above the Rio Grande near the turnoff for Rafter's Rest, 6km west of Port Antonio. The house, built into the remains of a plantation house has enviable views across the river and moun-tains. The villas and rooms are a bit old-fashioned but lovely nonetheless, while the Buccaneer restaurant (meals from US$12) offers great fare.

ℹ Getting There & Away

Both route taxis (J$150) and minibuses (J$100) pass Somerset Falls and Hope Bay between An-notto Bay and Port Antonio.

Charles Town

A couple of miles inland from the modest town of Buff Bay is the Maroon settlement of Charles Town, home to the Asafu Culture Yard (☑445-2861; admission by donation). The Yard is a sort of house complex/gardens/museum operated by Maroon Colonel Lums-den, who's happy to clue visitors in to the nuances of Maroon culture. You can also get a guide to take you on a three-hour hike to an 18th-century coffee plantation and Nan-ny's Look Out, a viewpoint over the coast.

One of the largest African heritage events in the Jamaican cultural calendar, Fi Wi Sinting (www.fiwisinting.com) is held on a Sun-day in February at Nature's Way, 5km east of Buff Bay. There's an African marketplace, children's village, I-tal food and live music. In a moving ritual, the official celebration comes to a close when libation is poured in remembrance of those who survived the 'middle passage,' a term designating the pas-sage of slaves to Jamaica from Africa. A boat covered in flowers is released into the sea. A Kumina drum circle keeps a sizable crowd dancing deep into the night.

DON'T MISS

RAFTING THE RIO GRANDE

Errol Flynn supposedly initiated rafting on the Rio Grande during the 1940s, and moon-light raft trips were considered the ultimate activity among the fashionable.

Today paying passengers make the 11km journey of one to three hours (depending on water level) from Grant's Level (Rafter's Village), about 2km south of Berridale, to Rafter's Rest at St Margaret's Bay. When the moon is full, unforgettable night-time trips are offered. These are less regimented; your guide will be happy to pull over on a moon-drenched riverbank so that you can canoodle with your sweetie or just open the ice chests to release the beer.

Reserve at Rio Grande Experience (☑993-5778; per raft US$65) or at Rafter's Village at Grant's Level if you don't have reservations. This is a one-way trip, so if you're driv-ing you need to hire a driver to bring your car from Berridale to St Margaret's Bay (Rio Grande Experience will help for US$15; the drivers are insured, but make clear to them that you expect them to drive slowly and safely) or take a taxi from Port Antonio (US$20).

A route taxi from Port Antonio to Grant's Level costs J$200; they depart from the cor-ner of Bridge St and Summers Town Rd. Licensed taxis cost about US$20 round-trip.

Buff Bay itself is of little interest, but anyone passing through should grab a bite at the fabulous **Blueberry Hill Jerk Centre** (jerk meat J$300-750), on the road out to Port Antonio. Some aficionados claim this to be the best jerk in Portland parish, which is really saying something. We're inclined to agree; the sauce alone is deliciously punishing.

Annotto Bay

This erstwhile banana port is a downtrodden one-street town that springs to life for the Saturday market. The paltry remains of Fort George, and some gingerbread colonial-era structures with columned walkways, stand on Main St. The most intriguing is the venerable yellow-and-red brick Baptist chapel, built in 'village baroque' style in 1894, with cut-glass windows and curious biblical exhortations engraved at cornice height.

There's no reason to stay in Annotto Bay, but every August it hosts the **St Mary Mi Come From** (www.facebook.com/AStMary MiComeFrom; ⊘1st Sat in Aug) music festival, headlined by Cappleton and featuring other popular dancehall artists.

The best place to eat in Annotto Bay is the **Human Service Station** (mains J$200-600) at the side of the road to Buff Bay as you're leaving town. It serves decent fish and chicken stews.

Robin's Bay

The paved road from Annotto Bay ends at Robin's Bay (known as Strawberry Fields in the 1970s, when it was a hippie free-love haven). There are persistent rumors about pirate's treasure still hidden away in the area's sea caves. The area has some of the most rugged and undeveloped country on the north coast.

◉ Sights & Activities

Kwaaman & Tacky Waterfalls   WATERFALL
Kwaaman and Tacky Falls are so pristine and isolated that, if you stumbled across them wandering up the coast from Robin's Bay, you might be tempted to claim them as your own. Kwaaman Waterfall is a 32m cascade that

tumbles into a clear pool you can swim in. It's a nearly one-hour hike from Robin's Bay.

Gazing up from the water at the contorted rockface behind the falls, you'll be able to make out what appears to be dreadlocks formed in the rock by the continual flow of water over centuries. Tacky Falls lacks the dreads but is equally worth the visit, particularly if the weather's calm and you can take a boat ride from Robin's Bay.

Hiking Port Maria to Robin's Bay   HIKING
You can reach Robin's Bay from Port Maria by a hiking trail that leads along one of the few stretches of Jamaican coastline that remains pristine. Locals can lead you to remote Black Sand Beach, and the Kwaaman and Tacky Waterfalls.

🛏 Sleeping & Eating

River Lodge   GUEST HOUSE $
(☑995-3003; www.river-lodge.com; s US$25, d US$50-60, cottages US$105-135; P) This atmospheric option has sprouted from the ruins of an old Spanish fort. The rooms have white bleached-stone walls and are lit by skylights. The bathrooms (cold water only) are festooned with climbing ivy; the bathroom in the upstairs 'tower' room is alfresco. Meals (on request) are a social affair, served in a small thatched restaurant.

Strawberry Fields Together   RESORT $$
(☑999-7169; www.strawberryfieldstogether.com; camping per person US$15, junior cottage US$70-90, deluxe cottage US$180-300; P❄) This series of cottages is also popular with those on a budget due to the campground (bring your own tent). The cottages (which can sleep four to six) all have views to the hills and sea (there's a private beach), and some come with whirlpool baths. The surrounding land is lovely to trek through. Meals available.

❶ Getting There & Away

Any public transport that travels between Ocho Rios and Annotto Bay or Port Antonio will let you off at the junction to Robin's Bay on the A3. It's then a 6km walk to Robin's Bay (route taxis are far and few between, but there's a daily bus from Robin's Bay to Kingston). The hotels can arrange transfers.

Montego Bay & Northwest Coast

Why Go?

Home to the nation's largest airport and a busy Caribbean cruise terminal, Montego Bay is many people's first view of Jamaica before they get whisked off to the surrounding beaches, golf courses and all-inclusive resorts. So it's ironic that some of the area's most interesting haunts are not to be found in MoBay itself – an unremarkable city of clamor and traffic – but in the crinkled mountains and jagged coastlines that surround it. Lethe is a verdant jungle-like domain where resort escapees can partake in adrenaline sports such as zip-lining and river-rafting. Falmouth is Jamaica's historical masterpiece that still retains the grit of its slave-era roots. Cockpit Country is a roadless wilderness of hidden caves and eerily silent hills that's disorientating, even to hardened locals. Filling in the gaps is a dense network of small towns and tiny villages that pulsate with the rawness and romance of everyday Jamaican life.

Best Places to Stay

➡ Polkerris B&B (p118)

➡ Richmond Hill Inn (p119)

➡ Hotel Rio Bueno (p130)

➡ Fisherman's Inn (p129)

Best Tastes of Local Life

➡ Far Out Fish Hut (p126)

➡ Chilli Pepper (p120)

➡ Miss Lilly's (p134)

➡ Lobster Bowl Restaurant (p130)

When to Go
Montego Bay

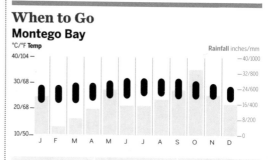

Dec–Mar High season is good for avoiding rain, but expect high rates.

Apr–Aug In low season the coast and mountains are cooler, and lodging is cheaper.

Sep–Nov Low-key festivals and moody weather characterize shoulder season.

Montego Bay & Northwest Coast Highlights

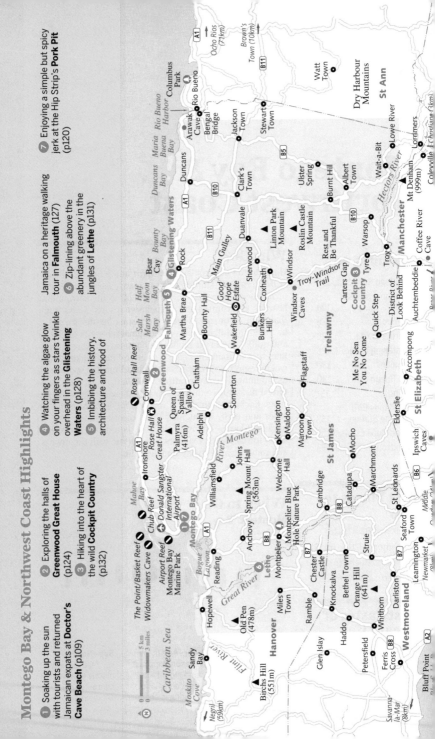

1 Soaking up the sun with tourists and returned Jamaican expats at **Doctor's Cave Beach** (p109)

2 Exploring the halls of **Greenwood Great House** (p124)

3 Hiking into the heart of the wild **Cockpit Country** (p132)

4 Watching the algae glow on your fingers as stars twinkle overhead in the **Glistening Waters** (p128)

5 Imbibing the history, architecture and food of Jamaica on a heritage walking tour in **Falmouth** (127)

6 Zip-lining above the abundant greenery in the jungles of **Lethe** (p131)

7 Enjoying a simple but spicy jerk at the Hip Strip's **Pork Pit** (p120)

MONTEGO BAY

POP 110,000

Montego Bay has two distinct faces: there's the smooth tourist countenance that grins contentedly from the pages of a thousand glossy Caribbean brochures; and there's MoBay proper, a pretty gritty city, second only to Kingston in terms of status and chaos. Most of the big all-inclusive resorts are located well outside the urban core in the fancy suburb of Ironshore. Stay in the city, however, and you're faced with an entirely different proposition – a riot of cacophonous car horns and bustling humanity that offers an unscripted and un-censored slice of Jamaican life, warts and all.

Hip Strip (aka Gloucester Avenue), with its mid-range hotels and ubiquitous souvenir shops flogging Bob Marley T-shirts, acts as a kind of decompression chamber between MoBay's two halves. You won't find many hipsters here, but, in among the hustlers and smoky jerk restaurants, there's a detectable Jamaican rhythm to the action on the street.

◉ Sights

◎ Hip Strip & the Beaches

★ Doctor's Cave Beach BEACH
(Map p116; ☑ 952-2566; www.doctorscavebathing club.com; adult/child US$6/3; ☺ 8:30am-sunset) It may sound like a rocky hole inhabited by lab-coated troglodytes, but this is actually Montego Bay's most famous beach. A pretty arc of sugary sand fronts a deep-blue gem studded with floating dive platforms and speckled with tourists sighing happily. Er, *lots* of tourists – and a fair few Jamaicans as well. The upside is an admission charge keeps out most of the beach hustlers.

Founded as a bathing club in 1906, Doc-tor's Cave earned its name when English chiropractor Sir Herbert Barker claimed the waters here had healing properties. People flocked to Montego Bay, kick-starting a tour-ism evolution that would culminate in the appearance of *Homo Margaritavillus* dec-ades later. There are lots of facilities on hand including a food court, grill bar, internet cafe and water sports, and lots of things to rent (beach chairs, towels, snorkeling gear).

Cornwall Beach BEACH
(Map p116; ☑ 979-0102; www.cornwallbeachja.com; admission $J350; ☺ 8am-6pm) Cornwall Beach has the most coolness cred out of Montego's beaches – if you're looking for a beach that feels like the spot where the cool locals hang

out (well, the cool locals willing to shell out $J350), this is your spot. There's a nice shal-low shelf for snorkeling, clear water for swim-ming and white sand for you to look good on. Every Wednesday an (open bar) beach party goes down here from 9pm til *oh-god-is-that-the-sun?*

Walter Fletcher Beach & Aquasol Theme Park BEACH
(Map p110; ☑ 979-9447; Gloucester Ave; adult/child US$5/3; ☺ 10am-10pm; ♠) While the theme park moniker is pushing it (the kid-orientated facilities consist of some blow-up water slides and a rusty go-cart circuit), this place on Wal-ter Fletcher Beach offers a decent spot to relax in a nonthreatening local environment; the cruise-ship day-trippers usually get bussed off to plusher Doctor's Cave up the road.

The beach is sandy and relatively clean and the water is safe for swimming with some limited snorkeling possibilities. Food and drink come courtesy of the onsite deck-bar with things heating up at sunset, especially at weekends. Look out for billboards advertising sporadic live-music events.

Dead End Beach BEACH
(Map p110) A meet-the-locals affair beside Kent Rd just north of Gloucester Ave, this narrow strip is also known as Buccaneer Beach. The lack of space promotes togetherness; at high tide it's pretty accurate to drop the 'beach' from 'dead end.' There are no facilities here, but the lack of crowds makes the sunsets over the bay all the more gorgeous.

◎ Downtown

Sam Sharpe Square SQUARE
(Map p114; Fort St) This bustling cobbled square is named for Samuel Sharpe (1801–32), na-tional hero and leader of the 1831 Christmas Rebellion. At the square's northwest corner is the **National Heroes Monument**, a bronze statue of Paul Bogle and Sam Sharpe, Bible in hand, speaking to three admirers. Nearby is the **Cage**, a tiny brick building built in 1806 as a lockup. The statue is the work of Jamai-can artist Kay Sullivan and has an appealing rawness to it. The Cage was originally built of wood, but unruly prisoners damaged it so much it was remodeled in stone. It now serves as a souvenir shop.

Civic Centre NOTABLE BUILDING
(Map p114; ☑ 952-5500, 971-9417; ☺ 9am-5pm Tue-Fri, 10am-3pm Sat, midday-5pm Sun) At the southwest corner of Sam Sharpe Sq you'll see

MONTEGO BAY & NORTHWEST COAST MONTEGO BAY

Montego Bay

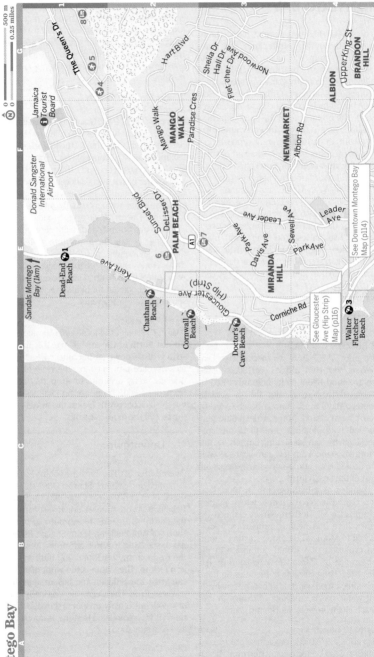

500 m
0.25 miles

The Queen's Dr

Jamaica Tourist Board

Donald Sangster International Airport

Sandals Montego Bay (1km)

Dead-End Beach 1

Kent Ave

Sunset Blvd

DeLisser Dr

PALM BEACH

A1

Chatham Beach

Gloucester Ave (Hip Strip)

Cornwall Beach

Doctor's Cave Beach

Corniche Rd

MIRANDA HILL

Davis Ave

Park Ave

Leader Ave

Sewell Ave

Park Ave

Leader Ave

NEWMARKET

Albion Rd

ALBION

Upper King St

BRANDON HILL

Hart Blvd

Sheila Dr

Hall Dr

Fletcher Ave

Norwood Ave

Mango Walk

MANGO WALK

Paradise Cres

See Downtown Montego Bay Map (p114)

See Gloucester Ave (Hip Strip) Map (p116)

Walter Fletcher Beach 3

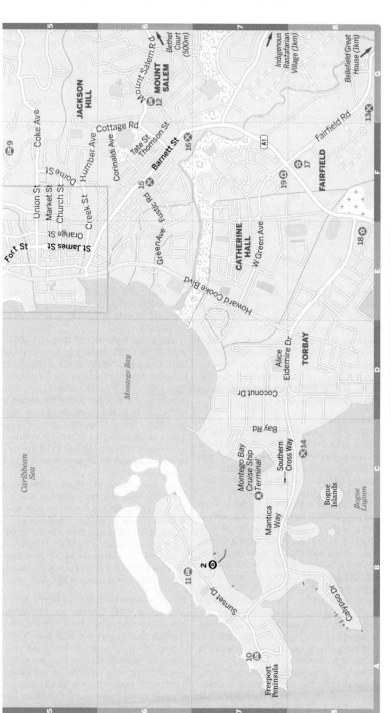

Montego Bay

the copper-domed Civic Centre, an elegant colonial-style cut-stone building on the site of a ruined colonial courthouse. It contains the small, not terribly well assembled, informative **Museum of St James**, replete with relics and other exhibits tracing the history of St James' parish from Taíno days to the present.

An art gallery and 200-seat theater are also on site, both of which host various events on the MoBay cultural calendar.

Church Street STREET
Many of the most interesting buildings in town are clustered along Church St, the most picturesque street in MoBay, although you shouldn't expect a quiet historic district – this thoroughfare is as alive and chaotic as anywhere else downtown.

The highlight is **St James Parish Church** (Map p114; 952-2775; Church St), regarded as the finest church on the island. It was built between 1775 and 1782 in the shape of a Greek cross, but was so damaged by the earthquake of March 1, 1957, that it had to be rebuilt. With luck, the tall church doors will be open (if they're not, call the rector at the above number) and you can view the interior, one of the most beautiful rooms in the whole of Jamaica. Note the wonderful stained glass and marble monuments, including some fine works by John Bacon, the foremost English sculptor of the late 18th century.

One is a memorial to Anne May Palmer, whose virtuous life was upended in literature to create the legend of the White Witch of Rose Hall. Look carefully at her neck and you'll detect faint purple marks. Locals con-

sider this proof of the fable that the 'witch' was strangled. Outside are the neglected (yet romantic, in a decaying way) gravestones of old planters.

The pretty **Town House** (Map p114; 952-2660; 16 Church St), fronted by a stately red-brick exterior, is buried under a cascade of bougainvillea and laburnum. The house dates from 1765, when it was the home of a wealthy merchant. It has since served as a church manse and later as a townhouse for the mistress of the Earl of Hereford, Governor of Jamaica. In the years that followed it was used as a hotel, warehouse, Masonic lodge, lawyer's office and synagogue (its current incarnation is a clothes store).

At the corner of Water Lane is a plantation-style octagonal structure that today houses a police station. About 50m west, at the corner of King St, is a redbrick Georgian building harboring the **National Housing Trust** (Map p114; 952-0063; 1 King St). A more impressive structure is the three-story **Georgian building** at 25 Church St – headquarters of Cable & Wireless Jamaica.

Burchell Memorial Baptist Church CHURCH
(Map p114; 952-6351; Market St) Two blocks east of Sam Sharpe Sq is one of the churches in which Sam Sharpe is said to have been a deacon. His remains are buried in the vault. The building, which dates to 1835, is a slice of British countryside architecture smoldering handsomely away in the tropical heat. The original church was founded in 1824 by Rev Thomas Burchell.

Creek Dome NOTABLE BUILDING

(Map p114; cnr Dome & Creek Sts) Lurking at the end of Creek St is the bizarre-looking Creek Dome, built in 1837 above the underground spring that supplied drinking water for Montego Bay. The structure is actually a hexagon with a crenellated castle turret in which the 'Keeper of the Creek' lived and collected a toll on the dispensation of drinking water.

◎ Around Montego Bay

Bellefield Great House GREAT HOUSE

(☑ 952-2382; www.bellefieldgreathouse.com; basic tour US$28, lunch tour adult US$40; ⊙ 11am-4pm Tue-Thu by reservation) The sea of sugarcane south of Montego Bay is part of the Barnett Estate, a plantation owned and operated since 1755 by the Kerr-Jarretts, one of Jamaica's preeminent families. Today the family holds the land and its accompanying Great House, the Bellefield, in trust for the government.

Built in 1735, Bellefield has been restored and is now a showcase of 18th-century colonial living and Jamaican culinary history, which makes for an interesting mash-up. You'll get to see the local gardens, meander past an on-site jerk pit, get pleasantly drunk on rum punch, wander the house and then gorge yourself at a delicious lunch buffet. Tours must be arranged at least 24 hours in advance, with a four-person minimum.

The estate is about 800m to the east of Doctor's Hospital, about 15 minutes from downtown Montego Bay heading southeast along Fairfield Rd. It's poorly signed: take the right turn at the Y-fork marked for Day-O Plantation, then the signed right turn at Granville Police Station.

**Montego Bay Marine Park
& Bogue Lagoon** NATURE RESERVE

(☑ 952-5619; www.mbmp.org) The waters of Montego Bay are gorgeous to behold both above and below the surface, but they have long been compromised by the effects of fishing, water sports and pollution. With the crea-tion in 1991 of the Montego Bay Marine Park, environmental regulations began to be strictly enforced to protect the area's coral reefs, flora and fauna, and shoreline mangroves.

The park extends from the eastern end of the airport almost 10km west to the Great River, encompassing the mangroves of Bogue Lagoon. You can hire canoes or a guide to spot herons, egrets, pelicans and waterfowl – swimming and crawling below are barracudas, tarpon, snapper, crabs and lobsters. Request a guide two days in advance; there's no charge but donations are gladly accepted. Authority is vested in the Montego Bay Marine Park Trust (MBMPT), which maintains a meager **resource center** (Map p114; ☑ 952-5619; Pier One Complex, off Howard Cooke Blvd; ⊙ 9am-5pm Mon-Fri), with a library on the vital ecosystem, where bookings can be made.

**Indigenous
Rastafarian Village** RASTAFARIAN VILLAGE

(☑ 285-4750; www.rastavillage.com; Fairfield Rd; 2hr/1-day tour US$25/100; ⊙ tours by appointment) If you want to learn about the Rastafari movement beyond the effort of popping in a Marley CD, come out to this...hmmm...'village', a good introduction to Jamaica's most famous indigenous religion. You'll be taken through a jungle settlement, shown medicinal plants (not what you're thinking), and given a breakdown of what the Rasta faith traditionally believed in. As most travelers don't learn much about Rastafari past the ramblings of dreadlocked hustlers, this is a valuable experience, and the all-day tour includes some lovely treks into the surrounding countryside, complete with swimming in paradisal natural pools.

If coming from downtown MoBay, head south on Barnett St and turn left at the Westgate Shopping Centre. You'll need either your own wheels (it's a lovely drive) or to pre-arrange a visit – which can easily be done through your accommodations. Even if you drive yourself, we recommend calling ahead; the village may not be ready to deal with drop-in visitors.

FORT MONTEGO'S QUIET CANNONS

At the southern end of the Hip Strip a set of stairs leads steeply up to a square of old rocks dubbed, somewhat ambitiously, **Fort Montego** (Map p114; Fort St) complete with rusty cannons. The cannons were only fired twice, and both times were a fiasco. The first shot, in celebration of the capture of Havana in 1762, was a misfire that killed an artilleryman. The second time the cannoneers screwed up and shot at one of their own ships, the *Mercury,* which was carrying a dangerous cargo of...dogs. Fortunately the cannon crews (as you may have guessed by now) weren't the best at their jobs and missed the *Mercury*. There's a fairly uninspiring craft market next to the fort.

Downtown Montego Bay

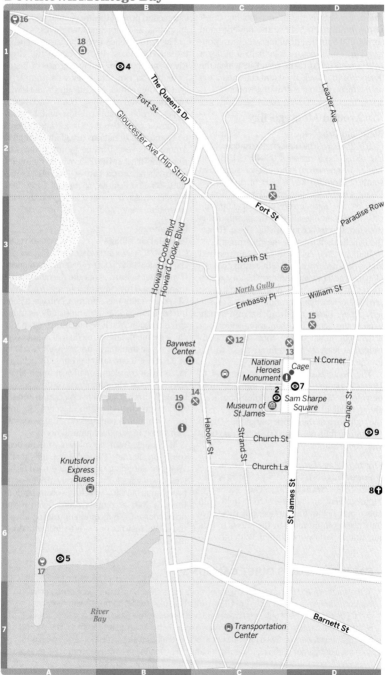

Leader Ave

The Queen's Dr

Fort St

Gloucester Ave (Hip Strip)

Fort St

Paradise Row

North St

Howard Cooke Blvd
Howard Cooke Blvd

North Gully

Embassy Pl

William St

Baywest Center

National Heroes Monument

Cage

N Corner

Sam Sharpe Square

Museum of St James

Orange St

Church St

Harbour St

Strand St

Church La

St James St

Knutsford Express Buses

River Bay

Barnett St

Transportation Center

N
0 ——— 200 m
0 ——— 0.1 mile

Downtown Montego Bay

Freeport Peninsula   NEIGHBORHOOD
The artificially made Freeport Peninsula, constructed by making a causeway between several small lagoon islands in the 1960s, is located southwest of downtown Montego Bay and serves, among other functions, as the docking point for cruise ships. It's also home to the city's two most centrally located all-inclusives (including the posh Secrets resort). It's a bit of a hike from downtown, but worth it for drinks at the yacht club or dinner at the Houseboat Grill that floats amid the mangroves of the Bogue Lagoon.

Montego Bay Yacht Club   MARINA
(Map p110; ☑979-8038; www.mobayyachtclub.com; Montego Bay Freeport, GPS N 18.462452°, W -77.943267°; ⊙10am-10pm) If you come out to the peninsula, try to stop by this pretty and posh yacht club for a meal or drink; the hours indicated are for the on-site restaurant, **Robbie Joseph's Seahorse Grill**. Technically the club is only open to members, but if you present yourself at the entrance and ask politely to look around, you'll likely be invited inside.

Gloucester Ave (Hip Strip)

🏃 Activities

Diving

MoBay offers a few good dive sites. For advanced divers the **Point**, north of the airport, has a good wall dive due to the fish, sharks, rays and dense coral that are fed by crystal-clear waters scoured by currents. The wall here starts at 20m and drops to at least 90m. **Airport Reef**, off the southwest edge of the airport, is considered by some to be the best site on the island, with masses of coral canyons, caves and tunnels, and a DC-3 wreck that's become a multicolored mansion for masses of fish.

Besides boasting the sort of name you'd expect in a *Pirates of the Caribbean* movie, **Widowmakers Cave** is an incredible tunnel filled with sponges, barracuda and schools of smaller fish. This is a site for experienced divers who can navigate through the 21.3m (70ft) passage and out the top of its chimney. **Chub Reef**, a 12.2m (40ft) dive site located to the northeast of the city, is named for the preponderance of Bermuda chub, rather than any physical squatness. **Rose Hall Reef**, about 10km east of the city, is a shallow reef more suitable for less-experienced divers. The main attraction is the **Fairy Castle**, a pretty coral pillar. With all this said, don't dive here expecting top-rate macrodiving (ie lots of big fish). There are mantas, nurse sharks and the like in these waters, but most divers report seeing nothing larger than barracuda, reef fish and rock lobsters. Most dive centers also offer snorkeling trips and the following provide multiple levels of PADI certification:

Dressel Divers   DIVING
(☑ 321-392-2338; www.dresseldivers.com; Iberostar Rose Hall Resort, Rose Hall) Acclaimed international diving outfit with scuba centre in Iberostar Rose Hall Resort, 20km east of MoBay. Non-hotel guests are welcome on trips. For customized dive-package prices, use the online form on their website.

Resort Divers   DIVING
(Map p116; ☑ 973-6131; www.resortdivers.com; 2 Gloucester Ave; 1-/2-tank dive US$50/95) Located on the Hip Strip in the Royal DeCameron Hotel.

Jamaica Scuba Divers   DIVING
(☑ 957-3039; www.scuba-jamaica.com; 1-/2-tank dive US$60/100) Jamaica-wide scuba outfit.

Fishing
The waters off Jamaica's north coast offer spectacular game fishing. Deep-water game fish such as blue marlin, sailfish, wahoo, kingfish and yellowfin tuna use the abyss known as Marlin Alley as a migratory freeway (June and August are peak months for marlin). The **Montego Bay Marlin Tournament** is held in late September; contact the **Montego Bay Yacht Club** (Map p110; ☑ 979-8038).

Charters can be booked through hotels, or you can contact Howard Martin at **Deep Drop Fishing Charters** (Map p110; ☑ 876-572-0010; www.fishinginjamaica.com; Montego Bay Yacht Club), usually based at the yacht club.

Boat Trips
The number of party boat tours in Montego Bay is stupefying. Most companies charge US$45 to US$80 for three-hour party cruises with open bars, and US$35 to US$45 for sunset and dinner cruises. You can also charter yachts for private sailing trips from the Montego Bay Yacht Club at Montego Freeport.

Dreamer Catamaran Cruises   BOAT TRIPS
(Map p110; ☑ 979-0102; www.dreamercatamarans.com; Shop 204, Chatwick Plaza; cruise US$65; ⊙ cruises 10am-1pm & 3-6pm Mon-Sat) An outfit that offers a catamaran adventure on swift boats specially designed for partying, with an open bar and a snorkeling stop in the marine park. Cruises depart from Doctor's Cave Beach Club. A bus will pick you up at your hotel.

Tours
Between your hotel or guesthouse and touts on the Hip Strip, someone's gonna approach you about taking a tour. There are always customization options available; trips to places such as Negril, Dunn's River Falls and Nine Mile (the birthplace of Bob Marley, south of Ocho Rios) are de rigueur. If you find a taxi driver you get along with who offers to give you a personalized tour, consider the option: your money may go directly to someone you like, rather than being split among commission-takers.

Winston Tours   SIGHTSEEING TOURS
(☑ 324-1419, 957-2075; www.winstontours jamaica.com) Call Winston for a personalized, intimate tour via his own Jamaica Union of Travelers Association (JUTA)-approved minibus. He'll tailor schedules for individual itineraries, which provides a nice level of flexibility.

Phillip Country Tours   SIGHTSEEING TOURS
(☑ 843-9840; www.phillipcountrytours.com) Phillip provides personal (and personable) tours of his home island catering for individual travelers. A nice break from being herded around in a big bus.

Marzouca Tours   SIGHTSEEING TOURS
(Map p116; ☑ 876-971-3859; www.marzouca.com; 39 Gloucester Ave; ⊙9am-5pm Mon-Fri) Has an office on the Hip Strip. For something a bit different try their Montego Bay History Tour (US$40).

Maroon Attraction Tours   CULTURAL TOURS
(Map p114; ☑ 971-3900, 700-8805; 32 Church St) Runs cultural, educational and historical tours (US$60, 8am to 3:30pm Tuesday, Thursday & Saturday) to Maroon Town, south of MoBay.

John's Hall Adventure Tours   ADVENTURE TOURS
(Map p110; ☑ 971-7776; www.johnshalladventuretour.com; 26 Hobbs Ave) Includes fairly comprehensive tours of the south coast.

Caribic Vacations   SIGHTSEEING TOURS
(☑ 953-9895, 953-9896; www.caribicvacations.com; 1310 Providence Dr, Ironshore Estate) Caribic is a pretty big outfit, with well-trained tour guides. You'll be in the tourist herd, but the service is very reliable.

Festivals & Events
Held in the fall, alternating between October and November, **Africa Jamfest** celebrates the African roots of Afro-Caribbean culture.

Red Stripe Reggae Sumfest MUSIC
(www.reggaesumfest.com) Jamaica's premier reggae festival typically includes over 50 world-class reggae artists. Held in July, it starts with a beach party on Walter Fletcher Beach, followed by a week of nonstop partying.

🛏 Sleeping

The following places are within Montego Bay proper; the top-end resorts and all-inclusives tend to cluster east of town in Ironshore. Note that all prices are high season (ie December to March) rates, which can be double or more during events like Reggae Sumfest.

🛏 Gloucester Ave (Hip Strip)

Hotel Gloriana HOTEL **$**
(Map p110; ☎970-0669; www.hotelgloriana.com; 1-2 Sunset Blvd; r US$46-65; P❄🛜☷) The word 'glorious' might be overdoing it, but the Gloriana, run by a pugnacious local lady, is excellent value for money, located within suitcase-dragging distance of the airport and safe walking distance of the Hip Strip action. Austere from the outside, the inside is a veritable mini-resort with a fountain-embellished pool, recently updated rooms and a restaurant where Jamaicans easily outnumber tourists.

Don Way HOTEL **$**
(Map p116; www.donwayja.com; 36 Gloucester Ave; d US$89; P❄🛜) A new mini complex that styles itself as 'a Jamaican village', Don Way claims boutique hotel status, though it lacks character. Rooms are clean and modern, but beware the onsite attractions – bar, grill, wine shop and pool tables – that sometimes draw in a lot of noisy outsiders.

Caribic House HOTEL **$**
(Map p116; ☎979-6073; 69 Gloucester Ave; d without/with seaview US$67/79; ❄🛜) This no-frills spot across the street from Doctor's Cave Beach is a favorite for the budget-minded. Rooms are basic, the hot water doesn't always work and there's no real communal area, but, what the hell – you're a backpacker, right?

★Polkerris B&B B&B **$$**
(Map p116; ☎876-877-7784; www.polvista.com; 31 Corniche Rd; r US$165-175; P❄🛜☷) The best B&B in Jamaica? Maybe. The best B&B in Montego Bay? No question. Hanging above the Hip Strip like a beautiful apparition, Polkerris, run by a Jamaican woman and her British husband, is sublime in every detail. There's a trickling waterfall, the inviting swimming pool, the view-embellished veranda,

the stupendous breakfast and – most importantly – the one-of-the-family style service that reminds you warmly that you're in the real Jamaica.

Gloucestershire Hotel HOTEL **$$**
(Map p116; ☎876-952-4420; www.hotelcomthegloucestershirehotel.com; 92 Gloucester Ave; s/d $97/112; P❄@🛜☷) A recent refurb at the venerable Gloucestershire has added some modern boutique touches to its glistening white frontage – the faux-grand facade wouldn't look out of place in a British seaside resort, circa 1973. Investigate closer and you'll find some welcome extras including a reasonably equipped gym, Jacuzzi, swimming pool and almost elegant bar and restaurant.

Altamont West HOTEL **$$**
(Map p116; ☎979-9378, 979-9378; www.altamontwesthotel.com; 33 Gloucester Ave; r US$110-180; P❄🛜☷) Bright Caribbean colors lure hotel window-shoppers into one of the Hip Strip's better accommodation options. A baby grand piano furnishes the front veranda (good sign!) and there are plenty of local Jamaican motifs dotted around to remind you this is the real deal. Rooms don't quite match the salubrious common areas, but they are clean, so who cares?

Tobys Resort HOTEL **$$**
(Map p116; ☎952-4370; www.tobyresorts.com; cnr Gloucester Ave & Sunset Blvd; s/d/tr US$140/150/170; P❄🛜☷) Located just off the 'top' of the Hip Strip, Tobys provides admirable local vibe with amenities geared for international travelers not averse to stepping outside the all-inclusive. Staff make Tobys feel like a gracious guesthouse, but with the benefits of large grounds, comfy rooms, a big pool, and a good bar and restaurant.

Wexford HOTEL **$$**
(Map p116; ☎952-2854; www.thewexfordhotel.com; 39 Gloucester Ave; s/d US$114/126; P❄@☷) This hotel has undergone quite a few sprucings, and they've all been for the better. Rooms in the older wings are efficient but comfortable, while the newer wing offers more expensive digs decked out in minimalist boutique-style elegance. The Wexford is convenient for Aquasol theme park and its beach, to which guests have free access.

Royal Decameron Montego Beach Resort RESORT **$$$**
(Map p116; ☎952-4340; www.decameron.com; 2 Gloucester Ave; all-incl r US$185-220; P❄@☷) The Hip Strip's only all-inclusive is a low-key

version of the genre where 143 rooms with creamy orange-and-white color schemes enjoy a pretty, private stretch of beach overlooked by a competent restaurant. Rooms all have ocean views and balconies and there is a wide range of activities including tennis, kids games and water sports to satisfy its savvy and loyal clientele.

Miranda Hill

Jamaica Grandiosa Resort   GUESTHOUSE **$$**
(Map p110; ☑979-3205; www.grandiosahotel. com; 3 Ramparts Close; s/d US$95/105; ⓟ✳☒) This unassuming hilltop property has 38 rooms with modest furnishings, cable TV, grandiose views and varying quality – some are kept quite clean, but others have faulty hot water and rusty furnishings. The dining room has a lofty vista. There's a small breeze-swept pool and sundeck, plus a pool table and an undistinguished bar.

El Greco   APARTMENTS **$$**
(Map p116; ☑940-6116; www.elgrecojamaica. com; 34 Queens Dr; 1-/2-bedroom apt US$105/195; ⓟ✳☏☒) More like a condorental than a hotel, El Greco is a nice choice for those who value comfort and independence. The apartments have cable TV, kitchens and private balconies that look out to a well-equipped complex that includes a pool, laundry service, tennis courts and kids play area. Relax. This is an efficiently run operation.

Around Montego Bay

In the following places you're a taxi ride (shared and public, or private and pricey) away from the Hip Strip.

Bethel Court   HOSTEL **$**
(☑971-0134, 476-7239; bethelcourt.wordpress.com; Federal Ave; dm/r from US$20/40; ⓟ✳☏) Located in the peripheral, sometimes volatile, neighborhood of Mt Salem, Bethel Court is one of the few dedicated hostels in Jamaica. Run by the friendly Steve, who works hard to help set up tours and arrange transportation, it offers dorms and pretty basic private suites. The slightly out-of-the-way location necessitates route taxis to get in and out of town.

The View Guest House   GUESTHOUSE **$**
(Map p110; ☑952-3175; www.theviewguesthouseja. com; 56 Jarrett Tce; r $50; ✳☒) On the southeast edge of town on the downslope of Mt Salem Rd is this family-run, friendly option. Rooms are basic but clean and come with a lot of love. Return guests are fanatic in their loyalty to this place. Home-cooked meals are served, and it has a communal kitchen and bar, plus a view overlooking the city.

★**Richmond Hill Inn**   HOTEL **$$**
(Map p110; ☑952-3859; www.richmond-hill-inn.com; Union St; s/d/ste US$85/115/189; ⓟ✳☏☒) Stay in a historic Great House within Montego Bay's city limits. This spectacularly located

MONTEGO BAY'S ALL-INCLUSIVE HOTELS

Most of Montego Bay's all-inclusive resorts are set apart from the city in the upper-crust districts of Ironshore and Rose Hall to the east, neighborhoods embellished by modern shopping malls and manicured golf courses. Cream of the crop is the **Half Moon** (☑953-2211, in the USA 877-626-0592; www.halfmoon.rockresorts.com; r from US$489, ste from US$750, villas from US$2000; ⓟ✳☏☒), the favored turf of queens and princes, which feels more like a utopian village than a resort. Also here is the **Hilton Rose Hall** (☑953-2650, in the USA 866-799-3661; www.rosehallresort.com; all-incl r from US$429-499; ⓟ✳@☏☒), a humungous place with its own golf course, water park and 300m-long beachfront.

Just east of the airport and closer to Montego Bay is **Coyaba Beach Resort & Club** (☑953-9150, 800-237-3237; www.coyabaresortjamaica.com; r US$300-380, all-incl US$412-492; ⓟ@☒), different from the other behemoths in that it is family run, relatively small (50 rooms) and boutique in style. Nearby are two of the popular Sandals hotels: **Sandals Montego Bay** (☑952-5510; www.sandals.com; N Kent Ave; all-incl r from US$435; ⓟ✳☏☒), one of the great-grand-daddies of all-inclusive resorts, and **Sandals Royal Caribbean** (☑953-2231; www.sandals.com/main/royal/rj-home; 3 nights all-incl r from US$1500, ste from US$2200; ⓟ✳☏☒), a couples-only outpost of the Sandals empire that lays on nostalgia for the British Empire.

Slightly closer to MoBay's city center on the Freeport Peninsula near the cruise ship terminal are two more all-inclusives: the high-rise **Sunset Beach Resort & Spa** (Map p110; ☑800-888-1199, 979-8800; www.sunsetbeachjamaica.com; Sunset Dr; all-incl r from $US260; ⓟ✳☒) and the closely guarded, couples-only **Secrets St James** (Map p110; ☑953-6600; www.secretsresorts. com; Freeport; r from US$450; ⓟ✳@☏☒).

gem atop a small hill once belonged to the Scotch whisky heirs and is bedizened with fine local art, antique furniture and the ghosts of prestigious former guests. Richard Nixon and James Bond in his third incarnation (Roger Moore) both stayed here. Spacious rooms are a relative bargain.

Relax Resort RESORT $$
(Map p110; ☑979-0656; www.relax-resort.com; 26 Hobbs Ave; r US$140, studio US$162, 1-/2-bed apt US$174/265; P❄@🛜🏊) This breeze-swept resort is often used as a layover for tourists whose flights have been delayed, which means it gets a bad rap in Tripadvisor reviews by people who have just sauntered out of a Sandals or a Hilton. Nonetheless, those without sky-high expectations will enjoy the ample grounds and large rooms adorned with floral prints, tile floors and ocean views.

✗ Eating

Montego Bay is a good place to sample 'haute' Jamaican food. The steady influx of free-spending vacationers, many desperate to escape the tyranny of the all-inclusive meal plan, means there are plenty of upmarket restaurants. Cheap local eats are tough to find on the Hip Strip. As usual, if you see a jerk stand on the side of the road billowing clouds of blue smoke and attracting lots of locals, eat at it.

✗ Downtown

Nyam 'n' Jam JAMAICAN $
(Map p114; ☑876-952-1922; 17 Harbour St; mains J$300-700; ⊙8am-11pm) On the cusp of the craft market, you can retreat into the red glow of a truly authentic Jamaican dining experience with none of the tourist get-out clauses of the Hip Strip. Settle down for snapper with a spicy sauce, jerk chicken or perhaps your first curried goat.

Adwa VEGETARIAN $
(Map p114; ☑940-7618; City Centre Mall; mains J$180-400; ⊙8am-9pm; 🍴) Tiny space in a health-food shop in a small shopping mall that mixes up fantastic cheap vegetarian and I-tal fare, fruit juice and silky smoothies. The curry tofu and soy patties are delicious, and can be boxed up and taken to the beach.

Pier One AMERICAN $
(Map p114; ☑286-7208; www.pieronejamaica.com; Howard Cooke Blvd; mains US$8-18; ⊙11am-11pm daily, till 2am Wed) Best known as a nightclub, Pier One also has a restaurant with a good,

clean, waterfront setting. Usain Bolt sometimes 'bolts' in.

✗ Gloucester Ave (Hip Strip)

★ Pork Pit JERK $
(Map p116; ☑952-1046; 27 Gloucester Ave; mains J$300-800; ⊙11am-11pm) 'Pit' is the operative word at this glorified food shack on the Hip Strip where a half-roasted chef slaves over a blackened barbecue fashioned from bamboo sticks laid over smoking hot coals. Notwithstanding, his meat-cooking travails send a delicious aroma wafting down Gloucester Ave and provide a perfect advert for the Pork Pit's obligatory jerk pork.

Get it scooped straight off the barbecue into a Styrofoam container and sit down at a picnic table under the Pork Pit's 300-year-old cotton tree. It's a MoBay rite of passage.

Chilli Pepper JAMAICAN $
(Map p116; ☑257-4850; Montego Arcade, Gloucester Ave; mains J$700; ⊙7am-midnight Mon-Wed, 7am-1:30am Thu-Sat, 7am-1:30pm Sun) Ask a local for eating directions and you could well end up in this six-table Hip Strip hole-in-the-wall where the flavorful food arrives fast (unusual for Jamaica). You can play away with so-so international options (pizzas, burgers), but the homemade curried goat and smoothies are best.

CC's Coffee & Cupcakes CAFE $
(Map p116; ☑633-7550; 36 Gloucester Ave; pastries from US$2; ⊙24 hr; 🛜) Dive in off the hot Hip Strip for gulps of refreshing air-conditioned air, passable lattes and sweet cupcakes. There's also wi-fi and some savory snacks. It practically never closes.

Berry College Restaurant JAMAICAN $
(Map p110; ☑979-0045; 1 Sunset Blvd, Hotel Gloriana; mains US$8-10; ⊙7am-10pm) In the courtyard of the Gloriana Hotel, this home-style Jamaican eatery demands a long wait for good food made from scratch. The menu features time-honored favorites like pepperpot soup, roast pumpkin and a unique, delectable snack that you'll want to take along for the ride: baked coconut chips. The breakfasts are equally robust.

Cafe Tease CAFE, SNACKS $
(Map p116; ☑618-3644; 55 Gloucester Ave; snacks J$300-600; ⊙10am-7pm Mon-Tue, 10am-5pm Wed-Sun) Simple walk-up window in the Hip Strip where you can escape the entreaties of the shopkeepers/taxi drivers with an iced coffee or a jerk hot dog.

Golden Dynasty
CHINESE $

(Map p116; ☑971-0459; 39 Gloucester Ave; mains J$400-800; ☺midday-10pm) Mid-priced, mid-flavor and mid-satisfying, Golden Dynasty represents MoBay's small Chinese population and provides an answer to your chow mein dilemma.

Candy Shack Ice Cream
ICE CREAM $

(Map p116; ☑979-5172; 75 Gloucester Ave; ice cream J$200-400; ☺10am-6pm) Just the ticket on a hot day on the Hip Strip. Try the reggae rainbow flavor.

Biggs BBQ Restaurant & Bar
AMERICAN $$

(Map p116; ☑952-9488; www.biggsbbq mobay.com; Gloucester Ave; mains US$13-22; ☺midday-midnight) This newcomer on the Hip Strip, perched on a terrace above a ribbon of beach, lives up to its name – the portions are big in an unashamedly American way, especially the double-decker sandwiches. Eschew the air-conditioned interior with its TVs showing American football and pose on the deck instead.

★Pelican
JAMAICAN $$$

(Map p116; ☑952-3171; Gloucester Ave; mains US$12-38; ☺7am-11pm) Loved by upper-crust Jamaicans and tourists on away-days from the all-inclusive buffets, Pelican is goat-curry heaven, though the oxtail's not bad either. Opened the same year Jamaica gained independence (1962) and armed with the same chef since the early 1980s, this seminal Hip Strip restaurant has fully earned its right to be called a MoBay institution.

Marguerite's
JAMAICAN, FUSION $$$

(Map p116; ☑952-4777; Gloucester Ave; mains US$32-48; ☺6-10:30pm) This celebrated restaurant provides a lovely setting from which to watch the sunset while drinking cocktails, followed by dinner on the elegant clifftop patio. The pricey (some would say overpriced)

menu edges toward nouvelle Jamaican and fresh seafood, but also includes sirloin steak and inventive pasta. The chef displays his culinary chops at a central flambé grill.

✕ Around Montego Bay

Evelyn's
JAMAICAN $

(☑952-3280; Kent Ave, Whitehouse; mains J$300-700; ☺9am-9pm Mon-Sat, 10am-6pm Sun) Fantastic choice: a true local's spot, this rustic seafood shack (near Sandals Montego Bay) is also patronized by some very in-the-know tourists. The food tends to be rich yet refined – layered and pleasantly oily without being overwhelmingly heavy (as is often the case in Jamaica).

Day-O Plantation
JAMAICAN $$

(Map p110; ☑952-1825; Fairfield Plantation; mains US$8-22; ☺9am-9pm Mon-Sat, 10am-6pm Sun; ☑) Ignore the cheesy name of this place if you can and just focus on the fact that this spot, about 3km southeast of Montego Bay proper, is hands-down romantic. Housed in a beautiful mansion, it elegantly makes use of colonial furnishings and serves some very fine food, including one of the best high-end vegetarian menus in the area.

★Houseboat Grill
JAMAICAN $$$

(Map p110; ☑979-8845; Southern Cross Blvd; mains US$15-32; ☺4-11pm Tue-Sun) Moored in Bogue Bay at Montego Bay Freeport, this converted houseboat is one of the best restaurants in the country. The changing menu offers eclectic Caribbean fusion cuisine: tiger shrimp in a fiery red curry, or beef medallions with goat's cheese and plantain mashed potatoes. You can dine inside or reclusively on the moondeck. Reservations are recommended, especially on weekends.

☗ Drinking & Nightlife

The nightlife in Montego Bay ranges from the obnoxious to the lethargic, with bits of 'that

MONTEGO BAY & NORTHWEST COAST MONTEGO BAY

QUICK EATS IN MOBAY

If you're in a rush or on the cheap, meat patties are a good snack. In MoBay, it's the usual toss-up between ubiquitous **Juici Patties** (Map p114; 36 St James St; J$150; ☺7am-10pm Mon-Sat) and equally common **Tastee Patty** (Map p110; ☑979-5537; www.tasteejamaica.com; 13 Barnett St; patties from J$150; ☺7am-10pm Mon-Sat). For a break from the chains try **Butterflake Pastries** (Map p114; ☑876-952-0070; 2 Union St; pastries from J$100; ☺8am-5pm Mon-Sat), good for cheap meat and vegetable patties. For bakeries that serve sweeter baked goods hit the **Viennese Bakery** (Map p114; cnr Union & Fort Sts; pastries from J$100; ☺9am-5pm Mon-Sat). There's also a good alfresco vegetarian place with I-tal rasta food called **Millennium Victory** (Map p110; ☑887-5545; www.millenniumvictory.weebly.com; 65 Barnett St; mains J$300-700; ☺8:30am-6pm Mon-Sat, 8:30am-3pm Sun; ☑); look for the colorful murals.

was actually pretty fun' sprinkled throughout. The Hip Strip can be surprisingly sedate while upscale hotels mostly have lackluster live bands, so if you're looking for the big party, it may be best to head over to Negril. Local bars outside of the Hip Strip can get lively, but if you plan to venture beyond Fort St after dark, you may want to do so with some Jamaican friends. That said, more locals party on the Hip Strip than you might think – the area is popular with middle-class Jamaicans.

Richmond Hill BAR
(Map p110; Union St, Richmond Hill Inn) This elegant Great House that flutters celestially over MoBay's shabby Canterbury neighborhood is a blissful place to go for cocktails at dusk when the sun's dying orb reflects onto the Italianate swimming pool. Beware the rum punch shaken (not stirred) by the convivial barman: it's a potent brew.

MoBay Proper BAR
(Map p114; Fort St; ☺ midday-midnight) Proper is often packed with locals and expats. It's a friendly, occasionally raucous spot, and probably the easiest bar for tourists to access off the Hip Strip. Beneath a 'chandelier' of Heineken bottles, the pool table generates considerable heat, while dominoes are the rage with an older crowd out on the patio.

Reggae Bar BAR
(Map p116; Gloucester Ave; ☺ midday-midnight) An upstairs bar in a two-story Hip Strip shack where the hustlers take time off from hustling to down a few Red Stripe beers to a backbeat of Bob Marley and the click of pool balls. Cheap, but not at all nasty.

Jimmy Buffett's Margaritaville BAR
(Map p116; www.margaritavillecaribbean.com; Gloucester Ave; entry after 10pm US$10; ☺ 11am-10pm) Of the three Margaritavilles in Jamaica, this one actually offers something like a local nightlife experience. Seriously – don't slam the book shut yet! By day, yes, it's a tourist trap, but as night falls, a lot of Jamaicans like to come here, and, well, dance. There are some big ugly tiki heads and a waterslide that carries revelers through the plumbing and flushes them ignominiously into the ocean, where their fellow booze cruisers await on a docked catarmaran.

Blue Beat Jazz & Blues Bar LOUNGE
(Map p116; Gloucester Ave; ☺ 10pm-2am) Blue Beat kind of feels like a collection of clichés of what a classy cocktail bar should look like (smooth metal furnishing, dim lighting, dark curtains and a general sense of heavily cologned polish throughout); but as Montego Bay's first jazz and blues martini bar, it rocks its style with live music nightly, along with Asian-Caribbean fusion cuisine.

Pier One NIGHTCLUB
(Map p114; Howard Cooke Blvd) If you're into big nightclubs, Pier One is the place to go in Montego Bay. It attracts a largely local crowd, all dressed to impress and dancing as if their lives depended on it. The music is earsplitting, the dance floor is crowded and sweaty (especially on Friday nights) and the light shows will leave you seeing spots for days afterward.

Montego Bay Yacht Club PRIVATE CLUB
(Map p110; ☎ 979-8038; www.mobayyachtclub.com; Montego Bay Freeport; ☺ 10am-11pm) This rum-happy haunt attracts an eclectic crowd that includes crusty old sea-salts and expats eager to talk about their new boats. Nonmembers must be signed in as guests, but this is rarely an issue.

☆ Entertainment

Fairfield Theatre THEATER
(Map p110; ☎ 952-0182; Fairfield Rd; ☺ shows 8pm) The home stage of MoBay's innovative Little Theatre Company; check its Facebook page (just search for 'Fairfield Theatre') for info on upcoming shows.

Palace Multiplex CINEMA
(Map p110; ☎ 979-8359; Alice Eldemire Dr, Fairview Shopping Centre) First-run Hollywood flicks.

🛍 Shopping

Craft Markets MARKETS
For the largest crafts selection head to the **Harbour Street Craft Market** (Map p114; Harbour St; ☺ 7am-7pm), which extends for three blocks between Barnett and Market Sts. **Fantasy Craft Market** (Map p116; ☺ 8am-7pm), at the northern end of Gloucester Ave, and **Fort Montego Craft Market** (Map p114; ☺ 8am-7pm), behind the fort, offer less variety and quality. You can expect a hard sell at all, so bring your haggling skills and don't be afraid to walk away from something you don't like.

Gallery of West Indian Art ART
(Map p110; ☎ 952-4547; www.galleryofwestindianart.com; 11 Fairfield Rd; ☺ 9am-5pm Mon-Wed & Fri, 9am-2pm Thu, 10am-3pm Sat) In the suburb of Catherine Hall, this is the best quality gallery in town. It sells genuinely original arts and crafts from around the Caribbean including Cuban canvases, hand-painted wooden ani-

mals, masks and handmade jewelry. Most of the work here is for sale.

ⓘ Information

DANGERS & ANNOYANCES

The well-policed Hip Strip (Gloucester Ave) is safe from criminals, but hustling may be an issue. There are aggressive hucksters in MoBay who will size you up and either try to charm or intimidate you out of a few bucks (or more) if they think you're green. Walk with purpose wherever you go; if you look lost or confused, you'll be an easier mark. That said, don't be afraid to ask for directions (shopkeepers are usually helpful, especially downtown).

Once you get downtown, the main drag (Fort St) is generally fine, but don't wander too far from it after dark; east of here, past Orange St, is a squatter neighborhood called Canterbury that's best avoided. You'll also want to steer clear of Flankers near the airport and parts of the Mount Salem neighborhood. Just across from the KFC that sits between the Hip Strip and downtown MoBay is a sparsely-vegetated field fronting a bit of sand known, pretty accurately, as Dump-Up Beach. It is best to avoid this area, especially at night. This is a popular spot for muggings, which are known to occur even in broad daylight.

Only ever use official taxis, identifiable by their red number plates and prescribed route emblazoned on the side of the car.

EMERGENCY

Police Stations Barnett St (☑ 952-1557, 952-2333; 14 Barnett St); Catherine Hall (☑ 952-4997, 953-6309; cnr Southern Cross Rd & Howard Cooke Blvd, Catherine Hall); Church St (☑ 952-5310, 952-4396; 29 Church St); Union St (☑ 940-3500; 49 Union St)

MEDICAL SERVICES

You'll find plenty of pharmacies downtown.
Cornwall Regional Hospital (☑ 952-5100; Mt Salem Rd) Has a 24-hour emergency ward.
Fontana Pharmacy (☑ 952-3860; Fairview Shopping Centre; ⊙ 9am-9pm Mon-Sat, 10am-9pm Sun) The best-stocked and largest pharmacy in town.

MONEY

At Donald Sangster International Airport (p212) there's a 24-hour money-exchange bureau and a branch of National Commercial Bank in the arrivals hall, but it doesn't change at good rates. You'll need local currency to take the bus into town, but taxis accept US dollars.

Better rates can be found on the main strip. Downtown, several bureaus can be found on St James St and Fort St; look for 'cambio' signs. Banks on Sam Sharpe Sq and in the Baywest Shopping Center all have 24-hour ATMs. Flanking the Doctor's Cave Beach Club are ATMs operated by National Commercial Bank and Scotiabank. The cruise-ship terminal is served by a branch of National Commercial Bank in the Montego Freeport Shopping Centre.

Cambio King (☑ 971-5260; Gloucester Ave; ⊙ 9am-2pm Mon-Thu, 9am-1pm Fri) Currency exchange, northern end of the street.
First Global Bank (☑ 971-5260; 53 Gloucester Ave; ⊙ 9am-3pm Mon-Thu, 9am-4pm Fri)

POST

Post Office Fort St (Map p114; ☑ 952-7016; Fort St); White Sands Beach (Map p116; ☑ 979-5137; Gloucester Ave, White Sands Beach)

TOURIST INFORMATION

Jamaica Tourist Board (Map p110; ☑ 952-3009; Donald Sangster International Airport; ⊙ for flight arrivals) In the arrivals hall at Donald Sangster International Airport.
Tourist Office (Map p116; Gloucester Ave, Old Hospital Park; ⊙ 8:30am-5pm Mon-Sat) On the Hip Strip.
Tourist Office (Map p114; ☑ 979-7987; Harbour St; ⊙ 8:30am-5pm Mon-Sat) The most helpful staff. It's in the Harbour Street Craft Market.

USEFUL WEBSITES

None of these sites are particularly good at updating.
Official Visitors Guide (www.montego-bay-jamaica.com) The most extensive online resource for MoBay and environs.
Visit Jamaica (www.visitjamaica.com) The official line on the city from the Jamaica Tourism Board.
What's On Jamaica (www.whatsonjamaica.com) Entertainment and culture listings.

ⓘ Getting There & Away

AIR

Air Jamaica (p212) operates jet and prop-plane services between MoBay's Donald Sangster International Airport and Kingston's Norman Manley International Airport and Tinson Pen (US$60 each way, several flights daily). Get tickets at the Montego Bay office or at the airport.

TimAir (p213), an 'air taxi' service, offers charter flights to Negril (US$179), Ocho Rios (US$362), Port Antonio (US$599) and Kingston (US$483).

BOAT

Cruise ships berth at the Montego Freeport, about 3km south of town. Taxis to downtown MoBay cost US$15. The savvy walk out of the port gates and flag cheaper route taxis.

Montego Bay Yacht Club (☑ 979-8038; www.mobayyachtclub.com; Montego Freeport) has hookups, gasoline and diesel, and will handle immigration and customs procedures.

BUS & MINIBUS

Comfortable **Knutsford Express buses** (Map p114; ☑ 971-1822; www.knutsfordexpress.com) run from their own bus terminal next to Pier One near downtown MoBay. Book tickets more than 24 hours in advance for a small discount. Be at the bus station 30 minutes before departure to register your ticket. Services:

Falmouth J$800, 30 minutes, six daily
Kingston J$2450, four hours, seven daily
Mandeville J$2000, three hours, one daily
Negril J$1400, 1¼ hours, two daily
Ocho Rios J$1600, two hours, six daily

Other public buses, minibuses and route taxis arrive and depart from the **transportation center** (Map p114) off Barnett St at the south end of St James St. There's an **inspector's office** (☉7am-6pm) inside the gate where you can ask for the departure point of the bus you're seeking.

Minibuses (ie vans) run directly to Ocho Rios (J$250 to J$300, two hours; onward transfers to Port Antonio and Kingston) and Lucea (J$200, one to 1½ hours; onward transfers to Negril), though some minibuses will continue on to Negril, thus eliminating the need for a transfer. More land routes can be accessed via share taxis.

PRIVATE TAXI

Jamaica Union of Travelers Association (JUTA; ☑ 952-0813) has taxi stands on Gloucester Ave at the Gloucestershire and Coral Cliff hotels and at Doctor's Cave Beach Hotel, downtown at the junction of Market and Strand Sts, and by the bus station. Identify JUTA members by the red plates and JTB decal emblazoned on their vehicles.

A list of official JUTA fares from Montego Bay is posted at the airport. At last visit, certified fares from the airport for up to four passengers: Falmouth (US$75), Kingston (US$200), Negril (US$100), Ocho Rios (US$100) and Port Antonio (US$250).

ROUTE TAXI

Shared (also known as route or public) taxis, identifiable by their red number plates, are located downtown at the junction of Market and Strand Sts, and by the Barnett St transportation center. Taxis run when full to locations like Falmouth (J$150), Lucea (J$200), Anchovy (J$150), Savanna-la-Mar (J$300), Ocho Rios (J$350) and smaller towns in between. You can almost always find a taxi early in the morning or around 4pm to 5pm (ie commuting hours); there will likely be a wait at other times of the day, and long-distance taxi service slacks off after sunset. It's always easier to get a ride to towns on the coast compared to towns in the interior.

❶ Getting Around

You can walk between any place along Gloucester Ave and downtown (it's about 2.5km from Kent Ave to Sam Sharpe Sq). You'll need a taxi for anywhere further.

TO/FROM THE AIRPORT

You'll find taxis outside the arrivals lounge at the airport. There is an official taxi booth immediately outside customs. Your taxi driver will probably call for a porter...who'll expect a tip for taking your luggage the 10m to your car. A tourist taxi to Gloucester Ave costs US$10. Alternatively, you can catch a minibus or route taxi from the gas station at the entrance to the airport (J$100).

PUBLIC TRANSPORTATION

Montego Bay Metro Line (☑ 952-5500; 19a Union St) bus service was introduced in 2001, linking MoBay with the suburbs and outlying towns (a flat fare of US$0.35 applies). Services depart and arrive at the transportation center (p124) near the junction of St James and Barnett Sts.

TAXI

Licensed JUTA taxis cruise Gloucester Ave; they charge a steep US$10 minimum. Published fares from Gloucester Ave are US$10 to the airport, US$23 to Greenwood, US$15 to Ironshore, US$15 to Montego Freeport and US$15 to Rose Hall.

EAST COAST TO RIO BUENO

East of Montego Bay the A1 hugs the coast all the way to Falmouth, 37km away, passing through the resort-heavy districts of Ironshore, Rose Hall and Greenwood.

Ironshore & Rose Hall

As you head east of Montego Bay the coast becomes a long stretch of screensaver-worthy beach, speckled with golf courses, all-inclusive resorts, high-end condos and expensive malls, all of which are marketed at wealthy tourists and the Jamaican upper class, many of whom opt to live here instead of the ritzier suburbs of Kingston. Ironshore, about 8km east of Montego Bay, is the epicenter of this little window of luxury. Further east is Rose Hall.

◉ Sights

★ **Greenwood Great House**   GREAT HOUSE
(☑ 953-1077; www.greenwoodgreathouse.com; adult/child US$20/10; ☉9am-6pm) This marvelous estate sits high on a hill 11km east of Ironshore. While the region's main attraction is Rose Hall, visiting Greenwood is a far more intimate and, frankly, interesting experience. The furnishings are more authentic, the tour less breakneck than Rose Hall's,

and there's none of the silly ghost stories – although the exterior edifice is admittedly not as impressive.

Construction of the two-story, stone-and-timber structure was begun in 1780 by the Honorable Richard Barrett, whose family arrived in Jamaica in the 1660s and amassed a fortune from its sugar plantations. (Barrett was a cousin of the famous English poet Elizabeth Barrett Browning.) In an unusual move for his times, Barrett educated his slaves.

Unique among local plantation houses, Greenwood survived unscathed during the slave rebellion of Christmas 1831. The original library is still intact, as are oil paintings, Dresden china, a court-jester's chair and plentiful antiques, including a mantrap used for catching runaway slaves (one of the few direct references we found in any Jamaican historical home to the foundations of the plantation labor market, ie slavery). Among the highlights is the rare collection of musical instruments, containing a barrel organ and two polyphones, which the guide is happy to bring to life. The view from the front balcony down to the sea is stunning.

Rose Hall Great House   GREAT HOUSE
(🖉 953-2323; www.rosehall.com; adult/child under 12yr US$20/10; ⏱9am-6pm, last tour 5:15pm) This mansion, with its commanding hilltop position 3km east of Ironshore, is the most famous Great House in Jamaica.

Construction was begun by George Ashe in the 1750s and was completed in the 1770s by John Palmer, a wealthy plantation owner. Palmer and his wife Rose (after whom the house was named) hosted some of the most elaborate social gatherings on the island.

Slaves destroyed the house in the Christmas Rebellion of 1831 and it was left in ruins for over a century. In 1966 the three-story building was restored to its haughty grandeur.

Beyond the Palladian portico the house is a bastion of historical style, with a magnificent mahogany staircase and doors, and silk wall-fabric that is a reproduction of the original designed for Marie Antoinette during the reign of Louis XVI. Unfortunately, because the house was cleaned out by looters back in the 19th century, almost all of the period furnishings were brought in from elsewhere, and quite a few are from the wrong century. With that said, the imported furnishings are the genuine article, and many are the work of past leading English master carpenters.

Much of the attraction is the legend of Annie Palmer, a multiple murderer said to haunt the house. Her bedroom upstairs has been (re)decorated in crimson silk brocades because, y'know, red is the color of blood. The cellar now houses an English-style pub and has a well-stocked gift shop haunted by the ghosts of tacky souvenirs. There's also a snack bar. Tours of the house are mandatory and commence every 15 minutes till 5:15pm.

🏃 Activities

Most all-inclusive resorts have scuba facilities and snorkeling gear for guests.

Half Moon Equestrian Centre   HORSE RIDING
(🖉 953-9489; www.horsebackridingjamaica.com; ⏱beach ride 7am & 4pm, pony ride 9am-midday & 2-5pm; ♿) The lovely grounds of this center, west of Half Moon Village, are a nice slice of the Kentucky bluegrass in paradise with well-kept horses. The main draw is the classic bareback beach ride (US$100) during which you and your horse splash straight into the turquoise sea. For the kiddies there's also a pony ride (US$25). Riding lessons cost US$80 per 30 minutes.

🛏 Sleeping

The Bird's Nest   HOSTEL $
(🖉 781-2190; www.thebirdsnestjamaica.com; 177 Patterson Dr, Ironshore; dm US$23-25, d US$35-45; ❄🛜🏊) Sporty hostel run by an enthusiastic group of kite-surfers who catch some gusts (and waves) in nearby Bounty Bay on the other side of Falmouth. In the true tradition of Jamaican hostels, it's small (two private doubles and two dorm rooms), but friendly. Pros: a pool, hammocks and a tranquil garden. Con: Ironshore location requires taxis or long walks.

Royal Reef Hotel & Restaurant   HOTEL $$
(🖉 953-1700; www.royalreefja.com; Hwy A1, Greenwood; s/d US$91/100; 🅿❄🏊) On the A1 at Greenwood, this modern Mediterranean-style hotel has 19 rooms. Its decor includes classical wrought-iron furnishings and exquisite tropical murals. An elevated amoeba-shaped pool is inset in the terracotta terrace, which has an outside grill overlooking a tiny beach overgrown by mangroves. The excellent continental cuisine is served both alfresco and in an intimate dining room.

Atrium   APARTMENTS $$
(🖉 953-2605; atrium@cwjamaica.com; 1084 Morgan Rd, Ironshore; apt US$120; ❄🏊) The Atrium bills itself as a collection of villas, but these are more like very modern, comfortable condominium units. Each one is blandly stylish in a freshly-furnished-by-Ikea kinda way, and

comes with a kitchen if you want to cook for yourself. Located near the Blue Diamond Shopping Centre.

Eating

Scotchies JERK $
(953-8041; Hwy A1, Ironshore; 0.5lb portion US$7; 11am-11pm Mon-Sat, 11am-9pm Sun) Many Jamaicans will tell you that (a) Scotchies serves the best 'sit-down' jerk in the northwest, if not all of Jamaica, and (b) the quality has slipped a bit with popularity. Savvy outsiders nod in agreement. 'Yah *mon*.' This is excellent quality jerk. But the locals are right – it's not the best on the island, despite the hype.

Far Out Fish Hut SEAFOOD $
(954-7155; Hwy A1, Greenwood; mains $J400-800; midday-11pm) East of Greenwood Great House, look along the coast for a trailer painted to look like a sea-blue slice of the ocean and you've found the Far Out Fish Hut, one of the finest purveyors of seafood on the north coast. This is a locals' spot where you sit under thatch and order fresh seafood at a good price.

Getting There & Away

A great number of minibuses and route taxis ply the A1 road, traveling to and from Donald Sangster International Airport and Montego Bay's transportation center, Gloucester Ave and downtown. You'll pay about J$100 to travel from MoBay to Ironshore; J$120 to Rose Hall. Private taxis cost US$35.

Falmouth

POP 9500

Built on riches amassed from sugar and slavery, and advanced enough by the early 19th century to have running water before even New York City, Falmouth feels like a sunken Titanic recently raised from the deep. Little altered architecturally since the 1840s when slave emancipation dramatically reversed its fortunes, the town retains one of the finest ensembles of Tropical-Georgian buildings in the Caribbean. For anyone with even a passing interest in Jamaican history and architecture, Falmouth is an essential stopover. Not only is the town attractive in a disheveled kind of way, it has recently introduced a trio of community-led walking tours that lucidly bring to life the people and stories that shaped it.

In 2011, Falmouth opened a massive new cruise-ship terminal furnished in mock Georgian style and kitted out with various shops and restaurants, all of them off-limits to unauthorized Jamaicans. Surprisingly, the development hasn't really spoiled the town's gritty Jamaican-ness. Most of the cruisers, who arrive on mega-liners that dock thrice weekly, are whisked off the gated port compound in air-conditioned minibuses on organized day-trips. Meanwhile, the town itself carries on much as it has always done; a vivid documentary of everyday Jamaican life. Old ladies in their Sunday best congregate outside the limestone-bricked English-style church, lazy dogs lie prostrate in quiet sun-bleached squares, and market traders ply roasted yam and sugar cane under the pretty gingerbread verandas of commerce-packed Harbour Lane. Stick around and join in the street theater.

History

Falmouth was laid out in 1769 and named for the English birthplace of Sir William Trelawny, then the governor of the island. The streets were planned as a grid and patriotically named after members of the royal family and English heroes. Planters erected their townhouses using Georgian elements adapted to Jamaican conditions.

With its advantageous position, Falmouth became the busiest port on the north coast. Outbound trade consisted mainly of hogsheads (large casks) of wet sugar and puncheons (casks) of rum, while slaves were offloaded for sale in the slave market.

The town's fortunes degenerated when the sugar industry went into decline during the 19th century and it was dealt a further blow with the advent of steamships, which the harbor was incapable of handling. By 1890 the port was essentially dead. The city has struggled along ever since.

A new cruise-ship dock was opened in Falmouth in March 2011 large enough to accommodate the world's second biggest cruise liner, the 6000-passenger *Oasis of the Seas*.

Sights

Water Square SQUARE
The best place to orient yourself is Water Sq, at the east end of Duke St. Named for an old circular stone reservoir dating from 1798, the square (actually a triangle) has a fountain topped by an old waterwheel. Today it forms a traffic roundabout, but back in the day this fountain pumped fresh water before New York City had any such luxury. Many of the wooden shop-fronts in this area are attractively disheveled relics.

Albert George Market   MARKET
The market structure on the east side of Water Sq, which dominates central Falmouth, was once the site of slave auctions. The current structure was built in 1894 and named, in honor of two of Queen Victoria's grandsons, Albert and George.

Courthouse   NOTABLE BUILDING
One block east of Water Sq is Seaboard St and the grandiose Georgian courthouse in Palladian style, fronted by a double curling staircase and Doric columns. The current building, dating from 1926, is a replica of the original 1815 structure that was destroyed by fire. The town council presides here.

Tharp House   NOTABLE BUILDING
(Seaboard St) Tharp House sags from age yet is still one of the best examples of an elegant period townhouse. Today housing the tax office, it was formerly the residence of John Tharp, at one time the largest slaveholder in Jamaica.

Phoenix Foundry   HISTORIC SITE
(cnr Tharpe & Lower Harbour Sts) One of Falmouth's most distinctive buildings, Phoenix Foundry was built in 1810 and sports a strange-looking conical roof. Behind the foundry, guarded by locked gates, is the Central Wharf where slaves were brought ashore, to be replaced in the holds by sugar, rum and other victuals borne of their back-breaking labor. The crumbling warehouses are on their last legs.

Baptist Manse   HISTORIC SITE
(cnr Market & Cornwall Sts) The restored Baptist Manse was formerly the residence of nonconformist Baptist preacher William Knibb, who was instrumental in lobbying for passage of the Abolition Bill that ended slavery. The porticoed post office is next door.

Methodist Manse   HISTORIC SITE
At the bottom of colonnaded Market St stands the Methodist Manse, a stone-and-wood building with wrought-iron balconies and Adam friezes above the doorways. A diversion along Trelawny St leads one block west to **Barrett House**, which is sadly in a state of advanced disrepair.

Police Station   HISTORIC SITE
(Rodney St) The oddly cute historic police station was constructed in 1814. The prison here once contained a treadmill: a huge wooden cylinder with steps on the outside. Shackled above the mill, slaves had to keep treading the steps as the cylinder turned. If they faltered, the revolving steps battered their bodies and legs. The ancient lockups are still in use.

William Knibb Memorial Church   CHURCH
(cnr King & George Sts) On July 31, 1838, slaves gathered outside William Knibb Memorial Church for an all-night vigil, awaiting midnight and then the dawn of full freedom (to quote Knibbs: 'The monster is dead'), when slave-shackles, a whip and an iron collar were symbolically buried in a coffin. In the grounds of the churchyard you can find Knibb's grave, as well as that of his wife.

A plaque inside the church displays the internment of these tools of slavery; to get in, ask for help at the Leaf of Life Hardware store on King St.

🛏 Sleeping & Eating

Falmouth Resort   HOTEL **$**
(☑954-3391; 29 Newton St; r J$4600; ꗃ❊) This 'resort' offers the only accommodations in the

MONTEGO BAY & NORTHWEST COAST FALMOUTH

DON'T MISS

FALMOUTH HERITAGE WALKS

Listed as an endangered historical monument, Falmouth, founded in 1769, harbors one of the Caribbean's most beguiling and architecturally homogenous townscapes. Preserving it is no easy task, not that this has dulled the efforts of robust local organizations run by people who are passionate about their town and its history. To gain a fuller appreciation of the settlement's historical importance and why it's worth protecting, join one of three tours offered by **Falmouth Heritage Walks Ltd** (☑407-2245 www.falmouthheritagewalks.com; 4 Lower Harbour St). The **Heritage Walking Tour** (adult/child US$25/15) is a two-hour ramble around Falmouth's small urban grid punctuated with handsome Tropical-Georgian architecture. The **Food Tour** (adult/child US$45/25) alternates cultural musings with tastings of street food, while the **Jewish Cemetery Tour** (adult/child US$15/10) visits a cemetery with gravestones etched in Hebrew. Walks usually take place on the days a cruise ship is in port (Tuesday, Wednesday and Thursday at the time of writing). Check online for an updated schedule.

center of Falmouth. If you want to get a feel for bustling Jamaican downtown life, this is a good option. Though it doesn't broadcast enough polish to qualify as a resort, it's a clean, friendly spot with welcoming, helpful staff. Meals are prepared on request. Take an upstairs room for privacy and a view.

★Club Nazz
Restaurant   BREAKFAST, JAMAICAN $
(☑617-5175; Market St, cnr Duke St; breakfast J$100-400, dinner J$450-600; ☺7:30am-9:30pm; ☎) You can't beat sitting on Nazz's unintentionally romantic streetside patio with a pot of piping hot Blue Mountain coffee and a piece of fruitcake watching the life of this historic city go cruising past. The word 'cruising' takes on a different meaning when a ship's in port and passengers pile in to order items off the extremely reasonable lunch menu.

Tropical Bliss Oasis   CAFE $
(Albert George Market; snacks J$150-450; ☺9am-5pm Mon-Sat; ☎) Enjoy a moment or two of bliss with a fruit smoothie and sandwich at this pleasant perch in Albert George Market.

❶ Information

Post Office (☑954-3050; cnr Cornwall & Market Sts; ☺8am-5pm Mon-Fri)

Scotiabank (☑954-3357; cnr Market & Lower Harbour Sts; ☺8:30am-2:30pm Mon-Thu, 8:30am-4pm Fri) Scotiabank also operates an ATM in the shopping center near the eastern edge of town.

❶ Getting There & Away

Buses, minibuses and route taxis arrive and depart on opposite sides of Water Sq for Martha Brae (J$100, 15 to 20 minutes), Montego Bay (J$150, 45 minutes) and Ocho Rios (J$300, 80 minutes). The Knutsford Express stops in Glistening Waters 2km east of Falmouth from where you can flag down a route taxi (J$50) to bring you into town.

Cruise ships arrive at the **Port of Falmouth** (☑876-617-2280; www.portoffalmouth.com; 2 King St) adjacent to the town center.

Martha Brae

Situated on a small hill and nearly encircled by the emerald-green waters of the scenic Martha Brae River, this small village 3km due south of Falmouth is justly famous for rafting. The river rises at Windsor Caves in Cockpit Country and spills into the sea at Glistening Waters, east of Falmouth.

A rafting trip down a 4.8km stretch of the Martha Brae River is a quiet thrill. The jour-

ney takes 90 minutes on 9m-long bamboo rafts, each carrying one or two passengers, poled by a skilled guide. You'll head through a green tunnel of jungle, vines and cold mountain water; the whole experience can be quite romantic, depending on your tolerance of other people (the river gets crowded, as this is the most popular rafting spot in Jamaica). The upper reaches tumble at a good pace before slowing further downriver, where you stop at 'Tarzan's Corner' for a swing and swim in a calm pool. At the end, after being plied with rum punch, you'll be driven back to your car or tour bus.

Trips begin from Rafters Village, about 1.5km south of Martha Brae. There you'll find an itinerant mento band and picnic area, bar, restaurant, swimming pool, bathrooms, changing rooms and a secure parking lot. Your captain will pause on request if you want to take a dip or climb a tree.

Just about any hotel on the north Jamaican coast, from Negril to Ocho Rios, offers rafting packages on the Martha Brae. Obviously transfer charges will be tacked on, so a smarter method is booking your adventure at the Rafters Village (p32) office in Montego Bay. It's customary to tip your raft guide.

Minibuses and route taxis regularly run to Martha Brae from Falmouth (J$100, 15 to 20 minutes).

Glistening Waters

Just east of Falmouth is one of the most incredible natural wonders of Jamaica, along with a smattering of good-value accommodations, clean beaches and one of the island's more innovative cultural exhibitions. The 25,000-seat Trelawny Greenfield Stadium is located opposite the small village of Rock. Built in 2007 for the Cricket World Cup, it also hosts football and music concerts.

◎ Sights & Activities

**Glistening Waters
(Luminous Lagoon)**   LAGOON
(½hr boat trip per person US$25; ☺tours from 6:45pm) Glistening Waters, also known as 'Luminous Lagoon,' actually lives up to the substantial hype. Located in an estuary near Rock, 1.6km east of Falmouth, the water here boasts a singular charm – it glows an eerie green when disturbed. The green glow is due to the presence of microorganisms that produce photochemical reactions when stirred; the concentrations are so thick that fish swimming by look like green lanterns.

Needless to say, swimming through the luminous lagoon is semi-hallucinogenic, especially on starry nights, when it's hard to tell where the water ends and the sky begins. The experience is made the more surreal thanks to the mixing of salt- and freshwater from the sea and the Martha Brae River; the fresh water 'floats' on the saltwater, so you not only swim through green clouds of phosphorescence, but alternating bands of cold and warm.

Half-hour boat trips are offered from **Glistening Waters Marina** (☎954-3229; per person US$25; ☉6:45-8:30pm). Any hotel from Ocho Rios to Negril should be able to organize a trip out here.

There's a good-value restaurant located at the marina where you can get fresh fish prepared just about any way you like; you're charged based on the size of the fish. The restaurant opens to coincide with the arrival and departure of tour groups.

Outameni   CULTURAL VILLAGE
(☎617-0948, 954-4035; www.outameni.com; admission US$30; ☉shows 3pm) Outameni is an interesting cultural village experience that takes visitors through Jamaican history, from the days of the Taíno to colonial settlement, slavery and up to the modern day via a 90-minute show that incorporates music, dance and film. It was being renovated at the time of research. It's located opposite the Royalton resort.

Kiteboarding Jamaica   KITEBOARDING
(☎781-2190;   www.kiteboardingjamaica.com;
rental per day US$80, 1hr lesson US$70) Jamaica has recently appeared on the radar for kite-boarders thanks, in part, to its inclusion in the 2010 World Cup. The island's small kite-boarding fraternity congregates near Burwood Beach in Bounty Bay (next to Royalton White Sands Hotel), an unkempt but beautiful stretch of sand which catches some stiff breezes. There is a handful of operators, but this one is arguably the best. Lessons and board rentals are available.

Fishing & Boating   FISHING
The river mouth in Glistening Waters is one of the few places in Jamaica that still offers good fishing for tarpon, known as the 'silver bullet' for its feisty defense on a line. No license is required. There are at least two dozen captains offering charter services at the Glistening Waters Marina; call the marina to pre-arrange, or just show up and pick the captain who seems friendliest. Charter prices of around US$500 can be split between six to eight passengers.

🛏 Sleeping

★ Time 'n' Place   RESORT **$**
(☎843-3625; www.mytimenplace.com; cottages US$80; P❄🔊) With four beach cabins set on a priceless patch of sand shaded by palms and pines, Time 'n' Place is the kind of place where you fall asleep to the throb of a distant reggae bass and wake up to the sound of lapping waves.

An added bonus comes in the shape of charismatic owner Tony, a legendary Jamaican character who has fiercely defended his slender slice of beach paradise from developers, environmental degradation and the criminal element for 23 years.

Fisherman's Inn   HOTEL **$$**
(☎954-4078, 954-3427; www.fishermansinnjamaica.com; s/d US$120/125; ❄🔊⊕) The perfect excuse to stay over in Glistening Waters after your psychedelic evening swim, Fisherman's Inn is a quiet, relaxed hotel with a good restaurant. All of the dozen bright white bedrooms face the bay with French windows opening directly onto a red wooden jetty with its own pool. A sublime place to relax.

N Resort   RESORT **$$$**
(☎876-617-2500; www.n-holidays.com; Oyster Bay; all-incl per person r US$273-336; P❄@🔊⊕) Check your clothes at the door: the N stands for 'nude.' Jamaica's only bona fide clothes-optional resort opened in the early 2010s in the shell of a former family-orientated all-inclusive. It's a rustic affair with clean wooden accommodation blocks set right on the beach, though the resort retains some bizarre reminders of its previous incarnation (water slides!).

Eschewing the party antics typical of some couples' resorts, N is for quieter, more discerning naturists – and all the better for it.

Royalton White Sands   RESORT **$$$**
(☎1-800-204-7982; www.royaltonresorts.com; all-incl r from US$439; ❄@🔊⊕) An old Breezes all-inclusive resort reborn as a Royalton in November 2013, this place is good for kids on account of its huge beachside waterpark. It's 3km east of Falmouth.

ⓘ Getting There & Away

Minibuses and route taxis frequently travel the A1 road to and from Falmouth (J$50 to J$80), which is about 36km east of Montego Bay and 42km west of Runaway Bay.

The Knutsford Express Falmouth station is actually situated at Glistening Waters Marina 2km east of the town. There are six buses daily to Kingston (J$2200) via Ocho Rios (J$1200), and six buses to Montego Bay (J$800), two of which carry onto Negril (J$1500). Buses are less frequent at weekends.

Duncans

This small town on a hillside 11km east of Falmouth is a pretty place to base yourself if you want to be removed from resort sprawl, although it appears developers are buying up surrounding real estate at a fast pace, so this may not be the case for long. The village is centered on an old stone clock tower in the middle of a three-way junction. The highway diverts ongoing traffic around the town; keep watch for the turnoff from the A1. Minibuses and route taxis pick up and drop off passengers to/from Duncans at the clock tower in the town center.

Kettering Baptist Church, built in 1893, is a creamy-colored building that commemorates William Knibb, the Baptist missionary and abolitionist who founded an emancipation village for freed slaves here in 1840.

The grandparents of singer and activist Harry Belafonte used to own the **Sober Robin** (🎯954-2202; r from US$35; P⚡) a cheerfully run-down inn-cum-pub situated on the old road that enters Duncans from the west. The lobby and lounge are atmospheric, with framed photos of classic movie stars, a small bar with table tennis and a pool table. Rooms are basic but clean and recently renovated.

Silver Sands Villa Resort (🎯888-745-7245, 954-7606; www.mysilversands.com; 1-/2-bed cottage from US$165/248, 3-/4-bed villas per week US$1650-2800; P⚡🏊) 1.5km west of Duncans, has more than 100 upscale one- to five-bedroom villas and cottages spread over 90 hectares. The cottages require a minimum three nights booking. The enclosed estate backs a private, 300m-long, white-sand beach which is kept pristine and gorgeous (nonguests can get access for US$25). Each unique villa is privately owned and individually decorated, and has a cook, housekeeper and gardener – this sort of personal service is frankly way above what you get at most all-inclusives. Most of the properties have TVs and their own pools. Weekly rates offer savings and include airport transfers. Facilities include a bar-grill, and there's a grocery store within the 'neighborhood' if you want to self-cater.

Just west of the Silver Sands is the undone public **Jacob Taylor Beach**, where you'll find a small, mellow craft market and a rum shop.

Rio Bueno

Rio Bueno is a tumbledown fishing village, 10km east of Duncans, where fishers tend their nets and lobster pots in front of ramshackle Georgian cut-stone buildings that featured in the 1964 movie *A High Wind in Jamaica*, which was filmed here. The town is set on the west side of a narrow bay that may be the site where Columbus first set foot in Jamaica on May 4, 1494. You can pick around the 18th-century ruins of **Fort Dundas**, the whitewashed remains of **St Mark's Anglican church** that dates to 1833, and a **Baptist church** erected in 1901 to replace another destroyed in anti-missionary riots of the abolitionist era. More modern ruins may be found after super-resort Breezes Rio Bueno closes its doors (scheduled to occur soon). As of research, it was not clear what would become of the enormous hulk of the 226-room hotel.

🏃 Activities

Braco Stables   HORSE RIDING
(🎯954-0185; www.bracostables.com; per person with/without transfers US$70/60; ⏰ rides 10:30am & 2:30pm) If riding a horse bareback into the sea sounds like your cup of tea, Braco Stables offers excellent group rides through sugarcane country that culminate in a bareback ride into the turquoise surf. The ride ends with refreshments at the renovated Braco Great House (clothing required).

🛏 Sleeping & Eating

Hotel Rio Bueno   HOTEL $$
(🎯954-0048; Main St; r/ste from US$110/250; P⚡🛜) Converted from a Georgian wharfside warehouse, this is the sort of wonderful old place eccentrics dream up for gawking visitors like yourself. In this case, said eccentric is Mr Joe James, father of former England and Liverpool goalkeeper David James who has turned the hotel into a museum/gallery of his paintings, carvings and masks.

It has 20 rooms, most with French doors opening onto balconies that overlook the bay.

Lobster Bowl Restaurant   SEAFOOD $$
(🎯954-0048; Hotel Rio Bueno, Main St; mains US$12-38; ⏰7am-10pm) This spacious restaurant has an old-time nightclub feel and, again, features the artwork of Joe James. As the name suggests, lobster and seafood figure prominently on the menu, and it's all fresh and prepared with love and attention.

❶ Getting There & Away

Rio Bueno is 60km east of Montego Bay and 20km west of Runaway Bay. The stretch of coastal road from here to Discovery Bay is known as the Queen's Hwy. Grab one of the route taxis that run between Falmouth (J$180) and Discovery Bay (J$150) and alight here.

INLAND: SOUTH OF MONTEGO BAY

The hill country inland of MoBay is speckled with villages clinging to rocky outcrops, narrow roads and large fields of fruit, vegetables and, deeper in the interior, ganja. This is friendly country, where locals aren't as jaded with tourists as their counterparts on the coast. Be on the lookout for brightly painted shacks decorated with off-the-wall bric-a-brac (pottery, feathers, whatever); these are often the homes of witchcraft-practicing bush doctors. The southeast quarter of St James parish culminates in the wild Cockpit Country.

Lethe

In Greek mythology Lethe was one of the rivers surrounding Hades, and to cross it caused you to lose memories of your previous life. This could happen to you in Lethe, Jamaica, if you spend enough time in this hilltop town. its turnoff is 3km south of Reading off the B8 (signs show the way). If you pass the sign for Rocklands Bird Feeding Station, you've gone too far. The stone bridge spanning the Great River was built in 1828, and from its pastoral span you can see the overgrown remains of an old sugar mill rotting on the riverbank.

❍ Sights & Activities

Animal Farm   FARM
(✆ 899-0040; www.animalfarmjamaica.com; adult/child US$25/10; ⊙ tours by arrangement Mon-Fri,

10am-5pm Sat & Sun; ⊕) ✐ While disappointingly light on revolutionary pigs corrupted by the acquisition of power (if you haven't read your Orwell, never mind), this Animal Farm does happen to be a great place to take your kids. This pretty little homestead is powered by ecofriendly solar power and pig crap.

Skilled guides take guests on bird-watching tours around the grounds (look for the funky-crested 'Rasta fowl'), and on site there's a friendly little petting zoo, donkey stable (rides available), access to swimming in the Great River and lovely views over Cockpit Country.

The farm is located just outside the tiny village of Copse, 3km west of Lethe in Hanover Parish. Follow the signs. The final approach is on a rough track.

Jamaica Zipline Adventure Tours   ZIP-LINING
(✆ 366-0124; www.ziplinejamaica.com) A relatively new fixture at the Lethe Estate is the increasingly popular pursuit of zip-lining. Not any old zip-line, mind. This is the longest in the Caribbean. The five lines add up to a total 'flying' distance of more than 1.3km, all of it through a lush jungley landscape.

The tours (US$89), run by a US-based company, also incorporate some sampling of local fruits.

Mountain Valley Rafting   RAFTING
(✆ 956-4920) Headquartered at Lethe Estate, this outfit offers tranquil one-hour river trips on the Great River from Lethe. You're piloted 3km downstream aboard long, narrow bamboo rafts poled by an expert rafter, who waxes poetic about the birds, flora and fauna as you glide along.

Trips cost US$65 for two passengers (children under 12 half price), including transfers. For an extra US$15 per person you'll get lunch, a plantation tour and a fresh piña colada at the end of the excursion. If you show up under your own steam, you'll pay US$50 for the raft trip alone.

MONTEGO BAY & NORTHWEST COAST LETHE

WORTH A TRIP

CROYDON IN THE MOUNTAINS PLANTATION

Reached via a side-road 1.5km from Catadupa on the edge of Cockpit Country, **Croydon in the Mountains Plantation** (✆ 979-8267; www.croydonplantation.com), a 54-hectare plantation, was the birthplace of national hero and icon of the abolitionist movement Sam Sharpe. It feels more like an Indian or Balinese rural community than Jamaica, with its well-groomed, deep green terraces sprouting fields and orchards of coffee, citrus and pineapples. A 'see, hear, touch and taste' tour is offered from 10:30am to 3pm Tuesday, Thursday and Friday (US$75 including lunch and transfers). Reservations are required, best organized through a Montego Bay tour company (p117) who will lay on transport.

❶ Getting There & Away

By car or taxi, head west out of Montego Bay on the coast road (A1/Howard Cooke Blvd). In Reading (4km west of downtown MoBay) take the B8 (Long Hill Rd) from Reading toward Anchovy; the signed turnoff for Lethe is about 5km inland. If traffic is light, the trip takes around 30 minutes. Route taxis heading towards Savanna-la-Mar and Black River can drop you off by the turnoff, but it's a short, steep hike up to Lethe from there.

Rocklands Bird Feeding Station

Rocklands (☏ 952-2009; admission US$20; ⊙ 2-5pm) is a favorite of birders, who have flocked here since 1958 when it was founded by noted ornithologist Lisa Salmon, who tamed and trained over 20 bird species to come and feed from your hand. More than 140 bird species have been recorded here, but the big draw are those little darting gems, hummingbirds, including the deep purple Jamaican mango hummingbird and ever-popular 'doctorbird,' all best seen around 4pm. You can also spot ground doves, orange and bananaquits, Jamaican woodpeckers (flickers) and orioles.

The station is run by Fritz Beckford, a champion of birds who will pour birdseed into your hand or provide you with a sugar-water feeder. Guests sit agog as humming-birds streak in to hover like tiny helicopters before finally perching on their outstretched fingers. Fritz estimates his feathered friends devour nearly 900kg of seed each year (so much for 'bird-sized' appetites). If you need more avian action, Fritz leads tours from the house into the bush (US$20 per person).

To get here from Montego Bay take the B8 (Long Hill Rd) from Reading toward Ancho-vy; turn left about 200m south of the signed turnoff for Lethe on Rock Pleasant Rd. The road leading to Rocklands is agonizingly steep and narrow in places. Alternatively, you can take a bus or route taxi from Montego Bay bound for Savanna-la-Mar or Black River, but be prepared for a tough 30-minute hike to and from your destination. If a taxi sounds better, be prepared to shell out at least US$75 for the round-trip journey.

HIKING THE TROY–WINDSOR TRAIL

Just over 30km from the roasting sunbathers of Montego Bay glowers a foreboding wilder-ness that challenges popular images of Jamaica as tame, well-trodden and bereft of back-country. Cockpit Country is a barely penetrable thicket of dense foliage and intricate karst topography scattered with caves, hollows and hills that resembles an upturned egg carton. In the 1700s, it provided a savage refuge for runaway slaves – the Maroons – who waged an in-termittent guerrilla war against the British. In an unsuccessful attempt to subjugate them, the British built a precarious military road across the Cockpits from Troy to Windsor that wound around hidden sinkholes and mosquito-infested jungle with paranoid place names such as The Land of Look Behind and Me No Sen You No Come. Many British soldiers disappeared into the Cockpits never to return, victims of ambush or sheer exhaustion.

Miraculously, the Troy–Windsor road still exists, though what remains of the route consists of a vague, overgrown trail that should not, under any circumstances, be tackled alone. If you mean to hike it, hire a guide with a machete from the Jamaican Caves Organisation form a small group, and ensure that your party has a GPS, plenty of water (a minimum of two litres per person), mosquito repellent, food and a torch. Additionally, leave your names, contact information and estimated time of arrival with a reliable source. The trail measures 15km between the hamlet of Tyre and Windsor (although add an extra 2km at Tyre and 5km at Windsor to walk to the nearest reliable transport source). As it's rarely walked in its entirety these days, parts of Troy–Windsor can be a bush-whack, making it easy to get lost (not a good idea seeing there are no settlements, surface water and no chance of helicopter res-cue). Six hours is the minimum time required, eight hours is average, 10 hours isn't uncom-mon. Start early!

Difficulties aside, the hike is one of Jamaica's greatest challenges. Tree cover and steep hills block any expansive views, meaning the most interesting aspect of the walk lies in stud-ying the remarkable endemism of the karst ecology. The Cockpit's bloody history, as related by any good guide, is equally fascinating. Look out for the stone walls of the old road which can be seen throughout much of the journey. The trail is easier done south to north starting from Troy. Beware, the mosquitoes are brutal! For a guided hike with the JCO, you'll need a minimum of five people and your own transport. The cost is US$100 per person.

NORTH COCKPIT COUNTRY

Look at a road map of Jamaica and you'll notice southwest Trelawny parish, inland of Falmouth is...blank. Just a big green eye of tantalizing mystery peeking at you from the tangle of towns, villages and roads that is the rest of Jamaica's face. So, what's that eye? Jamaica's most rugged quarter: a 1295-sq-km limestone plateau known as Cockpit Country, a vast network of eroded limestone studded with thousands of conical hummocks divided by precipitous ravines.

Activities

The Cockpits are laced with mostly uncharted **caves** that are a tempting draw for cavers. This is true adventure travel; guides lead trips into the better-known caverns, but past that, exploring is for experienced and properly outfitted cavers only. There is no rescue organization, and you enter caves at your own risk. The most accessible are Windsor Caves at Windsor.

The **Jamaican Caves Organisation** (JCO; ☎397-7488; www.jamaicancaves.org/main.htm) provides resources for the exploration of Jamaican caves, sinkholes and underground rivers. In 2005 the group completed a project to formally classify and evaluate more than 70 caves within Cockpit Country.

One of their more popular trips is to the **Peterkin-Rota cave system** near Maldon in St James. This excursion covers 1km with some swimming and spends three to four hours underground. Cost is US$100 per person (minimum US$250). Transport is extra (US$100 depending on location).

Tours

Cockpit Country Adventure Tours ADVENTURE TOURS
(☎610-0818; www.stea.net/ccat_main.htm; 3 Grants Office Complex, Albert Town; tours US$55-70) Sponsored by the Southern Trelawny Environmental Agency, local guides are used to lead hikes and cave exploration in the rugged Cockpit Country. Popular trips include the Quashie River and the Quashie Cave, featuring a 'cathedral room' and a nature hike along the semi-abandoned Burnt Hill/Barbecue Bottom Rd between Clark's Town and Albert Town.

Sun Venture Tours HIKING
(☎in Kingston 960-6685, in Ocho Rios 920-8348; www.sunventuretours.com; 30 Balmoral Ave, Kingston 10) Runs guided hikes and bird-watching trips into the Cockpits for US$85.

Good Hope Estate

Imagine 'Cotswold-on-Cockpit' and you'll get a sense of what this honey-hued Great House and working plantation looks like. The property, 13km south of Falmouth at the western end of Queen of Spains Valley, is set on the northern edge of Cockpit Country, and the views into that checkerboard of deep razor ridges and jungle domes has no rival.

The estate was owned by John Tharp (1744–1804), once the richest man in Jamaica, owner of over 40 sq km and 3000 slaves in Trelawny and St James parishes. Built around 1755, the estate still houses a collection of 18th-century Jamaican Georgian cut-stone buildings, including a sugar works and waterwheel.

Most Good Hope visits are organized through Chukka (p78) who run many of the facilities on the estate. Because Chukka buses in crowds of cruise ship and resort tourists, you'll often find the house tours busy and a little rushed. Tours can include lunch or high tea, plus Chukka also organizes zip-lining (US$99) and river tubing (US$69) on the estate (the Martha Brae River runs through it). Costs include transportation from Montego Bay hotels.

Acclaimed ceramicist David Pinto operates a **pottery studio** (☎954-4635) open to the public on the grounds, and pottery workshops are offered – though you'll need to contact the US-based **Anderson Ranch Arts Center** (☎954-4635, in the USA 970-923-3181; www.andersonranch.org) to attend.

The Great House first became a hotel in the early 1900s when an American banker came to Jamaica looking for antiques and happened upon Good Hope. Today the four-bedroom **Good Hope Treehouse** (☎881-6869; www.goodhopejamaica.com; s/d/tr US$195/270/330; P ⊖ ❄ ≋) is without doubt one of Jamaica's most opulent accommodations, where the architecture places the living space next to nature in a way that would make Frank Lloyd Wright swoon. Bank on high ceilings, gleaming hardwood floors and cut-stone walls hung with rustic Afro-Jamaican art.

Windsor

If you want to drive into Cockpit Country... well, you can't really. But you can get a taste

WORTH A TRIP

WINDSOR GREAT HOUSE

How often do you get to (affordably) sleep in a colonial mansion that happens to be a biological research station? Built in 1795 by John Tharp, **Windsor Great House** (☑ 997-3832; www.cockpitcountry.com; 1/2/3 people US$40/45/50) now serves as a scientific research center.and hostelry, decked out with several no-frills cut-stone rooms with shared bathroom (US$5 supplement for hot water). Breakfast/lunch/dinner is US$7.50/7.50/15 per person. Resident naturalists Mike Schwartz and Susan Koenig occasionally stage four-course 'Meet the Biologist' dinners (US$40, minimum four people). What better way of acquainting yourself with the background story on natural Jamaica than while enjoying nice food and wine? It's not marked by a sign; to find it, take a left at the junction at the end of the paved road.

of what's on offer by entering the narrow 5km-long valley southeast of Good Hope Estate. This passage, surrounded by towering cliffs, is most easily accessed from Sherwood at the north end. The paved road dead-ends at Windsor near the head of the valley; from here you can hike across the Cockpits to Troy, but this is as far as you can go into this wild country without hiking. And, to be fair, the natural beauty of the wild Cockpit Country interior is on display here in its truest form.

⊙ Sights

Usain Bolt is from Sherwood, the last real settlement before Windsor, and you'll see signs honoring him and his searing speed dotted around. You may also bump into his family. His father, Gideon, often shoots the breeze while playing dominoes in local bars, while his Aunt Lilly, who runs a bar/gift shop, cooks a mean goat curry.

Windsor Caves CAVES
These caverns may be off the beaten track to most people, but they're a major way-point for some 50,000 bats. Their egress and entrance, a massed cloud of skittering airborne mammalian tooth, fur, flap and claw, is a sight to behold (there's guano galore). Luckily, the caves were donated to the World Wildlife Fund in 1995 with the proviso that they never be developed.

The entrance is a 1km hike from the road, ending with a clamber up a narrow rocky path. Beyond the tight entrance you'll pass into a large gallery full of stalactites and a huge chamber with a dramatically arched ceiling; in rainy season you can hear the roar of the Martha Brae River flowing deep underground.

You'll need a local guide, they can usually be found at **Dango's shop** (www.jamaicancaves.

org/dango-jamaica) at the end of the road. It's emblazoned with the epithet 'Jah love is a burning flame'; here you'll likely find cave wardens Martell or Franklyn 'Dango' Taylor. One of them will lead the way with a flashlight or bamboo torch to visit Rat Bat Cave and the Royal Flat Chamber. Depending on how deep into the cave you wish to go and the size of your group, figure on around US$40 per person.

🛏 Sleeping & Eating

Miss Lilly's GUESTHOUSE $
(☑ 788-1022; www.jamaicancaves.org/lillys-jamaica. htm; Coxheath; r with shared bathroom US$40) In the hamlet of Coxheath, 5km north of Windsor, you'll find this bar, restaurant, guesthouse and Usain Bolt gift shop all rolled into one, run by the welcoming and jovial aunt of Mr Bolt, Miss Lilly. Two simply appointed rooms share a bathroom (cold water only), while Miss Lilly cooks some delicious yams, said to be the source of Usain's extreme speed.

This is a nice place to chill and meet locals, including a fair few members of the direct and extended Bolt family (and if you're really lucky) the fast man himself, who tend to congregate here for gossip, dominoes and other social pastimes.

❶ Getting There & Away

Windsor is reached by traveling the road from Falmouth to Martha Brae, then crossing the bridge to the east and turning right to follow the valley south into the hills. Minibuses and route taxis (around J$120) operate between Falmouth and Sherwood Content. Coxheath is a 10-minute walk from Sherwood (taxis will drop you there if you ask). Windsor is another 5km down the road (walk or cadge a lift in Coxheath).

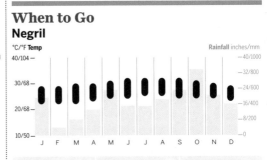

Negril & West Coast

Best Places for Breakfast

➡ Just Natural (p147)

➡ Pablo's Restaurant (p147)

➡ Cafe Goa (p145)

➡ Sips & Bites (p148)

Best Water Activities

➡ Mayfield Falls (p153)

➡ Blue Hole Mineral Spring (p154)

➡ Negril Tree House (p141)

➡ Cliff diving at Rick's Cafe (p148)

Why Go?

If you thought the north and east coasts of Jamaica were relaxed, head west to a land of long beaches and crimson sunsets where the pleasure-seeking resort of Negril shimmers like an independent republic of guilt-free sloth. Aside from producing sugar cane and surreptitiously growing Jamaica's best ganja, Western Jamaica's *raison d'être* is almost exclusively touristic; elongated Negril and its hotel developments stretch for more than 10 miles along the entire western coast. In the quiet bucolic hinterland little pockets of local life can still be glimpsed in places such as Lucea, a pretty coastal enclave bypassed by tourist traffic, wild and wet Mayfield Falls, and diminutive Little Bay, a non-resort that still feels like Negril circa 1969. Few come to the west with a to-do list, electing instead to enjoy life in the true spirit of the hippies who founded Negril. Join them on a sun-lounger and relax...*mon.*

When to Go
Negril

Apr–Jun It's not as wet here as the rest of Jamaica, but small thunderstorms do occur.

Jul–Oct Rooms dip into low-season rates, and short bursts of rain are common.

Nov–Mar Sunny, clear and dry. Weather-wise, it's the best time to be in town.

Negril & West Coast Highlights

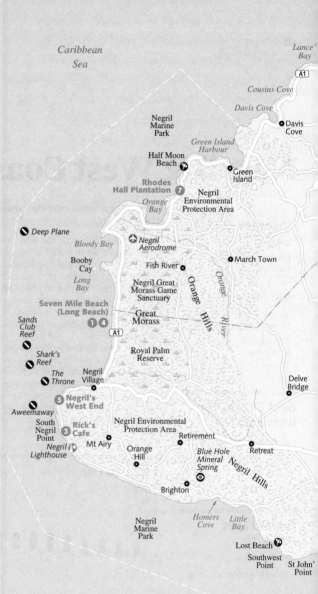

1 Plumbing the grottoes and reefs off **Negril** (p138) for some of the island's best scuba diving

2 Clambering, clawing and occasionally sliding around the slick rocks and white water of **Mayfield Falls** (p153)

3 Watching cliff divers pluck up courage (or lose their nerve) at **Rick's Cafe** (p148)

4 Gazing into the perfect sunsets that set on fire the sugary sand of **Seven Mile Beach** (p138)

5 Reclining in a hammock in a boutique hotel in **Negril's West End** (p143)

6 Disappearing into the country at one of Jamaica's most scenic and atmospheric caves at **Roaring River Park** (p154)

7 Riding a chestnut horse across the hills east of Negril from **Rhodes Hall Plantation** (p140)

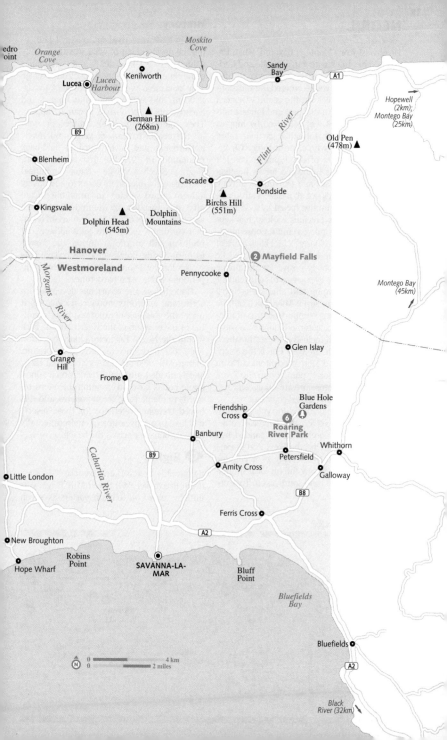

NEGRIL

POP 4200

Head west from Montego Bay and, when the air becomes thick with ganja smoke and horizontal pursuits take precedence over vertical ones, you'll know you've entered the vacationville of Negril. Stuck on the island's western tip and graced with its finest and longest natural beach, Negril was colonized by hippies in the early 1970s, though it is their more affluent offspring who claim it today. Unsurprisingly, 40 years of development has left its mark. Negril is renowned for its hustlers who push drugs, sex and trinkets on anyone who moves. But it's not all hassle: a strong local business community, fueled by a desire to safeguard Negril's precious ecology, has kept the area from becoming a circus. Consequently it remains, by and large, a laid-back place of impromptu reggae concerts and psychedelic sunsets where nobody – save for the manic route taxi drivers – ever seems to be in a hurry.

In both geography and character, Negril can be split in two. Seven Mile Beach (a little over four miles long) supports a strip of mid-range family-run accommodations plus some larger low-rise all-inclusives at its northern end. Further south, the West End is the Negril of hippy-era legend. Here precipitous cliffs, up to 50ft high in places, plunge into the azure ocean. Quirkier, more private hotels and restaurants inhabit this jagged coastline.

Save for a tiny pre-1970s fishing village, Negril has never supported a major Jamaican settlement. Thus, the nominal 'town' sandwiched between the beach and the West End doesn't really offer much in the way of a genuine Jamaica experience. For full-on local immersion, you'll have to head southeast to Treasure Beach (p173).

History

Only in 1959 was a road cut to Negril, launching the development of what was then a tiny fishing village. Electricity and telephones came later. The sleepy beachfront village soon became a popular holiday spot for Jamaicans, and at the same time, hippies and backpackers from abroad began to appear. They roomed with local families or slept on the beach, partook of ganja and magic mushrooms, and gave Negril its laid-back reputation. In 1977 the first major resort, Negril Beach Village (later renamed Hedonism II), opened its doors to a relatively affluent crowd seeking an uninhibited Club Med–style vacation. By the mid-1980s Negril was in the throes of a full-scale tourism boom that continues today. This let-it-all-hang-out tradition still overflows during the March to April Spring Break when US college kids swarm for wet T-shirt contests, drinking competitions and general party time.

Nonetheless, the resort has developed an active and environmentally conscious spirit under the guidance of expat residents, resulting in the creation of the Negril Marine Park within the Negril Environmental Protection Area. The park encompasses the shoreline, mangroves, offshore waters and coral reefs, and is divided into eight recreational zones. Some hotels have taken admirable steps towards implementing green policies, and it is hoped traveler preference for these resorts will lead to a copycatting of environmentally friendly behavior across the beach.

⊙ Sights

Seven Mile Beach (Long Beach) BEACH
(Negril Beach; Map p144) Seven Mile Beach was initially touted on tourism posters as 'seven

Negril Village

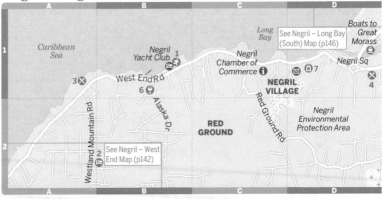

miles of nothing but you and the sea.' But the once-peaceful place that drew all those blissed-out sensualists in the early 1970s is now only a happy memory.

True, topless sunbathers still lie half submerged on lounge chairs in the gentle surf, and the sweet smell of ganja smoke continues to perfume the breeze, but otherwise the beach has changed in nearly every way. Today it's cluttered with restaurants, bars and nightspots and every conceivable water sport on offer. The swaying palms, clear waters and nearby coral reefs mean that the beach is still beautiful to behold – some contend it's the most beautiful in the Caribbean – but if you're looking for solitude, look elsewhere.

Bloody Bay Beach   BEACH
(Map p144) A splendid option, with no facilities and few people, save for a few travelers and a smattering of locals enjoying some repose away from the hubbub. There's a jerk shack selling snacks and drinks if you need 'em.

Negril Hills   HILLS
(Map p142) This range of low-lying hills rises inland of Negril's West End. The raised limestone upland is wild and smothered in brush. Tiny hamlets sprinkle the single road that provides access from Negril: Whitehall Rd leads south from Sheffield Rd to the hamlet of Orange Hill, swings east through the hills via the town of Retirement, and eventually links to the A2 for Savanna-la-Mar. The area is best explored on a bicycle.

Long Bay Beach Park   BEACH
(Map p144; J$150; ☉9:30am-5pm) Toward the north end of Seven Mile Beach, this beach is more peaceful and far less crowded than the

sand further south. Here you'll find more sugary sand and picnic tables, plus changing rooms. But there's also coarse grass here, so it's not quite as picturesque.

Booby Cay   ISLAND
This small coral island, just offshore from Rutland Point, was used as a South Seas setting in the Disney movie *20,000 Leagues Under the Sea*. The island is named for the seabirds – 'boobies' in local parlance – that make their nests here. Water-sports concessionaires can arrange boats for about US$35 return.

Negril Lighthouse   LIGHTHOUSE
(Map p142; West End Rd; ☉9am-sunset) FREE
The gleaming white, 20m-tall Negril Lighthouse, 5km south of Negril Village, illuminates the westernmost point of Jamaica. Erected in 1894 and originally powered by kerosene, the lighthouse is now solar powered and flashes every two seconds. The superintendent will gladly lead the way up the 103 stairs for a bird's-eye view of the coast.

Kool Runnings
Adventure Park   AMUSEMENT PARK
(Map p144; ☑957-5400; www.koolrunnings.com; Norman Manley Blvd; adult/child US$33/22; ☉11am-6pm Tue-Sun; ⊕) If you prefer your water fun doled out in a theme park, descend on this 2-hectare collection of 10 different rides, ranging from the 15m drop of the Jamaica Bobsled to the Rio Bueno Lazy River ride. Food is available at three restaurants, and children can be easily distracted at Captain Mikie's Coconut Island. It also offers kayak trips in the Great Morass.

NEGRIL & WEST COAST NEGRIL

Negril Village

☉ Activities, Courses & Tours
  1 Stanley's Deep Sea Fishing B1

☉ Sleeping
  2 Judy House Cottages & Rooms B2

☉ Eating
  3 Canoe Bar A1
  4 Hammond's Bakery.............................. D1
  5 Sweet Spice Restaurant F1

☉ Drinking & Nightlife
  6 Mi Yard B1

☉ Shopping
  7 A Fi Wi Plaza D1

🏃 Activities

Boat Trips

Companies offer two- and three-hour excursions that can be booked at most hotels. Many trips include snorkeling and booze, preferably in that order. **Negril Cruises** (Map p144; ☑ 430-0596; www.negril cruises.com; Hedonism II; US$30-50) operating out of Hedonism II, Couples Swept Away and Breezes resorts are perennial favorites, often stopping at Rick's Cafe for cliff diving. Glass-bottom boats are a great way to see fish and coral if you don't want to swim. There are several to choose from on Seven Mile Beach, and most trips will cost around US$35.

Cycling

The intense traffic along Norman Manley Blvd and West End Rd makes cycling a dicey proposition in town. The best place to ride is along Ocean Dr or in the Negril Hills, southeast of Negril. There are half a dozen bike rental place including **Gas Bike Rental** (Map p142; ☑ 957-4835; West End Rd) in the West End. Rates are normally US$15 per day.

Diving & Snorkeling

Negril has extensive offshore reefs and cliffs with grottoes, shallow reefs perfect for novice divers and mid-depth reefs right off the sands of Seven Mile Beach. Clusters of dwarf tube sponges are a noteworthy feature. The West End offers caves and tunnels; its overhangs are popular for night dives. Hawksbill turtles are still quite common here.

Visibility often exceeds 30m and seas are dependably calm. Most dives are in 10m to 23m of water. Several sites will be of interest to prospective divers. The Throne is a 15m-wide cave with massive sponges, plentiful soft corals, nurse sharks, octopuses, barracuda and stingrays. Aweemaway is a shallow reef area south of the Throne, and has tame stingrays. Deep Plane is the remains of a Cessna airplane lying 21m underwater. Corals and sponges have taken up residence in and around the plane, attracting an abundance of fish, and nurse sharks hang out at a nearby overhang. Sands Club Reef, sitting in 10m of water, lies offshore from the middle of Seven Mile Beach. From here, a drift dive to Shark's Reef leads through tunnels and overhangs with huge sponges and gorgonian corals.

Snorkeling is especially good at the southern end of Seven Mile Beach and off the West End. Expect to pay about US$5 an hour for masks and fins from concession stands on the beach. Most of the scuba-diving providers offer snorkeling tours (about US$25). Most

all-inclusive resorts have scuba facilities. Several companies offer PADI certification and introductory 'resort courses,' which are held in swimming pools.

Marine Life Divers   DIVING
(Map p142; ☑ 957-3245; www.mldiversnegril. com; Samsara Hotel, West End Rd; 1-/2-tank dives US$42.50/75) English- and German-speaking instructors.

Sun Divers   DIVING
(Map p144; ☑ 957-4503; www.sundiversnegril.com; Traveller's Beach Resort; 1-/2-tank dives US$50/90) 'Everything Irie' is their motto. Good start! Offers everything from snorkeling to advanced open-water diving courses.

Fishing

The waters off Negril – teeming with tuna, blue marlin, wahoo and sailfish – provide some excellent action for sport-fishing enthusiasts. **Stanley's Deep Sea Fishing** (Map p138; ☑ 957-0667; www.stanleysdeepseafishing. com; Negril Yacht Club; half-day trips for up to 4 people US$500, additional passengers per person US$50) offers custom fishing-trip charters. Three-quarter- and full-day trips are also available.

For a more offbeat experience, head out into the briny with a local fisher; ask around by the bridge over the South Negril River, or talk to the fishers near North Negril River.

Golf

Negril Hills Golf Club   GOLF
(☑ 957-4638; www.negrilhillsgolfclub.com; Sheffield Rd; green fees US$58, club/cart rentals US$18/35, caddies US$14; ⊙ 7:30am-4pm) An 18-hole par-72 course that borders the Great Morass, about 5km east of Negril. If you plop your ball in the water, forget it – the crocodiles will probably get to it first! Facilities here include a clubhouse, pro shop and restaurant.

Horseback Riding

Rhodes Hall Plantation   HORSE RIDING
(☑ 957-6422; www.rhodesresort.com; 2hr rides incl hotel transfers from US$70) Based 5km north of Negril on the A1 at Green Island, it offers rides through banana plantations and into the hills.

Water Sports

The waters off Negril are usually mirror calm – ideal for all kinds of water sports. Numerous concessions along the beach rent jet skis (about US$40 for 30 minutes), plus sea kayaks, sailboards and Sunfish sailboats (about US$20 per hour). They also offer waterskiing (US$25 for 30 minutes), glass-bottom boat rides (US$15) and banana-boat rides (US$15).

☞ Tours

Several tour operators offer a standard fare of excursions to the Black River Morass and Appleton Rum Estate (about US$85 to US$95) to the east in St Elizabeth parish, Mayfield Falls (US$65 to US$75) and Roaring River (US$60 to US$70).

Caribic Vacations   SIGHTSEEING TOURS
(Map p146; ☏ 953-9895; www.caribicvacations.com; Norman Manley Blvd) Negril's largest operator. Also has tours to the Royal Palm Reserve.

Clive's Transport Service   SIGHTSEEING TOURS
(☏ 956-2615;   www.clivestransportservicejamaica. com) Offers reliable, comfortable island-wide tours and airport transfers (US$50 for one to three people) in a nine-passenger minivan. Fill in the online form and Clive will pick you up.

JUTA Tours   SIGHTSEEING TOURS
(Map p146; ☏ 957-9197; Negril Crafts Market, Norman Manley Blvd) Run by the Jamaica Union of Travelers Association.

★★ Festivals & Events

Jamaica Beachfest   SPRING BREAK
(☉ Feb-Apr) Starting in late February and now spanning six weeks to early April is Negril's famous Spring Break celebration, featuring live music and plenty of booze.

Negril Music Festival   MUSIC
(☏ 968-9356; ☉ Mar) Three-day reggae and calypso festival.

Reggae Marathon & Half Marathon   MARATHON
(☏ 922-8677; www.reggaemarathon.com; ☉ Dec) Both a full and a half marathon, with a musical soundtrack staged on Norman Manley Blvd.

🛏 Sleeping

In general, beach properties are more expensive than hotels of equivalent standard in the West End.

🏖 Seven Mile Beach

Negril Yoga Centre   RESORT $
(Map p146; ☏ 957-4397; www.negrilyoga.com; Norman Manley Blvd; d US$45-91; ❋ 🛜) A hearkening back to hippie days of yore, these rustic yet atmospheric rooms and cottages surround an open-air, wood-floored, thatched yoga center set in a garden. Options range from a two-story, Thai-style wooden cabin to an adobe farmer's cottage; all are pleasingly, if modestly, furnished. The staff makes its own yogurt, cheese and sprouts. Naturally, yoga classes are offered (US$10 for guests and US$15 for visitors).

Travellers Beach Resort   HOTEL $
(Map p146; ☏ 957-9308; www.travellersresorts. com; Norman Manley Blvd; r US$76-96; ▣ ❋ 🛜 ⛱) Although overrun during Spring Break, Travellers is a real bargain the rest of the year. The family-owned resort is a lovely little midrange option, professionally run with clean, comfortable rooms that match the amenities of larger top-end resorts.

Roots Bamboo   RESORT $
(Map p146; ☏ 957-4479; www.rootsbamboo.com; Norman Manley Blvd; camping per person US$12, r US$35, d with shower US$60; ❋) Firstly, if you want peace and quiet, look elsewhere. On the other hand, if you need a party – well, stick around, *mon*. This complex of cottages, campsites and chalets attracts a mixed crowd of the middle-aged and backpackers who share a pretty similar desire to get crazy on the beach. There are regular reggae concerts and a perpetual party atmosphere.

★ **Negril Tree House**   RESORT $$
(Map p146; ☏ 957-4287; www.negril-treehouse.com; Norman Manley Blvd; r US$160-170; ▣ ❋ ⛱) Tree House feels exactly how Negril ought to feel: relaxing, but not too plush; friendly but never over-zealous; and welcoming and helpful, but in a very Jamaican kind of way. The rooms, set in bright white hexagonal rondavels, have everything you need for a successful sand-between-your-toes kind of holiday. The grill on the beach is to die for.

Rondel Village   RESORT $$
(Map p146; ☏ 957-4413; www.rondelvillage.com; Norman Manley Blvd; d US$120-190, 1-/2-bedroom villa US$250-295; ❋ 🛜 ⛱) 🍽 The Rondel is a charmer. Rooms encased in beautiful white chalets are set off with sharp purple color accents and are surrounded by snaking swimming pools and verdant (largely edible) natural foliage. Eschewing big resort ambitions, it is the epitome of Negrilian calm – relaxed, hassle-free and filled with all the ingredients of a week enjoyed doing absolutely nothing. Service is exemplary.

Kuyaba   HOTEL $$
(Map p146; ☏ 957-4318; www.kuyaba.com; Norman Manley Blvd; cottages US$70, r US$97, honeymoon ste US$106) 🍽 With considerable style, this tasteful family-run hotel offers six quaint,

NEGRIL & WEST COAST NEGRIL

Negril – West End

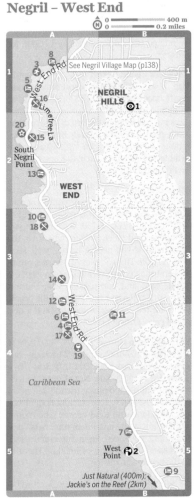

Negril–West End

rustic, wooden cabins with filigree trim, each done up in bright Caribbean colors. The cottages are nice enough, but the real draws are the deluxe rooms and suite with king-sized bed upstairs in a handsome stone-and-timber house tastefully decorated with terra-cotta floors and modern design touches.

White Sands   HOTEL **$$**
(Map p146; ☎957-4291, in the USA 305-503-9074; www.whitesandsjamaica.com; Norman Manley Blvd; r US$74-120, studio/villa US$138/540; ✳✉) This attractive property offers simple yet elegant one-bedroom octagonal units, and an excellent four bedroom, four-bathroom vil-

la that sleeps eight people and has its own pool. The latter is the real draw, as a group rental is a total steal. There's also a pleasant, well-maintained garden where you can relax while the resident parrot recites dub poetry.

Beachcomber Club & Spa   HOTEL **$$**
(Map p146; ☎957-4170; www.beachcomberclub.com; Norman Manley Blvd; r US$150-175, 1-bedroom apt US$250-275, 2-bedroom apt US$350-375; ⓟ✳@) Operating efficiently, this handsome multi-room hotel has an open-air beachside restaurant, Gambino's, that does great Italian, plus a nightly entertainment schedule, tennis and water sports. Yet for all this, it doesn't feel as corporate as an all-inclusive. All rooms are well furnished in a sort of standard high-midrange-hotel outlay of tans and beiges. Suites and apartments have kitchenettes.

Firefly Beach Cottages   HOTEL **$$**
(Map p146; ☎957-4358; www.jamaicalink.com; Norman Manley Blvd; s US$133, ste & apt US$190-250; ✳🛜) Not to be mixed up with the Noël

Coward estate (p86), Firefly Negril is a more modest affair where little wooden cabins and a pretty pink house have simple non-fancy rooms with an ocean breeze. In the communal areas you'll see hammocks slung between sea grapes, a rough-and-ready gym, and washing hung out to dry. It's rustic but real.

Charela Inn
HOTEL **$$**

(Map p146; ☑957-4277; www.charela.com; Norman Manley Blvd; s/d/tr US$170/190/240; P✳🛜🏊) Creating an individual style amid ubiquitous beach resorts, Charela has the feel of a Spanish hacienda with large comfortable rooms (some with king beds) built around an attractive courtyard embellished with a pool. The whole establishment sits on a hassle-free, fern-shrouded slice of Negril beach and is championed for its Jamaican-French fusion restaurant La Vendome.

★ Idle Awhile
HOTEL **$$$**

(Map p146; ☑957-9566, in the USA 877-243-5352; www.idleawhile.com; Norman Manley Blvd; r US$230-270, ste US$290-360; P✳🛜) Just what the therapist ordered! Idle Awhile is Negril in a nutshell: simple but stylish 14-room beachside abode where a hearty breakfast, a hammock and a lucid sunset are all you need to make things right in your life. Bonuses come with the aptly named Chill Awhile restaurant and complementary access to the fantastic Couples Swept Away Fitness Complex.

Moondance
VILLA **$$$**

(Map p146; ☑312-981-6344, in the USA 800-621-1120; www.moondanceresorts.com; Norman Manley Blvd; villas US$700-1900; P✳🛜🏊) The ultimate in Long Beach luxury, the Moondance villas put even the best all-inclusives to shame. You have a choice of gorgeous one- to five-bedroom villas – the one-bedroom honeymoon villa is akin to a lovely tropical home, whereas the three-bedroom 'Dream Walk' home looks like a medieval Chinese palace. For US$125 per adult per night you can get 24-hour all-inclusive service.

Nirvana on the Beach
RESORT **$$$**

(Map p146; ☑957-4314, in the USA 716-789-5955; www.nirvananegril.com; Norman Manley Blvd; d cottage US$160-350) The place to stay if you're seeking meditation, with the sort of bohemian ambiance you get when the counterculture decide to open up a tasteful boutique hotel. Pick from one-, two- and three-bedroom cottages, all set in elegantly subdued yet still vibrantly colorful Zen-like tropical gardens.

🏠 West End

★ Judy House Cottages & Rooms
COTTAGE, HOSTEL **$**

(Map p138; ☑957-0671; judyhousenegril.com; Westland Mountain Rd; dm/s US$20/25; 🛜) Offering the seclusion of the Negril of yore, this lush tropical garden on a hill above the West End guards two self-contained cottages with kitchens (US$75 to US$85) and five additional rooms (three singles and a couple of dorms all with shared bathroom) aimed at backpackers on a budget. The luxury here isn't in the gilded bath-taps, it's in the unscripted extras.

The English owner Sue is a mine of candid info on Jamaica, the honesty bar and shared kitchen encourage friendly discourse, and the hammocks in the garden are....zzzzzz.

Heaven for backpackers and anyone else who wants to have fun on a budget.

Seastar Inn
HOTEL **$**

(Map p142; ☑957-0553; www.seastarinn.com; Seastar Rd; s/d incl breakfast US$79-99; P✳🏊) This peaceful modern place is run by a charming Canadian-Jamaican couple. Pretty tiled rooms offset by tastefully frilly interior decor characterize the interior; outside the inn is fuzzed over with fecund trees and lush grounds. Hammocks are strung out over verandas, which is a bit of an issue, as you may never leave them. Cell phones are provided for guests.

Lighthouse Inn 2
GUESTHOUSE **$**

(Map p142; ☑957-4052; www.lighthouseinn2.com; West End Rd; studios US$70-80, cottages US$95-140) A small, family resort that brings to mind the old-school charms of Negril's heyday, the Lighthouse 2 is the sort of budget place with a gentle, fun vibe that you kind of want to export all over Seven Mile Beach, just to bring the madness there down a bit. Big efforts are made to accommodate guests with a disability guests. Rooms and apartments are sparse but sweet.

★ Blue Cave Castle
HOTEL **$$**

(Map p142; ☑957-4845; www.bluecavecastle.com; West End Rd; s/d US$60/125; ✳🛜) Winner of Negril's 'quirky hotel' prize is this mock castle that sits like a crenellated fortification warding off invaders on the cliffs of the West End. Fourteen fit-for-a-king rooms and a private grassy terrace create a less swashbuckling atmosphere inside. Lots of repeat visitors testify to fine, yet discreet service and a blissful ambiance. There's a swimming cave accessed via a slippery staircase.

Negril – Long Bay (North)

Negril – Long Bay (North)

◉ Sights
1 Bloody Bay Beach................................ B1
2 Kool Runnings Adventure Park...........B2
3 Long Bay Beach Park...........................B3
4 Seven Mile Beach (Long Beach) B3

◉ Activities, Courses & Tours
   Negril Cruises...............................(see 8)
5 Sun Divers...A2

🛏 Sleeping
6 Beaches Negril.......................................B4
7 Couples Swept Away.............................B4
8 Hedonism II...A2
9 Sandals Negril Beach Resort &
    Spa..B4
10 Sunset at the Palms B1

⊗ Eating
11 Cosmo's B4

🛍 Shopping
12 Rutland Point Craft Centre.................B2

Catcha Falling Star
HOTEL **$$**

(Map p142; ☎957-0390; www.catchajamaica.com; West End Rd; 1-/2-bedroom cottage incl breakfast from US$110-320; [P] [@] [🛜]) In inimitable West End style, these pleasant fan-cooled cottages – including several with two bedrooms – sit on the cliffs. Each is named for an astrological sign and the rooms do have the genuine variety of the zodiac; some peek into gardens all afire with tropical flowers, while others lip out onto the blue-on-blue vista of ocean. Breakfast is delivered to your veranda.

Home Sweet Home
HOTEL **$$**

(Map p142; ☎957-4478, in the USA 800-925-7418; www.homesweethomeresort.com; West End Rd; r US$189, ste US$249-299; [❄] [❄]) A cliffhanger with a dozen rooms plus two suites, all with private balconies and fans. The rooms are, naturally, done up in tropical pastels, but for some reason the execution works much better here than it does in other Negril hotels. It features a cliff-top bar and restaurant, a spa and multi-tiered sundecks overhanging the teal-blue waters.

Xtabi
HOTEL **$$**

(Map p142; ☎957-0120; www.xtabi-negril.com; West End Rd; r US$88-136, cottages US$222; [P] [❄] [🛜] [❄]) This chic and casual hotel bills itself as 'the meeting place of the gods.' Its clientele is decidedly human, but the setting is truly divine. You can choose from rooms, simple garden cottages or quaint octagonal seafront bungalows perched atop the cliff. They're pleasingly appointed, if nothing fancy.

Jackie's on the Reef
HOTEL **$$**

(☎957-4997, in the USA 718-469-2785; www.jackiesonthereef.com; West End Rd; r or cottage per person US$175; [❄]) This tranquil option is 11km south of the Negril roundabout, just north of the intersection with William Hogg Blvd. It operates as a New Age haven focusing on spiritual renewal. A natural stone 'temple' is divided into four rooms, each with two handmade wooden beds and an outdoor shower and bathroom enclosed within your own private backyard.

★ Rockhouse
HOTEL **$$$**

(Map p142; ☎957-4373; www.rockhousehotel.com; West End Rd; r/studios/villa US$180/220/410; [❄] [🛜] [❄]) One of the West End's most beautiful and well-run hotels, with luxury thatched rondavels (African huts) built of pine and stone, plus studio apartments that dramatically cling to the cliffside above a small cove. Decor is basic yet romantic, with net-draped poster

NEGRIL'S ALL-INCLUSIVE RESORTS

Although Negril's all-inclusives are low-rise (buildings must be lower than the tallest palm tree; ie three stories), they are not low-key. **Hedonism II** (Map p144; ☑ 957-5070; www.hedonism resorts.com; Norman Manley Blvd; all-inclusive r per person US$620-925; P ❈ 🕙 ☲) is an adult-only resort that soon gained notoriety for its risqué attitude, weekly lingerie parties and sheer tackiness. Prudes beware: nudity rules here (although technically it's optional). Couples are treated to a more romantic sheen at **Couples Swept Away** (Map p144; ☑ 957-4061; www. couples.com; Norman Manley Blvd; all-inclusive per person from US$700; P ❈ 🕙 ☲), a pleasure palace of villas and botanical gardens well known locally for its fantastic fitness complex, which non-guests can use for a fee. The Jamaica-founded Sandals hotels has two Negril outposts: **Sandals Negril Beach Resort & Spa** (Map p144; ☑ 957-5216; www.sandals.com; Norman Manley Blvd; all-inclusive r from $US400, ste US$1000-1250; P ❈ 🕙 ☲), another couples' resort popular with honeymooners; and **Beaches Negril** (Map p144; ☑ 957-9270; www.beaches.com; Norman Manley Blvd; 3 nights all-inclusive d US$2000-3200; P ❈ 🕙 ☲), which loosely resembles a castle and has loads of facilities for kids. For something less predictable, try the jungle cabin-style rooms at **Sunset at the Palms** (Map p144; ☑ 957-5350, in USA 877-734-3486; www.sunsetat thepalms.com; Norman Manley Blvd; all-inclusive d US$1500-2100, ste from US$1700; ❈ 🕙 ☲) ✐, an all-inclusive that likes to be eco-conscious.

beds and strong Caribbean colors. Catwalks lead over the rocks to an open-sided, multi-level dining pavilion (with one of the best restaurants in Negril) overhanging the ocean.

Caves   BOUTIQUE HOTEL $$$
(Map p142; ☑ 957-0269, in the UK 0800-688-76781, in the USA 800-688-7678; www.islandoutpost.com/ the_caves/; West End Rd; ste incl meals from US$608, all-inclusive cottage US$920-1865; P ❈ 🕙 ☲) One of the finest boutique hotels in Jamaica, and one beloved of the Hollywood elite (some of whom are helicoptered in), the Caves offers handcrafted, individually styled, wood-and-thatch cottages set in lush gardens above cave-riddled cliffs. If your credit card is up to it, rooms feature exquisite hand-carved furniture, batik fabrics and one-of-a-kind art; many have alfresco showers.

Banana Shout   CABIN $$$
(Map p142; ☑ 957-0384; www.banana shout.com; West End Rd; 2-/3-/4-person cabins US$200/200/250; P @ 🕙) Occupying a particularly choice bit of cliff-top turf, these cheerful green and orange cabins are perched over the sea in offbeat and homey seclusion. Tastefully decorated with Jamaican and Haitian art, they're unique and charmingly idiosyncratic, even for the West End. Step outside to a dramatic stairway descending to a sea cave with sundeck and freshwater shower.

Tensing Pen   RESORT $$$
(Map p142; ☑ 957-0387; www.tensingpen.com; West End Rd; r incl breakfast US$160-230, cottages US$370-720; ❈ 🕙 ☲) Among the more acclaimed accommodations in Negril is this

tranquil, reclusive option with 12 thatched cottages on a hectare of land. Most are 'pillar houses' – an architectural style closely associated with the West End – perched above the coral cliffs and set in natural gardens. All have exquisite bamboo and hardwood details, though otherwise rooms differ markedly in decor.

🍴 Eating

Local delicacies (besides hallucinogenic mushroom omelets and ganja muffins) include crab pickled in red peppers. Equally easy to find is pasta, pizza and plenty of good vegetarian (known as I-tal) fare. Many places price in US$, so in those cases we have followed suit.

🍴 Seven Mile Beach

Cosmo's   SEAFOOD $
(Map p144; ☑ 957-4784; Norman Manley Blvd; mains J$300-1000; ⊙ 10am-11pm) A tatty hippy outpost that sits like a island of good taste amid an ocean of insipid all-inclusive buffets. Cosmo's, in Negril-speak, is a synonym for 'fantastic seafood.' Eschewing fine-dining for a few rough-hewn beachside tables, the plates of melt-in-your-mouth lobster and curried conch are deliciously spicy.

Cafe Goa   BREAKFAST, JAMAICAN $
(Map p146; ☑ 957-9519; Norman Manley Blvd; mains US$5-16; ⊙ 8am-late) Replete with breakfasting locals and a few washed up hippies who look as if they fell asleep in 1973 and have just woken up, Goa is top of the morning for French toast, eggs and pancakes, or – should

Negril – Long Bay (South)

0 ____ 500 m
0 ____ 0.25 miles

Seven Mile Beach (Long Beach)

Norman Manley Blvd

Long Bay

Negril Enviromental Protection Area

Knutsford Express

Jamaica Tourist Board

S. Negril River

Negril Great Morass Game Sanctuary

Norman Manley Sea Park

See Negril Village Map (p138)

you be suitably acclimatized to Jamaican tastes – callaloo omelets, and ackee and saltfish. Sundays see a jazz band that draws a mixed bag of locals and visitors.

Kenny's Italian Cafe ITALIAN $
(Map p146; ☎957-4032; Norman Manley Blvd; pastas/pizzas US$8-10; ⊙3pm-late; ☜) A new operator winning the popular vote with this lovely half-indoor, half-outdoor cafe/restaurant, which sticks local fish on Italian pasta, steams up cappuccinos (rare in Jamaica), and has learned how to do a proper pizza. The decor is rustic but refined and the bar is a good place to swap your Red Stripe for a glass of wine.

Bourbon Beach JERK $
(Map p146; ☎957-4432; www.bbnegril.com; Norman Manley Blvd; mains J$300-800; ⊙midday-late) Though it's best known for its live reggae concerts, those in the know swear by Bourbon's jerk chicken. The sauce is thick and pastelike, and well complemented by a Red Stripe as you wait for a show.

Norma's on the Beach
at Sea Splash JAMAICAN $$
(Map p146; ☎957-4041; www.seasplash.com/normas-restaurant; Norman Manley Blvd; mains

US$15-32; ⏱7:30am-10:30pm) This Negril branch of Norma Shirley's celebrated Jamaican culinary empire seems to have escaped the hype surrounding her Kingston flagship, but the 'new world Caribbean' food at this stylish beach restaurant is just as adventurous. Expect to find the likes of lobster, Cornish game hen, jerk chicken and pasta, as well as tricolor 'rasta pasta.'

Le Vendôme
FRENCH $$$

(Map p146; ☎957-4648; Norman Manley Blvd; mains US$30-48; ⏱7:30am-10pm) Jamaican-French fusion means more than jerk croissant. Take your table on the terra-cotta terrace with garden view and choose from French classics like duck *à l'orange* and escargots Burgundy-style, or regional creations like curried shrimp or red snapper in coconut milk. What sets everything apart is the Gallic attention to final execution and the use of locally grown vegetables and spices.

Kuyaba on the Beach
FUSION $$$

(Map p146; ☎957-4318; www.kuyaba.com; Norman Manley Blvd; mains US$18-30; ⏱7am-11pm) 'Kuyaba' means 'Celebrate!' in the Arawakan language, which is exactly what happens here each evening at sunset as guests tuck into innovative dishes such as crab and pumpkin cakes with papaya mustard or coconut conch with a mango chutney. The lunch menu is a bit more laid-back: burgers, kebabs and gourmet sandwiches, plus superb pepper shrimp.

✖ West End

On the West End you'll find restaurants that mainly serve cheap Jamaican fare, although some of the nicer resorts have international fusion.

★3 Dives Jerk Centre
JERK $

(Map p142; ☎957-0845; West End Rd; quarter-/half-chicken J$350/600; ⏱midday-midnight) This unimpressive shack, which looks like it'll blow away in the next category one hurricane, serves up what may be the best food in Negril. Let your nose and taste buds be the judge. Feast your eyes on those sizzling lobsters or that smoking jerk and be prepared for a looooong, totally worthwhile, wait. The fresh food is prepared before your eyes.

Just Natural
BREAKFAST, JAMAICAN $

(☎957-0235; Hylton Ave; mains J$400-1500; ⏱8am-8pm Mon-Fri, to 9pm Sat & Sun) As quintessentially Jamaican as plastic wrist bands and gated hotel complexes aren't, Just Natural is a jumble of tables, trees and foliage at the southern end of the West End strip that serves up a formidable breakfast of fruit, porridge, smoothies and eggs. It's quite incredible what delicacies emerge from its wooden shack of a kitchen. Top of the morning!

Pablo's Restaurant
BREAKFAST, JAMAICAN $

(Map p142; ☎845-5108; West End Rd; mains J$750-1800; ⏱7am-11pm) A friendly fist appears through the kitchen window promptly followed by the words 'Respect, *mon*.' Return the greeting, take a seat and see what breakfast brings. Pablo's reinforces the view that, in Jamaica, the simpler the restaurant, the better the food and the friendlier the wait staff. Talking of respect – this place has it in spades.

Sweet Spice Restaurant
JAMAICAN $

(Map p138; ☎957-4621; Sheffield Rd; mains J$250-1200; ⏱8:30am-11pm) This unassuming bright-blue clapboard house is a favorite among several authentic Jamaican restaurants on Sheffield Rd that are frequented by locals. Portions are heaped, prices are inexpensive and the food is true blue Jamaican. The menu includes curried goat and fish, conch steak and pepper steak. No alcohol, but plenty of fruit juices.

Miss Brown's
CAFE $

(☎957-9217; Sheffield Rd; mains US$4-28; ⏱6:30am-midnight) Miss Brown's is one of Negril's most – ahem – famous restaurants, which may seem a bit odd given the menu. It's all just mushroom stuff, right? Mushroom omelets and mushroom tea and mushroom daiquiris...*They're hallucinogenic.* If you come here, make sure you have a trusted driver to get you back to your hotel (or a few hours to kill sitting around).

Hammond's Bakery
BAKERY $

(Map p138; ☎957-4734; Negril Sq; patties J$150; ⏱9am-6pm Mon-Thu, to 7:30pm Fri & Sat, to 4pm Sun) If you eat a patty in Negril, chances are it will have originated in Hammond's, a busy bakery with indoor seating that inhabits the small settlement's haggard main strip, aka Sheffield Rd. Donuts and cakes make up a good supporting cast.

Canoe Bar
FUSION $$

(Map p138; ☎878-5893; West End Rd; mains J$450-1400; ⏱7am-10pm) Simple wooden shack. Right on the water. Live steel drum performances. Fresh fish plucked from the nearby ocean. Thoroughly reasonable prices. Big portions. Gently lapping waves. Bloody Mary sunsets. What more do you want? Welcome to Canoe Bar – or should that be paradise?

RICK'S CAFE

This bar/restaurant-cum-entertainment venue is an essential pilgrimage, but be sure to arrive before 4pm when the unofficial diving 'show' kicks off. Daredevil locals and the odd brave tourist jump or dive off the adjacent 35ft cliffs into the azure Caribbean, while cocktail-sipping crowds applaud and tanned Adonises lounge by the swimming pool. When the sun sets, a middling reggae band take to the stage to support the equally middling food (nachos, pasta and international dishes mainly). The best part's over.

Rick's Cafe (Map p142; West End Rd; mains US$20-30; ⊙ midday-9pm) first took root in 1974 and was the first nominal drinking hole in the legendary hippie nirvana that was '70s Negril. Over the past 40 years two terrifying hurricanes have swept Rick's – quite literally – off the cliff. Its current incarnation was built after Hurricane Ivan in 2004. It has been voted one of the top ten bars in the world by – ahem – Caribbean Travel & Life Magazine.

Ciao Jamaica   ITALIAN $$
(Map p142; ☎ 957-4395; www.ciaojamaica.com; West End Rd; pastas US$12-18; ⊙ 3-10pm) It doesn't matter where you are in the world, it's always good to have a decent Italian to fall back on after seven straight nights of jerk chicken and curried goat have deadened your taste buds. Ciao makes a night off Jamaican cooking feel guilt-free, with fine create-your-own pasta (including jerk!), Naples-worthy thin crust pizzas and fantastic surprise desserts.

Ivan's Restaurant & Bar   JAMAICAN $$
(Map p142; ☎ 957-0390; www.catchajamaica.com; West End Rd; mains US$15-35; ⊙ 5-11pm) There's West End cliff-top romance at Catcha Falling Star hotel's affiliated restaurant. It's one of Negril's most lavish. The food is Caribbean with some creative fusion. The pineapple chicken is good, as is the lobster. Imaginative cocktails provide a good overture and generous desserts make an ideal coda.

Sips & Bites   JAMAICAN $$
(Map p142; ☎ 957-0188; West End Rd; mains J$350-1500; ⊙ 7am-10pm Sun-Fri) This large, welcoming open-air restaurant serves classic Jamaican fare, and it serves it done right: rich, filling and more compellingly seasoned than in many other Jamaican restaurants. The dishes include oxtail, curried goat, brown stew lobster and conch steaks. This is the go-to place for a slap-up ackee and saltfish breakfast.

★**Rockhouse Restaurant & Bar**   FUSION $$$
(Map p142; ☎ 957-4373; www.rockhousehotel.com/eat; West End Rd; mains US$15-30; ⊙ 7:30am-10pm) Lamplit at night, this pricey yet relaxed cliffside spot leads the pack when it comes to nouvelle Jamaican cuisine in the western parishes. Dine and gush over dishes such as vegetable tempura with lime and ginger, spe-cialty pastas and daily specials such as watermelon spare ribs and blackened mahimahi with mango chutney. At the very least, stop by for a sinful Bananas Foster.

Drinking & Nightlife

Negril gives Kingston a run for its money when it comes to the after-hours pursuits of cocktails and dancing. Dozens of bars and one big nightclub ensure things throb well into the night. Things really hop during Spring Break; in point of fact, it never really stops.

Nonguests can obtain passes (US$25 to US$50) for entry to the discos in the following upscale all-inclusive resorts: Sandals Negril, Hedonism II, Couples Swept Away, and Beaches Negril. Once inside the gates you can booze and party to your heart's content without having to shell out another cent, which is actually a pretty decent deal.

The booze starts flowing each evening along Seven Mile Beach in time to toast the setting sun, when many bars offer happy-hour incentives to lure you in. In the West End, bars are lively in the early evening before petering out as the beach bars take over.

Seven Mile Beach

Alfred's Ocean Palace   BAR
(Map p146; Norman Manley Blvd) Busiest bar on the Long Beach on some nights. Live music three nights a week.

Legends Beach Resort   BAR
(Map p146; Norman Manley Blvd) Corny music, cheesy vibes, good times.

Las Vegas   BAR
(Map p146; Norman Manley Blvd; ⊙ Mon, Thu & Sat) Formally known as Risky Business, this place goes all out during Spring Break. Covers sometimes budge into the expensive US$12 to

US$15 range. Sound-system parties rock the beachside.

Sunrise Club
BAR
(Map p146; www.sunriseclub.com; Norman Manley Blvd) At the hotel of that name, has a cool bar if you want to escape the beach mayhem.

Jungle
NIGHTCLUB
(Map p146; Norman Manley Blvd; admission US$5-10; ☺10pm-4am Thu-Sat) The only bona fide nightclub outside the all-inclusives, Jungle is not the most urbane place, with its tacky decor, but the DJs *definitely* know what they're doing; during the high season guest talent from Miami and New York regularly takes command of the turntables. The best nights are Thursday and Saturday. There's not much action before midnight.

West End

LTU Pub
BAR
(Map p142; West End Rd; ☺8am-11pm) A friendly and comfortable cliff-top haunt centered on a small yet lively tiki bar, LTU is the perfect place to strike up a conversation at sunset or to enjoy a Bloody Mary before noon.

Mi Yard
BAR
(Map p138; West End Rd; ☺24hr) Popular with locals, this place draws a late-night crowd into the wee hours, when you can swig shots of white rum and slap down dominoes with the Rastas.

☆ Entertainment

Negril's reggae concerts are legendary, with live performances every night in peak season, when there's sure to be some big talent in town. Several venues offer weekly jams, with a rotation system so they all get a piece of the action. The really big-name acts usually perform at **Samsara Cliff Resort** (Map p142; ☑957-4395; www.negrilhotels.com; West End Rd).

You will also find sound-system jams where the DJs ('selectors') play shatteringly loud music – usually dancehall with some Euro-disco – on speakers the size of railroad boxcars. The most popular jams are in the Negril Hills, near Little Bay. Most bars start the night playing reggae oldies (ie Bob Marley) early in the evening and bust out the dancehall later.

Information about upcoming events is posted on streetside poles. Covers are usually US$5 to US$10. Some venues stage free reggae concerts.

Bourbon Beach
LIVE MUSIC
(Map p146; ☑957-4405; Norman Manley Blvd; ☺Tue, Fri & Sun) The best spot for live reggae on Seven Mile Beach, Bourbon Beach occasionally hosts big-name acts.

Alfred's Ocean Palace
LIVE MUSIC
(Map p146; ☑957-4669; Norman Manley Blvd; ☺Tue, Fri & Sun) This Negril institution is one of the oldest beach bars. Shows begin around 10pm and continue deep into the night.

Roots Bamboo
LIVE MUSIC
(Map p146; ☑957-4479; Norman Manley Blvd; ☺Wed & Sun) With a rotating roster of musicians anchored by a rock-solid 'riddim' section, the house Hurricane Band shows tourists a thing or two about roots music here each Wednesday. On selected nights big dancehall shows rock the beach.

🛍 Shopping

Locals hawk carvings, woven caps, hammocks, jewelry, macramé bikinis, T-shirts and crafts on the beach and along West End Rd. Competition is fierce. Haggling is part of the fun. Don't be hustled into a purchase you don't want. Various shacks line Seven Mile Beach (and really, you can't walk without tripping on one) selling beach essentials like towels, lighters, sunscreen and bug spray.

Times Square Plaza
SHOPPING CENTER
(Map p146; www.timessquarenegril.com; Norman Manley Blvd; ☺9am-6pm Mon-Sat) Posh shopping center complete with duty-free shops such as Tajmahal's, and Cigar World (selling Cuban cigars) where you can wander unmolested. No haggling here though.

A Fi Wi Plaza
CRAFTS
(Map p138; West End Rd; ☺9am-5pm Mon-Sat) Probably the best crafts market around.

Kuyaba Arts & Crafts Boutique
CRAFTS
(Map p146; Norman Manley Blvd; ☺9am-5pm) At the Kuyaba hotel, with a nice craft selection and Caribbean art and assorted Africana.

Negril Crafts Market
CRAFTS
(Map p146; www.negrilcraftmarket.com; Norman Manley Blvd; ☺dawn-dusk) Just north of Plaza de Negril. Brave the hustlers and haggle hard.

Rutland Point Craft Centre
CRAFTS
(Map p144; Norman Manley Blvd; ☺9am-5pm) Next to the aerodrome. Sells some OK wood carvings and all the usual trinkets, plus some snacks. Prepare for lots of sales banter. Bargain hard.

NEGRIL & WEST COAST NEGRIL

GREAT MORASS

This virtually impenetrable 3km-wide swamp of mangroves stretches 16km from the South Negril River to Orange Bay. It is the island's second-largest freshwater wetland system and a refuge for endangered waterfowl.

The Great Morass acts like a sponge, filtering the waters flowing to the ocean from the hills east of Negril, and is a source of much-needed fresh water. Drainage channels cut into the swamp have lowered water levels, and sewage and other pollutants have seeped into the region's shallow water table, making their way to sea where they have poisoned coral reefs and depleted fish stocks. The easiest way to get a sense of the Great Morass is at the **Royal Palm Reserve** (Map p146; ☑ 957-3763; www.jpat-jm.net; adult/child US$10/5; ☉ 9am-6pm). Wooden boardwalks make a 1.5km loop around the reserve. Three distinct swamp forest types are present – royal palm forest, buttonwood forest and bull thatch forest. They're home to butterflies galore, doctorbirds, herons, egrets, endangered black parakeets, Jamaican woodpeckers and countless other birds. Two observation towers provide views over the mangroves.

If driving, take Sheffield Rd east of the roundabout for 10 minutes and turn left after the golf course. Local tour operators also run trips to the reserve. To explore the Great Morass outside the reserve, negotiate with villagers who have boats moored along the South Negril River northeast of Negril Village. It costs approximately US$45 for two hours. At the time of research, the reserve was officially closed. This is not uncommon, so check ahead. Nonetheless, it is still sometimes possible to get a guided tour with one of the staff who remain onsite.

❶ Information

DANGERS & ANNOYANCES

Do not walk between Seven Mile Beach and the West End at night. Tourists have been, and continue to be, mugged walking through this area. It's best to avoid dark patches of beach; the locals in Negril, police and civilian, are good about patrolling these areas, but sometimes a mugger slips through. At night you should definitely take taxis.

Hustlers stalk Negril like nowhere else in Jamaica. You can expect to be endlessly offered everything from drugs to the hustlers themselves. Usually – but not always – you can shake them off with a firm 'no,' but Negril hustlers can be pretty in your face, and some will try to cop an attitude with you if they think it will intimidate you into giving them some money. Tourist police now patrol the beach but, by law, all Jamaican beaches must permit public access so the hustlers are free to roam, like it or not.

Although ganja is smoked in plain view in Negril, undercover police agents have arrested many visitors throughout the years.

Prostitution is an established part of the local scene and short-term holiday liaisons are a staple. Female visitors should expect to hear a constant litany of well-honed lines enticing you to sample some 'Jamaican steel.'

EMERGENCY
Police Station (☑ 957-4268; Sheffield Rd)

INTERNET RESOURCES
Negril (www.negril.com) Commercial site with numerous listings.

Negril Jamaica (www.negriljamaica.com) Operated by the Negril Resort Association.

Negril Jamaica Videos (www.negril-jamaica-videos.com) A good clearing house of local information.

MEDICAL SERVICES
The nearest hospitals are in Savanna-la-Mar (p155) and Lucea (p153), and neither of those is very nice.

Negril Health Centre (☑ 957-4926; Sheffield Rd; ☉ 9am-8pm Mon-Fri) Government-operated center that offers basic non-emergency services.

Negril Pharmacy (☑ 957-4076; Plaza de Negril; ☉ 9am-7pm Mon-Sat, 10am-2pm Sun)

MONEY
Banks are open 9am to 2pm Monday to Thursday and 9am to 4pm Friday; 24-hour ATMs are on the north side of Plaza de Negril. While many hotels offer currency exchange, you'll get better rates at banks or a private enterprise. Avoid the black market currency-exchange touts that hang out around Negril Sq, or go there with a local.

National Commercial Bank (NCB; West End Rd)

Scotiabank (☑ 957-4236; Negril Sq) Northwest of Plaza de Negril; offers currency exchange and ATMs.

POST
Post Office (Map p138; West End Rd; ☉ 8am-5pm Mon-Fri) Between A Fi Wi Plaza and King's Plaza.

TOURIST INFORMATION
Jamaica Tourist Board (Map p146; ☑ 9314, 957-4803; Norman Manley Blvd; ☉ 9am-5pm

Mon-Fri) At Times Square Plaza, it's less an information center and more a tour booking agency.

Negril Chamber of Commerce (NCC; Map p138; www.negrilchamberofcommerce.com; West End Rd; ⊙9am-4pm Mon-Fri) Publishes an annual *Negril Guide*. You can pick it up at hotels or at the NCC office west of the post office.

🛈 Getting There & Away

Negril Aerodrome (p213), at Bloody Bay about 11km north of Negril Village, is served by the domestic charter company **TimAir** (☑957-2516; www.timair.net), an 'air taxi' service offering on-demand charter flights for small groups going to Montego Bay, Ocho Rios, Port Antonio and Kingston.

Dozens of minibuses and route taxis run between Negril and Montego Bay. The 1½-hour journey costs between J$350 and J$500, and you will likely need to change vehicles in Lucea. Minibuses and route taxis also leave for Negril from Donald Sangster International Airport in Montego Bay (the price is negotiable, but expect to pay about US$10 to US$15). Buses depart from the **transportation center** (Map p138; Sheffield Rd), 1km east of the Negril Sq roundabout.

The handy and comfortable **Knutsford Express** (Map p146; ☑971-1822; www.knutsford express.com; Norman Manley Blvd) has two daily buses to Kingston (J$2700) that also stop in Montego Bay (J$1400), Falmouth (J$1700), and Ocho Rios (J$2200). It stops opposite the Times Square Plaza on Norman Manley Blvd.

A licensed taxi between Montego Bay and Negril will cost about US$80-100. In MoBay, call the **Jamaica Union of Travelers Association** (JUTA; ☑979-0778).

🛈 Getting Around

Negril stretches along more than 16km of shoreline, and it can be a withering walk. At some stage you'll likely need transportation. Upscale resorts at the north end of Seven Mile Beach have shuttles to the village, and several hotels on the West End run shuttles to the beach.

Fortunately minibuses and route taxis cruise Norman Manley Blvd and West End Rd all the time. You can flag them down anywhere. The fare between any two points should never be more than J$130 (they'll always take you as far as Negril Sq from either the West End or Long Beach).

Local car-rental companies include **Vernon's Car Rentals** (☑957-4354, 957-4522; Norman Manley Blvd). High season rates start at around US$43per day.

More than a dozen places along Norman Manley Blvd and West End Rd rent motorcycles (US$40 to US$50 per day), scooters (US$25 to US$35) and bicycles (US$10 to US$15). For bicycle rentals, try **Wright's Bike Rental** (☑957-4908; Norman Man-

ley Blvd). **Dependable Bike Rental** (☑957-4354; Norman Manley Blvd) also rents scooters.

Tourist taxis display a red license plate. Fares are regulated by the government (per 3km about US$4) but few drivers use meters. Negotiate your fare before stepping into the cab. Do not get in a car if it doesn't have red plates and/or its route transfer displayed on the side. Your hotel will call a cab for you, or you can order taxis from **JUTA** (☑957-9197). There are taxi stands at the Negril Crafts Market and in front of Coral Seas Plaza.

NEGRIL TO MAYFIELD FALLS

Northeast from Negril, the A1 expressway leads to Tryall and on to Montego Bay. The only town of note is Lucea and the main draw in the area is Mayfield Falls.

Green Island Harbour

Immediately north of Negril, the A1 swings around a wide expanse of swampland – the Great Morass. After 16km you pass the shores of a deep cove – Green Island Harbour – where pirogues line the thin, gray-sand shore. Minibuses and route taxis between Negril and Lucea stop in Green Island Harbour.

Three miles west of Green Island, Half Moon Beach (☑957-6467; www.halfmoonbeach jamaica.com; admission US$5 cover; ⊙8am-10pm) is a beautiful, hassle-free stretch of sand beloved by locals and families. Here you get a sense of what originally brought tourists to Negril (speaking of which, there's a disused airstrip nearby once used for ganja smuggling – another original draw to the area). It's part of the Negril Marine Park; there are healthy reefs just offshore and no motorized watercraft. Nudism is permitted. Right on the beach are five simple but spacious wooden cabins (☑957-6467; cabins US$65) refurbished in 2013. The adjacent thatched restaurant has a lobster grill and bar and the owners offer boat tours to the tiny islands in the bay. It's a sublime and tranquil spot.

Rhodes Hall Plantation (☑957-6883; www.rhodesresort.com), 3km southwest of Green Island Harbour, is a picturesque 220-hectare fruit-and-coconut plantation with several thatched bars and a restaurant backing a small but attractive beach where hot mineral springs bubble up. Follow the beach west and you'll see a stand of mangroves where Jamaican crocodiles sometimes like to sun themselves. Horseback riding is offered (US$70 for two hours). This is lovely countryside, flat

WORTH A TRIP

BLENHEIM

This tiny hamlet, 6km inland of Davis Cove, is the birthplace of national hero Alexander Bustamante, the island's first prime minister. 'Busta' is honored with a memorial ceremony each August 6. The rustic three-room wooden shack where he was born has been reconstructed as the **Sir Alexander Bustamante Museum** (🖉 956-3898; admission J$250; ⊙ 9am-5pm). It includes memorabilia telling of the hero's life. It has public toilets and a picnic area to the rear.

and crisscrossed with natural water features, and being on horseback is the perfect way to access it.

If you've got some cash to blow, there's a beautiful villa to rent near here: the lovely **Cliffhouse** (🖉 in the USA 896-956-6076; www.cliffhousejamaica.com; Cousin's Cove; per week US$4000; P ❄ 🤶 🏊). Plenty of jerk stalls line the roadside at Green Island Harbour.

Lucea

POP 7500

The halfway point between Negril and Montego Bay, 'Lucy' is a pretty harbor ringed by hills on three sides, small enough for visitors to walk everywhere and charming enough to grab your attention for more than a quick blow-through.

The once-bustling port abounds in old limestone-and-timber structures in 'Caribbean vernacular' style, with gingerbread wood trim, clapboard frontages and wide verandas. The oldest dates to the mid-1700s, and although there is a general air of dishevelment, this is a well-preserved historic town. That said, Lucea is atmospheric enough to have made an appearance in several films, including *Cool Runnings* and *Wide Sargasso Sea*. The **Hanover Historical Society** (🖉 956-2584; Watson Taylor Dr; ⊙ 2-4pm Sat or by appointment) is active in the town's preservation.

◉ Sights

Sir Alexander Bustamante Square   HISTORIC SITE

Bustamante Square is centered on a small fountain fronting the handsome courthouse. Note the vintage 1932 fire engine beside the courthouse. The town's restored **courthouse** (🖉 956-2280; Watson Taylor Dr) has limestone

balustrades and a clapboard upper story topped by a clock tower supported by Corinthian columns. The clock was sent to Lucea in 1817 by mistake – it was actually intended for the Caribbean island of St Lucia. It has supposedly worked without a hitch ever since. On the east side of the square is **Cleveland Stanhope market**, bustling on Saturdays.

Hanover Parish Church   CHURCH

(Watson Taylor Dr) Although architecturally un-inspired, this church – established in 1725 – has several interesting monuments, one being a section of the walled cemetery that recalls the days when Lucea had a vibrant Jewish community. The walk north here from Bustamante Square curls past some of Lucea's finest historical houses, many in a state of near decrepitude, and deposits you atop the headland with a fine view east over Lucea Harbour. You'll find the church at the hillcrest.

Hanover Museum   MUSEUM

(🖉 956-2584; Watson Taylor Dr; admission J$150; ⊙ 8:30am-5pm Mon-Thu, to 4pm Fri) A side road that begins 200m west of Hanover Parish Church leads to the Hanover Museum, a tiny affair housed in an old police barracks. Exhibits include prisoners' stocks, a wooden bathtub and a miscellany of pots, lead weights and measures, but the poor place is pretty run-down, and thieves have stolen artifacts in the past.

Headland   LANDMARK

On the headland beyond the church is **Rusea High School**, a venerable Georgian-style red-brick building constructed in 1843 as an army barracks. The overgrown remains of **Fort Charlotte** overlook the channel a short distance beyond Rusea High School. It's named after Queen Charlotte, wife of King George III of England. The octagonal fortress still boasts cannons in its embrasures.

🛏 Sleeping & Eating

There are a few bare bones options in town, but they're poorly advertised. Most people press on to Negril or MoBay.

Global Villa Hotel   HOTEL $

(🖉 956-2916; www.globalvillahotel.com; Hwy A1; r J$3800-4700; ❄ 🤶) Eight kilometers west of Lucea on the A1, Global Villa is a pretty collection of rooms in a modern house with louvered windows and tiled floors. Tourist buses tend to stop here for drinks and the toilet, but the small restaurant serves good hearty Jamaican fare.

Chilli's Cocktail Bar JAMAICAN $
(Mosely Drive; J$400-700; ☺ midday-10pm) There's
no pampering for tourists' tastes in Lucea, so
pull up a chair with the locals at Chilli's and
pray that peppered steak and snapper are on
the day's menu.

ℹ Information

Lucea Hospital (☎ 956-2233/2733; Fort Char-
lette Dr) On the headland behind Hanover Parish
Church. Has an emergency department.
Police Station (☎ 956-2222; Watson Taylor Dr) In
Sir Alexander Bustamante Square.
Scotiabank (☎ 956-2553; Church St; ☺ 8:30am-
2:30pm Mon-Thu, to 4pm Fri) Faces the round-
about in the center of town.

ℹ Getting There & Away

Buses, minibuses and route taxis arrive at and
depart Lucea from the open ground opposite the
market. Lucea is a midway terminus for public
vehicles traveling between Montego Bay and
Negril, and you may need to change vehicles here.
A bus between Lucea and MoBay or Negril costs
about J$250. A minibus or route taxi costs about
J$300 to J$350.

Mayfield Falls

Jamaica specializes in paradisiacal waterfall
experiences, but, save perhaps for Reach Falls
in Portland parish, nowhere matches Mayfield Falls for wild, crowd-free natural beauty.
The key is that Mayfield is rarely included in
the standard tour operator itinerary that buses in people from Montego Bay and Negril.
As a result there's little frenzy here and few,
if any, hustlers.

Since Mayfield's falls are less ferocious than
West Jamaica's other big waterfall, YS Falls,
you can climb into the river and scramble
upstream for an hour without getting out of
the water. Highlights of this bracing escapade
include a high-diving pool, an underwater
swim-through tunnel, a 'kissing stone' and
a churning whirlpool known as the 'washing machine.' The land on either side of the
river is actually owned by two different families meaning you have a choice of operators.
House-a-Dread (Glenbrook; ☺ 9am-5pm) or the
so-called Original Mayfield Falls (☎ 792-2074;
www.mayfieldfalls.com; Glenbrook; ☺ 9am-5pm).
Both offer the same prices and facilities,
though House-a-Dread's excursion starts lower down the river and is thus longer. Entry
to the falls is US$15 per adult and US$10 per
child, and essential wet shoes can be rented
for US$6. The guides – who are usually fan-

tastic – earn money from your tips (10-20%
depending on service). Lockers, food and
toilets/changing are all available onsite.

From the A1, take the road inland from
Moskito Cove via Cascade. The route is signed
but it's quite complex and there are several
turnoffs; you should ask your way to be sure.
You can also reach Mayfield Falls from Tryall
or Hopewell via Pondside, or by turning north
at Savanna-la-Mar and taking the Banbury or
Amity Cross routes (about 24km) along a road
that is deplorably potholed.

NEGRIL TO SAVANNA-LA-MAR

Tourism has been slow to develop along the
southern shore of Westmoreland, with gritty
Savanna-la-Mar the only town of any import.
Roads fan out from Savanna-la-Mar through
the plains. This flat, mountain-rimmed area,
planted almost entirely in sugarcane, is
drained by the Cabarita River, which feeds
swamplands at its lower reaches. The fishing
is good, and a few crocodiles may still live in
more secluded areas, alongside an endemic
fish – the 'God-a-me' – that can live out of
water in moist, shady spots. The river is navigable by small boat for 19km. In the wetlands
you can spot rice paddies, originally planted
by Indian workers shipped here to work on
the sugar plantations.

Little Bay & Around

Southeast of Retirement, a badly eroded side
road loops down to Homers Cove (locals call
it 'Brighton Beach') and, immediately east, Little Bay, with handsome beaches and peaceful
bathing. Little Bay is imbued with the kind
of laid-back feel that pervaded Negril before
the onset of commercialization. It's a place to
commune with Rastas and other Jamaicans
who live by a carefree axiom in ramshackle
homes, dependent on fishing and their entrepreneurial wits. The area is popular for reggae
and dancehall sound systems.

Between Negril and Little Bay you'll first
pass the town of Orange Hill, (in)famous
around the island as a major marijuana cultivation and distribution center, although
you'd never guess it just looking around.
Ask around for directions to Jurassic Park
(☺ 10am-sunset) FREE; no, there's not real
velociraptors here (damn!), but you will
find giant cast-iron sculptures of dinosaurs

courtesy of local character Daniel Woolcock. Just look for the giant iron pterodactyl and you've found the entrance.

If you continue on to Little Bay, you may find the seaside **house** (now a private residence) where Bob Marley used to live with one of his girlfriends. The home stands next to imaginatively dubbed **Bob Marley's Spring**, where the legend used to bathe.

A mangrove swamp extends east of Little Bay, beyond which lies the fishing community of **Hope Wharf** and a long sliver of white sand called **Lost Beach**. Crocodiles and marine turtles can be found here. Dolphins and humpback whales frequent the waters offshore year-round.

Blue Hole Mineral Spring   SINKHOLE
(☑ 860-8805; US$10; ⊘ 9am-11pm) This sinkhole has long been a feature on the landscape, but its presentation as an attraction is relatively new with some elements ongoing – a hotel was being built at time of research. If you lacked the courage to leap off the cliffs at Rick's Cafe (no shame in that!) then you can have a second try here. The sinkhole requires a 30ft-plus plunge into refreshing mineral waters below, or you can descend via a ladder.

Acrobatic local divers provide plenty of entertainment. There's an adjacent swimming pool and bar/restaurant which cooks jerk – tasty enough to persuade you to linger for an hour or three.

Little Bay Cabins   CABIN $$
(☑ 588-6700; www.littlebaycabins.com; Beach Rd; s/d US$109/129; @) If you want total detachment from Negril-esque clamor, track down the coast to this haven of blissfulness where you can convene with the local Rastas rather than Rob and Carol from Rotherham. It's right on the water in Little Bay.

Frome

Frome lies at the heart of Jamaica's foremost sugar estate, in the center of a rich alluvial plain. The area is dominated by the Frome **sugar-processing factory** (☑ 955-6080), on the B9 north of Savanna-la-Mar and south of Grange Hill. Constructed in 1938, the factory became the setting for a violent nationwide labor dispute. During the 1930s Depression many small factories were bought out by the West Indies Sugar Company. Unemployed workers from all over the island converged here seeking work. Although workers were promised a dollar a day, the men who were hired received 15 cents a day and women only

10 cents. Workers went on strike for higher pay, passions ran high and violence erupted. When the crowds set fire to the cane fields, police responded by firing into the crowd, killing four people. The whole island exploded in violent clashes. The situation was defused when labor activist Alexander Bustamante mediated the dispute, giving rise to the island's first mass labor unions and the first organized political party, under his leadership.

A **monument** at a crossroads north of the factory gates reads: 'To Labour leader Alexander Bustamante and the Workers for their courageous fight in 1938. On behalf of the Working People of Jamaica.' Free tours of the factory can be arranged by reservation.

Frome also boasts two attractive churches, including **St Barnabas Anglican Church**, in a vaguely Teutonic style.

Roaring River & Blue Hole

If you're looking for a brief escape from the fun-in-the-sun ethos of Negril, an hour or two in and around the caves at **Roaring River Park** (cave tours adult/child US$15/8; ⊘ 8am-5pm) could do the trick, although it's not a patch on Mayfield Falls. This natural beauty spot contains mineral waters that gush up from the ground in a meadow full of water hyacinths and water lilies. A stone aqueduct takes off some of the water, which runs turquoise-jade. Steps lead up a cliff face gashed by the mouth of a subterranean passage lit by electric lanterns (you can enter the caves only with guides from the cooperative). Inside, a path with handrails leads down to chambers full of stalagmites and stalactites. Take your swimming gear to sit in the mineral spring that percolates up inside the cave, or in the 'bottomless' blue hole outside it. Harmless fruit bats roost in the recesses.

As you arrive an official guide will meet you to show the way to the ticket office, and then around the gardens and cave; ignore the touts who congregate outside posing as tour guides.

The lane then continues for about 1km uphill through the village to **Blue Hole Gardens** (☑ 955-8823; www.jamaicaescapes.com; admission US$10), a beautiful sinkhole that is surrounded by a landscaped garden full of ginger torch and heliconia. The sinkhole is privately owned and overpriced, but you'll get the chance to take a cool dip with the fish in the turquoise waters. The source of the Roaring River is about 400m further up the road, where the water foams up from beneath a matting of foliage. This is also a quintessential counterculture lifestyle retreat that offers two very rustic but charming **cottages** (☑401-5312; www.jamaicaescapes.com/villas/bluehole/bluehole. html; cottages US$40-80) set in gardens at the edge of the tumbling brook. The place acquired a new owner in 2013 and the cottages were in the process of being refurbished so prices may change. If you're hungry, pop into **Lovers Café** (mains US$3-8; ☑), known for its veggie feast, I-tal dishes, fruit juices and herbal teas.

Roaring River is at Shrewsbury Estate, about 2km north of the main crossroads in Petersfield (8km northeast of Savanna-la-Mar). You can catch a bus in Savanna-la-Mar as far as Petersfield (J$150, about once every hour). From there it's a hot walk or rough ride down the potholed road through the cane fields. Route taxis and coasters also run to Roaring River from Petersfield (J$100).

Organized tours to Roaring River are offered by companies in Negril (around US$75).

Savanna-la-Mar

POP 20,000

Although Savanna-la-Mar is the largest town in western Jamaica and capital of Westmoreland parish, 'Sav' offers few attractions save for its local shopping opportunities, strung out along the 2km-long main drag, Great George St. It gets a bad rap for its crime rate, so stick close to this road if you're staying in town and don't walk around after dark. Several petrol stations are also found on Great George St; where route taxis and minibuses congregate to take passengers on to Negril, Montego Bay, or further east to Black River.

◎ Sights

Savanna-la-Mar Fort   NOTABLE BUILDING
(Great George St) The English colonialists never completed the Savanna-la-Mar Fort at the foot of Great George St. Parts of it collapsed into the swamps within a few years of being built, and these discarded guts now form a small cove where locals swim. A bustling daily market, specializing in vegetables and local fish, has been built into the grounds.

Courthouse   NOTABLE BUILDING
(cnr Great George & Rose Sts) The most interesting building is the Sav courthouse, built in 1925, where there's a fountain made of cast iron, inscribed with the words, 'Keep the pavements dry.' There doesn't seem to be any deeper meaning to this highly literal commandment.

St George's Parish Church   CHURCH
(cnr Great George & Murray Sts) This church, opposite the courthouse, was built in 1905. It's uninspired, but has a stately **pipe organ** that was dedicated in 1914.

Manning's School   NOTABLE BUILDING
(Seaton St) At the north end of town by the roundabout known as Hendon Circle is the very handsome Manning's School, built in 1738 and named after Westmoreland planter Thomas Manning.

🛏 Sleeping & Eating

You can buy fresh fish and produce from the market at the base of Great George St, but the sanitary conditions aren't great; otherwise, cheap jerk and food stalls cluster in the center of Sav.

Lochiel Guest House   GUESTHOUSE **$**
(☑955-9344; Sheffield Rd; r US$35) On the A2, 2km east of town, is an old stone-and-timber, two-story great house that looks delightful from the outside. Inside it's a bit run-down, though some of the rooms are appealing. All have utilitarian furniture and hot water in private bathrooms. This place is decent as a last resort, but otherwise move along to Bluefields (17km to southeast) or Negril (29km to west).

Tan Tan Top Tasty Pastry   BAKERY **$**
(7 Great George St; patties J$120-150) Come here for Jamaica's default snack – a patti, plus a few sweeter treats. It's a quick skip from the transportation center.

ℹ Information

Police station (☑918-1865; Great George St) Near the courthouse.

Post office (☑955-9295; Great George St; ☺8am-5pm)

Savanna-la-Mar Hospital (☑955-2133; Barracks Rd; ☺emergency service 24hr) On the A2 on the northeast side of town.

Scotiabank (☑955-2601; Great George St; ☺8:30am-2:30pm Mon-Thu, to 4pm Fri)

ℹ Getting There & Away

Buses, minibuses and route taxis operate frequently along the A2/B8 between Montego Bay (J$350, 1½ to two hours) and Negril (J$300, 45 minutes). **Knutsford Express** (☑971-1822; ww.knutsfordexpress.com; Dunbar Mall) runs comfortable coaches once daily to Montego Bay (J$1200) and twice daily to Kingston (J$2400) via Mandeville (J$1600).

NEGRIL & WEST COAST SAVANNA-LA-MAR

South Coast & Central Highlands

Includes ➡

Why Go?

Cut off from the clamorous north coast by the natural bulwark of Cockpit Country and protected from resort development by local communities that seriously value their near-virgin beaches, southwest Jamaica feels like a clandestine paradise for the trickle of off-island visitors who make it this far. Its biggest present is Treasure Beach, an antidote to pretty much everything else in Jamaica you will have encountered so far, with its cow-filled pastures, crime-free country lanes, and semi-deserted scimitars of sand.

Rural St Elizabeth parish is often coined the breadbasket of Jamaica for the many crops that grow there, but fertile fields quickly give way to swamp around Black River and mountains around the lightly touristed, highland town of Mandeville. The region's most notable sights – the Black River, YS Falls and the Appleton Rum Estate – are usually visited by day-trippers on organized excursions from resorts in Negril and Montego Bay.

Best Places to Eat

➡ Little Ochie (p180)

➡ Jack Sprat Café (p177)

➡ Smurf's Cafe (p177)

➡ Jake's Country Cuisine (p177)

Best Places for a Red Stripe

➡ Frenchman's Reef (p178)

➡ Pelican Bar (p178)

➡ Little Ochie (p180)

➡ Manchester Arms Pub (p171)

When to Go

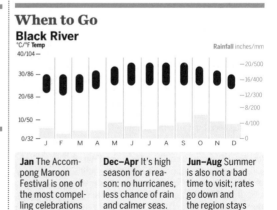

Black River

Jan The Accompong Maroon Festival is one of the most compelling celebrations of Afro-Caribbean culture.

Dec–Apr It's high season for a reason: no hurricanes, less chance of rain and calmer seas.

Jun–Aug Summer is also not a bad time to visit; rates go down and the region stays relatively dry.

BLUEFIELDS TO BLACK RIVER

Bluefields & Belmont

Bluefields in southeastern Westmoreland parish is appropriately named: look out the door and it's either big light-blue skies beyond the mountains or sea-blue harbors lapping the rocky beach. In 1519 this was Oristan, one of the first Spanish settlements in Jamaica; Bluefields Bay provided safe anchorage for Spanish explorers, British naval squadrons and pirates. In 1670, before he became a tacky rum mascot, infamous buccaneer Henry Morgan set out from Bluefields Bay to sack Panama City. Today Bluefields (population 2560) and adjacent Belmont (population 2880) are populated by a quiet collection of fishers, tourists, escape artists, regular artists, expats and returnees – the latter two attracted by a small housing-construction boom in the hills.

⊙ Sights

Peter Tosh Monument   MONUMENT
(Hwy A2; admission J$1000; ⊙ vary) Many monuments make a political statement, and the memorial to reggae superstar Peter Tosh, plunked a kilometer south of Bluefields on the beach road in Belmont, is no exception. And the cause here is, as Tosh once sang, to 'legalize it.' You can guess what 'it' is, but if not, just check all the murals, which depict a Rasta man with a huge joint, jumbo marijuana leaves, and, best of all, a red-eyed Lion of Zion on Tosh's actual tomb.

Behind the tomb is a garden where they ain't growing oregano. This is a casual place with few visitors, a stark contrast to the tourist maelstrom surrounding fellow Wailer Bob Marley's mausoleum in Nine Mile. It is run by the Tosh family – his nonagenarian mother lived on the property until her death in 2013 – and your money is taken by a caretaker who will give you a brief tour along with commentary on Tosh's political positions ('I'm like a smoke. Dat why we say legalize it.'). In mid-October the annual Peter Tosh Birthday Bash, an informal local affair, features live roots reggae music played deep into the night.

Bluefields House   HISTORIC SITE
Philip Gosse was one of the great polymaths of his time: the man who both popularized the aquarium and modified its design, and illustrator of gorgeously detailed renditions of Jamaican birdlife. His old home, naught but a

ruin located inland from the Bluefields police station, is worth visiting for historical novelty more than anything – to see where the author of *Illustrations of the Birds of Jamaica* and *A Naturalist's Sojourn in Jamaica* once laid his head. There's a lovely breadfruit tree on site, said to be the first on the island.

🏖 Beaches

Bluefields Beach Park   BEACH
(Hwy A2; ⊙ 8am-sunset) Well signed from the Winston Jones Hwy (A2), this beach is a swathe of pale sand that frames the dark-blue water like a ribbon; a beach as beautiful as it is ignored by foreign tourists, although it's quite popular with locals on weekends. During the early evening and on weekends you'll find a nice collection of food stalls featuring locally caught fresh fish and plenty of Red Stripe.

Belmont Beach   BEACH
There are actually two small Belmont Beaches, but one is too rocky to relax on and the other is a major mooring point for fishing boats. That said, if the day is clear the water will be as well, so you can swim out a little way and do some fine snorkeling or spear fishing. Most accommodations rent the required equipment.

☞ Tours

Travelers staying in the area can enjoy day trips and excursions to regional attractions including YS Falls, the Black River Great Morass, Ipswich Caves and Alligator Pond.

Natural Mystic Tours   NATURE TOURS
(☑ 851-3962; www.naturalmystic-jamaica.com) Run by a German expat; leads tours (in English and German) all across the island.

Nature Roots   NATURE TOURS
(☑ 955-8162, 384-6610; www.natureroots.de) Go with Brian the Bush Doctor out on the sea and into the jungle, or stay at his friendly little cottage.

Shafston Tours   NATURE TOURS
(☑ 869-9212; www.shafston.com; Shafston Estate Great House, Bluefields) A good choice for outdoor pursuits such as river kayaking (US$50 per person) and hiking.

🛏 Sleeping & Eating

For food, you can eat at any of the accommodation places listed. It's also worth pressing on to Scott's Cove for the full-on Jamaican fish and *bammy* (pancake of fried cassava) experience.

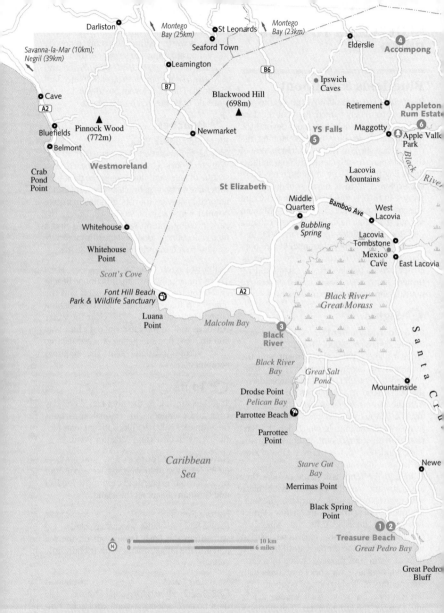

Darliston

Montego Bay (25km)

St Leonards

Seaford Town

Montego Bay (23km)

Elderslie

4 **Accompong**

Savanna-la-Mar (10km);
Negril (39km)

Leamington

B6

B7

Blackwood Hill
(698m)

Ipswich
Caves

Retirement

**Appleton
Rum Estate**

6

Cave

A2

Bluefields

Pinnock Wood
(772m)

Newmarket

YS Falls

5

Maggotty

Apple Valley
Park

Belmont

Westmoreland

Lacovia
Mountains

Black

River

Crab
Pond
Point

St Elizabeth

Middle
Quarters

Bamboo Ave

West
Lacovia

Whitehouse

*Bubbling
Spring*

Lacovia
Tombstone

Whitehouse
Point

Scott's Cove

Mexico
Cave

East Lacovia

Font Hill Beach
Park & Wildlife Sanctuary

A2

*Black River
Great Morass*

Luana
Point

Malcolm Bay

3

**Black
River**

*S
a
n
t
a
C
r
u*

*Black River
Bay*

*Great Salt
Pond*

Drodse Point
Pelican Bay

Mountainside

Parrottee Beach

7

Parrottee
Point

*Caribbean
Sea*

*Starve Gut
Bay*

Newe

Merrimas Point

Black Spring
Point

1 **2**

N

0 — 10 km
0 — 6 miles

Treasure Beach

Great Pedro Bay

*Great Pedro
Bluff*

South Coast & Central Highlights Highlights

1 Watching the fisherfolk
mending their nets on
otherwise deserted **Calabash
Bay Beach** (p175)

2 Enjoying a game of local
cricket at **Treasure Beach
Sports Park** (p178)

3 Exploring Jamaica's
longest river, **Black River**
(p161), by small watercraft
and seeing crocodiles in their
mangrove ecosystem

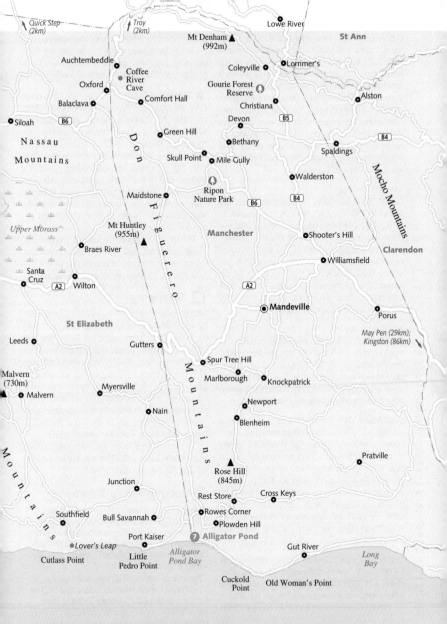

Quick Step
(2km)

Troy
(2km)

Lowe River

St Ann

Mt Denham
(992m)

Coleyville   Lorrimer's

Auchtembeddie

Coffee
River
Cave   Gourie Forest
Reserve   Alston

Oxford   Christiana

Balaclava   Comfort Hall   Devon   B5

Siloah   B6

Green Hill   Spaldings   B4

Nassau   Bethany

Mountains   Skull Point   Mile Gully

Walderston

Ripon   B6
Nature Park   B4

Maidstone   Mocho Mountains

Upper Morass   Manchester   Shooter's Hill

Mt Huntley   Clarendon
(955m)

Braes River   Williamsfield

Santa
Cruz   A2
Wilton   A2   Mandeville

St Elizabeth   Porus

Leeds   May Pen (29km);
Kingston (86km)

Gutters   Spur Tree Hill

Marlborough
Malvern   Myersville   Knockpatrick
(730m)

Malvern   Newport
Nain   Blenheim

Pratville

Rose Hill
(845m)

Junction   Rest Store   Cross Keys

Southfield   Rowes Corner

Bull Savannah   Plowden Hill

Port Kaiser   Alligator Pond

Lover's Leap   Gut River   Long
Bay
Cutlass Point   Little   Alligator
Pedro Point   Pond Bay

Cuckold   Old Woman's Point
Point

4 Heeding the call of the ancient *abeng* (goat horn) at the well-preserved Maroon village of **Accompong** (p166)

5 Soaring over the majestic **YS Falls** (p166) on a zip-line

6 Delving into the island's largest rum distillery, **Appleton Rum Estate** (p165), before sampling its wares

7 Watching your fish being caught, brought ashore and cooked at Jamaica's finest seafood restaurant, **Little Ochie** (p180), in Alligator Pond

Retro Roots Cabins
CABINS, HOUSE **$**

(☑ 876-521-0682; www.retrorootscabins.com; Belmont; cabins s/d US$25/50, mansion per month US$5000 ; 🅿 🛜 🌫) Opposite the ocean in the hamlet of Belmont, Retro Roots is a newly invigorated business with an interesting configuration of rooms: two simple but adequate cabins with front verandas, and a full-blown eight-room mansion with its own pool for groups keen to drop sticks for a month or more (easily done here). A new onsite grill was on the verge of opening at last visit promising seafood and kebabs.

Shades Cottage
HOMESTAY **$**

(☑ 441-1830, 955-8102; www.shadescottage.com; Belmont; r US$30-35; 🛜) Run by the hospitable Rasta Bigga (when you meet him, you'll understand the nickname), at Shades Cottage you'll be staying in a 'yard' – a compound of neighborly houses – arranged around a bar where fresh meals and cold beer can be ordered. The rooms are basic and clean; don't expect the Ritz. The spot attracts younger travelers and long-term expats.

Nature Roots
HOMESTAY **$**

(☑ 955-8162, 384-6610; www.natureroots.de; Belmont; r US$25-30) Nature Roots, the home base for the tour outfit of the same name, offers chilled-out accommodations in a yard with good vibes, easy access to the beach (it's about 50m away) and a lovely, indolent air.

South Sea View Guest House
GUESTHOUSE **$**

(☑ 963-5172; www.southseaviewjamaica.com; Whitehouse; r without/with air-con US$70/90; 🌫🌫) With a bit of imagination you could call South Sea View Greek Island-ish in its aesthetics, all white-walled and open to the pale-blue sky and winds. Rooms are fresh and modern, with fluffy king-size beds, tropical murals and cable TV for those days when you need to veg. It's located 14km southwest of Belmont in the town of Whitehouse.

Shafston Estate Great House
GUESTHOUSE **$$**

(☑ 869-9212; www.shafston.com; Bluefields Bay; all-incl s/d US$100/160; 🅿🌫) Poised on a hilltop with exquisite coastal views stretching as far as Savanna-la-Mar, this creaky Great House is an 'all-inclusive' that is nothing like the other all-inclusives on the island. In the original manor house there are atmospheric, spacious rooms ranging from basic to modest; a few have bathrooms.

For even cheaper digs, there are 12 simple yet charming rooms in a newer block with screened windows and clean, tiled communal unisex showers and bathrooms. Note: this is not a luxury resort; rather, it's a more rustic Jamaican experience. Behold the sunsets.

To get here from the A2, take the dirt road opposite Bluefields police station, then it's a precipitous 3km climb over bad roads.

★ Bluefields Villas
VILLAS **$$$**

(☑ in the USA 1-877-955-8993; www.bluefieldsvillas.com; Hwy A2, Bluefields Bay; per week US$6440-10,828; 🅿🌫🛜🌫) Exquisite is an understatement for these six private villas scattered around the Bluefields Bay waterfront that offer all-inclusive services (chef, cleaners, butlers, etc) fit for Marie Antoinette. All have pools and luxury furnishings, and three of them even have their own tiny private islands. Villa sizes vary; some fit four, the largest caters for 13 people.

Throw in unique organized excursions, private nannies, and spectacular service that doesn't miss a single beat and you've got the holiday of a lifetime pretty much guaranteed.

🛍 Shopping

Studio Black
CRAFTS, ART

(☑ 459-9918; www.studioblack-jamaica.com; Hwy A2; ⏰ 9am-5pm) Warning: don't walk past this artistically attired Rasta shack that's been defying hurricanes, dodgy drivers and all else in Belmont since 1977; it's simply too good to miss. Run by amiable local artist, Jah Calo, it's replete with one-of-a-kind art and sculptures immersed in Rastafarian imagery. Calo's painted many murals in the area, including those at the Peter Tosh Memorial (p157).

The shop-shack is on the main beach road (A2) running through Belmont. With its colorful decoration, you can't miss it.

ℹ Getting There & Away

The A2 is the only road that runs through Bluefields and Belmont, and buses will drop you off wherever you ask in either town; otherwise they'll likely leave you in Bluefields 'square,' a centrally located patch of open land with a small general-purpose shop.

Buses and minivans run frequently (every hour during the day) up the coastal road (A2) to Savanna-la-Mar (J$200, one hour), and from there to Montego Bay and Negril, but try to go before late afternoon – you don't want to be stuck in Savanna-la-Mar, especially after dark.

In the opposite direction (southeast) most buses go through Black River (J$350, 1½ to two hours), from where you can get buses or taxis to Treasure Beach or Mandeville, or travel onwards to May Pen, from where you can find reliable transportation to Kingston. Getting stuck in Black River is fine, for the record.

FONT HILL BEACH PARK & WILDLIFE SANCTUARY

This **beach park** (adult/child J$350/175; ⊙9am-5pm), situated on almost 13 sq km southeast of Scott's Cove, is owned by the Petroleum Corporation of Jamaica, which has not tarnished its natural beauty in the slightest after the company realized that the oil it initially sought offshore didn't exist. Two golden-sand beaches (connected by a trail) are fringed by a reef offering great snorkeling and bathing. Dolphins come into the cove, as do turtles for nesting season. There's a small cafe and bar, changing rooms, picnic booths, volleyball, a boardwalk and a lackluster interpretive center and marina. Horseback rides are also offered.

You can only visit the wildlife sanctuary if accompanied by a guide, but it's worth it for the good intro to the odd marsh-and-scrub coastal ecosystem of southwest Jamaica. There's scrubby acacia, logwood thickets, and closer to the shore, a maze of connected lagoons and swamps with a population of a couple of hundred American crocodiles (made all the more vulnerable after being displaced from other parts of the south coast by large-scale construction projects). The bird-watching is fabulous, highlighted by a flock of bald-pate pigeons as well as assorted black-billed whistling ducks, jacanas, herons and pelicans.

Black River

POP 4230

The capital of St Elizabeth and the parish's largest town, Black River occupies an interesting median point in terms of tropical energy. A big city this may be for these parts, but a bustling metropolis it most certainly is not. At the same time it's no sleepy backwater either – Black River may be off the beaten path, but there's a buzz here, a colorful, open-air chaos offset by Georgian architecture peeling away in a state of elegant rot and buckets of liquid gold sunlight. The namesake river is a slow-moving slick of moldering tannins patrolled by straight-arrow alligators and boats full of curious tourists. Although most visitors understandably opt to stay in nearby Treasure Beach, a few people do use this town as a base for visiting attractions like YS Falls and the Appleton Rum Estate.

The town's Georgian buildings attest to its 19th-century prosperity, when Black River exported local logwood from which Prussian blue dye was extracted for textiles. Locals proudly point out the Waterloo Guest House, which in 1893 became the first house in Jamaica to have electricity installed. The racetrack and spa that attracted the wealthy have sadly not survived the passage of time.

☉ Sights

**Black River
Heritage Buildings** HISTORICAL BUILDINGS
Foremost among the structures worth checking out is the yellow-brick **Parish Church of St John the Evangelist** (cnr Main & North Sts), built in 1837. From the outside it's a bright, mustard-colored supermarket. The wind-pocked interior is graced by wooden porticoes and a stately balcony, while the graves around the back cemetery date from the 17th century. Two blocks west are the porticoed courthouse and the town hall, with lofty pillars, and beyond that a simple Roman Catholic church, a rare denomination in Jamaica.

Two of the most impressive buildings are both hotels. The 1894 **Invercauld Great House & Hotel** and the **Waterloo Guest House**, both west on Main St, are splendid examples of the Jamaican vernacular style; with their shady wooden verandas and gingerbread trim they look like the sort of place where you should don a safari hat and demand a sherry in an imperious voice.

High Street STREET
Although it's as frenetic and chaotic as any other High St in Jamaica, Black River's High St (note: High St and Main St are used interchangeably here) is also lined with colonnaded Georgian timber houses, all musty and fading away in the intense sunshine, which gives it a prettily entropic quality. At the east end is the **Hendricks Building** (2 High St), dating from 1813, a fine example of period British-Caribbean architecture.

Immediately east is an old iron bridge, a good spot for watching American crocodiles waiting for tidbits thrown by tourists from the riverside berths. Trawlers lie at anchor immediately south of the bridge, from where you can watch fish being hauled ashore onto the wharfs.

🏊 Beaches

Heavy Sands BEACH
Long stretches of dark sand still undiscovered by most international tourists. Just don't

Black River

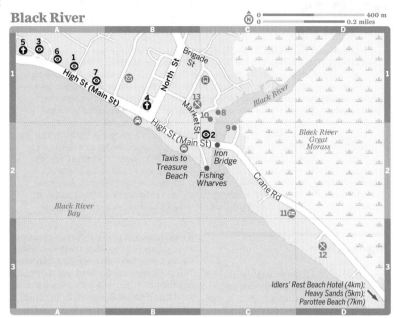

swim near the river mouth – crocodiles like to congregate here! You'll be fine in the sea, but beware the tides as there will likely be no one around. Abutting it is Parottee Beach.

☞ Tours

A river trip is the main reason many tourists come to Black River and it has become a popular day-out from the all-inclusives. Loads of boats cluster by the old warehouse on the east bank of the river, waiting to chug people into the vine-laden interior of the Great Morass. You'll be escorted along water that resembles a mossy oil slick, and while nothing can be guaranteed when speaking of spotting wildlife, there's a good chance you'll see white marsh cranes and herons skimming the banks like pterodactyls, sword-beaked, fish-spearing anhinga, and, of course, crocodiles. Thanks to all the visitors these reptiles are tame around people now, and they're pretty small to boot. Many operators let people go swimming in the river with them, which they insist is a safe endeavor. If you do choose to swim, do so at your own risk.

J Charles Swaby's Black River Safari (☑965-2513, 965-2086; tour US$19; ☺tours 9am, 11am, 12:30pm, 2pm & 3:30pm), on the east side of the river just north of the bridge, offers 60- to 75-minute journeys aboard the *Safari Queen* and is the oldest operator. Similar tours and

prices are offered by **St Elizabeth River Safari** (☑965-2229, 965-2374; ☺tours 9am, 11am, 2pm & 3:30pm), behind the Hendricks Building, and **Irie Safaris** (☑965-2211; Riverside Dr; ☺tours every 90min 9am-4.30pm), wharfside from a jetty just southeast of the bus station (Irie can also arrange kayaking trips in the area, which come highly recommended). At the time of writing tours ran around US$20 to US$30; thanks to the price of petrol these rates can swing up and down at short notice.

For a less regimented (and more authentic) experience, you can easily hire a guide to take you upriver by canoe or boat for about US$50 to US$60 round-trip. Ask near the bridge in town or anywhere in Treasure Beach. If you're continuing on to Treasure Beach, you can hire a boat there for a round-trip tour (US$75) that includes a stop at the Pelican Bar and a journey up the Black River.

Midday tours are best for spotting crocodiles; early and later tours are better for birding. Take a hat and some mosquito repellent.

🛏 Sleeping

Spring Garden Hotel HOTEL $
(☑876-965-2361; 14 Crane Rd; s/d J$4000/7000; [P][❄][📶]) This recently refurbished and re-named bay-side hotel, just a short stroll from Black River's main drag, could provide a good excuse to layover in town en route for

Black River

Sights

Activities, Courses & Tours

Sleeping

Eating

Treasure Beach. Rooms are simple but freshly painted and, most importantly, clean. The ocean is stone-lobbing distance and there are a periodically open bar and restaurant on site.

Waterloo Guest House HOTEL $
(☑965-2278; 44 High St; r US$40-50; P❄☀) The Waterloo, the first home in Jamaica with electricity, looks like an elegantly ruined throwback of British-Caribbean architecture. Though if you're staying here you won't have much appreciation for the withered wood and broken fixtures as rooms scream 'gimme a refurb.' Indeed, the ones in the main building were closed altogether at last research. Be careful when you dive into that swimming pool – it may not have any water in it. For the non-fussy on a budget only.

Idlers' Rest Beach Hotel HOTEL $$
(☑965-9000; www.idlersrest.com; r from US$100; P❄🛜) A worthwhile non–Treasure Beach option a little way out of town, Idlers' Rest redefines 'Irie.' Owned by a friendly lawyer, the hotel is a tasteful boutique decorated in a comfy mix of modern chic, Caribbean color and pan-African art. Rooms are cooled by sea breezes and you can wander the beach while gazing at dolphins frolicking on the waves.

✕ Eating

There's a supermarket in the Hendricks Building, and another one 100m north. You can buy fruit, vegetables and meats at the open-air **produce market** (Market St; ☺sunrise-sunset).

Waterloo Guest House JAMAICAN $
(44 High St; mains J$300-900; ☺7am-10pm) The Waterloo's on-site restaurant is as decrepit as its guesthouse although there's a raffish quality to the colonial bar that looks like it could have sprung from a Graham Greene novel. OK for a quick drink or a too-simple-to-get-wrong grilled cheese sandwich.

Cloggy's on the Beach SEAFOOD $$
(☑634-2424; www.cloggysonthebeach.webs.com; 22 Crane Rd; mains J$600-2000; ☺midday-10pm) This beachside joint is your best culinary bet in Black River; it's an all-round pleaser with a relaxed vibe, great bar ambience and excellent chow. It occasionally throws well-attended beach sound-system parties; ask the bartender for the lowdown. Try a cup of conch soup for a revelation, and follow that up with some gorgeous fresh lobster.

ℹ Information

Black River Hospital (☑965-2212/2224; 45 Main St) A kilometer west of town.
Police Station (☑965-2232; North St)
Post Office (☑965-2250; ☺8am-5pm) Immediately west of the police station.
Scotiabank (☑965-2251; 6 High St; ☺8:30am-2:30pm Mon-Thu, 8:30am-4pm Fri)
St Bess Pharmacy (☑634-4526; 1a Brigade St; ☺8:30am-7pm Mon-Sat)

ℹ Getting There & Away

Black River is a nexus for route taxis that shoot off in all directions, including Santa Cruz (J$180), Whitehouse (J$100) and Treasure Beach (J$250). Change at Whitehouse for Bluefields and Belmont. Minibuses go to Montego Bay (J$250 to J$300) and Savanna-la-Mar (J$200). The transportation center is behind the market, just west of the river. Taxis arrive and depart from a lot at the junction of Main and North Sts, though Treasure Beach taxis have a separate departure point close to the corner of High and Market Sts.

SOUTH COCKPIT COUNTRY

St Elizabeth is the driest parish in Jamaica thanks in part to the rugged Cockpit Country, which joins St Elizabeth to Trelawny parish in a rocky fist-bump and blocks the south coast from the rains whipping off the ocean. South Cockpit Country is as beautiful, rugged and remote as its northern counterpart, and perhaps a better area from which to access the unique, if fading, culture of the Maroons. Few roads penetrate the hills, where the sparse population is mostly involved in subsistence farming and, deeper in the valleys, ganja cultivation. We warn you away from trying to discover marijuana plots; if you come upon one uninvited, it could cost you your life (see p210 for more information). Between the Nassau Mountains and the Cockpit Country is the wide Siloah Valley, carpeted with sugarcane.

From the hamlet of Troy you can plunge into the depths of Cockpit Country on foot (see p132) and come out on the northern side.

Middle Quarters

This small village on the A2, 13km north of Black River, is a tiny vortex of good eats. First, it's renowned for women *higglers* or street vendors, who stand at the roadside selling delicious and spicy pepper shrimp – pronounced 'swimp' in these parts – cooked at the roadside grills. The shrimp are caught in traps made in centuries-old West African tradition from split bamboo. Around J$300 will buy a spicy bagful. The women come on strong in the sales pitch, but many of these vendors are related, so don't let guilt direct your purchase.

Jog, jump, or do whatever it takes to get hungry again, because now you have to try a Jamaican trucker favorite: **Howie's Healthy Eating** (☑378-8714; A2 Hwy; mains J$200-500; ☺24hr), on the A2 at the turnoff for YS Falls. Do you have a great 24-hour diner or greasy spoon in your town? If so, come to Howie's for the same vibe Jamaican-style. The cooking is done in big pots bubbling over wood fires. Choose from a number of soups, stews, fried fish, curried goat, of course, and huge help-

ings of 'swimp'; the fried chicken is a feast – even with the trucks roaring past.

If you want to shed some of your newly accumulated weight via a quick dip, stop by **Bubbling Spring** (☑850-1606; A2 Hwy; admission US$15; ☺8am-6pm), 1.5km south of Middle Quarters on the A2. Cool, slightly carbonated spring water is fed into long, shallow pools. If you're driving yourself around, this can be a lovely break from the road, but it may be a bit underwhelming if you're coming here by public transportation. Simple Jamaican fare is served at nearby stalls.

Santa Cruz

POP 7000

Santa Cruz is a bustling market town and the most important commercial center in southwest Jamaica. Black River may be the capital of St Elizabeth parish, but Santa Cruz is arguably the more important settlement thanks to its economic clout. Unfortunately it's less attractive. Back in the day Santa Cruz was a market center for horses and mules bred locally for the British army, and a livestock market is still held on Saturday, but by and large this is a bauxite town that has grown too fast.

While there's nothing here to keep the average tourist busy for long, it's a good place to stop for a bite to eat or money, and it's a major transportation hub as well.

Hind's Restaurant & Bakery (☑966-2234; Santa Cruz Plaza, Main St; mains US$1-6; ☺7:30am-5pm Mon-Thu, 7:30am-7pm Fri & Sat) sells baked goods and is a clean, simple place to enjoy Jamaican fare such as brown stew and curried goat. **Paradise Patties** (Shop 30, Beadles Plaza, Main St) sells veggie and beef patties for cheap (under J$100). **Fruity's** (Shop 27, Philip's Plaza, Main St) serves delicious ice-cream cones.

DON'T MISS

BAMBOO AVENUE

The soothing sound of a million leaves rustling in the wind is one of the quiet pleasures of this photogenic archway of towering bamboo. The 4km-long stretch of the A2 between Middle Quarters and Lacovia is shaded by dense 100-year-old stands of *Bambusa vulgaris*, the largest species of bamboo in Jamaica. Cool and pretty, Bamboo Avenue is the perfect place to stop for a coconut jelly, accompanied by a bag of pepper shrimp brought from Middle Quarters. In Lacovia, ask locals for help finding the **twin tombs** (near the Texaco) where, according to local lore, two young victims of a 1738 duel are buried. One of the dead is identified: Thomas Jordan Spencer, a descendant of the Duke of Marlborough and distant ancestor of Lady Diana Spencer and Winston Churchill. Infrequent minibuses connect Lacovia to Black River and Santa Cruz, but it makes more sense to drive here; a nice add-on to a trip to Mandeville.

There's a **Scotiabank** (☑966-2230; 77 Main St; ⊙8:30am-2:30pm Mon-Thu, 8:30am-4pm Fri) on the main drag.

Santa Cruz is a main stop for buses, mini-buses and route taxis going between Kingston, Mandeville and Black River. They arrive and depart from the transportation center on the A2, at the east end of Santa Cruz. **Knutsford Express** (www.knutsfordexpress.com) coaches also stop here on their way between Mandeville (J$800, 45 minutes) and Savanna-la-Mar (J$1000, 1¼ hours).

Maggotty

POP 1400

Maggotty is a forgettable town with an unforgettable name, laid out on a bend of the Black River at the western end of the Siloah Valley. It thinks of itself as a sleepy regional center, but it can also be a viable base for exploring YS Falls and the Appleton Rum Estate. Plus, Maggotty is the closest base for trips into the Black River Gorge, a rocky rent in the jungle speckled with 28 pretty waterfalls and intermittent natural swimming pools. The name, by the way, can be attributed to the missionary Rev John Hutch, who named Maggotty after his English birthplace.

◎ Sights

Apple Valley Park   PARK
(☑487-4521, 894-5947; www.applevalleypark.com; adult/child J$450/350; ⊙10am-5pm daily by reservation only) Owned by Patrick Lee and his lovely Chinese-Jamaican family, Apple Valley Park is a little triumph of green sensibility and community tourism. The park grounds consist of an 18th-century home, a manicured lake, an artificial pool and, further on, a forest reserve that stretches past the waterfalls and swimming holes of the Black River Gorge. You can kayak and paddleboat in the park itself or hike into the woods or fish or order a meal – it's all relaxing.

The prettiness of the place is all the more remarkable when one considers this was once the scarred remains of a bauxite mine; Patrick Lee helped bring the area back to nature after hiring locals and subsequently boosting the surrounding economy, and for this reason we give some of the wear and tear evident on the grounds a pass. The 169-hectare family nature park is only open by appointment, so call ahead. The owners also operate a tractor-pulled jitney from the old train station in Maggotty.

🛌 Sleeping & Eating

Apple Valley Guesthouse   GUESTHOUSE $
(per person camping/dm/d US$5/15/20) Patrick and Lucille Lee, the Chinese-Jamaican couple who run Apple Valley Park, keep bunks and private rooms in the 18th-century red-roofed Great House south of town. The house was undergoing refurbishment at the time of research. Ask about availability at Apple Valley Park.

Happy Times Restaurant   JAMAICAN $
(☑963-9807; Shakespeare Plaza; mains J$300-500; ⊙Mon-Sat) This place serves simple, well-prepared meals, including curried goat, snapper, curried chicken and brown-stew pork.

❶ Getting There & Away

Public vehicles infrequently arrive and depart from opposite Shakespeare Plaza at the north end of Maggotty, connecting to Mandeville (J$200) and Black River (J$180).

Appleton Rum Estate

You can smell the yeasty odor of molasses wafting from the **Appleton Sugar Estate and Rum Factory** (☑963-9215; www.appletonrumtour.com; factory tour & rum tasting US$25; ⊙9am-3:30pm Mon-Sat, closed public holidays) well before you reach it, 1km northeast of Maggotty in the middle of the Siloah Valley. This is the largest distillery in Jamaica and the oldest: the factory has been blending Appleton rums since 1749.

The 45-minute tour of the factory explains how molasses is extracted from sugarcane, then fermented, distilled and aged to produce the Caribbean's own rocket fuel, which you can taste in the John Wray Tavern. Around 17 varieties – including the lethal Overproof – are available for sampling. Unsurprisingly, the well-stocked gift shop does brisk business with visitors whose inhibitions have understandably been lowered over the course of the tour (and by the way, you get a complimentary bottle of the stuff at the end of the tour, so don't get too soused!).

Every tour company in Jamaica can get you onto one of the busloads of tourists that truck to and from (the 'from' part is pretty fun after 17 varieties of rum) the Appleton estate. Otherwise, it's easiest to get here from Maggotty: the factory is 1km east, and taxis will take you there and back for around J$500.

SOUTH COAST & CENTRAL HIGHLANDS MAGGOTTY

YS Falls

Jamaica prides itself on her waterfalls, but for our J$ the title of most beautiful cascades in the country is a dead heat between Reach Falls and the south-coast stunner, YS – a series of eight **cascades** (☑ 997-6360; www.ysfalls.com; adult/child US$17/7.50; ☉ 9:30am-3:30pm Tue-Sun, closed public holidays) hemmed in by limestone cliffs, surrounded by lush jungle and brimming with an energy that is positively Edenic. If you wander around early in the morning, before the falls are swarming with tourists, there is, well…a natural mysticism in the air. The waters of YS – *why-ess;* the falls take their name from the original landowners, ranchers John Yates and Richard Scott – look like a whitewater necklace laid over deep green, falling 36m from top to bottom, separated by cool pools just screaming to be swum in.

If you're so inclined, you can tube down a bamboo-shaded stretch of river through five mini-rapids for US$6; depending on the flow of the water, this should take about 30 minutes. If you're feeling more daring, whiz down a canopy **zip-line** (adult/child US$30/20) or just take a dip in the local spring-fed pool.

A tractor-drawn jitney takes visitors to the cascades, where you'll find picnic grounds, a tree house and a rope-swing over the pools. Be careful: the eddies are strong, especially af-

ter rains when the falls are torrential. A stone staircase and pathway follow the cascades upriver. There are no lockers, however, so you'll need to keep an eye on your stuff while you bathe. Admission includes a guide. There's a gift store and a cheap restaurant on site.

Almost every tour operator in Jamaica (and many hotels) offers trips to YS Falls, but if you want to get here ahead of the crowds, drive yourself (or charter your own taxi) and arrive right when the grounds open.

The YS Falls entrance is just north of the junction of the B6 toward Maggotty. From the A2 (a much smoother road if you're driving) the turnoff is 1.5km east of Middle Quarters; from here you'll head 5.5km north to the falls. On the B6, buses travel via YS Falls from Shakespeare Plaza in Maggotty. On the A2, buses, minibuses and route taxis will drop you at the junction to YS Falls, from where you can walk or catch an Ipswich-bound route taxi and ask to be dropped at the falls (J$80 to J$100).

Accompong

POP 3000 / ELEV 448M

The Maroons and their legacy make up a significant chapter in the Jamaican national narrative, yet the truth of the matter is there are very few actual Maroon communities re-

DON'T MISS

ACCOMPONG MAROON FESTIVAL

In many ways, the best sight in Accompong is…well, Accompong. The village is more than politically autonomous; despite the fact the native Coromantee language has vanished and knowledge of local rituals is fading among the young, Accompong still feels *different* from the rest of Jamaica. Locals will proudly tell you there is no crime, police or taxes in Accompong, and while they may be guilty of some exaggeration, the town certainly feels tranquil compared to settlements in other parts of Jamaica. Although it is anything but calm, the best time to get a sense of Accompong's uniqueness is during the Accompong Maroon Festival, held on January 6. Because of the time of year, many Jamaicans call it 'Maroon New Year,' but it actually marks the signing of the 1739 peace treaty between Cudjoe of the Maroons and the British Empire. The provisions of that agreement guaranteed the Maroons significant personal freedom and 15,000 acres out of which to make their own community; a clerical error reduced said land to 1500 acres, still a source of some tension in these parts. The Maroon Festival celebrates Accompong's nominal independence and is a riot of traditional dancing, drumming, mento bands and local tonics and herbs. Between the storytellers, chanting, rhythmic drumbeats and appeals to pre-Christian spirits, this is an intense invocation of Afro-Caribbean heritage – perhaps the most raw meshing of Old Africa and the New World many people will see in their lifetime (outside of certain parts of Brazil). The festival culminates in a traditional march to the revered Kindah Tree, where a specially prepared Maroon dish of unsalted and unseasoned pork is consumed with yams; afterwards (because, after all, this is still Jamaica) an all-night sound-system party rocks into the wee hours. You'll never see Jamaica so quiet as Accompong sometime around 11am on January 7.

maining on the island. Accompong, named for the brother of Maroon hero Cudjoe and embedded in the outer edges of southwestern Cockpit Country, is the sole remaining outpost in western Jamaica. This unique cultural lineage alone makes the town worth a visit, but it is also a good base for exploring the region of Cockpit Country, also known as 'Me No Sen, You No Come,' a landscape that, by dint of its ruggedness, is as responsible for Maroon independence as Maroon battle prowess.

The village still enjoys aspects of quasi-autonomy and is headed by a colonel elected by secret ballot for a period of five years. The colonel appoints and oversees a council, and it is considered proper etiquette to introduce yourself upon visiting (you should be directed to him upon entering the village, but if not, just ask around).

◎ Sights & Activities

If you arrive in Accompong under your own steam you'll be quickly greeted by locals offering to give you a tour of the town; the going rate at time of writing was US$20, which pays for a full tour of everything mentioned here, except the Peace Caves. Try asking for Tackie (☑864-4462), a good local guide who also lets out his house as a homestay.

Accompong is centered on the tiny Parade Ground, where the Presbyterian church looks over a small monument that honors Cudjoe, the Maroon leader (the statue next to it is that of Leonard Parkinson, another Maroon freedom fighter). Opposite the monument, the Accompong Community Centre & Museum is a veritable peek into the Afro-Caribbean world's cultural attic: *goombay* drums, a musket, a sword, baskets and other artifacts from the Maroon era stacked alongside Ashanti art and Taíno tools. Other sections of the tour take in a Maroon burial ground, a small herbal garden, Bickle Village, studded with traditional thatch-roofed homes, and the Kindah Tree, a stately, sacred mango tree where the elders of the community congregate.

There are several tours offered into the beautiful surrounding countryside, including a one-hour trek down to the Peace Caves (about US$60), where Cudjoe signed the 1739 peace treaty with the British.

☞ Tours

There are many hotels in Treasure Beach and Mandeville, and a few in Montego Bay and Negril, that can hook you up with tours into Accompong.

Original Trails of the Maroons   CULTURAL TOURS
(☑475-3046; www.jamaicanmaroons.com) This is an excellent ecotourism collaboration between an expat and the local Accompong community. It offers cultural tours of Accompong, and arranges tours with local guides into the rugged interior of the Cockpit Country.

Sun Venture Tours   CULTURAL TOURS
(☑960-6685, 408-6973; www.sunventuretours.com; 30 Balmoral Ave, Kingston 10) An excellent Kingston-based tour operator that specializes in cultural and environmental tours of off-the-beaten-path Jamaica.

🛏 Sleeping & Eating

Most residents of Accompong will offer to put you up for around US$20 to US$30; meals will be a 'likkle' bit extra.

Mystic Pass Villas   GUESTHOUSE $
(☑770-3680; r US$50-60; 🅿) These simple yet well-kept, thatch-roofed, wooden-floored cottages constitute some surprisingly luxurious digs considering how far off the beaten path Accompong is. There are refreshing outdoor hot showers, worth the price of the stay alone if you've been out hiking.

Maroon Restaurant   JAMAICAN $
(mains J$300-400; ⊙9am-9pm) One of two excellent restaurants in the Accompong community which will enthusiastically rustle up traditional food with ingredients plucked from within a 100m radius of your plate.

🛍 Shopping

Local artisans still make *goombay* drums here. These – along with an array of medicinal herbs, calabash shells and *abengs* (goat horns) – are for sale in the tiny red-and-green craft shop as you enter town. The hand-carved *goombay* drum is box-shaped and covered with goatskin, and makes a wonderfully deep and resonant racket. A large one will set you back at least US$150.

ⓘ Getting There & Away

Route taxis run from Shakespeare Plaza in Maggotty (J$200), where you'll have to change for Black River. If you're driving, the route from Maggotty is well signed, but the winding road is horribly potholed. All the better to go slow as the views over the crinkled broccoli-colored mountains are spectacular.

Troy & Around

Three kilometers northeast of the tiny settlement of Balaclava the B6 turns southeast for Mandeville; another road, the B10, leads north and climbs to Troy on the border with Trelawny parish. The latter is a spectacular drive as you climb through a series of dramatic gorges, with the road clinging to the sheer face of the Cockpits.

Troy, plunked in a valley bottom and surrounded by sugarcane fields, is the southeastern gateway to Cockpit Country. It is also a center for the cultivation of yams, which grow on tall runners spaced throughout the valley. St Silas Church, still in use by the locals, is worth a look for its blue-tinted corrugated iron roof.

Auchtembeddie, 5km south of Troy, is a choice spot for cavers, who head to Coffee River Cave, known for some magnificent rockfalls and a whole lotta bats. The area is totally undeveloped for tourism, but local guides will escort you for a negotiated fee.

A dirt road leads 3km north from Troy to Tyre, a hamlet on the edge of the Cockpits. Beyond Tyre the road fades into a bush-enshrouded trail that leads all the way to Windsor (about 21km). Don't attempt this trek alone, as there are several forks and it is easy to get lost.

To hire a guide, contact the Jamaican Caves Organisation (www.jamaicancaves.org).

Christiana

POP 8430

The harvesting heart of the western highland agricultural yam-basket, Christiana, some 16km north of Mandeville and 900m above sea level, is a pleasant town set in a lovely backdrop of rippling hills and shallow valleys.

The area was settled by German farmers during the 18th and 19th centuries, which is a little bit evident in the complexion of some locals and the local Moravian church, located at the northern end of sinuous Main St. During the 19th century, Christiana became a hill-town resort popular with European dignitaries and Kingstonians escaping the heat of the plains. Today Christiana makes a good base for exploring YS Falls and the Appleton Rum Estate.

This is a fairly sleepy place – farmers go to bed early and get up around 4am or 5am – which you may find refreshing if you're tired of Jamaica's usual cacophony. That said, if you're here on Thursday when the hagglers come to sell their produce, the roads are so thick you can hardly drive through town. It's a sight worth seeing.

Around Christiana you'd be forgiven for imagining yourself in the Pyrenees or the Costa Rican highlands. The air is crisp, clouds drift through the vales and pine trees add to the alpine setting. This is an important center for growing Irish potatoes, cacao, yams and coffee, and during picking season you can watch women with baskets moving among the rows, plucking cherry-red coffee berries.

◉ Sights & Activities

Christiana Bottom   VALLEY

The main reason for stopping here is to discover this beautiful riverside valley bottom, located below the town at the base of a shimmering waterfall. Two sinkholes full of crystal-clear water offer refreshing dips; collectively they're known as the Blue Hole. You can hike from the center of Christiana, though the going at the lower reaches can be muddy and slippery (but pretty, once you start pressing through a tangle of moss and ferns).

Take the road that leads east from the National Commercial Bank; it's 3km from here. Take the first left and then the second left and press on through the green; if you get lost, locals are happy to provide directions.

Gourie Forest Reserve   NATURE RESERVE

(☉ sunrise-sunset) An unexpected bloom of pine trees, plus mahogany and mahoe, grows atop the flinty heads of the Cockpits 3km northwest of Christiana, near Coleyville. This park is laced with hiking trails and is most noteworthy for having one of Jamaica's longest cave systems. Two routes into the Gourie Caves have been explored, but this is advanced caving; ask at Hotel Villa Bella for a guide.

You'll find magnificent columns, narrow fissures and an icy river with overhead air passages that barely clear 30cm. As such, Gourie should only be attempted in dry weather, as flooding is a distinct possibility. You'll also want to bring warm clothes; the water is seriously cold.

To get to the park from Christiana, turn uphill (southwest) at the radio tower immediately south of the junction that leads west for Coleyville and Troy. Immediately take the left at a Y-fork, then right at the next Y-fork and follow the green wire fence. The road isn't in very good condition, but it's doable in a 2WD if you proceed carefully.

🛌 Sleeping & Eating

Main St has numerous undistinguished restaurants and pastry shops including the ever-dependable **Juici Patties** (☎964-2568; Lewis Plaza, Main Street; patties from J$150).

Hotel Villa Bella   HOTEL **$**
(☎964-2243, in the USA 888-790-5264; www.hotel villabella.com; r US$72-96; **P**) A charming, cozy country inn perched on a hill at Sedburgh, at the south end of town, this villa is a former grande dame that retains her original mahogany floors, now somewhat squeaky, and Victorian and deco furniture and trappings. The polite service matches the old-school elegance of the furnishings.

The rooms don't entirely keep pace with all this grandeur, but they're still lovely, if a little plain. Villa Bella also offers a reasonably priced dining experience – a melange of Jamaican, Japanese and Chinese cuisines. Afternoon tea can sometimes be procured.

ℹ️ Getting There & Away

Christiana is well served by route taxis and minibuses from both Kingston and Mandeville (J$120); from Mandeville you can access other major towns in the south coast and central highlands. To get to Montego Bay and Ocho Rios, head north in a route taxi to Albert Town (J$100) and change.

MANDEVILLE & AROUND

Mandeville

POP 48,000 / ELEV 628M

An antidote to Jamaica's busy, sometimes blemished, coast, Mandeville is a cool inland town, meaning you can traverse its busy streets without collapsing from heat exhaustion and enjoy a slice of everyday Jamaican life bereft of the iPad wielding, camera-clicking tourists in evidence elsewhere. While the town center remains boisterously Jamaican with uniformed schoolchildren playing cat and mouse with the speeding taxis, Mandeville's salubrious suburbs exhibit a posher, more refined, veneer. Mock Georgian mansions with manicured gardens provide second homes for Kingston entrepreneurs or returning expats who have made their money abroad. Devoid of major sights per se, Mandeville is best enjoyed as a pit stop for people who want to see the island from a different (Jamaican) perspective. Grab a patty from a scruffy shopping mall, be a spectator to an alfresco game of dominoes, or just shoot the breeze with the local taxi drivers/shop assistants/rastas in the busy central square. Welcome to the real Jamaica, *mon*!

History

Established in 1816, Mandeville began life as a haven for colonial planters escaping the heat of the plains. In the 19th century, the city prospered as a holiday retreat for wealthy Kingstonians, and attracted soldiers and British retirees from other colonial quarters. Many early expats established the area as a center for dairy farming and citrus and pimento production. Jamaica's unique seedless citrus fruit, the *ortanique*, was first produced here in the 1920s and is grown in large quantities.

North American bauxite company Alcan opened operations here in 1940 (in 2000 it sold its operations to a Swiss company, Glencore). Relatively high wage levels lured educated Jamaicans, bringing a middle-class savoir faire to the town.

⊙ Sights

Marshall's Pen   GREAT HOUSE
(☎904-5454; Mike Town Rd; admission US$10; ⊙by appointment) One of the most impressive historical sights in the central highlands, Marshall's Pen Great House has a story that manages to encapsulate the sweep of Jamaican history from Taíno times through colonialism to abolition, independence and the modern day. Also, it's a great spot to watch birds.

Taíno people once inhabited this property, and archaeological digs still turn up their artifacts. The stone-and-timber Great House itself, built in 1795, dates back to the first British Provost General of Jamaica. Throughout its history the home has been a coffee plantation and cattle-breeding property (hence Marshall's 'Pen'). The 120-hectare grounds are owned by Jamaica's leading ornithologist, Ann Haynes-Sutton, an environmental scientist.

The exterior of the building, all cut-stone and Spanish windows surrounded by landscaped gardens, is beautiful. The interior is equally arresting, a honeycomb of wood-paneled rooms brimming with antiques, leather-bound books, Taíno artifacts, historical and original artwork and lots of other museum-quality pieces, many from Japan and China (this may be the best collection of Asian art on the island). You can tour the mini-museum by appointment only.

Marshall's Pen is splendid for birdwatching: more than 100 species have been

Mandeville

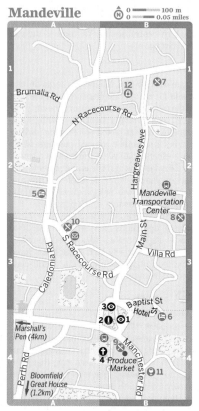

recorded here, including 25 of the 27 species endemic to Jamaica. Organized bird-watching trips often stay here. If you would like to visit, phone ahead first.

To get to the property, take Oriole Close off Winston Jones Hwy (A2), about 5km northwest of the town center (there's a sign for 'Somerset Quarries' at the junction). Turn left on Nightingale Dr and then, after about 100m, right on Mike Town Rd; the estate entrance – an unmarked stone gateway – is about 400m further on the right. Take insect repellent.

Cecil Charlton Park　　　　　　SQUARE
This tiny English-style 'green', also known as Mandeville Sq, lends a slight Cotswoldian village feel to the town center – assuming Cotswold greens are dominated by dozens of people hailing taxis, selling produce and hawking Digicel scratch cards. On the north side is the Mandeville Courthouse, the oldest building on the square. Built by slaves in 1817

out of cut limestone, the edifice is fronted by a horseshoe staircase and raised portico supported by Doric columns. The rectory, attached to the courthouse, was completed in 1820 and is the oldest home in town.

On the south side is a produce market and a cenotaph commemorating Jamaican dead from the two world wars.

St Mark's Anglican Church, on the south side of Cecil Charlton Park, was established in 1820. There's a lot of Gothic accents, which makes it stand out from other Jamaican churches built around the same period. The building still functions as the parish church for Manchester.

Bloomfield Great House　　GREAT HOUSE
(☑ 962-7130; bloomfield.g.h@cwjamaica.com; 8 Perth Rd; ☉ midday-10pm Tue-Sat) This immaculate historic home stands atop a hill at the end of a very winding road southwest of the town center. The two-story structure is built in traditional Caribbean vernacular and gleams today thanks to some fine renovations. It is about 170 years old (the exact date is uncertain) and began life as the center of a coffee estate and, later, a citrus plantation, cattle farm and dairy. It's now one of Jamaica's finest art galleries and a premier restaurant.

The art gallery features works by many of Jamaica's leading artists and is a popular function space for Mandeville's many well-to-do and the local expat population. Most of the work you see is available for purchase; if you want something cheaper than an original work of art, there's a gift and crafts shop on site that sells woodwork, prints and assorted goodies that are a bit more exciting than the stuff you see in a standard Jamaican souvenir shack. The entrance is 200m south of Manchester College, on the opposite side of the road at the crossroads. It's easily walkable from the town center.

🖝 Tours

Jack Mandora Tours SIGHTSEEING TOURS
(☏ 530-6902; www.real-jamaica-vacations.com/jack-mandora) These tours are conducted by the affiliated Real Jamaican Vacations, which tailors special packages for small groups (one to four individuals) at good rates (whole day trips are US$150). Affiliated with local **Allison Morris** (☏ 965-2288), a clever, witty joy who can expound for hours on her beloved home island, and offers steel drumming lessons; her website is a fantastic clearinghouse of island information.

🛏 Sleeping

Golf View Hotel HOTEL $
(☏ 962-4477; www.thegolfviewhotel.com; 51/2 Caledonia Rd; s US$70-90, d US$75-95, ste US$110; ⓟ ✱ @ 🛜 🏊) This rambling, conference-oriented property features 60-odd rooms centered on a small pool in a concrete courtyard. The complex has a clean, if slightly sterile, feel, but the rooms – decent mid-range standard – are acceptable. The interior decor is surprisingly modern; the four-poster beds are pretty comfy and yes, there's a view of – surprise, surprise – a golf course.

Kariba Kariba Guest House GUESTHOUSE $
(☏ 962-8006/3039; 1 McKinley Rd; r incl breakfast US$50) North of the town center, Kariba is a beautiful fieldstone home run by a surpassingly friendly English-Jamaican couple. Admittedly, the exterior grounds and lobby are a good deal more attractive than the actual rooms, which are a bit middling, but the staff make a big effort to accommodate guests. The owner can point out nature trails, and also leads customized excursions.

Proceed west on Brumalia Rd for 800m; turn right (north) into McKinley Rd and follow for 1km to the junction with the A2 ring-road. The house is on the right.

Mandeville Hotel HOTEL $$
(☏ 962-2460/9764; www.mandevillehoteljamaica.com; Hotel St; r J$8100, ste J$9975; ⓟ ✱ 🛜 🏊)

This dependable 1875-vintage hotel (one of the oldest on the island) is a well-run establishment with huge, if slightly institutionalized rooms, a decent restaurant and pub, and friendly down-to-earth staff. It caters mainly to Jamaican businesspeople and holidaymakers and you'll feel nicely integrated with them here in a town where tourism isn't really a big deal.

🍴 Eating

Fresh produce can be found at the market on the south side of Cecil Charlton Park.

A Little Pastry Place CAFE $
(59 Main St; snacks J$150-350) Perk up on coffee, sugar up on doughnuts, or chill out on local Devon House I Scream.

Manchester Arms Pub & Restaurant JAMAICAN $
(Mandeville Hotel, Hotel St; mains J$500-1500; ⊘ 4:30-11pm) The Manchester Arms goes all out to give you that pub-in-the-midst-of-Jamaica feeling, an effort that's vaguely successful. The broad menu encapsulates fairly overpriced Jamaican and continental food, but the setting is pretty lovely, especially for the poolside barbecues held on Wednesday night. The last Wednesday of every month is Jamaica Night, with Jamaican food and entertainment, including a live mento band.

Star Grill JAMAICAN, INTERNATIONAL $$
(☏ 632-3834; 20 South Racecourse Rd; mains J$700-3000; ⊘ 10am-10pm Mon-Thu, 10am-11pm Fri & Sat, midday-8pm Sun) Suspend your judgment on Mandeville's newest restaurant. On first impressions, it looks like a modern run-of-the-mill fast food joint, but peer upstairs and you're in different, more skillful, hands. The menu's Jamaican with some international inflections, such as quesadillas, the service is as fresh as the decor, and the conversation is mainly patois.

Bloomfield Great House Restaurant & Bar FUSION $$
(8 Perth Rd; mains J$800-2200; ⊘ midday-10pm Mon-Sat) The on-site restaurant at Bloomfield Great House is one of Jamaica's preeminent eateries and purveyors of Caribbean fusion cuisine, though it doesn't quite live up to the setting. But it's still quite good: callaloo fettuccine, jumbo shrimp stuffed with jalapeño pepper, filet mignon and, many say, the best fish-and-chips on the island; no mushy peas, though.

WORTH A TRIP

HIGH MOUNTAIN COFFEE FACTORY

In the village of Williamsfield, 300m below and northeast of Mandeville, at the base of the Winston Jones Hwy (A2), you can take a free tour of the **High Mountain Coffee Factory** (☑963-4211; Winston Jones Hwy; tour incl drink US$10; ☺10am-4pm Mon-Fri, tours by appointment). Both the factory and the tour are pretty small, but the whole affair is fascinating, especially the sections where the tour guides explain how coffee is categorized, tasted, packaged and exported (mainly to Japan). We might add the whole place smells amazing. Obviously, you can purchase fresh bags of coffee (plus Scotch bonnet sauce) after the tour is done.

Little Ochie SEAFOOD **$$**
(☑625-3279; Leaders Plaza; mains J$500-2000; ☺11am-11pm) A satellite of the famous fish restaurant at Alligator Pond, this Little Ochie branch is good. Very good. Not as good as its parent, but hey – we can't all approach perfection. The menu is seafood done in all the traditional Jamaican ways served in a slightly less salubrious setting to its cousin next to the bus station.

Drinking & Entertainment

This town has a reputation for being popular with newlyweds and seniors, which should tell you how exciting the place can get. The Manchester Arms has a quiet English-style pub that's open late, while Bloomfield Great House has live music on Friday night.

Vineyard WINE BAR
(Manchester Rd; ☺4:30pm-midnight Mon-Thu, 4pm-until last person leaves Fri) As posh as Mandeville gets, with flashy small plates and, of course, a good wine menu.

Shopping

Bookland BOOKSTORE
(Manchester Shopping Plaza; ☺9am-5pm Mon-Sat) You can struggle to find a decent book shop in small town Jamaica, so all hail to Bookland in the Manchester Plaza, which is notable for its encyclopedic and nicely laid-out Caribbean fiction section, and multitude of tomes on Bob Marley and his legacy.

Information

Fontana Pharmacy (☑962-3129; Manchester Shopping Plaza; ☺9am-8pm Mon-Thu, 9am-9pm Fri & Sat, 10am-5pm Sun)

Mandeville Hospital (☑962-2067; 32 Hargreaves Ave)

Police Station (☑962-2250; Park Cres)

Post Office (Map p170; ☑962-2339; South Racecourse Rd; ☺8am-5pm Mon-Fri)

Scotiabank (☑962-1083; cnr Ward Ave & Caledonia Rd; ☺8:30am-2:30pm Mon-Thu, 8:30am-4pm Fri)

Getting There & Around

Mandeville has direct bus, minibus and route-taxi services from virtually every major town in Jamaica. Most buses, and many minibuses and route taxis, depart and arrive from the transportation center, off Main St. Others depart and arrive near the market on the main square. The island-wide **Knutsford Express** (www.knutsfordexpress.com) connects daily to all of the island's main towns including Kingston (J$1600), Montego Bay (J$2000, four hours), Santa Cruz (J$1400, one hour) and Savanna-la-Mar (J$1600, 2½ hours).

Shooter's Hill

Shooter's Hill begins 3km northwest of Williamsfield and climbs steadily and steeply (430m in elevation) to Christiana. A lookout point midway offers splendid views. On the west side of the road, atop a hillock, is the Moravian-built **Mizpah Church**, topped by a four-faced German clock.

If you've ever eaten at a Jamaican restaurant anywhere in the world, you've undoubtedly seen bottles of spicy Pickapeppa sauce. If you've ever wondered where the stuff is made, ponder no more and come to the **Pickapeppa Factory** (☑603-3439/3441; www.pickapeppa.com; tours J$200; ☺9am-3pm Mon-Thu), on the B6 at the foot of Shooter's Hill. The plant offers 30-minute tours by appointment. There's honestly not much to see but workers stirring giant pots of simmering scallions, mangoes, peppers and some other ingredients – we'd tell you, but then we'd have to kill you. (Joke!)

Mile Gully & Around

The village of Mile Gully sprawls along a valley that runs northwest from Mandeville in the lee of the forested north face of the Don Figuerero Mountains. The B6 leads northwest from Shooter's Hill, winding, dipping and rising past lime-green pastures dotted with guango- and silk-cotton trees and crisscrossed with stone walls and hedgerows.

About 1km west of Mile Gully at Skull Point, you'll find a venerable blue-and-white 19th-century police station and courthouse at the junction for Bethany, plus the atmospheric remains of a defunct train station. The name Skull Point has nothing to do with the police station, though; it comes from the local church – or at least the ruins of that church. It's a genuinely creepy place, all rotted and burnt out and infested with bats. The local consensus is the grounds are very much haunted (folks were literally yelling at us from their cars to beware of duppies – ghosts – when we arrived), supposedly by beheaded local slave James Knight.

The Bethany road climbs sharply and delivers you at the Bethany Moravian Church – a simple gray stone building dating to 1835, dramatically perched foursquare midway up the hill with fantastic valley views. The church is rather dour close up, but the simple interior boasts a resplendent organ. Another beautiful church – St Simon's Anglican Church – sits on a hillside amid meadows at Comfort Hall, 6km west of Mile Gully, with huge spreading trees festooned with old-man's beard.

To the south of the B6, perched atop the Don Figuerero Mountains, at Maidstone, is the humble Nazareth Moravian Church, which would look as comfortable on the American prairie as it does in the Jamaican bush. Founded in 1840, Maidstone is one of Jamaica's post-emancipation pre-planned 'free villages,' an early experiment at the intersection of urban planning and social policy. The annual Emancipation Day Fair is celebrated at Maidstone on August 1, with mento bands, Jonkanoo celebrations, and maypole and quadrille dancing.

Coasters and route taxis operate on the B6 between Mandeville and Maggotty via Mile Gully. If you're driving from Mandeville, the B6 continues west about 8km to Green Hill and a T-junction. About 1.5km north (to the right) of the junction, en route to Balaclava, is a *very dangerous* spot: you'll climb a short hill that tempts you to accelerate. Unfortunately there's an unmarked railway crossing on the crest and a hairpin bend *immediately* after. Drive slowly!

TREASURE BEACH & AROUND

The sun-kissed land southeast of Black River is sheltered from rain for most of the year by the Santa Cruz Mountains, so there is none of the lush greenery of the north coast. Instead, you'll find a thorny, surreally beautiful semidesert, a landscape almost East African in its scorched beauty. Acacia trees and cacti tower over fields of scallions guarded by fencerows of aloe vera. The region remains unsullied by resort-style tourism; here you can slip into a lazy, no-frills tropical lifestyle almost impossible to achieve elsewhere on the island's coast.

Dividing the plains north to south is the aforementioned Santa Cruz range, a steepfaced chain that slopes to the sea and drops 520m at Lover's Leap.

Treasure Beach

A person who is tired of Treasure Beach is probably lacking in a few essential life forces – like a pulse. Welcome to a unique and wonderfully old-fashioned part of Jamaica that gets all the facets of the quintessential Caribbean experience exactly right without even trying. Winding country lanes, close to zero crime, a dearth of hustlers, sublime deserted beaches, no gimmicky resorts (as yet), and – above all – a proud, foresighted local community that promotes sustainability and harbors a bonhomous but mellow culture. Too good to be true? Not at all. Wander into the new local sports park when a cricket match is in full swing, or walk along deserted Frenchman's Beach where the fisherfolk are more likely to ask you to help them pull in the boats than sell you a trinket.

Treasure Beach is the generic name for four coves – Billy's Bay, Frenchman's Bay, Calabash Bay and Great (Pedro) Bay. It's said Scottish sailors were shipwrecked near Treasure Beach in the 19th century, accounting for the presence of fair skin, green eyes and reddish hair among the local population. The area's residents are known for their strong community spirit. Collectives like the Treasure Beach Women's Group and the Treasure Beach Foundation bring locals and expats together to work on projects relating to housing, education and local culture. There's a burgeoning cultural scene, with artists, poets and other luminaries continuing to put down roots.

Treasure Beach

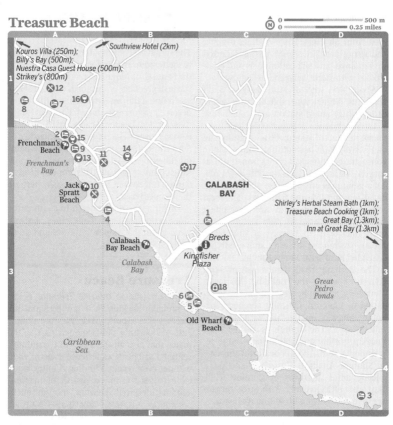

Kouros Villa (250m);
Billy's Bay (500m);
Nuestra Casa Guest House (500m);
Strikey's (800m)

Southview Hotel (2km)

Frenchman's
Beach

*Frenchman's
Bay*

Jack
Spratt
Beach

Calabash
Bay Beach

*Calabash
Bay*

*Caribbean
Sea*

CALABASH
BAY

Shirley's Herbal Steam Bath (1km);
Treasure Beach Cooking (1km);
Great Bay (1.3km);
Inn at Great Bay (1.3km)

Breds

Kingfisher
Plaza

Old Wharf
Beach

*Great
Pedro
Ponds*

0   500 m
0   0.25 miles

Activities

With a long history, and large population, of seafaring fishers, it's no wonder Treasure Beach is a great place from which to take to the sea. The best time to book a trip is during the early morning or late afternoon; the winds tend to pick up during the middle of the day. On bright moonlit evenings it is possible to take to the silvery waters for an enchanting tour of the coast.

Popular boating excursions include the Pelican Bar, Black River Great Morass, and Sunny Island and Little Ochie, both near Alligator Pond. From Frenchman's Beach, boat captain and fisher **Dennis Abrahams** (☑965-3084, 435-3779; dennisabrahams@yahoo.com) offers a sunset cruise by motorboat to Great Pedro Bluff and Billy's Bay, as well as fishing and on-demand trips to the Pelican Bar and Black River Great Morass. Other recommended captains include **Allan Daley** (☑366-7394, 423-3673), **Teddy Parchment** (☑854-5442) and

Joseph Brown (☑847-1951, 376-9944). Expect to pay around US$35 for a trip out to Pelican Bar and US$70 for a trip to Black River, although bear in mind the shifting cost of petrol makes prices subject to change.

Everyone with a boat in Treasure Beach is involved in some way with the pursuit of fishing, and it's easy to talk someone into taking you out to pull a trap or drop a line. Or you can book a fishing trip at Jake's Hotel (p177), which includes rods and bait. Fish frequently caught include grouper, kingfish and snapper; most restaurants are happy to prepare them for the night's dinner.

Beaches

Several fishing beaches, all sparsely sprinkled with tourists, beckon within easy walking distance of the major accommodations. Water sports haven't yet caught on, but the waves are good for bodysurfing. Beware, as sometimes a vicious undertow tugs at area beaches.

Treasure Beach

🛏 Sleeping
1 Bay Villa...C2
2 Golden Sands Beach Hotel..................A2
3 Ital Rest D4
4 Jake's Hotel B2
5 Kudeyha Guesthouse...........................B3
6 Marblue Villa Suites Boutique
   Hotel...B3
7 Shakespeare Cottage..........................A1
8 Treasure Beach Hotel A1
9 Waikiki Guest House.............................A2

✕ Eating
10 Jack Sprat Café......................................A2
    Jake's Country Cuisine ....(see 4)
11 Pardy's B2
12 Smurf's Cafe A1

🍸 Drinking & Nightlife
13 Eggy's Bar..A2
14 Fisherman's Nightclub.........................B2
15 Frenchman's Reef..................................A2
16 Wild Onion...A1

🎭 Entertainment
17 Treasure Beach Sports Park...............B2

🛍 Shopping
18 Treasure Beach Women's Group C3

If you head east from Great Bay, across Great Pedro Bluff (it's about a 20-minute walk; ask for directions), you'll discover waves of grassy hills studded with tall cacti, seabirds, very few (if any) people and cow-paths. The sunlight seems to melt into this utterly pastoral coastscape, named by locals Back Seaside.

Frenchman's Beach   BEACH
This is the most centrally located beach running east from the Treasure Beach Hotel as far as Jack Sprat's. It is watched over by a landmark buttonwood tree that has long attracted the attention of poets, painters and woodcarvers who ply their wares. Local boat captains congregate here, as does everyone else in the area once the sun starts to set. It's a great place to arrange trips to the Pelican Bar or Black River.

Jack Spratt Beach   BEACH
At the western edge of Jake's Place brightly painted wooden fishing boats are pulled up on the sand, and there is invariably a fisher or two on hand tending the nets. This is the safest beach for swimming.

Calabash Bay Beach   BEACH
Heading east from Jack Spratt Beach, there's Calabash Bay Beach, with a few beach shacks plying rum and – if you're lucky – some basic potluck cuisine, mainly fish.

Old Wharf Beach   BEACH
The most private of the bunch, although still accessible by anyone who makes the effort to totter down to the sand.

Great Bay Beach   BEACH
All the way at the eastern 'bottom' of Treasure Beach you'll find Great Bay, a pretty, rural patchwork of fields and beach; this is the least-developed portion of Treasure Beach, where the main business remains a Fisher-men's Co-op building.

🖝 Tours

Every hotel in Treasure Beach can hook you up with their own recommended tour guides.

Treasure Tours   SIGHTSEEING TOURS
(📞965-0126;   www.treasuretoursjamaica.com)
Does tours all around the south coast and across the island.

🎉 Festivals & Events

**Calabash International
Literary Festival**   LITERARY
(📞965-3000; www.calabashfestival.org; ⏰ late May)
A daring, acclaimed literary festival at Jake's Hotel, drawing literary voices both domesti-cally and internationally.

🛏 Sleeping

New villa rentals open in Treasure Beach all the time. Some provide bona fide luxu-ry and considerable style, while others are more modest and practical, providing good value for groups or families. Details can be found at www.treasurebeach.net, www. jamaicaescapes.com and www.treasure toursjamaica.com. Parking is included at all of the accommodations listed here; prices quoted are high-season rates.

★**Nuestra Casa Guest House** GUESTHOUSE **$**
(📞965-0152; www.billysbay.com; d US$50; ❄🛜)
Nuestra Casa is just gorgeous; it's a pretty house run by the lovely Roger and his mum Lillian, who together with their Jamaican staff are the epitome of hospitality.

Their laid-back property consists of a beautiful arid flora garden built into porous rocks, a wide veranda peppered with rockers and highly personalized rooms kitted out in quirky, individual (yet also intellectual; the books on hand are amazing) decor.

Southview Hotel
HOTEL **$**

(☑ 876-965-0654; www.southviewhoteljamaica.com; r US$30-80; 🖥 🕸) 🏊 Being set back from the main beach area needn't be a disadvantage, especially as Southview is accessed via a pretty, winding lane that cuts through bucolic grassy pastures full of munching cows and goats. The main bonus here is the service – the convivial owners will go out of their way to help you – including picking you up from the beach after dinner.

Set in fertile gardens replete with fruit trees and endowed with two swimming pools, the hotel is partly powered by its own wind turbine.

Ital Rest
GUESTHOUSE **$**

(☑ 473-6145, 421-8909; www.italrest.com; r US$50) In the right setting, a lack of electricity rockets a property right into the super-romantic category. Two exquisite all-wood thatched cabins is the deal here. Hang with the Rasta owners as the sun sets, then retire to a candlelit room with a loved one. All rooms have toilets and the upstairs room has a great sundeck. Kitchen facilities are shared.

Waikiki Guest House
GUESTHOUSE **$**

(☑ 345-9669, 965-3660; s/d US$25/50) Location, location, location: this excellent budget option abuts Frenchman's Beach. The rooms are clean and simple; nothing special and nothing to complain about either. The 2nd-floor double in Waikiki's odd concrete tower (prettier than it sounds) is awesome; you can step out onto a little veranda and watch the sun set into the ocean.

Waikiki also has a one-bedroom cottage, two two-story cottages and a small house with three bedrooms and kitchen.

Golden Sands Beach Hotel
HOTEL **$**

(☑ 965-0167; www.goldensandstreasure beach.com; r US$55-70, 3-bedroom apt US$165-215; 🕸) Golden Sands is one of the few traditional hotels in Treasure Beach, and could be a good choice for those who don't like the intimacy of sharing a guesthouse, or the length of time needed to book a villa or private house. Rooms vary; some have ceiling fans, others boast sea views, while one- and three-bedroom cottages come with air-con and TV, but they're all clean and quite serviceable.

Shakespeare Cottage
GUESTHOUSE **$**

(☑ 965-0120; www.marycroteau.com; r with shared/ private bathroom US$20/50, studio US$70; 🕸) This simple budget option has five rooms with fans and bathrooms with cold water only. There's a communal kitchen. The building itself doesn't have much character, but Shakespeare is popular with backpackers, so there's a good social vibe going on.

Bay Villa
VILLA **$**

(☑ 837-0430; bayvillaja@yahoo.com; d US$50, 8-person villa US$170; W) This pleasant red-roofed house is in as central a location as you can get in Treasure Beach, across from the Kingfisher Plaza and a quick jaunt to the beach. Rooms are standard Jamaican: tiled floors, clean walls, chintzy furniture and friendly staff if you need someone to help organize more trips in the area.

Kudeyha Guesthouse
HOTEL **$$**

(Old Wharf Rd; US$70-110; 🅿 🕸) 🏊 The only common link in Treasure Beach accommodations is they're all wonderful – but for different reasons. Kudeyha is a newish offering within splashing distance of the waves that carries a Rastafarian theme in its three drop-dead-gorgeous suites. One has a kitchenette, all have private bathrooms and coffee machines. I-tal meals can be arranged with ingredients plucked from the garden.

Treasure Beach Hotel
HOTEL **$$**

(☑ 965-0114; www.jamaicatreasurebeach hotel.com; d garden/sea view US$108/132; 🕸 🖥 🕸) This rambling property, dotted with palms and nestled on a hillside overlooking the beach, has a good variety of midrange-quality rooms, including spacious, deluxe oceanfront

---

TREASURE BEACH FOUNDATION

The **Treasure Beach Foundation** (☑ 965-3434, 965-0748; www.breds.org; Kingfisher Plaza) or Breds (short for brethren) – is dedicated to fostering heritage pride, sports, health and education among the community, and represents a partnership between the Treasure Beach community, expats and stakeholders (Jamaican and foreign) in the local tourism industry. Work includes restoring decrepit housing, sponsorship of both a soccer team and a basketball team, the introduction of computer labs at local schools and education for the children of fishers lost at sea.

suites that have king-size four-poster beds and breezy patios. The Yabba Restaurant is on the premises, and the front desk can hook you up with a good range of tours and activities across the region.

Inn at Great Bay
HOTEL **$$**

(☎876-848-3818; s/d US$60/100; ❋🎧) The economical choice over in Great Bay is this small inn cum hotel with eight rooms, two of them equipped with kitchenettes and two double beds. The rooms on the upper floor have ocean views and there are a couple of beachside eating places so close you can smell the fish frying.

Marblue Villa Suites Boutique Hotel
BOUTIQUE HOTEL **$$**

(☎840-5772, 848-0001; www.marblue.com; Old Wharf Rd; junior ste US$111-122, ste US$255-275; ❋🎧❄) One of Jamaica's most stylish boutique hotels, this well-run, welcoming property pampers its guests with thoughtful service and considerable streamlined luxury. Five one-bedroom villa suites are appointed with furniture designed by the owners, Axel, an architect, and Andrea Wichterich. Each veranda suite features living areas that open to spectacular views of the sea. Weekly barbecues, two dramatic pools, superb cuisine and a spa/meditation room round out the offerings. It's accessible for travelers with disabilities.

★ Jake's Hotel
HOTEL **$$$**

(☎965-3000, in the UK 020-7440-4360, in the USA 800-688-7678; www.jakeshotel.com; r US$150-395; @🎧❄) 🏊 If you haven't been to Jake's, you haven't really been to Treasure Beach. This romance-drenched boutique hotel is the nexus of pretty much everything in the area – cooking courses (US$35), yoga classes (9am; US$20) and mosaic workshops all happen here. Furthermore, it's owned by Jason Henzell, son of film director Perry Henzell who conceived Jamaica's great seminal movie *The Harder They Come* in 1972.

Individually crafted rooms spurn TVs but are big on style and atmosphere.

Kouros Villa
VILLA **$$$**

(☎965-0126; www.villa-kouros.com; per day US$550, per week US$3600; ❋🎧) A slice of Santorini in Jamaica, Kouros consists of a whitewashed, Greek Island–style Great House clustered over a cliff with roof terrace, sundeck, enclosed courtyard and oodles of romance. The interior is as simple and breezy – yet luxurious – as the digs you'd expect in the most

romantic Aegean village. Located about halfway between Frenchman's Beach and Billy's Bay.

✖️ Eating

★ Smurf's Cafe
JAMAICAN **$**

(☎483-7523; meals J$300-700; ⏲6:30am-1pm) Smurf's is Treasure Beach's most improbable legend. On the surface it's an open-all-hours bottle shop constructed from breeze-blocks and adorned with kitschy blue Smurf motifs. But out the back is a morning-only cafe that cooks up some of the best breakfasts in Jamaica and roasts and brews the most delicious and dangerously addictive coffee this side of... Seattle. Don't be put off by the smudged and dented coffee urn. Indulge in the breakfast of champions.

Strikey's
JAMAICAN **$**

(Billy's Bay; mains J$400-800; ⏲4-10pm daily Nov-Apr) A seasonal affair run by the energetic, ever-friendly Chris Strikey, who has worked as a professional chef in the US and at Jake's place, this understated food shack in Billy's Bay is anchored by secret recipes and a hand-built jerk smoker. The food is sublime: Jamaican favorites, home-cooked and mouth-watering, especially the jerk.

Pardy's
CAFE **$**

(☎326-9008; mains J$300-500; ⏲7am-3pm Mon-Sat) On the main road across from Frenchman's Bay, Pardy's does some delicious breakfast and lunch-style fare: lovely callaloo omelets, and pancakes and French toast served with generous helpings of homemade honey in the morning, or light sandwiches as the day beats on.

★ Jack Sprat Café
FUSION **$$**

(☎965-3583; mains US$7-20; ⏲10am-11pm) Seafood and pizza aren't obvious bedfellows until you wander into Jack Sprat's, where they dare to put fresh lobster on their thick Italian-style pies. For many it's the start of a beautiful friendship enhanced by the dreamy location: candlelit tables beside a near perfect scimitar of sand, and bohemian interior of a dandy mix of retro reggae posters and old album covers. The star dish out of many is the homemade crab cakes and *bammy*. The star drink: the incredible fruit smoothies.

Jake's Country Cuisine
FUSION **$$**

(☎965-3000; mains US$5-27; ⏲7am-11pm ☎) This atmospheric spot in the eponymous hotel serves excellent fare in an open-sided wooden restaurant with low

SOUTH COAST & CENTRAL HIGHLANDS TREASURE BEACH

lighting and hip music – you can also dine poolside on the patio. The menu shifts daily based on what's growing in the local gardens and what's fresh from the market. Jake's is friendly to vegetarians, although meat eaters will be equally at home.

Typical dishes include pumpkin soup, baked lamb, stuffed crab, and chocolate cake for dessert.

🍷 Drinking & Nightlife

At night, Treasure Beach appears to be a sleepy place, but local bars party late into the night until the last person leaves. Jake's Hotel has an infamous poolside cocktail hour, while Jack Sprat Café hosts small concerts, poetry readings and outdoor movies.

★ Pelican Bar   BAR
(Caribbean Sea; ⊙ 10:30am-sunset) The Pelican Bar may be Jamaica's most famous spot for a drink: a thatched hut built on a submerged sandbar 1km out to sea, where you can chill with a Red Stripe while watching dolphins flip in the surf a few meters away. This eatery on stilts provides Jamaica's – and perhaps the planet's – most enjoyable spot for a drink.

Getting there is half the fun: hire a local boat captain (most charge around US$40), who will call ahead to arrange things if you want to eat. This is essential for those who want to take a meal out here (mains are US$5 to US$15), which is novel but frankly not necessary – you'll get better food on land. It's best to come here for the beer (or rum, if such is your fancy). The clientele is a mix of enchanted travelers and repeat-business fishers who while away the hours playing dominoes, talking on their cell phones, checking the cricket scores or exchanging pleasantries with the self-satisfied owner. In between Red Stripes, or perhaps before your meal of lobster, shrimp or fish, feel free to slip into the water for a dip.

Frenchman's Reef   BAR
(🖉 965-3049; www.frenchmansreeftreasurebeach. com; Frenchman's Bay; ⊙ 8am-11pm) Four words: draught Red Stripe beer; a rarity in Jamaica. Everything else is a footnote, although the strawberry milkshakes are good, and there's often live music to serenade the sunset.

Eggy's Bar   BAR
Off the main road by Frenchman's Bay, Eggy's is the place to go at sunset; everyone in Treasure Beach, locals and tourists alike, gathers here to drink beer, watch the sunset and pass around torpedo-sized spliffs.

Fisherman's Nightclub   BAR, NIGHTCLUB
(⊙ midday-late) Up a dirt road near Jake's Hotel, the Fisherman's has an open wooden bar where everyone plays dominoes and watches cricket, and an appealing reggae bar out the back with a rickety stage and powerful sound system where you can relive your Rude Boy days.

Wild Onion   NIGHTCLUB
(⊙ 8am-2am) Located in Frenchman's Bay, the Onion attracts a mix of locals and visitors with its spacious dance floor and pool tables.

☆ Entertainment

★ Treasure Beach
Sports Park   SPORTS GROUND
(Map p174) FREE This badge of the local community was opened in 2012 and contains tennis courts, several football pitches and – pride of place – a cricket oval. Look out for local posters for upcoming events or ask at Jack Sprat Café.

DON'T MISS

COMMUNITY CRICKET IN TREASURE BEACH

You'll hear it before you see it; the unmistakable thud of leather on willow, followed by a gentle ripple of appreciative applause. For a dedicated follower of cricket, this quintessential scene needs no further explanation. For those of you who haven't got a clue about the LBW law or how to bowl a 'googly', welcome to an integral part of Jamaican culture. Slow, unassuming Treasure Beach might have been designed with the rhythms of cricket in mind and great excitement met the opening of the Treasure Beach Sports Park in 2012 and its cricket oval. Games – accompanied by wry commentaries and snippets of skanking reggae music – take place most Sunday afternoons year round. The park's cute clapboard pavilion provides an ideal place to mingle with cricket-savvy locals over an icy Red Stripe. Ply them gently and they might even get around to explaining the LBW law.

Cooking Classes Prepare local delicacies such as *bammy* (pancake of fried cassava), ackee, curried goat and jerk. Private classes can be organized at Marblue Villa (p177), while for a more comprehensive course try **Treasure Beach Cooking** (☑457-5885; www.treasurebeachcooking.com) by chef Roddy Drake.

Eating During a full moon, **Jake's Hotel** (p177) organizes a special farm-to-table banquet at a nearby farm for US$90 including transport.

Spas The most well-known spa is **Driftwood Spa** at Jake's Hotel (p177). Equally popular is **Shirley's Herbal Steam Bath** (☑965-3820; bath & massage US$70-90) in Great Bay.

Cycling With its quiet country lanes, minimal traffic and scenic coastal paths, there is no better place in Jamaica to cycle. Many hotels rent bikes for approximately US$15 per day.

Movie Nights There's no cinema in Treasure Beach, but films are shown on an alfresco screen at **Jack Sprat Café** (p177) every Thursday night at 7pm.

Sport Many sports can be seen (and played) at the new **Treasure Beach Sports Park** (p178). Sunday afternoons are good for cricket, with periodic boxing and tennis tournaments.

Shopping

People don't come to Treasure Beach to shop per se, but, truth be told, it's an excellent place to amass some unique Jamaican souvenirs. The lady at the breakfast shack Smurf's Cafe sells bags of her delicious micro-roasted Jamaican coffee for J$1000, the gift shop at Jack Sprat Café plies hip retro film posters of *The Harder They Come,* while the **Treasure Beach Women's Group** (☑965-0748; Old Wharf Rd; ⊙9am-3pm Mon-Fri, 9am-1pm Sat) runs a craft shop selling batiks, calabash shells and the like off Old Wharf Beach.

Information

For information online, a good starting point is www.treasurebeach.net. There are no banks serving international travelers here, but there is a 24-hour ATM in the Kingfisher Plaza in Calabash Bay.

Breds (☑965-9748; Kingfisher Plaza; ⊙9am-5pm) Unofficial information center.

Police Station (☑965-0163) Between Calabash Bay and Pedro Cross.

Getting There & Away

There is no direct service to Treasure Beach from Montego Bay, Negril or Kingston. Jake's Hotel is now served by its own aerodrome. It's hoped that the building will eventually take public domestic flights, but for now only private charters are landing there – contact Jake's directly for information on fares, and expect them to run for at least a few hundred US dollars.

A private taxi will run around US$20 from Black River and US$40 to US$50 from Mandeville. Most hotels and villas arrange transfers from Montego Bay for US$100.

Via route taxi or minibus, you can connect to Treasure Beach from Black River (J$250); from Mandeville, you'll need to get a route taxi to Junction or Santa Cruz (J$150) and another taxi to Treasure Beach (J$200).

Most accommodations can help with car and motorcycle rental, which, thanks to quiet roads, is quite popular here. If driving, from Black River take the A2 to Santa Cruz and turn south; follow the many signs to Jack Sprat's.

Getting Around

A bicycle is a good means of getting around quiet Treasure Beach; most hotels and guesthouses rent them out for a small fee. There is one main road connecting all of the beaches, plus many smaller cow-paths and dirt trails.

It takes about 30 minutes to walk from Jake's Place to Billy's Bay and 30 minutes to get from Great Bay to Jake's Place. Beautiful walk too!

Lover's Leap

The Santa Cruz Mountains don't tend to slope very gently into the coast even at their most gentle, but at **Lover's Leap** (☑965-6577; admission US$3; ⊙10am-6pm), 1.5km southeast of Southfield, they positively plunge over 500m into the ocean. This headland provides a very photogenic, end-of-the-world-esque view, and is tipped by a red-and-white-hooped solar-powered lighthouse.

Far below, waves crash on jagged rocks and wash onto Cutlass Beach. You can hike down, a stiff one-hour trek to the bottom, made more difficult by the mocking stare of herds of smug mountain goats.

Lover's Leap is named for two young slaves who supposedly committed suicide here in 1747. Legend says the woman was lusted after by her owner, who arranged for her lover to be sold to another estate. When the couple heard of the plot, they fled and were eventually cornered at the cliffs, where they chose to plunge to their deaths. The power of this heartbreaking story is not diminished by the children's play area, souvenir shop, small museum and restaurant that have been set up at the spot where they made their sacrifice.

Just over 1½km beyond Lover's Leap (follow the signs), you'll find the spectacularly perched **Ocean Breeze Hotel** (⏱ 965-6000; www.oceanbreezejamaica.com; Southfield; r garden/ocean view US$34/51) with 23 bright tropical rooms, a restaurant, pool, garden and – well, behold the view!

Alligator Pond

Jamaica is a huge holiday destination for foreigners, but where do Jamaicans go when they want to chill out? Well, if you're from Kingston or the surrounding area, you may very likely drive over to Alligator Pond, hidden at the foot of a valley between two steep spurs of the Santa Cruz and Don Figuerero mountains. This is about as far from packaged-for-foreigners tourism as you can get in Jamaica, but it's got an offbeat Jamaican vacation vibe that's tough not to love.

The hamlet is set behind a deep-blue bay backed by dunes. The main street is smothered in wind-blown sand. Each morning, local women gather on the dark-sand beach to haggle over the catch – delivered by fishers, whose colorful old pirogues line the long shore. Local youths surf wooden planks. Among all this low-key charm, the main reason to come here is for quite possibly the best dining experience in Jamaica: Little Ochie.

◉ Sights & Activities

The Sandy Cays, about 32km offshore, are lined with white-sand beaches. The snorkeling and scuba diving are good at Alligator

Reef, about a 20-minute boat ride from shore; you'll need to organize an outing with a local boat captain, who'll likely charge around US$30 to US$40 for the experience.

West of Alligator Pond you may see the cranes of Port Kaiser, one of the major bauxite shipping ports on the island.

🛏 Sleeping & Eating

Sea-Riv Hotel   HOTEL $
(⏱ 360-7609, 450-1356; r US$25-40; P ❄) If you need to stay over in Alligator Pond, try this hotel on the black-sand beach next to a river mouth. There are 18 unspectacular, fan-cooled rooms, water sports and many in-the-know guides.

★ **Little Ochie**   SEAFOOD $$
(⏱ 965-4449; www.littleochie.com; mains J$800-2000; ☺ 8am until last guest leaves) Little Ochie is a culinary phenomenon that, despite a cult following, refuses to sell out. Set on an unkempt but romantic slice of beach, it uses the same charcoal-blackened kitchen and scribbled chalkboard menu it has for eons, although the staff has morphed from one to 30 since 1989. The secret? Fish so fresh you can catch them yourself – if you have time.

If not, make your choice from what the fishers just brought in and then elect how you want it cooked. The jerk is always a good bet, though it can be HOT. Grilled lobster and steamed snapper also have a dedicated following. And 'dedicated' is the word. Little Ochie is one of Jamaica's few bona fide destination restaurants and has established itself as the No 1 attraction in otherwise sleepy Alligator Pond. Jamaicans drive from Kingston just to eat here; stick your fork in that lobster and you'll soon find out why.

❶ Getting There & Around

Minibuses and route taxis operate between Alligator Pond and the Beckford St transportation center in Kingston (about J$500), and from Mandeville via Gutters (about J$400). The route from Treasure Beach is trickier and you'll have to change route taxis in Southfield. Hotels and guesthouses in Treasure Beach usually offer 'tours' to Little Ochie for around US$50 round-trip.

Understand Jamaica

Jamaica Today

It's quite possible to visit Jamaica and do little more than lie on a beach with a rum cocktail in hand, taking in sunset after spectacular sunset. It's a seductive option (to be fair, we've done plenty of that ourselves), but engage a little further and Jamaica reveals itself to be a far more interesting, exciting and complicated place than you could ever have imagined.

Best on Film

The Harder They Come (1972) A classic rags-to-rude *bwai* (rude boy) story of a country boy turned Kingston criminal. One of the best soundtracks in film history.

Marley (2012) Exemplary documentary about the life and music of reggae superstar Bob Marley.

Better Mus Come (2013) Acclaimed feature about Jamaica's gang troubles of the 1970s.

Life and Debt (2001) A powerful documentary on the impact of globalization on the Jamaican economy.

Best in Print

The Book of Night Women (2009) Gripping tale of a female-led plantation revolt, by Marlon James.

The Lunatic (1987) Comic novel revolving around a village madman and his affair with a tourist, by Anthony Winkler.

Lionheart Gal (1986) A lively short-story collection that reveals much about patois and the lives of women.

White Witch of Rose Hall (1928) Herbert de Lisser's classic Gothic horror, set in colonial Jamaica.

Global Position

Modern Jamaica looks less and less to Britain, its old imperial ruler, instead turning its head more toward the USA. Far from just being that slice of tropical paradise sold through the brochures of all-inclusive resorts, Jamaica is a developing country negotiating its way through the 21st century, with all the challenges – and opportunities – that presents. A troubled economy has meant an increasing number of Jamaicans (and the majority of those with a post-high school education) are emigrating. Remittances from the Jamaican diaspora made up nearly 20% of the economy in 2013.

In keeping with many developing nations, Jamaica has also looked to China, and Prime Minister Portia Simpson-Miller has been keen to pursue closer economic ties to Beijing. The biggest project to come out of this policy has been the controversial Goat Island infrastructure plan. This seeks to turn the Portland Bight Protected Area near Kingston, the largest protected conservation area in Jamaica, into a huge transshipment port and logistics hub. The passionate voices from both those for and against the project raised key questions about the discontents of globalization: are economic development and environment protection mutually exclusive, and who benefits from the scheme – the people, the government or the corporations? The answers that Jamaica finds to these questions will be key in determining its future development.

Courtroom Drama

Throughout the first half of 2014, Jamaica was in thrall to a courthouse drama unfolding in downtown Kingston. Vybz Kartel, who has spent a decade as both the country's most popular and infamous dancehall star, was found guilty of the murder of his associate Clive 'Lizard' Williams.

The trial, which was the longest in Jamaica's history, became the nation's equivalent of the OJ Simpson affair, holding a mirror up to society and reflecting back the prejudices of the individual viewer. Church-goers condemned the slack morality of dancehall and spoke of the need to return to Christian virtues; Uptown society saw it as a come-uppance for a public life that repeatedly blurred the lines between DJ and criminal don; and those in the ghetto saw a hero unfairly punished while corrupt politicians and policeman act with impunity.

For one brief moment, all the anxieties of modern Jamaican life seemed to bubble to the surface.

Running Pride

The country celebrated its 50th anniversary of independence from Britain in 2012, a year of remarkable highs. Fittingly in London, Jamaica again showed the strength of its stride on the international scene, with Usain Bolt and Shelly-Ann Fraser-Pryce leading the Jamaican athletics team to Olympic triumphs. Their medals emphasized the golden nature of the jubilee, and proved the little island punches far above its weight. Bolt and Fraser-Pryce shone again in 2013, winning six golds between them at the World Championships in Moscow, though the year was marred by the positive drug tests of Jamaican legends Asafa Powell and Veronica Campbell Brown. Jamaica's pride in their athletic prowess can not be underestimated, nor can their shock and disappointment at seeing two of their Olympic gold medal heroes fall.

Jamaican Conversations

Jamaicans tend to be passionate people. Their full-bore approach to life is what often attracts (and occasionally intimidates) visitors to their island. The easiest way to hear lively patois is to talk politics with a Jamaican; most, including deceptively laid-back Rastas, have well-crafted and informed opinions on current affairs in Jamaica, and even the optimistic ones have their gripes.

On this island there are as many opinions on how to fix things as there are Jamaicans. Travelers, however, remain well regarded by the average Jamaican. Tourism – an industry where Jamaica was an early pioneer of globalization – is the second-largest segment of the economy, and remains a testament to the fact that despite the challenges, Jamaicans are determined to share their island with the world.

POPULATION: 2.93 MILLION

GDP: **US$25.13 BILLION**

GDP PER CAPITA: **US$9000**

PUBLIC DEBT: **123% OF GDP**

INFLATION RATE: **9.4%**

UNEMPLOYMENT RATE: **16.3%**

if Jamaica were 100 people

92 would Black
6 would Mixed
1 would East Indian
1 would be Other

belief systems
(% of population)

64.8 Protestant

2.2 Roman Catholic

1.9 Jehovah's Witness

1.1 Rastafarian

8.8 other

21.3 none

population per sq km

JAMAICA   USA   UK

≈ 10 people

History

Through conquest, settlement and plantocracy, Jamaica's history is to be found at the sharp edge of Western colonialism. Sugar and slavery led to the island briefly becoming Britain's wealthiest colony, yet resistance to that project helped create a national identity that led to reform, and the path to independence. The legacy of those 300 years leaves its mark on the island still, with color lines drawn and with post-independence discontent leading the have-nots to turn upon each other. Yet the passion and the perseverance of the Jamaican people, which have made the island and its culture so vital, still leads you to imagine a brighter future.

Xaymaca

The Caribbean was inhabited long before Christopher Columbus sailed into view, colonized by a successive wave of island-hopping incomers originally from South America. Most notable were the Arawaks, and then the Taínos who first settled 'Xaymaca' ('land of wood and water') around AD 700–800.

The Taínos were both farmers and seafarers, living in large chiefdoms called caciques, and honing their skills as potters, carvers, weavers and boat builders. They worshipped a variety of gods believed to control rain, sun, wind and hurricanes, and who were represented by zemes, idols of humans or animals.

The Killing Time: The Morant Bay Rebellion in Jamaica by Gad Heuman explores the roots and the political aftermath of the rebellion that was brutally suppressed by the British authorities.

Clothing was made of cotton or pounded bark fibers, along with jewelry of bone, shell, and gold panned from rivers. While Taíno artifacts remain relatively few, the crops they bequeathed to the world were revolutionary, from tobacco and yams to cassava and pineapples.

Columbus & Spanish Settlement

Christopher Columbus landed on the island in 1494 on his second voyage to the New World, landing at Bahía Santa Gloria (modern St Ann's Bay) and making first contact with the Taínos along the coast at Discovery Bay. Although he didn't linger, he claimed the island for Spain and christened it Santo Jago.

TIMELINE	AD 700–800	1494	1503
	Taínos settle on the island, calling it 'Xaymaca,' meaning 'land of wood and water.'	Christopher Columbus first lands on Jamaica, which he names Santa Jago; it later becomes his personal property.	Columbus returns to Jamaica for the fourth time, convinced he can forge a passage to Asia. However, his decrepit ships are ruined and he and his party become stranded.

Columbus returned disastrously in 1503, when his poorly maintained ships sank beneath him. He and his crew spent almost a year marooned, and suffered from disease and malnutrition. Finally, two officers paddled a canoe 240km to Hispaniola to raise a rescue expedition.

Jamaica became Columbus' personal property and when he died in 1506 it passed to his son Diego, who appointed a governor to establish a capital called Nueva Sevilla, near present-day Ocho Rios.

Within three decades of their first meeting with Europeans, the Taínos were quickly reduced to a shadow of their previous numbers, stricken by European illnesses and the forced labor required to dig for gold. In response, the Spaniards began importing West African slaves.

In 1534 a new settlement was founded on the south coast, Villa de la Vega (Spanish Town). However, Spain had become distracted by the immense riches coming from its new possessions in Mexico and Peru, and Jamaica languished as a post for provisioning ships sailing between Spain and Central America.

Visit the ruins of the first Spanish settlement on the island at the Maima Seville Great House & Heritage Park near St Ann's Bay.

HISTORY THE ENGLISH INVASION

The English Invasion

On May 10 1655, an expeditionary force of 38 ships landed 8000 troops on weakly defended Jamaica as part of Oliver Cromwell's 'Grand Western

JAMAICA'S NATIONAL HEROES

After independence, Jamaica honored seven heroes for their special roles in forging the national identity. Memorialized at National Heroes Park in Kingston, they're also depicted on the currency.

➡ Paul Bogle (c 1820–1865) staged the 1865 protests that became the Morant Bay Rebellion.

➡ Alexander Bustamante (1884–1977) was a firebrand trade unionist and founder of the Jamaica Labour Party, who became independent Jamaica's first prime minister.

➡ Marcus Garvey (1887–1940) was a key proponent of Pan-Africanism and father of the 'black power' movement.

➡ George William Gordon (1820–65), a lawyer, assemblyman and post-emancipation nationalist, was a powerful advocate of the rights of the poor.

➡ Norman Manley (1893–1969) founded the People's National Party and became the self-governing island's first prime minister, prior to independence.

➡ Nanny of the Maroons (c 1686–c 1733) was a leader of the Windward Maroons in the 18th century. Folklore attributes her with magical powers.

➡ Samuel Sharpe (1801–1832), a slave and Baptist deacon, was hanged for his leadership of the Christmas Rebellion of 1831.

1517	1643	1655	1670
The Spanish bring enslaved West Africans to do their bidding on the island in place of the Taínos, whose population has been decimated by European disease and appalling treatment.	Jamaica is sacked by English pirate William Jackson, raising doubt about the security of the Spanish colony.	The English capture Jamaica from the Spanish, who retreat to Cuba.	At the Treaty of Madrid, the Spanish cede Jamaica to the English. Both nations agree to cease trading in each other's territories.

Design' to destroy the Spanish trade monopoly and amass English holdings in the Caribbean.

The British had to fight both Spanish loyalists and the *cimarrones* (runaways) – freed slaves left in the Spaniards' wake. The guerrilla warfare lasted several years until the last Spanish forces were finally routed at the Battle of Rio Bueno (outside Ocho Rios) in 1660.

By 1662 there were 4000 colonists on the island, including exiled felons as well as impoverished Scots and Welsh who arrived as indentured laborers. Port Royal, across the bay from Spanish Town, became the island's capital, and a viable trading economy slowly began to evolve.

The Age of the Buccaneers

Throughout the 17th century, Britain was constantly at war with France, Spain or Holland. The English sponsored privateers to capture enemy vessels, raid their settlements and contribute their plunder to the Crown's coffers. These buccaneers became the Brethren of the Coast, committed to a life of piracy, and grew into a powerful and ruthless force, feared throughout the Antilles.

In 1664 the Jamaican governor Sir Thomas Modyford invited the Brethren to defend Jamaica, with Port Royal as their base. Their numbers swelled astronomically, and within a decade Port Royal was Jamaica's largest city – a den of iniquity and prosperity.

When England and Spain finally made peace, the pirates' days became numbered. Mother Nature lent a hand in their suppression when a massive earthquake struck Port Royal on June 7, 1692, toppling it into the sea. More than 2000 people – one-third of the city's population – perished, and survivors fled to newly founded Kingston, believing the earthquake to be punishment from God.

Sugar & Slavery

Europe's sweet tooth had been growing for years, and sugar – cultivated by African slaves – helped turn Jamaica into Britain's wealthiest colony and helped provide the capital that fueled the Industrial Revolution.

Planters built 'great houses' in Georgian fashion high above their cane fields, and lived a life of indolence, but many were absentee landlords, forming the powerful sugar lobby back in London. Many overindulged in drink and had sexual relations with slaves – some of the mulatto offspring were freed; known as 'free coloreds,' they were accorded special rights and often sent to study in England.

Plantations were both farm and factory, growing the cane and refining the sugar. The by-product molasses was turned into cheap rum for export. Sugar production was back-breaking work, and while some planters nurtured their slaves, most resorted to violence to terrorize the

Jamaica National Heritage Trust (p209) provides a guide to Jamaica's history and heritage, covering all sites of importance on the island.

The Story of the Jamaican People by Philip Sherlock and Hazel Bennett offers a new interpretation of Jamaica's history that eschews the imperial perspective, instead looking to Africa for the keys to understanding the island's complex culture.

1692	1700	1720	1760
Port Royal slides into the harbor after an earthquake, killing more than 2000 people. Kingston is founded the following year as a replacement to the port.	There are more than five slaves for every English settler on Jamaica. The practice of slavery creates enormous economic bounty for the English, at terrible cost to the enslaved.	Notorious pirate 'Calico Jack' Rackham is executed in Port Royal, his body hung in a cage above Rackham Cay.	Tacky, a runaway slave, starts an uprising in St Mary that is brutally suppressed with the aid of the local Maroons.

population into obedience. The extreme treatment was eventually regulated, but plantation society remained tied to the rule of the whip.

Most slaves worked on plantations; others were domestic servants. During their few free hours, the slaves cultivated their own tiny plots, and could sell produce at market. By 1800, the slave population of 300,000 outnumbered the free population twenty to one.

Maroon Resistance

Colonial life was paranoid over the possibility of slave rebellion. The first major revolt occurred in 1690 in Clarendon parish, when escaped slaves joined the descendants of slaves that had been freed by the Spanish, coalescing into two powerful bands called Maroons. The Windward Maroons lived in the remote Blue Mountains, while the Leeward Maroons colonized the almost impenetrable Cockpit Country. Both groups raided plantations and attracted runaway slaves.

Colonial troops fought several prolonged campaigns against the Maroons, who were led by Nanny in the Blue Mountains and Cudjoe in Cockpit Country. The thickly forested mountains, however, were ill-suited to traditional British military tactics and perfect for the Maroons' ambush-style guerrilla warfare. Nonetheless, after a decade of costly campaigning, the English gained the upper hand.

In March 1739, the English signed a peace treaty with Cudjoe, granting the Maroons autonomy and 1500 acres of land. In return, the Maroons agreed to chase down runaway slaves and return them to the plantations and to assist the English in quelling rebellions. The Maroons of the Blue Mountains, now led by Quao, signed a similar treaty one year later. To this day, the Maroons still practice a semi-autonomous form of government.

Before his execution on May 23 1832, Sam Sharpe is quoted as saying, 'I would rather die upon yonder gallows than live in slavery.'

THE ATLANTIC SLAVE TRADE

The Atlantic slave trade was dubbed 'the triangular trade.' European merchants sailed to West Africa with goods to exchange for slaves. Although domestic slavery had long been an established part of many African societies, European demand (and trade goods such as firearms) turned African states into asset-strippers, sucking in captives in insatiable numbers, often from tribes living 1000 miles from African slave ports.

Traders packed hundreds of shackled captives into the bowels of their ships. Around one in eight died during the voyage, which lasted two to three months. The slaves were sold for sugar, which was then exported back to Europe – the third profitable leg of the trade.

During the lifetime of the trade, around 12 million slaves were brought to the Americas, of whom around 1.5 million ended up in Jamaica.

1814	1834	1845	1865
Jamaican sugar production peaks at £34 million. During the latter half of the 18th century and the first half of the 19th, Jamaica is the world's largest producer of sugar.	Slavery is abolished throughout the British Empire, causing economic chaos in Jamaica.	To fill the labor gap left by the abolition of slavery, 30,000 Indians are brought to Jamaica as indentured laborers.	The Morant Bay Rebellion, led by Paul Bogle, is brutally suppressed by the British authorities.

Revolt & Reform

After a prolonged campaign by abolitionist campaigners such as Thomas Clarkson and William Wilberforce, Britain abolished the slave trade in 1807, although the institution of slavery itself was left untouched. Jamaica's 1831 Christmas Rebellion lent particular focus to the debate.

Inspired by 'Daddy' Sam Sharpe, an educated slave and lay preacher, up to 20,000 slaves razed plantations and killed their masters. The rebellion was violently suppressed, and 400 slaves were hanged as a result. The brutality of the response lent weight to British abolitionist debates. In 1834 the British Parliament finally passed antislavery legislation, emancipating the empire's slaves.

The resulting transition from a slave economy to one based on paid labor caused economic chaos; most slaves rejected the starvation wages offered on the estates, choosing to fend for themselves. Desperation over conditions and injustice finally boiled over in the 1865 Morant Bay Rebellion.

Mavis Campbell's *The Maroons of Jamaica* is a serious study of the origins of the Maroons and their evolution as a culture through to the late-19th century.

'Come Mr Tallyman, tally me banana...'

In 1866 a Yankee skipper, George Busch, arrived in Jamaica and loaded several hundred stems of bananas, which he transported to Boston and sold at a handsome profit. He quickly returned to Port Antonio, where he encouraged production and soon had himself a thriving export business. Captain Lorenzo Dow Baker followed suit in the west, forming the United Fruit Company. Within a decade the banana trade was booming. Production peaked in 1927, when 21 million stems were exported.

To help pay the passage south to Jamaica, banana traders promoted the island's virtues and took on passengers. Thus, the banana-export trade gave rise to the tourism industry, which continues to grow and flourish.

Matthew Parker's *The Sugar Barons* is a gripping account of the founding of Britain's Caribbean slave empire, with Jamaica taking center stage.

Birth of a Nation

During the Depression of the 1930s, sugar and banana sales plummeted, causing widespread economic hardships. Strikes and riots erupted in 1938, but out of the clamor stepped the charismatic labor leader Alexander Bustamante and his Bustamante Industrial Trade Union. That same year, his cousin Norman Manley formed the People's National Party (PNP), Jamaica's first political party.

Separately they campaigned for economic and political reforms, putting the working class into political life and securing constitutional changes. Not content with trade union activism, Bustamante formed the Jamaica Labour Party (JLP) in 1943.

A year later, a new constitution granted universal suffrage and Jamaica's first elections, which were won by Bustamante's JLP. There was a

1907	1930	1938	1941
A great earthquake topples much of Kingston on January 14, causing widespread destruction and killing more than 800 people.	Haile Selassie is crowned emperor of Ethiopia, encouraging the rise of Rastafarianism in Jamaica.	Jamaica's first political party, the People's National Party (PNP), is formed by Norman Manley, who works with the Bustamante Industrial Trade Union to make working-class issues a main focus of Jamaican politics.	Thousands of Jamaican servicemen volunteer to fight for Britain during WWII.

brief flirtation with the fledgling West Indies Federation of British colonies, but on August 6 1962, Jamaica finally gained full independence. The Union Jack was replaced by Jamaica's new flag, in glorious black (for the people), green (for the land) and gold (for the sun).

The Manley–Seaga Era

The legacies of Bustamante and Manley have dominated post-independence politics. Manley's son Michael led the PNP toward democratic socialism in the mid-'70s. His policy of taxation to fund social services deterred foreign investment but caused widespread capital flight, and bitterly opposed factions engaged in open urban warfare before the 1976 election. Amid a controversial state of emergency, the PNP won the election by a wide margin.

The US government was hostile to Jamaica's socialist turn, withdrew aid and purportedly planned to topple the Jamaican government. The economy (tourism in particular) went into sharp decline. JLP–PNP violence escalated until a ceasefire was finally brokered, celebrated by the famed 'One Love' concert in April 1978, when Bob Marley got Manley and the JLP's Edward Seaga to hold hands in a symbol of unity. Nevertheless, almost 800 people were killed in the lead-up to the 1980 elections, which were won by Seaga. Seaga opened the door to the free market and International Monetary Fund, and became a staunch ally of the Reagan administration.

Relatively peaceful elections in 1989 returned a reinvented 'mainstream realist' Manley to power; when he retired in 1992, he handed the reins to his deputy, Percival James Patterson, who became Jamaica's first black prime minister.

Pieces of the Past (www.jamaica-gleaner.com/pages/history) is a compendium of thematic essays about Jamaican history.

HISTORY THE MANLEY–SEAGA ERA

THE MORANT BAY REBELLION

In the 1860s Paul Bogle, a Black Baptist deacon in St Thomas parish, preached resistance against the post-emancipation injustices of the local authorities. He was supported by George William Gordon, a mulatto planter and assemblyman.

On October 11, 1865, Bogle and his supporters marched to the Morant Bay courthouse to protest the trial of a vagrant for trespass. A riot ensued and the courthouse and town center were razed. As the countryside erupted, Bogle fled with a bounty on his head, but was captured by Maroons and hanged from the burned-out courthouse. Gordon was arrested in Kingston, condemned by a kangaroo court and also hanged.

Governor Edward Eyre ordered vicious reprisals. Martial law was declared and some 439 people were killed in arbitrary executions and more than 1000 homes were burned down. Such was the subsequent outrage in Britain that Eyre was stripped of his post along with the powers of the Jamaican House of Assembly, turning the island into a Crown colony.

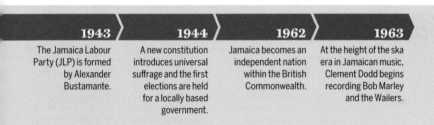

1943	1944	1962	1963
The Jamaica Labour Party (JLP) is formed by Alexander Bustamante.	A new constitution introduces universal suffrage and the first elections are held for a locally based government.	Jamaica becomes an independent nation within the British Commonwealth.	At the height of the ska era in Jamaican music, Clement Dodd begins recording Bob Marley and the Wailers.

The PNP Years

The Patterson-led PNP triumphed in the 1993 and 1997 elections. In spring 1999 the country erupted in nationwide riots after the government announced a 30% increase in the tax on gasoline. Kingston and Montego Bay, where sugarcane fields were set ablaze, were particularly badly hit. After three days of arson and looting, the government rescinded the tax.

In the lead-up to the 2002 elections, violence in West Kingston soared to new heights as criminal posses battled to control electoral turf and profit from the largesse that victory at the polls in Jamaica brings. Rival political gangs turned the area into a war zone, forcing residents to flee, and schools, businesses and even Kingston Public Hospital to close.

In 2004 Hurricane Ivan bounced off Jamaica en route to the Cayman Islands, causing widespread damage, and Edward Seaga – still representing the JLP as opposition leader – retired after more than three decades in politics. Two years later Prime Minister Patterson resigned, giving

Tony Sewall's *Garvey's Children: The Legacy of Marcus Garvey* provides a look at the rise of black nationalism inspired by national hero Marcus Garvey.

UP YOU MIGHTY RACE!

Marcus Garvey was born of working-class parents in St Ann's Bay on August 17 1887. After traveling to Costa Rica, Panama and England, he returned a firm believer in self-improvement and he founded the Universal Negro Improvement Association (UNIA) in 1914 to unite 'all the Negro peoples of the world to establish a state exclusively their own.' When Jamaica's middle classes proved largely unreceptive to his message, he moved in 1916 to the US, where he received a rapturous welcome and formed a branch of the UNIA in New York. The UNIA is credited for giving birth to the Black Panther movement, which in turn paved the way for the civil rights movement. Garvey, a gifted orator, established a weekly newspaper, the *Negro World,* and built an enormous following under the slogan 'One God! One Aim! One Destiny!'

Garvey set up the Black Star Line, a steamship company, with the aim of eventually repatriating blacks to Africa, though it ultimately failed due to poor management. Garvey's greatest achievement was to instill the post-colonial black community with a sense of self-worth and pride: 'Up you mighty race, you can accomplish what you will.'

Considering Garvey a dangerous agitator, the American and British governments conspired against him, and in 1922 they arrested him on dubious mail-fraud charges. He served two years in Atlanta Federal Prison before being deported to Jamaica, where he founded the reformist People's Political Party. Universal franchise did not then exist in Jamaica, and he failed to gather enough support at the polls. In 1935 he departed for England, where he died in poverty in 1940.

His remains were repatriated to Jamaica in 1964 and interred with state honors in National Heroes Park in Kingston. The advent of reggae music in the 1970s gave rise to a new wave of Garveyism.

1966	1976	1978	1980
On the second stop of his Caribbean trip, HIM Haile Selassie I is greeted by nearly 100,000 chanting Rastafarians at the airport.	In the lead-up to the election, tensions between Jamaica's two political parties erupt into open warfare in the streets between politically aligned gangs. A state of emergency is declared.	The One Love peace concert is held in Kingston, following Bob Marley's homecoming; 100,000 people attend. The PNP and JLP declare a peacefire in its honor.	The JLP's Edward Seaga is elected to power, and begins transforming Jamaica's foreign engagement, cutting ties with Cuba, and positioning himself as a friend of the Reagan administration.

way to Portia Simpson-Miller, Jamaica's first female prime minister and Michael Manley's protégé. 'Mama P' was initially popular with the masses, but 18 years of PNP rule bred voter disillusionment with the party. In the 2007 elections, Bruce Golding of the JLP carried the day, inheriting high rates of crime and illiteracy as well as threats to the environment through deforestation and overdevelopment.

From Dudus to the Present

Politics and gang crime came to a head in 2009, when the US called for the extradition of Christopher 'Dudus' Coke, the don of the pro-PNP Tivoli Gardens ghetto and one of the most powerful men in Jamaica, on alleged gun- and drug-running charges. The demand for extradition was originally refused, but after US pressure the Jamaican authorities finally agreed to pursue him. In May 2010, a joint police-military force underwent the controversial Tivoli Incursion, which left some 74 dead – including many bystanders, with others the victims of alleged extra-judicial executions. Dudus himself remained on the run for a month before being apprehended and extradited. He is now serving a 23-year sentence in the US, although his absence left a power vacuum in the poverty-stricken Tivoli area.

In 2011, Portia Simpson-Miller was returned as prime minister. In a reflection of the changing geopolitical climate, her government has looked to China as much as America, using Jamaica's long-standing Chinese community to leverage increased investment from Beijing. A stabilizing political scene, coupled with the country's renewed image following the Olympic success of its athletes, has buoyed tourism returns, although long-standing foreign debt problems meant that in 2013 the government had to go cap in hand to the IMF for restructured loans. Jamaicans still require their vaunted resolve and good humor to face the challenges of the new century.

Jamaica carries a debt to foreign banks exceeding US$800 billion. *Life & Debt*, a documentary film by Stephanie Black, takes a provocative look into the island's burden.

David Howard's *Kingston* is an engaging exploration of the capital's history, from Spanish to modern times.

HISTORY FROM DUDUS TO THE PRESENT

2004	2006	2008	2010
At least 15 people are killed by Hurricane Ivan, with Negril being particularly hard hit. The banana-tree population is ravaged, and the following year banana exports drop by 68%.	Portia Simpson-Miller, of the PNP, becomes Jamaica's first female prime minister.	At the Beijing Olympic Games, world records are broken by sprinter Usain Bolt in the 100m and 200m and with the Jamaican men's team in the 400m relay.	Christopher 'Dudus' Coke, don of the Tivoli Gardens ghetto, is extradited to the US after an armed standoff between gang members and the Jamaican police and military.

Jamaican Culture

Oh Jamaican clichés, how do we love thee? Let us count the ways: Spliff-puffing Rastas, violent rude boys from the Kingston ghettoes, deep reggae vibes and slack dancehall lyrics – come one, come all! We're not saying that the stereotypes don't exist, but exploring Jamaica is about discovering a culture as diverse as the island's geography is varied. Born of an often-troubled history, it's both complicated and exciting – as smooth as a cup of Blue Mountain coffee, as buzzing as a shot of white overproof rum.

'Out of Many, One People'

The nation's motto reflects the diverse heritage of Jamaica. Along with the many West Africans imported as slaves, the population was salted with English, Scots, Irish, Welsh and Germans, along with Hispanic and Portuguese Jews and 'Syrians' (a term for all those of Levantine extraction), as well as Chinese and Indians, who arrived as indentured workers following emancipation.

Jamaica proclaims itself a melting pot of racial harmony. Still, insecurities of identity have been carried down from the plantation era. The issue of class lines drawn during the colonial era has left profound societal divisions and is closely tied to color; lighter-skinned Jamaicans are far more likely to hold better-paid jobs, and skin bleaching is a common phenomenon. The middle classes have always sought to distance themselves from the inhabitants of shanty towns. There is some lingering resentment against whites, particularly among the poorer segment of society, and disillusionment with post-independence Jamaica.

Jamaicans can be the most gracious people you'll ever meet: hardworking, helpful, courteous, genteel and full of humility. However, charged memories of slavery and racism have continued to bring out the spirit of anarchy latent in a society divided into rich and poor. Jamaicans struggling hard against poverty are disdainful of talk about a 'tropical paradise.'

Jamaicans love to debate, or 'reason.' They tend to express themselves forcefully, turning differences of opinion into voluble arguments with some confounding elliptical twists and stream-of-consciousness associations.

Jamaicans' sarcasm and sardonic wit is legendary. The deprecating humor has evolved as an escape valve that hides their true feelings. In a country where it is hard to make a living, the saying that 'everyt'ing irie' – no problems – can mark black humor indeed.

Living in Jamaica

Jamaica is classed as a middle-income country, and it has a small but significant middle class – well educated, entrepreneurial and frequently with close ties to the UK and America.

Despite this, many Jamaicans live in pockets of extreme poverty, either in the countryside, eking out a life as farmers, fishers or plantation laborers, or scraping by in Kingston's ghettoes and shanties. Job

PATOIS

When Jamaicans speak patois, often they drop their 'h's' (thus, *ouse* instead of 'house') and add them in unexpected places (eg, *hemphasize*). Jamaicans usually drop the 'h' from 'th' as well: hence, *t'anks* for 'thanks.' 'The' is usually pronounced as *de* and 'them' as *dem*. They also sometimes drop the 'w,' as in *ooman* (woman).

HOMOPHOBIA IN JAMAICA

Ever since Buju Banton's 1990s dancehall hit *Boom Bye Bye* made international headlines for its apparent celebration of the murder of gay men, Jamaica has gained an unfortunate reputation as one of the most homophobic countries in the world – a reputation thrown into even sharper relief with the 2013 lynching of transsexual teenager Dwayne Jones at a Montego Bay dance party.

Dancehall homophobia is merely a reflection of deeper currents within Jamaican society. This is a deeply devout Christian country, where homosexuality is preached against as a Biblical sin, and often seen as a Western colonial import – a threat to the fabric of society itself.

Homophobic violence is common, from verbal and physical abuse to 'corrective rape' against lesbians (in a country where sexual violence against women is sadly all too commonplace). Pejorative terms such as 'batty man' and 'fish' are still thrown about, despite 2007's Reggae Compassionate Act, which sought to strip dancehall of its homophobic elements. Homelessness is a particular problem for young gay men, who are often ostracized by their families. Jamaica has the highest rate of prostate cancer in the world, with anecdotal evidence suggesting a link to a perceived homosexual stigma attached to getting a rectal check-up.

For all this, Jamaica's LGBT community is increasingly visible and assertive, from organizations such as **J-Flag** (Jamaica Forum for Lesbians, All-Sexuals and Gays; www.jflag.org) and **Quality of Citizenship Jamaica** (www.qcjm.org), to the campaign to repeal the 1864 buggery law which criminalizes all anal sex. Despite pushback from Christian organizations, societal attitudes remain in flux, from the wild popularity of the outrageously camp comedy actor Keith 'Shebada' Ramsey, to the influence that gay fashion has had on the hyper-masculine dancehall world. Like many things in Jamaica, homophobia is a lot more complicated than it first appears.

opportunities are difficult to come by without a proper education, which doesn't come cheap, so many low-income Jamaicans hustle, waiting for an opportunity to present itself. The average per capita income is only US$4390 (J$371,615) and many Jamaicans are reliant on remittances sent by family members living abroad.

Religion & Spirituality

Jamaica professes to have the greatest number of churches per square kilometer in the world. Although most foreigners associate the island with Rastafarianism, more than 80% of Jamaicans identify themselves as Christian.

Christianity

On weekends, it's common to see adults and children walking along country roads holding Bibles and dressed in their finest outfits. Every church in the country seems to overflow with the righteous, and the old fire-and-brimstone school of sermonizing is still the preferred mode. It's hard to over-emphasize the social and cultural influence of the church in Jamaica.

The most popular denomination is the Anglican Church of Jamaica, followed by Seventh-Day Adventists, Pentecostals, Baptists, Methodists and Catholics.

Revivalism

Jamaica has several sects that are generically named Revivalist cults after the post-emancipation Great Revival, during which many blacks converted to Christianity. The most important Revivalist branches are

Jamaican proverbs are a proud celebration of heritage and dialect. A sample: 'So cow a grow so him nose hole a open.' This roughly translates to 'Live and learn.'

A UNIQUE LEXICON

One of the 21 tenets of Rastafarianism is the belief that God exists in each person, and that the two are the same. Thus the creed unifies divinity and individuality through the use of personal pronouns that reflect the 'I and I.' 'I' becomes the id or true measure of inner divinity, which places everyone on the same plane. Thus 'I and I' can mean 'we,' 'him and her,' 'you and them.' (The personal pronoun 'me' is seen as a sign of subservience, of acceptance of the self as an 'object.')

Rastafarian reasoning sees the English language as a tool in the service of Babylon, designed to 'downpress' the black people. The belief that language itself is biased has led to a whole lexicon laced with cryptic intent and meaning, that has profoundly influenced 'Jamaica talk.'

Zionism and Pocomania (Pukkumina), the former being more Bible-centered, and the latter involving ancestor worship.

A core Revivalist belief is that spirits live independently of the body and can inhabit inanimate objects and communicate themselves to humans.

Revivalist ceremonies are characterized by the flowing robes of the congregation, chanting, drumming, speaking in tongues and spirit possession. They are held in designated poco yards, led by a 'shepherd' or 'mother,' who interprets the messages of the spirits.

Rarer these days, Kumina is the most African of the Revivalist cults, combining evocation of ancestral spirits with call-and-response chanting and intricate drumming rhythms and dancing.

Barry Chevannes' *Rastafari: Roots and Ideology* and *Rasta Heart: A Journey Into One Love* by Robert Roskind are noteworthy books on Jamaica's most-talked-about creed.

Rastafarianism

Dreadlocked Rastafarians are as synonymous with Jamaica as reggae. Developed in the 1930s, the creed evolved as an expression of poor, black Jamaicans seeking fulfillment, boosted by Marcus Garvey's 'back to Africa' zeal.

Central to Rastafarianism is the concept that the Africans are one of the displaced Twelve Tribes of Israel. Jamaica is Babylon, and their lot is in exile in a land that cannot be reformed. The crowning of Ras Tafari (Haile Selassie) as emperor of Abyssinia in 1930 fulfilled the prophecy of an African king and redeemer who would lead them from exile to the promised land of Zion, the black race's spiritual home.

Ganja smoking is a sacrament for many (if not all) Rastas, allowing them to gain wisdom and inner divinity through the ability to 'reason' more clearly. The parsing of Bible verses is an essential tradition, helping to see through the corrupting influences of Babylon. The growing of dreadlocks is an allegory for the mane of the Lion of Judah.

Despite its militant consciousness, the religion preaches love and nonviolence, and adherents live by strict biblical codes advocating a way of life in harmony with Old Testament traditions. Some Rastas are teetotalers who shun tobacco and keep to a strict diet of vegetarian I-tal food, prepared without salt; others, like the 12 Tribes Rastafari, eat meat and drink beer.

Jamaica's tiny Jewish community is the oldest in the New World. Visit www.ucija.org for more information on the Kingston-based community band synagogue.

Jamaica's Sporting Legacy

If anyone can wrest away Bob Marley's mantle as the world's most recognizable Jamaican, it's Usain Bolt, currently the fastest man on the planet, who exploded onto the global stage with a double 100m and 200m gold at the 2008 Beijing Olympics, and did it again four years later in London. Sprinter Shelly-Ann Fraser-Pryce repeated the golden trick for the women's 100m at the same games.

Jamaica is cricket mad, and cricketers such as fast bowler Courtney Walsh and batsman Chris Gayle are revered. Jamaica plays nationally as part of the West Indies team, who were quarter-finalists in the 2011 World Cup, but champions in the 2012 World Twenty20. Jamaican cricket's home is Sabina Park in Kingston, which hosts national and international test matches as well as the new Caribbean Premier League (CPL).

Football is Jamaica's second sport. It was given a huge boost by the success of the Reggae Boyz – Jamaica's national soccer team – in qualifying for the 1998 World Cup, though they haven't qualified since. Spirited international matches are played at Kingston's National Stadium.

A Woman's Lot

While Jamaican society can appear oppressively macho to outsiders accustomed to dancehall lyrics, women tend to be strong and independent (in 40% of households, a woman is the sole provider). This spirit often translates into the self-assurance so apparent in Portia Simpson-Miller, the current prime minister. Jamaican women attain far higher grades in school and have higher literacy rates than Jamaican men, and middle-class women have attained levels of respect and career performance that are commensurate with their counterparts in North America and Europe. Women also make up about 46% of Jamaica's labor force, although the majority are in extremely low-paying jobs.

The darker side of a Jamaican woman's life is the proliferation of sexual violence. According to statistics, one in four women is subject to a forced sexual encounter during the course of her life. While 47% of pregnancies in Jamaica are unplanned, and Jamaica has one of the highest rates of teenage pregnancy in the region, abortion remains illegal except under medical grounds.

The lavishly illustrated *Reggae Routes: The Story of Jamaican Music* by Wayne Chen and Kevin O'Brien Chang is required reading for anyone exploring the island's musical culture.

Jamaican Arts

Literature

Through the years Jamaican literature has been haunted by the ghosts of slave history and the ambiguities of Jamaica's relationship to Mother England. Best known, perhaps, is Herbert de Lisser's classic Gothic

OBEAH & MYAL

Jamaica has its own folk magic system, based on practices derived from West Africa, and similar to Haiti's Vodou or Cuba's Santería. Myal is essentially 'white magic' to obeah's 'black magic.' Largely a rural practice, it involves invoking the services of a practitioner who can cast or dispel a curse, bring you luck, or force your partner to be faithful, using an arsenal of herbs, powders (including grave dust), specially shaped candles and power rings to achieve their objective.

The summoning of duppies, or spirits, is central to the practice. Jamaicans believe that your spirit roams the earth for nine days after you die, and in that time it can be summoned to do good or evil. Many Jamaicans still observe Nine Night, a 'wake' held for nine nights after someone's death to ensure that the spirit of the deceased (duppy) departs to heaven – these can be pretty big parties complete with sound-systems.

Invoking duppies involves a ritual circle comprised of bottles topped with candles. The entrance or 'gateway' to the circle is barred with a cutlass or machete and the circle may contain food offerings to the spirits, as well as chalked symbols.

Nonbelievers dismiss obeah as superstitious nonsense, but everyone knows where the nearest obeah shop is, and local newspapers often feature hilarious 'duppy' stories in their news round-ups. Judging by the charms you find in many Jamaican homes, obeah still has a powerful grip on the nation's psyche.

horror, *White Witch of Rose Hall,* about the murderous Annie Palmer, the wicked mistress of Rose Hall.

The novels of Anthony Winkler are celebrated for the wry eye they cast over Jamaican life, most notably in *The Lunatic, The Duppy* and *The Family Mansion.*

The streets of Kingston are also the setting for the gritty novels of Roger Mais, notably *The Hills Were Joyful Together* and *Brother Man.* Orlando Patterson's *The Children of Sisyphus* mines the same tough terrain from a Rastafarian perspective.

In recent years, a number of Jamaican female writers have gained notice: they include Christine Craig *(Mint Tea),* Patricia Powell *(Me Dying Trial),* Michelle Cliff *(Abeng, Land of Look Behind)* and Vanessa Spence *(Roads Are Down).*

Current stars on Jamaica's literary scene include Olive Senior *(Dancing Lessons),* Garfield Ellis *(For Nothing At All),* Kei Miller *(The Last Warner Woman),* Marlon James *(The Book of Night Women)* and Diana McCaulay *(Huracan).*

Bridging the gap between literature and performance is the patois-rich genre of dub poetry. Louise Bennett *(Selected Poems)* and Linton Kwesi Johnson *(My Revolutionary Fren)* are essential texts.

Jamaica Art by Kim Robinson and Petrine Archer Straw is a well-illustrated treatise on the evolution of the island's art scene.

Film

For many, Jamaican cinema begins with cult classic *The Harder They Come* (1973), starring Jimmy Cliff as a 'rude bwai' in Kingston's ghettoes. *Smile Orange* (1974) tells the story of Ringo, a hustling waiter at a resort – a theme not irrelevant today. *Rockers* (1978), another music-propelled, socially poignant fable is a Jamaican reworking of *The Bicycle Thief* featuring a cast of reggae all-stars.

The Lunatic (1991), based on the Anthony Winkler novel, is a humorous exploration of the island's sexual taboos.

Rick Elgood's 1997 film *Dancehall Queen* found an international audience for its tale of redemption for a struggling street vendor, who escapes the mean streets of Kingston through dancehall music. Jamaica's highest-grossing film is Chris Browne's 2000 crime drama *Third World Cop,* in which old friends straddling both sides of the law must come to terms with each other. *Shottas* (2002) follows in its footsteps, featuring two Kingston criminals trying their luck in the US. *One Love* (2003) explores Jamaica's social divides against the backdrop of a controversial romance between a Rasta musician and a pastor's daughter.

Currently making waves on the Jamaican movie scene is director Storm Saulter, whose communal approach to film-making has brought many admirers, most notably for his 2013 movie *Better Mus Come,* about Kingston's gang troubles in the 1970s, one of the most critically acclaimed films coming out of the Caribbean in the last 10 years.

The Birth of Visual Nationalism

Jamaica's most celebrated theater company is the National Dance Theatre Company, which performs at the Little Theatre in Kingston and incorporates Kumina movements into their routines.

British trends and colonial tastes traditionally shaped Jamaican art, but in the 1920s the Jamaican School of local artists began to develop its own style, shaped by realities of Jamaican life. There were two main groups: the painters who were schooled abroad, and island-themed 'intuitives.'

Jamaican Independence leader Norman Manley's wife, Edna, an inspired sculptor and advocate for indigenous Jamaican art, became a leading catalyst for change. Through the example of seminal works such as *Negro Aroused* (1935) and *Pocomania* (1936), which synthesized African and Jamaican archetypes within a deeply personal vision of the national psyche, Manley provided an electrifying example of the potential of Jamaican art. At a grassroots level, Manley organized free art classes and training courses to energize and organize rising talent.

This fertile ground gave birth to three of Jamaica's great painters. Self-taught artist John Dunkley was 'discovered' by Manley in his brilliantly decorated Kingston barbershop. His brooding landscapes of sinister tropical foliage, never-ending roads and furtive reptiles and rodents, spoke of a vision that resonated with the historical traumas of the nation. In contrast, Albert Huie produced intricately detailed and beautifully composed works depicting an idyllic dreamscape of rural scenes far removed from the urban strife of his native Kingston. More rooted in his immediate surroundings, David Pottinger's primary interest is in the urban landscape. His portrayals of downtown life reveal the melancholy of poverty while also suggesting the indomitable spirit of life.

Leading lights of the contemporary Jamaican visual arts scene currently include the painter Ebony Patterson and the photographer Marvin Bartley. Both have strong links to Kingston's Edna Manley College of Visual and Performing Arts, which remains an important crucible for the country's artistic scene. Good annual events for taking the temperature of Jamaica's visual arts are the Kingston on the Edge festival and the National Gallery of Jamaica's Biennial Art Exhibition.

One of the most electrifying voices of Jamaican dub poetry today is that of Mutabaruka. Learn about his work and read his poems at www.mutabaruka.com.

Music

Few places are as defined by their music as Jamaica. Thanks to Bob Marley, reggae is the island soundtrack that went on to conquer the world, helping permanently brand the country and bestow it a global cultural influencer well out of proportion to the island's tiny size. In fact, there's a lot more to Jamaican music than just reggae, as Jamaica's relentlessly busy studios attest. Per capita, Jamaica is the world's most prolific creator of recorded music. Or as the patois proverbs put it, 'We likkle but we talawah.' *We're small, but we're powerful.*

A Brief History

Modern Jamaican music starts with the acoustic folk music of mento. In the early 1960s, this blended with calypso, jazz and R&B to form ska, the country's first popular music form in the early 1960s. This evolved, via the intermediate step of rocksteady, into the bass-heavy reggae of the 1970s, the genre that ultimately swept all before it. Dancehall, a faster and more clubby sound than its predecessors, followed thereafter, and continues to dominate the contemporary music scene today. For all that

Timothy White's *Catch a Fire* remains the go-to Bob Marley biography. Pair it with a screening of Kevin Macdonald's superb 2012 feature documentary, *Marley*.

OUR TOP PLAYLISTS

Reggae

007 (Shanty Town) Desmond Decker & the Aces
Picture of Selassie I Khari Kill
Legalize It Peter Tosh
One Love Bob Marley and the Wailers
Cool Rasta The Heptones
The Harder They Come Jimmy Cliff
Rivers of Babylon The Melodians
Pass the Koutchie The Mighty Diamonds
Funky Kingston Toots & the Maytals
Is This Love Bob Marley and the Wailers

Dancehall

Who Am I Beenie Man
Murder She Wrote Chaka Demus and Pliers
Sycamore Tree Lady Saw
Get Busy Sean Paul
Ting-A-Ling Shabba Ranks
Under Me Sleng Teng Wayne Smith
It's a Pity Tanya Stephens
Ring the Alarm Tenor Saw
Clarks Vybz Kartel ft. Popcaan & Gaza Slim
Zungguzungguzeng Yellowman

these styles are distinct, they constantly blend and feed off each other – this syncretism is the true magic of Jamaican music.

Reggae Roots

Carolyn Cooper's *Sound Clash: Jamaican Dancehall Culture at Large* is a key text for exploring contemporary Jamaica's dominant music form.

In his song 'Trench Town', Bob Marley asked if anything good could ever come from Jamaica's ghettoes. In doing so, he challenged the class-based assumptions of Jamaican society, where minority elite rule over the disenfranchised masses. Of course the answer came in the message of pride and spiritual redemption contained in the music itself, as reggae left the yard to conquer the world, in the process turning Bob Marley into a true global icon.

Bob Marley's band, The Wailers, sprang from the ska and rocksteady era of the 1960s. Producers such as Lee 'Scratch' Perry, Clement 'Sir Coxsone' Dodd and King Tubby played a key role in evolving the more spacious new reggae sound, while the resurgence of Rastafarianism that followed Haile Sellassie's 1966 visit to Jamaica inspired the music's soul. Through his signing of The Wailers, Jamaican-born founder of Island Records, Chris Blackwell, helped introduce reggae to an international audience.

Reggae is more than just Marley. His original band-mates Peter Tosh and Bunny Wailer both became major stars, joining a pantheon that runs from Desmond Dekker and Dennis Brown to Burning Spear and Gregory Isaacs. While dancehall has since taken over as Jamaica's most popular domestic music, in recent years there has been something of a roots reggae revival, with artists like Chronixx, Proteje and Jah9 bringing back some rasta consciousness to rejuvenate the genre for the new century.

Dancehall Culture

The modern sound of Jamaica is definitely dancehall: rapid-fire chanting over bass-heavy beats. It's simplistic to just call dancehall Jamaican rap, because the formation of the beats, their structure and the nuances of the lyrics all have deep roots in Jamaica's musical past.

The new sound sprang up at the close of the 1970s with DJs such as Yellowman and Lone Ranger and Josey Wales, who grabbed the mic, and powered the high-energy rhythms through the advent of faster, more digital beats. This was a period of turmoil in Jamaica, and the music reacted by moving away from political consciousness towards a more hedonistic vibe. The scene centered on the sound systems and 'sound clashes' between DJs, dueling with custom records to win the crowd's favor and boost their reputation.

DUTTY WINE

Dancehall's iconic dance move is the (female only) dutty wine. Wining involves bending over and a gymnastically rotating posterior and head. The male equivalent is 'daggering' – rough drysex on the dancefloor. Prudes need not apply.

By the 1990s, the success of artists such as Shabba Ranks turned dancehall global, but stars including Buju Banton, Beenie Man, Bounty Killer and Sizzla continue to be criticized for lyrics celebrating violence and homophobia. An infamous feud between 'World Boss' Vybz Kartel and Mavado spilled onto the street before a publicly brokered 'peace deal', but in 2014, Vybz Kartel was convicted of the murder of an associate. Criticism of dancehall's more outlandish facets is a staple of the Jamaican press, but for all this, dancehall remains in rude health – Sean Paul and Konshens have long ascended into international stardom, while acts such as Cham and Tommy Lee ride the riddims at home.

Experiencing Jamaican Music

It's a surprise to some, but there's not much of a live music scene in Jamaica. The sound system rules supreme here; many working musicians often head to the resort hotels to earn a crust playing reggae for package tourists. If you're in Kingston, one of the best venues to catch a band is at Red Bones, which has excellent live music several times a week, but keep your eyes open for posters advertising one-off concerts elsewhere.

There are also some excellent reggae festivals, most notably Montego Bay's Sumfest every July, and Rebel Salute held every January in St Ann. February is designated 'Reggae month' in Jamaica (in part to honor Bob Marley's birthday on the 6th) when there's lots of live music to be had, especially in Kingston.

If you want to hear dancehall, there are plenty of clubs, but the street parties in Kingston are by far the most vibrant. For the sound systems, the toasting, the street fashion and the dancing, they're hard to beat. Ask locals, especially those working in your hotel or guest house, where you'll find the best parties and promoted events. Don't be scared off by the city's reputation – they're on the whole well-run, community-policed events. Parties run late though – don't even think of arriving before midnight.

Jamaican Music Glossary

dubplate a specialized version of a popular tune recorded specifically to bug up a sound system, especially in a clash!

dancehall fast, beat-led offspring of reggae, currently Jamaica's most popular form of music

dub a subgenre of reggae with more emphasis on mixing reverb, echo and other production techniques, plus 'dubbing' instrumental and vocal sections

jonkonnu a carnival parade with West African and Bahamian origins; particularly associated with Christmas

mento traditional folk music that predates modern Jamaican genres. The sound is acoustic: guitar, fiddle, banjo, drums and rhumba box (a wooden box with metal keys)

ragga synonymous with dancehall, but more commonly used in the UK rather than Jamaica

reggae Jamaica's most famous music, generally played in 4/4 time with a dominant bass. The guitar is (usually) played on the second and fourth beat; this 'plink...plink' sound is known as a 'skank.'

riddim can just mean 'rhythm,' but also refers to instrumental versions of songs, the beat and bassline to be toasted over; popular riddims spread like wildfire

rocksteady the genre bridge between ska and reggae, rocksteady is characterized by strong bass lines and a mellow sound

roots reggae sub-genre of reggae that focuses on Rastafarian spirituality and social change

selector basically, a DJ (in the sense that they 'selects' the riddims)

ska a uniquely Jamaican genre, blending mento, calypso and American R&B, with a walking bassline and strong upbeat

slackness while 'slack' can refer to any kind of vulgarity (particularly sexual), it is often used as an adjective to describe dancehall lyrics

soca combination of soul and calypso music

sound system mobile disco/party using giant speakers, such as a dancehall. Sound systems tend to have specific names, sounds and followings.

toasting at a party, a toaster starts a rhythmic chant over a pre-laid beat (riddim). There's a convincing case to be made that this is the origin of modern rap and hip-hop.

JAMAICAN CULTURE MUSIC

Listen to the story of Jamaican music, from ska and rocksteady to roots reggae and dancehall, with *Reggae Golden Jubilee*, a 100-track retrospective released in 2012 to celebrate 50 years of independence, compiled by ex-prime minister (and record producer) Edward Seaga.

The Maytals' 1968 song 'Do the Reggay' was one of the first records to use the term 'reggae.' Prior to this the music was known as rocksteady.

Jamaican Landscapes

It's important to note there is a distinction between Jamaica the island and Jamaica the country. The nation is actually an archipelago, with the main island of Jamaica overwhelmingly the dominant land mass. Other small islands in the chain, called cays, are all uninhabited except for some temporary stints by local fishers, include the Port Royal Cays south of Port Royal (such as Lime Cay), the Pedro Banks, an important fishing area 160km to the southwest, and the Morant Cays, which lay off the east coast.

The Archipelago

At 10,991 sq km (roughly equal to the US state of Connecticut, or half the size of Wales), Jamaica is the third-largest island in the Caribbean and the largest of the English-speaking islands. It is one of the Greater Antilles, which make up the westernmost Caribbean islands.

'Mainland' Jamaica is rimmed by a narrow coastal plain, except for the southern broad flatlands. Mountains form the island's spine, rising gradually from the west and culminating in the Blue Mountains in the east, which are capped by Blue Mountain Peak at 2256m. The island is cut by about 120 rivers, many of which are bone dry for much of the year but spring to life after heavy rains, causing great flooding and damage to roads. Coastal mangroves, wetland preserves and montane cloud forests form small specialized ecosystems that contain a wide variety of the island's wildlife.

Caves

Two-thirds of the island's surface is composed of soft, porous limestone (the compressed skeletons of coral, clams and other sea life), in places

TIPS FOR TRAVELERS

➡ Never take 'souvenirs' such as shells, plants or artifacts from historical sites or natural areas.

➡ Keep to the footpaths. When hiking, always follow designated trails. Natural habitats are often quickly eroded, and animals and plants are disturbed by walkers who stray from the beaten path.

➡ Don't touch or stand on coral. Coral is extremely sensitive and is easily killed by snorkelers and divers who make contact. Likewise, boaters should never anchor on coral – use mooring buoys.

➡ Try to patronize hotels, tour companies and merchants that act in an environmentally sound manner, based on their waste generation, noise levels, energy consumption and the local culture.

➡ Many local communities derive little benefit from Jamaica's huge tourism revenues. Educate yourself on community tourism and ways you can participate. Use local tour guides wherever possible.

➡ Respect the community. Learn about the customs of the region and support local efforts to preserve the environment and traditional culture.

several miles thick and covered by red-clay soils rich in bauxite (the principal source of aluminum). The constant interplay of water and soft rock makes Jamaica an especially good destination for spelunkers – for more information see p30.

Animals

Birds

When it comes to sheer variety of color and song, birds are Jamaica's main animal attraction. Over 255 bird species call Jamaica home, 26 of which are endemic, while others are passing through on migration routes to and from North America.

Jamaica's national bird is the 'doctor bird' or red-billed streamertail – an indigenous hummingbird with shimmering emerald feathers, a velvety black crown with purple crest, a long bill and curved tail feathers. It's image is reproduced everywhere. In total four of the 16 Caribbean species of hummingbird are represented in Jamaica.

Stilt-legged, snowy-white cattle egrets are ubiquitous, as are 'John crows,' or turkey vultures, which are the subject of many proverbs. The *patoo* is the Jamaican name for the owl, which many islanders regard as a harbinger of death. Jamaica has two species: the screech owl and the endemic brown owl. There are also four endemic species of flycatcher, a woodpecker and many rare species of dove.

In the extensive swamps, bird-watchers can spot herons, gallinules and countless other waterfowl. Pelicans can be seen diving for fish, while magnificent frigate birds soar high above the coast.

Jamaica is a particularly rewarding destination for bird-watching; for more information see p29.

Mammals

Jamaica has few mammal species. Small numbers of wild hogs and feral goats still roam isolated wilderness areas, but the only native land mammal is the endangered Jamaican coney (or *hutia*), a large brown rodent akin to a guinea pig. Habitat loss now restricts the highly social, nocturnal animal to remote areas of eastern Jamaica.

The mongoose is the one you're most likely to see, usually scurrying across the road. It was imported from India in 1872 to rid sugarcane fields of rats. Unfortunately, they proved more interested in feeding on snakes, a natural predator of the rat, and is now considered a destructive pest.

Amphibians & Reptiles

Jamaica harbors plenty of both. The largest are American crocodiles (called 'alligators' in Jamaica), found along the south coast, but also in and around Negril's Great Morass and adjacent rivers. Abundant until big-game hunters appeared around the turn of the century, crocs are now protected. Crocodile river-safaris are big business in Black River.

Jamaica has 24 species of lizard, including the Jamaican iguana, which hangs on to survival in the remote backwaters of the Hellshire Hills. Geckos can often be seen hanging on ceilings by their sticky feet. Local superstition shuns geckos, but their presence in your hotel room means fewer bugs.

Jamaica has five snake species, none venomous and all endangered thanks mostly to the ravages of the mongoose, which has entirely disposed of a sixth species – the black snake. The largest is the Jamaican boa, or yellow snake – a constrictor (called *nanka* locally) that can grow 2.5m in length.

If you're into caving, refer to Alan Fincham's *Jamaica Underground*, which plumbs the depths of Cockpit Country.

There are 17 frog and one toad species. Uniquely, none of Jamaica's 14 endemic frog species undergoes a tadpole stage; instead, tiny frogs emerge in adult form directly from eggs. All over Jamaica you'll hear the whistle frog living up to its name. While it makes a big racket, the frog itself is smaller than a grape.

Insects

Jamaica has mosquitoes, bees and wasps, but most bugs are harmless. A brown scarab beetle called the 'newsbug' flies seemingly without control and, when it flies into people, locals consider it a sign of important news to come. Diamond-shaped 'stinky bugs' are exactly that, advertising themselves with an offensive smell. Fireflies (called 'blinkies' and 'peeny-wallies') are also common.

Jamaica has 120 butterfly species and countless moth species, of which 21 are endemic. The most spectacular butterfly is the giant swallowtail, *Papilio homerus,* with a 15cm wingspan. It lives only at higher altitudes in the John Crow Mountains and the eastern extent of the Blue Mountains (and in Cockpit Country in smaller numbers).

Marine Life

Coral reefs lie along the north shore, where the reef is almost continuous and much of it is within a few hundred meters of shore.

More than 700 species of fish zip in and out of the reefs: wrasses, parrotfish, snapper, bonito, kingfish, jewelfish and scores of others. Smaller fry are preyed upon by barracuda, giant groupers and tarpon. Sharks are frequently seen, though most of these are harmless nurse sharks. Further out, the deep water is run by sailfish, marlin and manta rays.

Three species of endangered marine turtle – the green, hawksbill and loggerhead – lay eggs at the few remaining undeveloped sandy beaches.

About 100 endangered West Indian manatee – a shy, gentle creature once common around the island – survive in Jamaican waters, most numerously in the swamps of Long Bay on the south coast.

Plants

Jamaica is a veritable garden, with some 3582 plant species (including 237 species of orchid and 550 species of fern), of which at least 912 are endemic. Although much of the island has been cultivated for agriculture, there are large stretches, especially in the interior, where the flora has largely been undisturbed since human settlement. Probably the most famous indigenous plant species is pimento (allspice), the base of many Jamaican seasonings.

Introduced exotics include bougainvillea, brought from South America via London's Kew Gardens in 1858; ackee, the staple of Jamaican breakfasts, brought from West Africa in 1778; and mangoes, which arrived in 1782 from Mauritius. Breadfruit was introduced in 1793 by Captain Bligh (of 'Mutiny on the Bounty' fame) as a food crop for the slave population. Closer cousins to local plants are cocoa, cashew and cassava, native to Central America and the West Indies. A native pineapple from Jamaica was the progenitor of Hawaii's pineapples (the fruit even appears on the Jamaican coat of arms).

Needless to say, ganja (marijuana) is grown beneath tall plants in remote areas to evade the helicopters of the Jamaica Defense Force. The harvest season runs from late August through October. Originally imported to the island by laborers from India, Rastafarians will tell you the plant was first cultivated off the grave of King Solomon in Ethiopia.

Bird-watchers should turn to *Birds of Jamaica: A Photographic Field Guide* by Audrey Downer and Robert Sutton. James Bond's classic *Birds of the West Indies,* another reference for serious bird-watchers, was republished as *Peterson Field Guide to Birds of the West Indies.*

The Nature Conservancy (www.nature.org/wherewework/caribbean/jamaica) has been instrumental in protecting the Blue Mountains-John Crow National Park.

Tree Species

The national flower is the dark-blue bloom of the lignum vitae tree, whose timber is much in demand by carvers. The national tree is blue mahoe, which derives its name from the blue-green streaks in its beautiful wood. You'll also want to keep your eyes peeled for the dramatic flowering of the vermilion 'flame of the forest' (also called the African tulip tree).

Logwood, introduced to the island in 1715, grows wild in dry areas and produces a dark blue dye. Native species include rosewood, palmetto, mahogany, silk cotton (said to be a habitat for duppies, or ghosts), cedar and ebony; the latter two have been logged to decimation during the past two centuries. Over the last decade, deforestation has also led to the deterioration of more than a third of Jamaica's watersheds.

National Parks

Jamaica's embryonic park system comprises four parks: Blue Mountains-John Crow National Park, Montego Bay Marine Park, Port Antonio Marine Park and Negril Marine Park.

The 780-sq-km Blue Mountains-John Crow National Park (Jamaica's largest) includes the biologically diverse forest reserves of the Blue and John Crow mountain ranges. Both marine parks are situated around resort areas and were developed to preserve and manage coral reefs, mangroves and offshore marine resources.

There is also a fistful of other wilderness areas with varying degrees of protection, such as the Portland Bight Protected Area.

Proposals to turn Cockpit Country into a national park have been met with stiff resistance from the Maroons who live there and fear increased governmental authority will infringe on their hard-won autonomy.

Environmental Issues

Today, the island the Taínos called Xaymaca (or 'Land of Wood and Water') faces significant environmental issues. The aggregation of government agencies into the National Environmental & Planning Agency and its partnering with the University of the West Indies at Mona on research issues, has been a positive step. But in Jamaica, the fact remains that top-down policy enactment can occur very slowly, and the nation's environment is on a tight schedule.

In the mid-1990s, Jamaica had the highest rate of deforestation (5% per year) of any country in the world and, although there is now greater awareness of the problem, it is still a threat. Many of Jamaica's endemic wildlife species are endangered, largely due to habitat loss, including

Those captivated by Jamaica's astonishingly beautiful butterflies should grab a copy of *An Annotated List of Butterflies of Jamaica* by A Avinoff and N Shoumatoff.

THE MARVELLOUS MANGROVES

The spidery mangrove, which grows along the Jamaican coast, is crucially important to coastal preservation, besides functioning as a nursery for countless marine and amphibian species. By acting as a shield between the ocean and the mainland, mangroves maintain the integrity of the Jamaican coast; it is estimated their destruction, due to agriculture, resort development, timber cutting, human settlement and pollution, has resulted in the erosion of up to 80 million tons of topsoil per year. This habitat destruction obviously sets off an ecological chain reaction of disaster; as mangroves die, so too do the nurseries of important fisheries. As a result, the National Environment & Planning Agency (NEPA; www.nepa.gov.jm), in concert with local community organizations, has identified over a dozen areas for mangrove rehabilitation across the country; check the agency's website for more information.

the American crocodile, Jamaican boa, Jamaican iguana, coney, green parrot and giant swallowtail butterfly.

Bauxite mining – the island's second-most lucrative industry after tourism – is considered to be the single largest cause of deforestation in Jamaica. Bauxite can only be extracted by opencast mining, which requires the wholesale destruction of forests and topsoil. The access roads cut by mining concerns are then used by loggers, coal burners and yam-stick traders to get to trees in and around designated mining areas, extending the deforestation. Local pressure has blocked periodic attempts to open Cockpit Country to bauxite (and limestone) mining. Deforestation has also damaged parts of the Blue Mountains, where farmers felled trees to clear land to grow lucrative coffee plants. As we went to press, environmental groups were fighting a controversial joint Jamaican-Chinese project to develop the reef- and mangrove-rich Portland Bight Protected Area into a US$1.5 billion transhipment hub.

NEPA is entrusted with responsibility for promoting ecological consciousness among Jamaicans and management of the national parks and protected areas under the Protected Areas Resource Conservation Project (PARC).

The following organizations are also taking the lead in bringing attention to ecological issues:

➡ **Cockpit Country** (www.cockpitcountry.com)

To visit Cockpit Country in an ecologically responsible manner, check out the Southern Trelawny Environmental Agency's website, www. stea.net.

➡ **Environmental Foundation of Jamaica** (☑960-6744; www.efj.org.jm; 1B Norwood Ave, Kingston 5)

➡ **Jamaica Conservation & Development Trust** (☑960-2848; www. jcdt.org.jm; 29 Dumbarton Ave, Kingston 10) Responsible for the management and supervision of the Blue Mountains-John Crow National Park. Can advise on guides and routes.

➡ **Jamaica Environment Trust** (☑960-3693; www.jamentrust.org; 58 Half Way Tree Rd, Kingston 10)

➡ **Jamaican Caves Organisation** (www.jamaicancaves.org)

➡ **North Jamaica Conservation Association** (☑973-4305; http://n-j-c-a.yolasite.com; Runaway Bay)

Survival Guide

Directory A–Z

Accommodations

Low season (summer) is usually mid-April to early December; the high season (winter) is the remainder of the year, when hotel prices increase by 40% or more. All-inclusive packages are usually based on three-day minimum stays.

All-Inclusive Resorts

Rates for all-inclusive resorts presented in listings here are guidelines based on unpublicized 'rack' or 'standard' rates. (Note: reviews for all-inclusive options will include a mention of 'all-incl' in the practicalities details where costs are shown.) You will likely spend considerably less depending on the source of booking, season and current specials, which are perpetually publicized.

Major all-inclusive resort chains include the following:

Couples (www.couples.com)

Riu (www.riu.com)

Sandals (www.sandals.com)

Camping

Jamaica is not developed for campers, and it's unsafe to camp in much of the wild. Many budget properties will let you pitch a tent on their lawns for a small fee. Some even rent tents and have shower, toilet and laundry facilities.

Guest Houses

Most guest houses are inexpensive and good places to mix with the locals. Breakfast is often included. Some are homely houses, others are indistinguishable from hotels.

Villa Rentals

Jamaica boasts hundreds of private villas for rent. Rates start as low as US$100 per week for budget units with minimal facilities. More upscale villas begin at about US$750 weekly and can run to US$10,000. Rates fall as much as 30% in summer. A large deposit (usually 25% or more) is required. Try the following:

Airbnb (www.airbnb.com) House and apartment rental as well as villas. Good for Kingston.

Jamaican Association of Villas & Apartments (JAVA; 800-845-5276, in North America 773-463-6688; www.villasinjamaica.com; 2706 W Agatite, 2nd Fl, Chicago, IL)

Jamaican Treasures (in North America 877-446-7188; www.jamaicantreasures.com; 14629 SW 5th St, Pembroke Pines, FL)

Children

All-inclusive resorts cater to families and have an impressive range of amenities for children. Many hotels offer free accommodations or reduced rates for young children in their parents' room; many provide a babysitter/nanny with advance notice. Increasingly, resorts and upscale hotels offer free childcare centers.

It's a good idea to pre-arrange necessities such as cribs, babysitters, cots and baby food at hotels other than family resorts. Many car-rental agencies in Jamaica do not offer safety seats. Negril, Ocho Rios and Montego Bay are perhaps the best towns for children, each replete with kid-friendly attractions and activities, most notably Dunn's River Falls (outside Ocho Rios), Kool Runnings Water Park (Negril), Aquasol Theme Park

SLEEPING PRICE RANGES

Unless otherwise stated, the following price ranges refer to a double room in high season with European Plan (room only) with bathroom), with the compulsory 6.25% to 15% GCT included in the price.

$	less than US$90 (J$9400)
$$	US$90–200 (J$9400–20,800)
$$$	more than US$200 (J$20,800)

(Montego Bay) and horse-back riding (all three).

Some vaccines are not approved for use in children and pregnant women, so check with your doctor before traveling. Be particularly careful not to drink tap water or consume any questionable food or beverage; hand-sanitizer gel is recommended (and widely available in Jamaica). Breastfeeding in public is somewhat taboo but not illegal.

Lonely Planet's *Travel with Children* gives you the lowdown on preparing for family travel.

Climate

Coastal temperatures are consistently warm, and while temperatures fall steadily with increasing altitude, even in the Blue Mountains the thermometer averages 18°C (64°F) or more. The annual rainfall averages 1980mm (78in), but nationwide there are large variations, with the east coast receiving considerably more rain than elsewhere. Despite wet and dry seasons, rain can fall any time of year and normally comes in short, heavy showers, often followed by sun. Jamaica lies in the Caribbean 'hurricane belt.' Officially the hurricane season lasts from June 1 to November 30; August and September are peak months.

Customs Regulations

➡ Passengers may bring into Jamaica duty-free goods in amounts that they 'might reasonably be expected to carry with them for personal use.'

➡ It's possible (though highly unlikely) that you may need to show proof that laptop computers and other expensive items (especially electronics) are for personal use; otherwise you may be charged import duty.

➡ For more information, see **Jamaica Customs** (www.jacustoms.gov.jm).

Electricity

110V/50Hz

110V/50Hz

Embassies & Consulates

If your country isn't represented in this list, check Em-

bassies & High Commissions in the yellow pages of the Greater Kingston telephone directory.

Canada High Commission (☎926-1500; www.canada international.gc.ca/jamaica-jamaique; 3 West Kings House Rd, Kingston); Consulate (☎952-6198; 29 Gloucester Ave, Montego Bay).

French Embassy (☎946-4000; www.ambafrance-jm-bm.org; 13 Hillcrest Ave, Kingston 6)

German Embassy (☎631-7935; www.kingston.diplo.de; 10 Waterloo Rd, Kingston 10)

Italian Embassy (☎968-8464; 10 Surbiton Rd, Kingston 10)

Japanese Embassy (☎929-7534; www.jamaica.eab-japan.go.jp; NCB Tower, Nth Tower, 6th fl, 2 Oxford Rd, Kingston 5)

Netherlands Embassy (☎926-2026; Victoria Mutual Bldg, 53 Knutsford Blvd, Kingston 5)

UK High Commission (☎936-0700; www.gov.uk/government/world/organis ations/british-high-commis sion-jamaica; 28 Trafalgar Rd, Kingston)

US Embassy (☎702-6000, after hours 702-6055; http://kingston.usembassy.gov; 142 Old Hope Rd, Kingston); Consulate (☎953-0602, 952-5050; Unit EU-1, Whitter Village, Ironshore)

Gay & Lesbian Travelers

There is a gay scene in Kingston, but it is an underground affair as Jamaica is a largely homophobic society. Sexual acts between men are prohibited by law and punishable by up to 10 years in prison. Many reggae dancehall lyrics by big-name stars could be classified as anti-gay hate speech. Gay-bashing incidents are almost never prosecuted, with law enforcement in most cases looking the other way.

Nonetheless, you shouldn't be put off from

visiting the island. In the more heavily touristed areas you'll find more tolerant attitudes, and hotels that welcome gay travelers, including all-inclusives. Publicly, though, discretion is important and open displays of affection should be avoided.

For more information see the Homophobia in Jamaica boxed text p197.

Gay Jamaica Watch (http://gayjamaicawatch.blogspot.com)

J-FLAG (www.jflag.org)

Purple Roofs (www.purpleroofs.com/caribbean/jamaica.html) Lists specifically LGBT-friendly hotels in Jamaica.

Health

Availability & Cost of Health Care

Acceptable health care is available in most major cities and larger towns throughout Jamaica, but may be hard to locate in rural areas. Most travelers will find the quality of health care will not be comparable to that in their home country. To find a good local doctor, your best bet is to ask the management of the hotel where you are staying or contact your embassy in Kingston or Montego Bay.

Many doctors and hospitals expect payment in cash, regardless of whether you have travel health insurance. If you develop a life-threatening medical problem, you'll probably want to be evacuated to a country with state-of-the-art medical care. Since this may cost tens of

thousands of dollars, be sure you have insurance to cover this before you depart.

Many pharmacies are well supplied, but important medications may not be consistently available. Be sure to bring along adequate supplies of all prescription drugs.

No See Ums

No see ums, also known as midges, are tiny biting insects that live near water. Females are blood suckers, and while their bites are not painful, they are awfully itchy. No see ums congregate in large swarms near bodies of water, puddles etc; to avoid them, wear insect repellent and skirt around their swarm areas, as the bugs will not fly too far from their 'home' body of water.

Traveler's Diarrhea

Throughout most of Jamaica tap water has been treated and is safe to drink, but in some far-flung rural areas it is safest to avoid it unless it has been boiled, filtered or chemically disinfected (with iodine tablets). Eat fresh fruits or vegetables only if cooked or peeled; be wary of dairy products that might contain unpasteurized milk; and be highly selective when eating food from street vendors. If you develop diarrhea, be sure to drink plenty of fluid, preferably an oral rehydration solution containing lots of salt and sugar.

ABC of Healthy Travel by E Walker et al, and *Medicine for the Outdoors* by Paul S Auerbach, are other valuable resources.

Internet Resources

Lonely Planet (www.lonelyplanet.com) A good place to start.

MD Travel Health (www.mdtravelhealth.com) Provides complete travel health recommendations for every country, updated daily, at no cost.

World Health Organization (www.who.int/ith) Publishes a superb book called *International Travel and Health*, which is revised annually and is available for free online.

Internet Access

Wi-fi is increasingly widespread in Jamaican hotels, but internet access is still restricted in rural areas. Most town libraries now offer internet access (US$1 for 30 minutes), though you may find there's only one or two terminals and waits can be long. Most towns have at least one commercial entity where you can get online. Jamaican businesses aren't very good at maintaining (or even creating) their web presence, so don't rely too heavily on online research before your trip.

Internet Resources

Dancehall Reggae (www.dancehallreggae.com) The place to go for the latest on the island's music scene.

Jamaica Gleaner (www.jamaica-gleaner.com) Best news source from the island's most reliable newspaper.

WATER

Water is generally safe to drink from faucets throughout the island except in the most far-flung rural regions. It is safest, however, to stick with bottled water, which is widely available. It's a good idea to avoid ice, particularly that sold at street stands as 'bellywash,' 'sno-cones' or 'skyjuice' – shaved-ice cones sweetened with fruit juice. Unless you're certain that the local water is not contaminated, you shouldn't drink it. In Jamaica's backwaters, clean your teeth with purified water rather than tap water.

Jamaica National Heritage Trust (www.jnht. com) Excellent guide to Jamaica's history and heritage.

Jamaica Yellow Pages (www.jamaicayp.com) Handy online version of the Jamaican phone directory.

Lonely Planet (www.lonely planet.com) Succinct summaries on travel in Jamaica, plus the popular Thorn Tree bulletin board, travel news and a complete online store.

Visit Jamaica (www.visit jamaica.com)

Legal Matters

Jamaica's drug and drink-driving laws are strictly enforced. Don't expect leniency just because you're a foreigner. Jamaican jails are distinctly unpleasant. If arrested, insist on your right to call your embassy in Kingston to request its assistance.

Maps

The Jamaican Tourist Board (JTB) publishes a *Discover Jamaica* road map (1:350,000). No topographical details are shown.

The best maps are Hildebrandt's *Jamaica* map (1:300,000) and ITMB Publishing's maps (1:250,000), available online or at travel bookstores.

The most accurate maps are the Jamaica Ordnance Survey maps published by

the **Survey Department** (922-6630; 23 1/2 Charles St, PO Box 493, Kingston 10).

Money

→ The unit of currency is the Jamaican dollar, the 'jay,' which uses the same symbol as the US dollar ($).

→ Jamaican currency is issued in bank notes of J$50, J$100, J$500, J$1000 and (rarely) J$5000. Prices for hotels and valuable items are usually quoted in US dollars, which are widely accepted.

→ Commercial banks have branches throughout the island. Those in major towns maintain a foreign-exchange booth.

→ Most towns have 24-hour ATMs linked to international networks such as Cirrus or Plus. In more remote areas, look for ATMs at gas stations.

→ Traveler's checks are little used and attract fees for cashing.

→ Major credit cards are accepted throughout the island, although local groceries and the like will not be able to process them even in Kingston.

Tipping

A 10% tip is normal in hotels and restaurants. Some restaurants automatically add a 10% to 15% service charge to your bill. Check your bill carefully.

Some all-inclusive resorts have a strictly enforced no-tipping policy.

Outside Kingston, tourist taxi drivers often ask for tips but it is not necessary; JUTA (Jamaica Union of Travelers Association) route taxis do not expect tips.

Opening Hours

The following are standard hours for Jamaica; exceptions are noted in reviews. Note that the country virtually shuts down on Sunday.

Banks 9:30am to 4pm Monday to Friday.

Bars Usually open around midday. Jamaicans tend to go out late. Although some clubs and drinking establishments claim set opening hours, many just stay open until the last customer stumbles out, or the owner decides it's time to call it a night.

Businesses 8:30am to 4:30pm, Monday to Friday.

Restaurants Breakfast: dawn to 11am; lunch: midday to 2pm; dinner: 5:30pm to 11pm.

Shops 8am or 9am to 5pm Monday to Friday, to midday or 5pm Saturday, late-night shopping to 9pm Thursday and Friday.

Safe Travel

The **Jamaica Tourist Board** (hotline 929-9200; www. visitjamaica.com; 64 Knutsford Blvd) publishes a pocket-size pamphlet, *Helpful Hints for Your Vacation,* containing concise tips for safer travel. You can also call the hotline for non-emergency assistance.

Crime

In 1978, The Clash sang 'I'd stay an' be a tourist but I can't take the gunplay,' in *Safe European Home,* about their trip to Jamaica during the height of its political violence. Attitudes towards safe travel to the country sometimes seem barely to have moved on since.

Jamaica has the highest murder rate in the Caribbean, although recent statistics show this decreasing. While areas like Spanish Town and some parts of Kingston are best avoided due to gang trouble, crimes against tourists have also dropped greatly, and the overwhelming majority of visitors enjoy their vacations without incident.

Travel advice is common sense: keep hotel doors and windows locked at night, and lock car doors from the inside while driving. Don't open your hotel door to anyone who can't prove their identity. If

PRACTICALITIES

➡ **Newspapers** The *Jamaica Gleaner* is the high-standard newspaper; its rival is the *Jamaica Observer*.

➡ **TV & Radio** There are 30 radio stations and seven TV channels; most hotels have satellite TV.

➡ **Measurements** Metric and imperial measurements are both used. Distances are measured in meters and kilometers, and gas in liters, but coffee (and ganja) is most often sold by the pound.

➡ **Smoking** In 2013, smoking in public places (including bars and restaurants) was banned.

you're renting an out-of-the-way private villa or cottage, check in advance to establish whether security is provided.

Carry as little cash as you need when away from your hotel. Keep the rest in a hotel safe, and don't flash your valuables (particularly smartphones).

Finally, while taking care to be sensible, it's important not to get too hung up about Jamaica's reputation. Many travelers fear the worst and avoid the country; those who do make it here are far more likely to come away with positive impressions than horror stories.

Drugs

Ganja (marijuana) is everywhere in Jamaica and you're almost certain to be approached by hustlers selling drugs. Cocaine is also widely available (Jamaica is a major trans-shipment point for the Colombia–US route), along with hallucinogenic wild mushrooms. The globalisation of the drugs trade has undoubtedly helped fuel gang violence in Jamaica.

Despite their ubiquity and cultural eminence, drugs are strictly illegal and penalties can be severe. Roadblocks and random searches of cars, undertaken by well-armed police in combat gear, have been common. Professionalism is never guaranteed, and 'dash' – extortion – is often extracted to boost wages. Drug checks at airports can be particularly strict.

However, in June 2014 Jamaica's justice minister announced that the government was going to reform its drug laws, with possession of less than 57 grams (2 ounces) of ganja becoming a non-arrestable, ticketable infraction. The drug would also be decriminalised for religious, scientific and medical reasons. The changes were expected to be approved by parliament in September 2014. Check the situation before you travel

Harassment

Usually the traveler's biggest problem is the vast army of hustlers (mostly male) who harass visitors, notably in and around major tourist centers. A hustler is someone who makes a living by seizing opportunities, and the biggest opportunity in Jamaica is you.

Be polite but firm in repressing unwanted advances; never ignore them, which is taken as an insult. Aggressive persistence is the key to their success and trying to shake them off can be a wearying process. Hustlers often persist in the hope that you'll pay just to be rid of them. Try pretending to be a tourist from a non-English-speaking country (few Jamaicans speak Croatian). If harassment continues, seek the assistance of a tourist police officer or the local constabulary.

BAD TRIP?

While some travelers are keen to seek ganja out, even those wanting to avoid it are unlikely to get through their trip without at least a whiff of secondhand smoke. You'll undoubtedly be approached by people offering to sell you ganja, whether a 'nudge wink' hustler, or a vendor at a dancehall street party openly selling it alongside candies and rum. If you want to smoke, we recommend doing so discreetly, at your hotel. Some local strains are particularly strong, and tourists have reported suffering harmful side effects from ganja, especially from ganja cakes.

While we've heard rumors of winery-style 'tasting' tours to ganja plantations, if you're hiking in the Jamaican back country and come across a field of ganja, get out of there. At best, you've found someone's personal home-grown plot. Jamaicans are fiercely protective of these secret spots and there's a good chance they will loudly (and perhaps aggressively) demand you leave the area. At worst, you'll have found plants grown by gangsters – and the repercussions of this situation cannot be overstated.

Telephone

Jamaica's country code is ☎876. To call Jamaica from the US, dial ☎1-876 + the seven-digit local number. From elsewhere, dial your country's international dialing code, then ☎876 and the local number.

For calls within the same parish in Jamaica, just dial the local number. Between parishes, dial ☎1 + the local number. We have included only the seven-digit local number in Jamaica listings.

Cell Phones

You can bring your own cellular phone into Jamaica (GSM or CDMA). Be aware of hefty roaming charges. If your phone is unlocked buy a local SIM card (around US$20 including credit) from one of the two local cellphone operators, **Digicel** (☎888-344-4235; www.digiceljamaica.com) or **Lime** (☎888-225-5295; www.timeforlime.com.jm), or you can buy a cheap handset. You'll need to bring ID to buy either. Prepaid top-up cards are sold in denominations from JS$50 to J$1000, and you'll find them at many gas stations and grocery stores.

Time

In fall (autumn) and winter, Jamaican time is five hours behind Greenwich Mean Time, and the same as in New York (Eastern Standard Time). Jamaica does not adjust for daylight saving time. Hence, from April to October, it is six hours behind London and one hour behind New York.

Toilets

There are few public toilets, and those that do exist are best avoided. Most restaurants have restrooms, but many require you to make a purchase before you can use them.

GOVERNMENT TRAVEL ADVICE

British Foreign & Commonwealth Office (☎0845-850-2829; www.fco.gov.uk; Travel Advice Unit, Consular Division, Foreign & Commonwealth Office, 1 Palace St, London)

US State Department (☎202-663-1225; www.travel.state.gov) US State Department publishes travel advisories that advise US citizens of trouble spots.

Tourist Information

The **Jamaica Tourist Board** (JTB; www.visitjamaica.com) has offices in key cities around the world. You can request maps and literature, including hotel brochures, but they do not serve as reservation agencies.

Travelers with Disabilities

Very few allowances have been made in Jamaica for travelers with disabilities. Some useful resources:

Council for Persons with Disabilities (☎922-0585; www.mlss.gov.jm; 4 Ellesmere Rd, Kingston 5)

Disabled Peoples' International (☎268-461-1273; www.dpinorthamericacaribbean.org; PO Box W1529, Potters Main Rd, St John's, Antigua)

Visas

For stays of six months or less, no visas are required for citizens of the EU, the US, Commonwealth countries, Mexico, Japan and Israel. Nationals of Argentina, Brazil, Chile, Costa Rica, Ecuador, Greece and Japan don't need a visa for stays of up to 90 days.

All other nationals require visas (nationals of most countries can obtain a visa on arrival, provided they are holding valid onward or return tickets and evidence of sufficient funds).

Women Travelers

Many Jamaican men display behavior and attitudes that might shock visiting women, often expressing disdain for the notion of female equality or women's rights. Despite this, women play pivotal roles in Jamaican society.

If you're single, it may be assumed you're on the island seeking a 'likkle love beneat' de palms.' Protests to the contrary will likely be met with wearying attempts to get you to change your mind. If you go along with the flirting, your innocent acceptance will be taken as a sign of acquiescence. Never beat about the bush out of fear of hurting the man's feelings.

Rape is not uncommon in Jamaica and occasionally involves female tourists. Women traveling alone may reduce unwanted attention by dressing modestly when away from the beach. Women should avoid walking alone at night and otherwise traveling alone in remote areas.

Work

Visitors are admitted to Jamaica on the condition that they 'not engage in any form of employment on the island.' Professionals can obtain work permits if sponsored by a Jamaican company, but casual work is very difficult to obtain.

Transportation

GETTING THERE & AWAY

Entering the Country

Expect a wait in the immigration halls at the airports in Kingston and Montego Bay. There are often only two or three immigration officers on hand to process the planeloads of passengers, and often multiple flights land within minutes of each other, increasing the burden on officials.

Passport

Passports valid for at least six months from the date of entry are required for all visits to Jamaica.

Air

Airports & Airlines

Jamaica's international airports are in Montego Bay and Kingston. For flight arrival and departure information, call the airports, visit their websites or call the airline directly.

Donald Sangster International Airport (MBJ; ☎952-3124; www.mbjairport.com) The majority of international visitors arrive at Sangster, 3km north of Montego Bay. There's a Jamaica Tourist Board (JTB) information booth in the arrivals hall and a 24-hour money-exchange bureau immediately beyond immigration. There is also a transportation information counter plus desks representing tour companies, hotels and rental cars immediately as you exit customs, as well as a booth for taxis. The adjacent terminal serves domestic flights. The terminals aren't linked by walkways but there are connecting shuttles.

Norman Manley International Airport (KIN; ☎924-8452; www.nmia.aero) Around 11km southeast of downtown Kingston, Manley also handles international flights. There's a JTB desk in the arrivals hall, and a money-exchange bureau before customs. As you exit there's a bank, car rental booths and a booking station for official taxis.

Jamaica is well served by international carriers for cities across North America and Europe, as well as two national carriers and a regional Caribbean airline.

Air Jamaica (☎922-3460; www.airjamaica.com) Kingston (☎888-359-2475; 4 St Lucia Ave); Montego Bay (☎922-4661, 888-359-2475, in the USA 800-523-5585; 9 Queen's Dr; ☺8:30am-4:30pm Mon-Fri)

Caribbean Airlines (☎744-2225; www.caribbean-airlines.com) Kingston (☎800-744-2225; 7 Trafalgar Rd, Kingston)

Fly Jamaica (☎656-9832; www.fly-jamaica.com)

Sea

Jamaica is a popular destination on the cruise roster,

CLIMATE CHANGE & TRAVEL

Every form of transport that relies on carbon-based fuel generates CO_2, the main cause of human-induced climate change. Modern travel is dependent on airplanes which might use less fuel per mile per person than most cars but travel much greater distances. The altitude at which aircraft emit gases (including CO_2) and particles also contributes to their climate change impact. Many websites offer 'carbon calculators' that allow people to estimate the carbon emissions generated by their journey and, for those who wish to do so, to offset the impact of the greenhouse gases emitted with contributions to portfolios of climate-friendly initiatives throughout the world. Lonely Planet offsets the carbon footprint of all staff and author travel.

mainly for passenger liners but also for private yachts. Arrival by freighter is another option.

For maps and charts of the Caribbean, contact **Bluewater Books & Charts** (📞800-942-2583; www.bluewaterweb.com). The **National Oceanic & Atmospheric Administration** (📞888-990-6622; www.nauticalcharts.noaa.gov) sells US government charts.

Cruise Ship

More than 800,000 cruise-ship passengers sail to Jamaica annually, making it one of the world's biggest cruise-ship destinations. Most ships hit four or five ports, sometimes spending a night, other times only a few hours. The typical cruise-ship holiday is the ultimate package tour. While the majority of mainstream cruises take in fine scenery along the way, the time spent on the islands is generally limited and the opportunities to experience a sense of island life are more restricted. Port visits are usually one-day stopovers at either Ocho Rios, Montego Bay or Falmouth.

Private Yacht

Many yachties make the trip to Jamaica from North America. Upon arrival in Jamaica, you *must* clear customs and immigration at Montego Bay, Kingston, Ocho Rios or Port Antonio. In addition, you'll need to clear customs at *each* port of call. The main ports for yachts:

Errol Flynn Marina (📞993-3209, 715-6044; www.errolflynnmarina.com; Port Antonio, GPS N 18.168889°, W -76.450556°)

Montego Bay Yacht Club (📞979-8038; www.mobayyachtclub.com; Montego Bay Freeport, GPS N 18.462452°, W -77.943267°; ⊗10am-10pm)

Royal Jamaican Yacht Club (📞924-8685; www.rjyc.org.jm; Norman Manley Dr, Kingston, GPS N 17.940939°, W -76.764939°)

GETTING AROUND

Air

There are four domestic airports: **Tinson Pen Aerodrome** (Marcus Garvey Dr) in Kingston, **Ian Fleming International Airport** (📞975-3101), formerly Boscobel Aerodrome, near Ocho Rios, **Negril Aerodrome** (📞957-5016) and **Ken Jones Aerodrome** (📞913-3173) at Port Antonio. Montego Bay's **Donald Sangster International Airport** (MBJ; 📞952-3124; www.mbjairport.com) has a domestic terminal adjacent to the international terminal. It's a bit of a walk – Air Jamaica Express provides a shuttle.

In Kingston, most domestic flights use Tinson Pen, 3km west of downtown, but it's a 40-minute ride to the domestic airstrip from Norman Manley International Airport.

Airlines in Jamaica

Jamaica's small size makes domestic flights largely redundant, but charters are available with **TimAir** (📞952-2516; www.timair.net;

Domestic terminal, Donald Sangster International Airport). It has ridiculously expensive charter flights between its hub in Montego Bay and Kingston, Negril, Ocho Rios and Port Antonio. Rates start at around US$320 for two passengers; fares go up or down for fewer or more passengers.

Helicopter

You can charter your own helicopter for transportation or for personalized tours from **Jamaica Customised Vacations & Tours** (📞979-2021; www.jcvtt.com; 19 Austin Ave, Mt Salem, Montego Bay; tours per person from US$460). Tours depart from Montego Bay, Negril and Ocho Rios.

Bicycle

Mountain bikes and 'beach cruisers' (bikes with fat tires, suitable for riding on sand) can be rented at most major resorts (US$10 to US$30 per day). Road conditions can be poor when off the main highways, and Jamaican drivers are not considerate to cyclists. For serious touring, bring your own mountain or multipurpose bike.

Bus & Public Transportation

Traveling by public transportation is a great way to explore Jamaica. An extensive transportation network links virtually every village and comprises several options that range from standard public buses to private taxis, with minibuses and route taxis in between.

For the adventurous traveler who doesn't mind getting up close and personal with fellow passengers without the comfort of air-conditioning, and is unfazed by the wild manoeuvres of the drivers, this is the cheapest way to get around Jamaica. There is usually no set timetable – buses leave when the driver considers them full – and passengers are crammed in with little regard for comfort. Taxis and buses tend to fill quickly early in the morning (before 8am) and around 5pm as people depart for work or home. There are fewer public transport options on Sunday.

Public buses, minibuses and route taxis depart from and arrive at each town's transportation station, which is usually near the main market. Locals can direct you to the appropriate vehicle, which should have its destination marked above the front window (for buses) or on its side.

Public buses and minibuses are regulated by the **Ministry of Transport & Works** (☑754-2584; www.mtw.gov.jm; 138 Maxfield Ave, Kingston 10).

Buses

Large buses are few and far between in Jamaica due to the narrow twisting roads. Throughout the island there are bus stops at most road intersections along routes, but you can usually flag down a bus anywhere except in major cities. When you want to get off, shout 'One stop!' The conductor will usually echo your request with, 'Let off!'

A worthwhile exception is the big, comfortable, air-conditioned buses of **Knutsford Express** (☑971-1822; www.knutsfordexpress.com; 18 Dominica Dr, New Kingston Shopping Center parking lot). Destinations include Kingston, Ocho Rios, Falmouth, Montego Bay, Negril, Savanna-la-Mar, Sant Acruz and Mandeville. Sample fares/times are Kingston–Ocho Rios (J$1600, three hours) and Kingston–Montego Bay (J$2450; five hours). Online booking is available, along with student, senior and child fares.

Minibuses

Private minibuses, also known as 'coasters,' have traditionally been the workhorses of Jamaica's regional public transportation system. All major towns and virtually every village in the country are served.

Licensed minibuses display red license plates with the initials PPV (public passenger vehicle) or have a JUTA (Jamaica Union of Travelers Association) insignia. JUTA buses are exclusively for tourists. Public coasters don't run to set timetables,

but depart their point of origin when they're full. They're often overflowing, and the drivers seem to have death wishes.

Route Taxis

These communal taxis are the most universal mode of public transportation, reaching every part of the country. They operate like minibuses, picking up as many people as they can squeeze in along their specified routes. They're very convenient and are a cheap and easy way of getting around the island. Simply pick them up at their terminal in town (they go when full), or flag them down on the road and tell the driver where you want to get off. If you get in an empty taxi – particularly at the taxi station – you might get asked if you want to hire the vehicle outright, so be clear if you just want to pay the regular fare instead of a charter.

Most route taxis are white Toyota Corolla station wagons marked by their red license plates. They should have 'Route Taxi' marked on the front door, and they are not to be confused with similar licensed taxis, which charge more. Avoid any taxi that lacks the red license plate.

Car & Motorcycle

Automobile Associations

There is no national roadside organization to phone when you have car trouble. Most car-rental agencies have a 24-hour service number in case of breakdowns and other emergencies. If you do break down, use a local mechanic only for minor work; otherwise the car-rental company may balk at reimbursing you for work it hasn't authorized. If you can't find a phone or repair service, seek police assistance. *Never* give your keys to strangers.

COSTS

Taking public transportation is terrifically inexpensive. Buses and minibuses charge in the neighborhood of J$100 per 50km, and route taxis charge about J$150 to J$250 per 50km, with short rides of around 10 minutes costing J$100. As an example of longer routes, at the time of writing, a coaster from Kingston to Port Antonio (two hours) cost J$450.

Driver's License

To drive in Jamaica, you must have a valid International Driver's License (IDL) or a current license for your home country or state, valid for at least six months.

Fuel & Spare Parts

Many gas stations close at 7pm or so. In rural areas, stations are usually closed on Sunday. At the time of writing, gasoline cost about US$1.20/J$125 per liter. Most gas stations only accept cash for payment, although a growing number of modern gas stations in larger towns accept credit cards.

Rental

Several major international car-rental companies operate in Jamaica, along with dozens of local firms. Car-rental agencies are listed in the local yellow pages.

INTERNATIONAL RENTAL COMPANIES

Avis (www.avis.com.jm); Donald Sangster International Airport (☑952-0762); Norman Manley International Airport (☑924-8542)

Budget (www.budgetjamaica. com) Donald Sangster International Airport (☑952-3838); Norman Manley International Airport (☑924-8762); Ocho Rios (☑974-1288; 15 Milford Rd)

Hertz (www.hertz.com) Donald Sangster International Airport (☑979-0438); Norman Manley International Airport (☑924-8028)

Jamaica Airport Car Rental (www.jamaicaairport carrental.com) Clearing house on local car rentals.

Thrifty (☑952-1126; www. thrifty.com; Donald Sangster International Airport)

DOMESTIC RENTAL COMPANIES

Local rental agencies often provide better daily rates than the international chains, but cars are sometimes road-worn.

Reputable agencies include the following:

Beaumont Car Rentals (www.beaumont-car-rental. com) Kingston (☑926-0311; 56C Brentford Rd); Montego Bay (☑971-8476; 34 Queens Dr)

Caribbean Car Rentals (☑974-2513, in North America 877-801-6797, in UK 0800-917-9904; www.caribbeancarrentals. net; 31 Hope Rd, Kingston)

Island Car Rentals (www. islandcarrentals.com) Donald Sangster International Airport (☑952-7225); Kingston (☑926-8012; 17 Antigua Ave); Norman Manley International Airport (☑924-8075); North America (☑866-978-5335)

COSTS

High-season rates begin at about US$45 (J$4000) per day and can run as high as US$150 (J$12,700) or more, depending on the vehicle. Cheaper rates apply in the low season. Some companies include unlimited distance, while others set a limit and charge a fee for excess kilometers driven. Most firms require a deposit of at least US$500 (J$40,000), but will accept a credit-card imprint. Keep copies of all your paperwork. Renters must be 21 years old (some companies will rent only to people aged 25 or older).

RESERVING

You can reserve a car upon arrival, but in the high season be sure to make your reservation in advance. Reconfirm before your arrive.

Before signing, go over the vehicle with a fine-tooth comb to identify any dents and scratches. Make a note of each one before you drive away. You're likely to be charged for the slightest mark that wasn't noted before. Don't forget to check the cigarette lighter and interior switches, which are often missing.

WHAT KIND OF CAR

Most of the companies rent out modern Japanese sedans. A big car can be a liability on Jamaica's narrow, winding roads. Some companies also rent 4WD vehicles, which are highly recommended if you intend to do *any* driving away from main roads.

Stick shift is preferable because frequent and sudden gear changes are required when potholes and kamikaze chickens appear out of nowhere. Remember that you'll be changing gears with your *left* hand. If this is new to you, you'll soon get the hang of it.

INSURANCE

Check in advance whether your current insurance or credit card covers you for driving while abroad. All rental companies will recommend damage-waiver insurance, which limits your liability in the event of an accident or damage.

Road Conditions

Jamaica's roads run the gamut from modern multilane highways to barely passable tracks. You can expect any road with the designation 'A' to be in fairly good condition. 'B' roads are generally much more narrow and often badly potholed, but still passable in the average rental car. Minor roads, particularly those in the Blue Mountains and Cockpit Country, can be hellish. If you plan to drive off the major routes, it's essential to have a stalwart 4WD.

Signage on main roads is good, but directional signs are few and far between as soon as you leave them. Many B roads are not shown on maps. And what may appear on a map to be a 30-minute journey may take several hours. More often than not there are no signs to indicate sharp curves, steep ascents or work in progress.

In addition roads are often poorly lit at night, if at all.

Road Hazards

Jamaicans undergo a psychological mind flip when they get behind the wheel, shifting from laid-back folks who rarely rush anything to some of the world's rudest and most dangerously aggressive drivers. Cars race through towns and play chicken with one another with daredevil folly. Use extreme caution and drive defensively, especially at night when you should be prepared to meet oncoming cars that are either without lights or blinding you with high beams (there's never a middle ground for some reason). Use your horn liberally, especially when approaching blind corners.

Road Rules

➡ Always drive on the left.

➡ Jamaica has a compulsory seatbelt law.

➡ Speed limits range from 50km/h to 80km/h and vary from place to place across the island.

Hitchhiking

Hitchhiking is common enough among Jamaicans but, because public transportation is absurdly cheap, few tourists stick out their thumbs.

Hitchhiking is never entirely safe in any country in the world and we don't recommend it, especially in Jamaica where there are a lot of bad men looking to take advantage of naive tourists. Travelers who decide to hitchhike should understand that they are taking a small but potentially serious risk. If you choose to take that risk, you will be safer if you travel in pairs and let someone

TAXI FARES

The following are typical fares, based on up to four people per taxi:

ROUTE	FARE
Kingston–Montego Bay	US$200
Kingston–Ocho Rios	US$100
Kingston–Port Antonio	US$100
Montego Bay–Ocho Rios or Negril	US$100
Norman Manley International Airport–Kingston (Uptown)	US$35
Donald Sangster International Airport–Montego Bay	US$10

know where you are planning to go.

Local Transportation

Boat

A new tourist ferry between Ocho Rios, Montego Bay and Negril had been announced at the time of research, with services expected to commence by mid-2015.

Buses

Kingston's **municipal bus system** (Jamaica Urban Transport Co Ltd; ☎749-3196; fares J$100; ⊙5am-10pm) operates a fleet of Mercedes-Benz and Volvo buses. Buses stop only at official stops. Fares are J$100, but students, children, disabled passengers and pensioners pay half fare.

Motor Scooter & Motorcycle

Dozens of companies hire motorcycles and scooters; they're available at any resort town. These companies are far more lax than the car-rental companies; you may not even have to show your driver's license. If you are not an experienced motorcycle driver, it might

be better to rent a scooter, which is far easier to handle. Scooters cost about US$35 to US$50 (J$3000 to J$4000) per day and motorcycles about US$45 to US$60 (J$4000 to J$5000) per day; note that deposits can be high.

Road conditions in Jamaica are hazardous. Always wear a helmet.

Taxi

Licensed taxis – called 'contract carriages' – have red PPV license plates (those without such plates are unlicensed). They're expensive, but affordable if you share the cost with other passengers.

Jamaica Union of Travelers Association (JUTA; ☎957-4620; www.jutatours jamaica.com) operates island-wide and is geared almost exclusively to the tourist business. Other taxicab companies are listed in the yellow pages.

The Transport Authority has established fixed rates according to distance (different rates apply for locals and tourists, who pay more). Licensed cabs should have these posted inside. Taxis are also supposed to have meters, but many don't use them.

Behind the Scenes

SEND US YOUR FEEDBACK

We love to hear from travelers – your comments keep us on our toes and help make our books better. Our well-traveled team reads every word on what you loved or loathed about this book. Although we cannot reply individually to your submissions, we always guarantee that your feedback goes straight to the appropriate authors, in time for the next edition. Each person who sends us information is thanked in the next edition – the most useful submissions are rewarded with a selection of digital PDF chapters.

Visit **lonelyplanet.com/contact** to submit your updates and suggestions or to ask for help. Our award-winning website also features inspirational travel stories, news and discussions.

Note: We may edit, reproduce and incorporate your comments in Lonely Planet products such as guidebooks, websites and digital products, so let us know if you don't want your comments reproduced or your name acknowledged. For a copy of our privacy policy visit lonelyplanet.com/privacy.

AUTHOR THANKS

Paul Clammer

Bless up to those who were great help on the road: David 'Scotty' Scott (Reggae Hostel), Karen Hutchinson (Jamaica Cultural Enterprises), Annie Paul (University of the West Indies), Karin Wilson Edmonds (Yard Edge), Christopher Edmonds (Red Selecter), Josh Chamberlain (Alpha Boys), Nate (driver-extraordinaire in Ocho Rios), Carla Gullotta (Drapers San Guest House) Leonard Welsh (Reach Falls) and staff at the Jamaica Conservation & Development Trust. Thanks also to Erin MacLeod for remote input, and my co-author Brendan Sainsbury: I owe you both a Red Stripe or three.

Brendan Sainsbury

Thanks to Garth, Leroy and Chucky for their rally-driving skills; to Sue in Negril for her recommendations and insights; all the ladies at the wonderful Falmouth Heritage Walks; Tony at Time & Place; Stefan at the Jamaican Caves Organisation; and all my Jamaican companions on the arduous Troy–Windsor hike. Special thanks to my wife Liz and eight-year-old son Kieran for their company in MoBay and Negril.

ACKNOWLEDGMENTS

Climate map data adapted from Peel MC, Finlayson BL & McMahon TA (2007) 'Updated World Map of the Köppen-Geiger Climate Classification', Hydrology and Earth System Sciences, 11, 1633¬44.

Cover photograph: Dunn's River Falls, Ocho Rios; Franz Marc Frel/Alamy ©

THIS BOOK

This 7th edition of Lonely Planet's *Jamaica* guidebook was researched and written by Paul Clammer and Brendan Sainsbury. The previous two editions were written by Anna Kaminski, Adam Karlin and Richard Kloss. This guidebook was commissioned in Lonely Planet's Oakland office, and produced by the following:

Commissioning Editors
Catherine Craddock-Carrillo, Kathleen Munnelly

Destination Editor
Matt Phillips

Product Editor
Amanda Williamson

Senior Cartographer
David Kemp

Book Designer
Clara Monitto

Assisting Editors Katie Connolly, Bruce Evans, Rosie Nicholson, Erin Richards

Assisting Cartographer
Mark Griffiths

Cover Researcher
Naomi Parker

Thanks to Sasha Baskett, Brendan Dempsey, Fredrik Divall, David Marty, Claire Naylor, Nikta Nilchian, Karyn Noble, Ellie Simpson, Angela Tinson, Tracy Whitmey, Dean Wray

Index

Map Legend

Sights
- Beach
- Bird Sanctuary
- Buddhist
- Castle/Palace
- Christian
- Confucian
- Hindu
- Islamic
- Jain
- Jewish
- Monument
- Museum/Gallery/Historic Building
- Ruin
- Sento Hot Baths/Onsen
- Shinto
- Sikh
- Taoist
- Winery/Vineyard
- Zoo/Wildlife Sanctuary
- Other Sight

Activities, Courses & Tours
- Bodysurfing
- Diving
- Canoeing/Kayaking
- Course/Tour
- Skiing
- Snorkelling
- Surfing
- Swimming/Pool
- Walking
- Windsurfing
- Other Activity

Sleeping
- Sleeping
- Camping

Eating
- Eating

Drinking & Nightlife
- Drinking & Nightlife
- Cafe

Entertainment
- Entertainment

Shopping
- Shopping

Information
- Bank
- Embassy/Consulate
- Hospital/Medical
- Internet
- Police
- Post Office
- Telephone
- Toilet
- Tourist Information
- Other Information

Geographic
- Beach
- Hut/Shelter
- Lighthouse
- Lookout
- Mountain/Volcano
- Oasis
- Park
- Pass
- Picnic Area
- Waterfall

Population
- Capital (National)
- Capital (State/Province)
- City/Large Town
- Town/Village

Transport
- Airport
- Border crossing
- Bus
- Cable car/Funicular
- Cycling
- Ferry
- Metro station
- Monorail
- Parking
- Petrol station
- Subway station
- Taxi
- Train station/Railway
- Tram
- Underground station
- Other Transport

Routes
- Tollway
- Freeway
- Primary
- Secondary
- Tertiary
- Lane
- Unsealed road
- Road under construction
- Plaza/Mall
- Steps
- Tunnel
- Pedestrian overpass
- Walking Tour
- Walking Tour detour
- Path/Walking Trail

Boundaries
- International
- State/Province
- Disputed
- Regional/Suburb
- Marine Park
- Cliff
- Wall

Hydrography
- River, Creek
- Intermittent River
- Canal
- Water
- Dry/Salt/Intermittent Lake
- Reef

Areas
- Airport/Runway
- Beach/Desert
- Cemetery (Christian)
- Cemetery (Other)
- Glacier
- Mudflat
- Park/Forest
- Sight (Building)
- Sportsground
- Swamp/Mangrove

Note: Not all symbols displayed above appear on the maps in this book

OUR STORY

A beat-up old car, a few dollars in the pocket and a sense of adventure. In 1972 that's all Tony and Maureen Wheeler needed for the trip of a lifetime – across Europe and Asia overland to Australia. It took several months, and at the end – broke but inspired – they sat at their kitchen table writing and stapling together their first travel guide, *Across Asia on the Cheap*. Within a week they'd sold 1500 copies. Lonely Planet was born.

Today, Lonely Planet has offices in Franklin, London, Melbourne, Oakland, Beijing and Delhi, with more than 600 staff and writers. We share Tony's belief that 'a great guidebook should do three things: inform, educate and amuse'.

OUR WRITERS

Paul Clammer

Coordinating Author; Kingston, Blue Mountains & Southeast Coast; Ocho Rios, Port Antonio & North Coast Paul Clammer has contributed to more than 25 Lonely Planet guidebooks and worked as a tour guide in countries from Turkey to Morocco. In a previous life he may even have been a molecular biologist. Having spent a year living in post-earthquake Port-au-Prince, Haiti, Jamaica was always high on his travel list. One of the most important lessons he learned on this research trip was that if you stay out until 4am drinking rum at a dancehall street party in a Kingston ghetto, don't expect to get too many hotel reviews done the next day.

Read more about Paul at:
lonelyplanet.com/members/paulclammer

Brendan Sainsbury

Montego Bay & Northwest Coast; Negril & West Coast; South Coast & Central Highlands Originally from Hampshire, England, Brendan grew up appreciating Jamaica from his safe European home; coupling a teenage penchant for punk-reggae with a lifelong love of cricket. His curiosity was further piqued while living in London's quintessential Jamaican district, Brixton, during the 1990s. When Lonely Planet came knocking, Brendan jumped at the chance to track 90 miles south from his customary haunt, Cuba to sample Negril's sunsets and Treasure Beach's beautiful languor. He has since developed a healthy appetite for Red Stripe beer, Blue Mountain coffee and saying the words 'yah mon!' at the end of every sentence.

Read more about Brendan at:
lonelyplanet.com/members/brendansainsbury

Published by Lonely Planet Publications Pty Ltd
ABN 36 005 607 983
7th edition – October 2014
ISBN 978 1 74220 443 7
© Lonely Planet 2014   Photographs © as indicated 2014
10 9 8 7 6 5 4 3 2 1
Printed in China